W9-AXN-024

WOMEN AND MONARCHY IN MACEDONIA

Women and Monarchy in Macedonia

ELIZABETH DONNELLY CARNEY

University of Oklahoma Press : Norman

Portions of the following chapters were first published, in different versions, as follows: chapter 4 in *American Journal of Philology* 117 (1996), 563–83; chapter 5 in *Ventures into Greek History*, ed. I. Worthington (Oxford: Clarendon Press, 1994), 357–80, by permission of Oxford University Press; chapters 6 and 8 in *Ancient History Bulletin* 8 (1994), 123–31.

Carney, Elizabeth Donnelly, 1947–
    Women and monarchy in Macedonia / Elizabeth Donnelly Carney.
        p.   cm.
    Includes bibliographical references and index.
    ISBN 0-8061-3212-4 (cloth: alk. paper)
    1. Queens—Macedonia Biography.   2. Women in public life—
Macedonia Biography.   3. Women—Macedonia—History   I. Title.
DF233.2.C37   2000
938' .1'0082—dc21   99-37790
                                                CIP

Text design by Gail Carter

The paper in this book meets the guidelines for permanence and durability of the Committee on Production Guidelines for Book Longevity of the Council on Library Resources, Inc. ∞

1 2 3 4 5 6 7 8 9 10

Dis manibus

Emma Louise Maynard Carney Babbit
Elizabeth Donnelly Chapman Carney

Contents

Preface

The origins of this book lie far back in my scholarly career. In 1980 I began work on an article about Olympias, mother of Alexander the Great. This research followed logically from a dissertation on the relationship between Alexander the Great and the Macedonian aristocracy and a subsequent series of articles dealing with various aspects of relations between Macedonian rulers and the Macedonian elite. At that time I had no sense that research on Olympias would be any different from research on Macedonian men.

Meanwhile, in the years since the completion of my dissertation in 1975, like many other women classicists of my generation, I had begun to teach myself about the role of women in Graeco-Roman antiquity. In 1977 I taught a course on women in the ancient world for the first time. I had, at first, no reason to think my personal and pedagogical interest in the history of women in the ancient period, still comparatively trendy in the 1970s, could or would intersect in any way with my much more traditional research in Macedonian political history.

To my surprise, my two seemingly separate areas of interest intersected and collided. I soon discovered that, obvious though it seemed to me that Olympias had played an important role in the reigns of her son and grandson and perhaps in that of her husband, little work had been done on her. The work that had been done was based largely on remarkably uncritical use of ancient sources as well as sexual stereotypes and caricatures. My initial publication on Olympias was comparatively polite about this phenomenon. I had discovered a considerable void in the very heart of one of the grand topics of Graeco-Roman history, the reign of Alexander the Great.

When I looked at the careers of other royal women in the Argead period, I began to realize that my own views were shaped not only by a rejection of sexist interpretations but also by an understanding of monarchy in

Macedonia that was very different from the traditional, constitutional views of many scholars. The messier, less tidily constitutional views of Errington, Lock, Anson, and, later, Borza made more sense to me. Indeed, the role many women played in the monarchy confirmed the more personal, less structured reading of Macedonian monarchy these scholars advanced.

As I continued to look at the role of women in Macedonian monarchy, I encountered the work of William Greenwalt, who shared my understanding of women as part of Macedonian monarchy but looked at the question from a more institutional and less individual perspective. We planned to write this book together, but in the end that proved impractical. Many of Greenwalt's ideas have, however, influenced and informed my work.

A number of others have helped with the writing of this book. John Oates, my dissertation director, has continued to offer advice through the years. Peter Green read the manuscript twice, with great care, and offered many helpful suggestions. Gene Borza discussed many aspects of the work and was particularly helpful in bringing it to publication. Jenny Roberts also offered good advice. Bob Milns, Suzanne Dixon, and Kate Mortensen read earlier versions of parts of the manuscript and often functioned as sounding boards for my ideas. Maureen Flory and Kathryn Gutzwiller read and commented on portions of the text. Beryl Barr-Sharrar helped with art historical material. Conversations over the years with Stan Burstein, Waldemar Heckel, Lindsey Adams, Michael Flowers, Stella Miller Collet, and Frank Holt broadened my understanding of ancient Macedonia. Pierre Briant, Sylvie Le Bohec, and Argyro Tataki were kind enough to send me material that was difficult to obtain.

My family also helped me to write this book. I owe a great debt to my husband, William Aarnes, who has come to know more about ancient Macedonia and royal women than a poet and scholar of nineteenth-century American literature has any good reason to do. He patiently read over my manuscript and tried to make it at least a bit more readable. My daughter, Emma, and my father and brother have always supported my work. I am grateful to the two women to whom this book is dedicated, my paternal grandmother, Emma Carney Babbit, and my mother, Elizabeth Chapman Carney; they instilled in me a love for the ancient world and for scholarship.

Introduction

My mother claimed—more whimsically than seriously—that electric power must leak from household outlets. She never explained why, but I have always supposed that it was because, in her experience with Irish-American machine politics, power did not stay put. It flowed; sometimes it even leaked; and it certainly moved in two directions.

This book is about how power in one ancient society, Macedonia, flowed from the one person often supposed to have had a near-monopoly on it, the king, to others in his clan, particularly to the women of his family. It is also about how at moments of crisis various royal women used the power they possessed as members of the king's family to shore up the monarchy and preserve the throne for their sons or grandsons.

This is a study of the role of women in the monarchy of Macedonia from early classical times until the Roman conquest of 167 B.C. abolished the monarchy itself. In dynastic terms this means that both the Argead and Antigonid dynasties, as well as the transitional period between them, are dealt with. The bulk of our evidence about royal women in Macedonia, however, comes from a much narrower period, the fourth century (particularly the second half) and the early third century. My concentration here on the same period reflects the limited nature of available evidence.

This study has two parts. The main narrative considers the role of women in the Macedonian monarchy from an institutional point of view and proceeds in chronological order. Essays on the careers of individual royal women (all named wives, daughters, and sisters of Macedonian rulers as well as any women who produced or may have produced sons who were considered eligible for the throne) supplement the narrative. These biographical essays appear as inserts in the main text. (Cross-references to the biographical essays appear in capital letters with additional numerals if more than one woman bore the same name.) An index at the back of the book lists the biographical essays in alphabetical order. Essays on those women whose careers spanned several reigns have been divided into parts, included in several chapters. In general, the biographical essays focus on motivation and personal perspective, whereas the main narrative is more concerned with general issues and repeated patterns.

Women and Monarchy in Macedonia is, primarily, a work of political history, a consideration of the role of women in the power structure of one critical ancient society. It is also a work of women's history, intended to challenge some aspects of our conventional understanding of Macedonian society and to provide a more nuanced view of the lives of individual royal women. Royal women were hardly typical, and much of women's history has, quite rightly, focused on typicality, on the lives of ordinary women. So little, however, is known about the lives of individual women from the ancient period that we must regard the knowledge we have about various royal Macedonian women as precious.

Although I run the risk of displeasing both traditional political historians by being too trendy and historians of women and gender by being not trendy (and theoretical) enough, I have tried to write a work of political history that is informed by the history of women. I find that my personal copy of *Hellenistic Queens*, the work of my distinguished predecessor Grace Macurdy, tends to wander back and forth in my library between the section devoted to the history of Macedonia (largely political) and the one dedicated to the history of women in antiquity (largely not political). This suggests the mixed nature of my own study.

Inevitably, this study will be compared to Macurdy's *Hellenistic Queens*, the only previous scholarly work that looked at royal Macedonian women in a consistent way. My book is different from hers. Macurdy looked at royal women not only in Macedonia itself but also in the Hellenistic dynasties that derived from Macedonian monarchy. My work focuses on monarchy in Macedonia itself and only touches on its Hellenistic offshoots elsewhere. *Hellenistic Queens*, published in 1932, is dated. Subsequent research and discoveries have altered the factual base Macurdy worked with, but some of her analysis is also outmoded. Her anxiety about the sexual propriety of royal women now seems to be quaint and even distracting. More important, her work was primarily biographical. Her interest in the relationship of women to the institution of monarchy was secondary and intermittent. My work attempts to integrate the study of royal women into the study of monarchy, whereas Macurdy, to some degree, segregated it.

Unlike Macurdy, I have consciously avoided calling any of the women I discuss "queens" and prefer the more accurate, if vague, term "royal women." The meaning of "queen" and its cognates in other modern European languages is too vague to be useful. By any definition, many of the women I deal with would never be termed queens.

The subject of this book, then, is the role that royal wives, daughters, and mothers played in the central political institution of ancient Macedonia, the monarchy. My thesis is that the explanation for fluctuations in the prominence of royal women in the public life of Macedonia can be found in changes in Macedonian monarchy itself. Once one recognizes that women were part of Macedonian monarchy, one can understand more about the nature of this powerful and much-imitated institution by looking at the role women played in it. Conventional analysis of Macedonian monarchy has often stressed continuity, but the changing role of women in it suggests that continuity was actually limited. In reality, the public presentation of the monarchy narrowed significantly in Hellenistic times. Monarchy only then began to be understood as an office held by a series of individuals rather than as the hereditary possession of a large clan.

WOMEN AND MONARCHY IN MACEDONIA

CHAPTER ONE

Women and Monarchy in the Argead Period

Women were excluded from political power in the classical Greek polis, or city-state. Political and cultural ideology, particularly in Athens, divided life between the private world of the family, in which women had an important role, and the public world of the polis, in which women had little place, except in the area of religion.[1]

In Macedonia things were different. Monarchy, not the polis, was the dominant political structure, and one family, the Argeads, ruled Macedonia from the seventh century B.C. until the death of the last male Argead ca. 309 B.C. After a brief transitional period, another dynasty, the Antigonids, reigned until the Roman conquest of 168 B.C. brought an end to independent ancient Macedonia.[2] In this ancient kingdom, *dunasteia* (power, dominion) was truly synonymous with dynasty. The sexual and political dichotomies of southern Greece could not apply: in a personal monarchy, drawing a hard line between private and public matters was impossible, and in a country where membership in the royal family determined power, female members of the royal family could not entirely be excluded from power, or even understood to have no appropriate role to play in the manipulation of power.

This is not to say that ancient Macedonia was a society in which men and women were in any respect equal. It was a patriarchal world in which at least some degree of the sexual segregation displayed by other Hellenic societies was practiced. No woman ever held the throne, and most royal women, as we shall see, were usually pawns in the power struggles of the males in their family. Nonetheless, the separation of the worlds of men and women and the degree of inequality between men and women, at least among the elite, was not so extreme as elsewhere in the Hellenic world. On occasion, particularly toward the end of the Argead

3

period, women in the Argead clan could and did exercise real power and sometimes played vital roles in power struggles. In a sense women had no part in the political history of southern Greece in the classical period, but in Macedonia they did.

Macedonian monarchy, despite its origins in the remote border regions of the Greek world, had a very broad impact and influence on the political institutions of the rest of the ancient world. The part royal women played in Macedonian monarchy had a similarly long life in political history. The conquests of Philip II (359–336 B.C.) and those of his son, Alexander III, commonly known as Alexander the Great (336–323), built an empire that stretched from northern Greece to the borders of modern India.³ After the death of Alexander, his Macedonian generals, the Successors or Diadochi, engaged in a vicious struggle to seize various chunks of his former empire for themselves and their families.

By the early third century B.C., his generals and their heirs had carved out of Alexander's world empire three large kingdoms that they and their descendants ruled until each, in turn, was conquered by the Romans. Although the monarchy in each of these Successor kingdoms was different and was profoundly affected by previous monarchical tradition in the area ruled, a number of traditions were retained, sometimes even after they had disappeared from the Macedonian homeland. The Roman conquerors of these Hellenistic kingdoms appropriated a number of aspects of Hellenistic monarchy, although altered to fit Roman need and circumstance.⁴

THE NATURE AND EARLY HISTORY OF MACEDONIAN MONARCHY (7TH C.–393)

The heartland of the kingdom of ancient Macedonia was the region around the Thermaic Gulf, between the Haliacmon and Axios rivers, in the northeast of the Greek peninsula. By sometime in the seventh century B.C. the Argeads had established a monarchy in this region. For centuries, however, Macedonia remained a Balkan backwater, little noticed by other and more powerful ancient states, especially by the Greek city-states to the south. The first scattered references in Greek sources to the Macedonian kingdom appear in connection with the Persian invasion of the Greek peninsula early in the fifth century B.C. Probably only shortly before Darius' invasion of 490 B.C., Macedonia came under Persian domination and remained so until the failure of Xerxes' invasion in 479 B.C. Alexander I, the first Macedonian ruler about whom much is known, was able to capitalize on the Persian failure to expand his kingdom and to begin to increase cultural connections with southern Greece.

Nonetheless, throughout the remainder of the fifth century and the first half of the fourth century B.C., Macedonia continued to be a kingdom on the frontier of Greek culture. Macedonia, despite its rich pastures and timber and mineral resources, remained weak and comparatively unurbanized. Its kings were unable to control the upland regions above the coastal plain or to prevent the development of Greek, particularly Athenian, colonies on Macedonian borders. Incursions by neighboring tribal peoples, particularly the Illyrians, were frequent. During the Peloponnesian War (431–404), the long-lasting confrontation between the great powers of Athens and Sparta, Macedonia was buffeted by intervention from both powers but allied itself more permanently with Athens in the later stages of the war, primarily under the leadership of Archelaus (413–399 B.C.). An able ruler, Archelaus improved both the internal and external security of the kingdom, built roads, strengthened the army, and sponsored Hellenization. After his assassination in 399 B.C., succession to the throne was chaotic and sometimes violent until Amyntas III, father of Philip II and grandfather of Alexander the Great, came to the throne ca. 393.[5]

Monarchy was the central institution of ancient Macedonia. Macedonian rulers, neither isolated nor insulated by elaborate ceremony, dress, or protocol, stood out little from the rest of the elite. Kings were warriors, not infrequently killed in battle. In peace and in war they were surrounded by *hetairoi* (companions), similar to those of Homeric heroes. Some of the elite received land in return for service. Macedonian kings had an important religious role, although comparatively little is known of this aspect of monarchy. They presided over a society that, although increasingly urban, remained more rural than that of southern Greece. Both Macedonian monarchy and Macedonian society are often characterized as "Homeric."[6]

The evidence for most periods of ancient Macedonian history is poor. Extant literary evidence dates largely from the Hellenistic and Roman periods, and none of these surviving sources was written by a Macedonian. Much of this evidence relates to the second half of the fourth century B.C., the comparatively brief period of the reigns of Philip II and his son, Alexander the Great. Archaeological evidence supplements the uneven coverage of our written sources, as does epigraphic evidence (although it is concentrated in the Hellenistic period). The reality remains, however, that we know comparatively little about Macedonia before the fourth century and much less than we would like to about Hellenistic Macedonia.

The poor and uneven nature of our sources affects attempts to understand even the most fundamental aspect of ancient Macedonian society, the monarchy, and creates a basic disagreement among scholars about the nature of that monarchy. Some have argued that the Macedonian king was limited in a constitutional way by law and by an army assembly. Others, including me, see the power of the kings as unlimited in the abstract but in reality as often hemmed in by circumstance, particularly by the machinations of groups within the royal family and Macedonian elite.[7] Macedonian kings had to take custom (no evidence for written law exists) into account but could and did flout it if doing so seemed to be necessary or opportune.[8]

Despite the theoretically absolute nature of royal power, the history of Macedonian monarchy in the Argead period was a chaotic and violent one. Rival branches of the royal dynasty struggled for dominance over generations, often invoking foreign assistance and thus intervention; invasions and even royal exile were common. Regicide was frequently attempted and sometimes successful. Virtually every succession to the throne was, in some degree, contested. Argead seemed to supplant Argead with relative ease, but no clear plan for succession developed.[9] One Argead was apparently as good as another, so long as he was able to defeat the others. Granted such long-standing practice, emphasis in Argead monarchy was not, primarily, on the individual ruler whose identity was so subject to change.

Stability lay not with the individual Argead but with the clan.[10] Despite centuries of violent intrigue and confusion, one thing remained unchanged: the king was an Argead. As far as we know, only Argeads ruled Macedonia from its historical beginnings until the death of the last male in the direct line, Alexander IV.[11] Whereas the deaths of individual Argeads do not seem to have precipitated long-lasting trouble, the demise of the Argead dynasty certainly did. Their immediate successors, the Antipatrids, were unable to retain control of the throne that Cassander, son of Antipater, had in effect seized from the last of the Argeads. A generation of anarchy followed before the Antigonids managed to reestablish order and secure a firm hold on the throne. Antigonid manipulation of nostalgia for Argead rule contributed to this achievement. I shall argue, however, that this reestablished monarchy was significantly different because it had been detached from its relationship to one dynasty. The weight of centuries of Macedonian history argues for an understanding of Macedonian kingship, at least in classical times, not as an office held by an individual, but rather as the domination of a clan.[12]

More than the remarkable longevity of the Argeads points in the direction of this understanding of Macedonian monarchy. Only in the reign of Alexander the Great, the last Argead to rule in his own right, did the king begin to employ a title, and even then the title was not employed consistently. Typically Argead kings designated themselves by a personal name and a patronymic.[13] The existence of a title and the conceptualization of kingship as an office held by an individual are not identical issues. Nonetheless, the absence of a regularly used title suggests that the king's power was determined not by title or by office but rather by his position as the dominant Argead. The practice of having a king sign a treaty first, followed by other Argeads, apparently in status order, implies much the same.[14] Indeed, Macedonian society in general in the classical period tended to conceptualize power in terms of individual personalities rather than offices.[15] In terms of the monarchy, it is significant that when the first non-Argeads, Alexander's Successors, began to call themselves and each other *basileus* (king), the title was still so undefined, so personal a term, that it was tied neither to the rule of a specific people nor to an area.

Another sign that kingship was seen not as an office with well-defined powers but rather as the domination of a clan is the messy and undefined situations that tended to develop in Macedonia whenever the king himself was not present for a considerable time. It has proved virtually impossible to clarify the distribution of power on such occasions, suggesting that the powers of kingship could not easily be defined and thus transferred. A certain tendency for power to accumulate around available Argeads is observable, even if they appeared to be ineligible because of age or sex. Apparently it was difficult to dissociate royal power from the royal clan, especially over time. Moreover, even after Alexander's death, during the long period of the minority of Alexander's son, Alexander IV (and Philip Arrhidaeus, Alexander's mentally limited half-brother), no clear understanding or terminology for substitute kingship developed. This lack of development in terminology is unsurprising given that, before the death of Alexander the Great, instances involving a person who held power in the place of the king for any length of time were rare. Ordinarily what we might term a regency constituted a brief transition period that allowed the Argead acting as king to become king in fact.[16]

Problems arose when the person acting as king was not an Argead and no one was available to replace him. The cultural shock precipitated by the final collapse of the Argead dynasty and the ensuing anarchy it caused may well have created a growing perception of monarchy as an office to be held, exactly because dominion and dynasty, after a period in which they had been dissociated, had to be reunited and their relationship somewhat rationalized in the process. *Basileia* (monarchy) belonged to the Argead clan, and the dismay and disorientation the end of the dynasty generated are certain signs of the importance of the idea of *dunasteia* of the clan.[17]

THE ROLE OF ROYAL WOMEN IN ARGEAD MONARCHY

Although no woman ever reigned in ancient Macedonia, the wives, daughters, and sisters of the Argead clan nonetheless participated in monarchy. Female Argeads, whether by blood or marriage, played a role in the exercise of power, particularly in issues related to royal succession.

SCHOLARSHIP AND THE SOURCES

Those who wish to understand the role of women in Macedonian monarchy encounter special problems, quite apart from the paucity of sources familiar to all students of antiquity and different even from the chronic problem of doing Macedonian history without Macedonian sources. There are four major difficulties peculiar to the study of royal Macedonian women. First, information on women is scarcer, generally, than information on men. Even, for instance, in the comparatively well documented reign of the Antigonid ruler Philip V, we have no good evidence about the women of his family. Second, extant sources frequently suffer from a variety of biases about women, almost in direct proportion to the degree of power these women attained. Third, in considering both individual women and the general role of women in monarchy, modern scholarship has too often suffered from uncritical use of biased ancient sources. Fourth, distortion created by the modern retention of ancient preconceptions about women (and, occasionally, by more recent preju-dices) also affects scholarship.

The dearth of references to women in extant sources has various consequences for both the study of individual royal women and analysis of the role of royal women in general. In the case of individual women, we often lack critical information about even the best-known and best-documented women, for instance, Olympias, mother of Alexander the Great. Ancient and modern writers have suggested that Olympias was behind the murder of her husband, Philip II, but we cannot know if Olympias was in Macedonia at the time (see OLYMPIAS: PART I). Simi-larly, we cannot be certain of the location of either Olympias or her daughter, Alexander's full sister, during much of the reign of Alexander (see OLYMPIAS and CLEOPATRA 2).

Scarcity of information has a different effect on understanding royal women in general. Although we can arrive at a rough understanding of the life of ordinary and elite male Macedonians as compared to that of their kings, the same does not apply to women. We know nothing about the lives of ordinary women in Macedonia and little more than nothing about women in the elite, and we have specifics about the lives of only a handful of royal women.[18] Thus we cannot establish a societal norm to which we can compare the actions of individual royal women.

This absence of normative material leads to another problem. Schol-ars tend to assume that, in the absence of specific contradictory evi-dence, things must have been done in the same way in Macedonia that they were in Athens.[19] Behind this assumption lies a kind of wishful thinking: we know or think we know more about the role of women in classical Athens than in other places and periods in the Hellenic world, so what we know must be relevant. Yet the assumption of similarity in Athenian and Macedonian female roles is particularly dubious because so many aspects of the role and status of women in Athens were directly con-nected to the development of citizenship in the democratic system. In fact, the role of women in classical Athens is the least preferable model for that of royal women in Macedonia. Rather than assume that whatever was true of Athenian women was true of Macedonian women, it would be wiser to begin with the reverse assumption. We should wonder whether superficial similarities are significant or the consequence of self-conscious Hellenizing. In terms of similarities between Macedonian and Athenian female roles, there may well have been change over time. Macedonia seems considerably more Hellenized in Antigonid times than earlier. Doubts entertained by many scholars about the Hellenic ethnicity of the Macedonians only compound the problem.[20] That so many royal women were neither Greek nor Macedonian adds yet more difficulty. As we shall see, some foreign royal wives brought with them very different expectations about their roles than those apparently held by local Macedonians, yet, despite this alien context, at least some of these atypical customs and attitudes were retained and even passed on to the descendants of these women.

Those who attempt to understand the role of women in monarchy must determine the significance of silence. What, for instance, should we make of the fact that royal women in the Antigonid period are virtually invisible in the literary sources, yet fairly well documented in epigraphic sources (see chap. 7)? What we do know about the lives of individual royal women suggests that we should not automatically assume that they lacked influence simply because we do not hear of them in a given period: the careers of Olympias, Cynnane, and Thessalonice provide examples of women whose sudden prominence in the sources presumes earlier, behind-the-scenes activity. It is easy to underestimate the clout of royal women because they usually had influence but not direct authority. It is much simpler to document power exercised in an overtly public way than it is to demonstrate the private, often consciously discreet implementation of power. Indeed, royal males may publicly deny the influence of the women of their family yet privately tolerate and even encourage it (see OLYMPIAS). Sarah B. Pomeroy has noted how women in general, because of their role and the interests of the ancient sources, tend to be a "muted group," whose influence is often underestimated.[21]

The prejudice of the ancient sources is a significant problem, particularly for the careers of the more aggressive women like Olympias or Arsinoe whose actions seemed not only to ignore Hellenic expectations about female behavior but also actually to invert them. That our surviving sources are Greek, not Macedonian—not the product of the Macedonian political system but that of the polis world of the south—makes them hostile to the power at least some women exercised in monarchy. One might even conclude that the Greeks disliked monarchy partly because women played a part in its politics as they did not in the politics of the city-state. The mingling of public and private that characterized Macedonian monarchy and that enabled royal women to play some occasional political role seemed to Greeks anathema, a sort of cultural heresy and proof of the essentially barbarian nature of those who violated the norms of the polis world.[22]

Anecdotes present particular problems for those who look at the lives and actions of royal women. First, scholars need to take into account the nature of anecdotes. Even when they refer to men, they should be used with much more caution than most scholars exercise.[23] Especially over time, narratives tend to develop a life and force of their own. For instance, a story may be told simply because it is entertaining, or it may be altered to apply to someone else because he is more famous than the individual to whom the original event occurred.[24] The same story may be told about different people, particularly if there is a desire to demonstrate that the protagonist of the tale is the equal of some earlier hero. From the storyteller's point of view, the tale may be more important than the identities of those involved.[25] It is not uncommon for anecdotes to assume an assortment of circumstances that are probably not true.[26] Some anecdotes show obvious signs of being influenced by drama or epic (see, e.g., ADEA EURYDICE for the accounts of her death). More insidious are anecdotes that in themselves seem quite plausible but whose accurate preservation in a historical source is unlikely.[27]

Second, when an anecdote focuses on a woman, scholars should exercise even greater caution. Contemporary documentary evidence is clearly preferable to that furnished by anecdotal sources, but the less public role of women makes the former rather scarce and the latter, however dubious, necessary to examine. Anecdotes about women often reflect the sources' prejudiced attempts to reinforce conventional behavior.[28] Such attempts are particularly likely if the women in question have pursued or demonstrated political power in an overt way. Information offered obliquely by an anecdote may be more trustworthy than the main thrust of the anecdote.[29]

The third problem relating to the study of royal women in Macedonia is continuing late-twentieth-century prejudice. On some occasions the apparent retention of prejudice is simply the consequence of uncritical use of the sources. On the one hand, the unconscious, false, assumption is made that the point of view of the sources and that of the scholars is identical. It seems self-evident that societal norms and gender expectations differ dramatically when one compares the ancient Hellenic world and our own postmodern one. Moreover, scholars sometimes treat assertions encountered in the sources as objective facts rather than subjective assessments. We know that judgments made about contemporary controversial figures (e.g., Hillary Clinton, wife of the current U.S. president) vary tremendously depending on the partisan point of view of the person making the judgment, but we somehow forget that statements made about ancient personalities should be looked at in the same way and not taken as universal truths.[30] On the other hand, ancient prejudice is also perpetuated when a scholar fails to notice that a source has different, more moralistic expectations for the behavior of prominent women than for the behavior of men.[31]

Our culture shares the prejudices of our sources about powerful women; many stereotypes about women with power persist comparatively unchanged and continue to have tremendous appeal, even for those who should know better. For instance, in both modern and ancient sources women's motivation is often assumed to be private and personal and men's as more likely the result of reasons of state; the former is condemned and the latter approved. When Olympias kills one hundred people, her action is disapproved of as irrational vengeance, whereas the atrocity of male Successors is tacitly approved of or at least not criticized because it is seen as politically motivated.[32] Perhaps the most dangerous aspect of these stereotypes is that the stories that perpetuate them are often seen as gruesome, if unacknowledged, fun. It is difficult, for instance, to find any other reason for repeating Pausanias' (8.7.5) improbably bizarre version of the execution of Cleopatra and her baby by Olympias.[33]

The long history and success of patriarchy prevented women from exercising power directly and often meant that women were criticized for being manipulative when they tried to exercise power indirectly. Excluded from participation in public violence usually deemed legitimate (i.e., war), women who pursued power turned to (or were believed to turn to) private violence, which was usually considered illegitimate.[34] Accusations of witchcraft and poisoning, often with a sexual undertone, arise

from this fear of the private violence of women.[35] Such crimes are paradoxically seen as both typically feminine and as betrayals of a woman's
role. Justin (14.6.1), for instance, says that Olympias' murder of Adea Eurydice and Philip Arrhidaeus was more like that of a woman than a
ruler.[36] It is often difficult to determine whether women did or did not
conform to stereotypical expectations in a given incident.[37]

Finally, scholarship sometimes invents new prejudices about women
where none exists in the ancient source.[38] We must be careful not to attribute our own reactions to ancient peoples unless evidence suggests that
they were indeed similar, and we should be sensitive to differences between
our perceptions and conceptualizations and those of ancient people.

INFLUENCES AND CONTEXTS
Much of this study concerns internal influences on the role and status of
royal women in ancient Macedonia, but there were external influences
as well. Although it is difficult to demonstrate the absolute existence of
influence (mere similarity of custom is not sufficient proof), it is possible to demonstrate that royal women had access to information about the
role of royal women in other cultures and times.[39]

The most obvious possible influence is that of Homer. Macedonian society, in particular, the monarchy, is often said to be Homeric in nature;
royal Macedonian burial customs certainly owe more to Homer than to
southern Greeks; Olympias and her son and daughter believed themselves
to be descendants of both Andromache and Achilles (Eur. *Andr.* 1239–49;
Paus. 1.11.2; Pind. *Nem.* 4.51, 7.35–40); and the further Hellenization of
Macedonia sponsored by various kings would hardly have limited the influence of Homer.

Royal women in Homer, although not generally the equal of their
husbands and sons, move in and out of the world of men.[40] Penelope, wife
of the long-absent hero Odysseus, spends much time in the women's
quarters but often enters the great hall and talks to the men there, and
she summons people to her quarters for interviews and listens in on
events below (*Od.* 1.329–35; 4.675–714, 735–41). When she deals with
men, she is always attended by women and semiveiled, but deal with men
and public events she does (*Od.* 1.331–35; 4.791; 16.409–33). Other royal
women act in a similar way, sitting in the hall with their husbands and oc-

casionally entering into male conversation (*Od.* 4.120–47, 235–46; 6.305–15; 7.233–39; 8.243). Even the unmarried Nausicaa appears in her father's hall (*Od.* 6.458–62). Penelope's interactions with men are usually in her son's or her husband's interest; it is easy to imagine her actions being used by various Macedonian royal women to justify their own.[41]

Although royal Macedonian women did not lead lives like those of contemporary women to the south, there are similarities between their roles and the roles of elite women in the Archaic period, particularly in the families of tyrants. Anna Maria Prestianni-Giallombardo and N. G. L. Hammond have both compared the polygamous marital situation of Macedonian women and aristocratic women in the Archaic period.[42] The latter were less circumscribed than were women in the same class in the classical period. They had considerable freedom of action and some political influence, functioned as vehicles for the display of family wealth (in their dress, their burials, their weddings), and often were involved in international marriage alliances.[43] Women in tyrant's families had quasi-public roles and, like later Macedonian women, might suddenly take a very public role in moments of crisis. They made offerings at major shrines, demonstrating the wealth of their families, and their names, like those of Argead women, might be changed to glorify men in the family.[44]

Other possible influences on royal women's roles and actions were not Hellenic. For one thing, many royal wives were not Macedonian. Despite our very limited evidence, it seems clear that what these women did in their new context was affected by the role of women, particularly royal women, in their homelands. It is likely that women had a greater and more institutionalized role in the Molossian monarchy than in the Macedonian: the careers and expectations of Olympias and her daughter, Cleopatra, almost certainly reflect this Molossian experience (see OLYMPIAS). Audata, one of the wives of Philip II, her daughter, Cynnane, and her granddaughter, Adea Eurydice, continued an Illyrian tradition of military action by royal women (see CYNNANE). When one recalls that royal mothers were the primary influences on their daughters and that they seem to have remained associated even when their daughters were adults, it is reasonable to conclude that many foreign customs and viewpoints came to affect royal women in Macedonia.

The practices of nearby contemporary monarchies may also have affected Macedonian practice concerning royal women. Although monarchy had largely disappeared from southern Greece, it remained dominant on the edges of the Greek world (e.g., Macedonia and Molossia) and outside it. It is possible that the unusually prominent role of women in the Hecatomnid dynasty of Caria had some influence on the role of women in Macedonian monarchy, but the Persian monarchy was much better known to the Greek world, particularly to the Macedonians. The Hellenic world was, on the one hand, fascinated by the externals of Persian monarchy and, on the other, repelled by what Greeks understood to be its basic nature. Much of this "understanding" was a misunderstanding, generated by the Greek predilection for thinking in terms of complete opposition rather than mere difference and the tendency to associate different sorts of "others," the foreign and the female.[45]

This distorted image of Persian monarchy applies particularly to the role of women. Greek literary tradition insists that Persian royal women, especially kings' mothers, were important to Persian monarchy and played critical roles in the succession of their sons. Greek sources also tend to associate Persian monarchy with effeminacy, luxury, and lack of freedom and to blame the influence of royal women for these qualities. Persian evidence, although confirming the wealth of royal women, offers no support for the idea that they had any political role. Greek sources should therefore be used with caution.[46]

Whatever the reality of the role of women in Persian monarchy, there can be no doubt that both men and women at the Macedonian court were familiar with it, not simply with literary tradition about it. Macedonia was once under Persian domination.[47] A sister of Alexander I named Gygaea married a high-ranking Persian (see GYGEA 1). Artabazus, a Persian satrap with Achaemenid blood, spent years in exile at the court of Philip II, along with his Greek wife and their children (Diod. 16.52.3; Curt. 5.9.1, 6.5.2). According to a curious tale in Athenaeus (6.256c–d), the women of Artabazus' family had a harmful influence on the women of Philip's family because they brought to them the ways of the Persian court. After Alexander's conquests began, elite Macedonians had increasing contacts with Persian royal women, and many married into the Persian elite. Harpalus, at least, seems to have found the role of Persian royal women worthy of imitation (Ath. 13.586c, 597c). It seems likely that just as males were influenced by Persian monarchy, so were females, but the specifics are virtually impossible to ascertain.[48]

GYGAEA 1

Gygaea, daughter of Amyntas I and sister of Alexander I, married Bubares (Herod. 5.21), son of Megabazus and a high-ranking Persian official. According to Herodotus (5.21), Gygaea's brother arranged his sister's marriage as part of a bribe intended to conceal Alexander's supposed murder of members of a Persian embassy (Herod. 5.18–21). Herodotus (8.136) later reports that Gygaea and Bubares had a son, Amyntas, named after his maternal grandfather. The son commanded the revenues of a Phrygian town.

Much of Herodotus' information about Gygaea is unlikely to be true. The murder of the Persian ambassadors is widely recognized as a fiction. Macedonia was probably not a vassal state of Persia's until just before the invasion of 490.[49] Moreover, it is unlikely that Gygaea's brother arranged her marriage while her father was still alive,[50] so one must conclude either that Amyntas himself arranged it ca. 510 or that Alexander did so, after his father's death, sometime after his accession ca. 498.

In either event, this marriage of the first historical Argead woman whose name is preserved in our sources[51] is clearly a marriage alliance, the first of many recorded for royal Macedonian women. The alliance doubtless was an element in Macedonian-Persian diplomatic relations, but the uncertainty of its date makes it impossible to say.

APPROPRIATE PARALLELS OR MODELS

Given the comparatively poor surviving evidence on royal women in Macedonia, it is helpful to examine the role of women in similar situations (see discussion of polygamy below) and monarchies. Such models can offer confirmation for hypotheses initially based only on Macedonian material.

These are not the only possible grounds for a comparison of medieval and Macedonian monarchy. Alan Samuel has argued that in a general way Macedonian monarchy resembled Merovingian monarchy. Not all his arguments are convincing, but undeniable parallels existed.[52] It is even possible that the changes in monarchy in the high medieval period that led to a more circumscribed role for royal women can help us to understand the apparent changes in the role of royal Macedonian women in the Antigonid period.

WOMEN AND MONARCHY IN MACEDONIA

The circumstances of royal women in early medieval monarchy were in many ways analogous to those of royal Macedonian women,[53] at least in the Argead period, and these circumstances are much better documented than those of Macedonian women. Like Macedonian rulers, Merovingian kings were polygamous and had no titular queens or chief wives. As in Macedonia, no clearly established system of succession existed. In both cases sources with a monogamous orientation (Greek in the case of Macedonia, Christian in the case of Merovingian monarchy) often labeled royal wives "concubines" (Simache is a good Macedonian example of this phenomenon) and tended to be hostile to aggressive royal women, caricaturing them as manipulative and sometimes murderous schemers and workers of magic.[54]

SIMACHE

Simache was the mother of Archelaus (Ael. *VH* 12.43). Despite the statements of Aelian and Plato (Grg. 471a–c) that Archelaus' mother was a slave of Perdiccas II's brother Alcetas, she must have been a wife of Perdiccas II or her son could not have been treated as legitimate well before his father's death (*IG* I 89).[55] Servile status may have been imputed to her because of the failure of non-Macedonian sources to understand royal polygamy,[56] her probable nonroyal status,[57] and subsequent attempts by rivals and contenders to attack Archelaus through his parentage.[58]

The date of her marriage to Perdiccas II is unknown,[59] but the marriage probably occurred comparatively early in his reign.[60] Nothing is known of Simache's lineage, but the most plausible surmise is that she was a member of the Macedonian elite and that her marriage to Perdiccas was part of efforts early in his reign to stabilize the kingdom and establish a secure political base.

However, the two monarchies differed in important ways. Whereas royal polygamy produced numerous competing heirs in both Argead and Merovingian times, the struggle between competing heirs tended to come after a man became king in Macedonia but before he became king in the case of the Merovingian Franks.[61] Christian institutions and values in the Merovingian period offered possibilities for power and manipulation as well as disadvantages to Frankish royal women.[62] It seems likely that Merovingian royal women, in keeping with the generally broader role women played in Frankish society, were less circumscribed in their actions than were Macedonian women.[63]

Conclusions reached by Pauline Stafford and others about these early medieval royal women have relevance to the Macedonian situation and tend to confirm my conclusions. Among them are the following: the absence of a titular queen or chief wife meant that the general status of royal wives remained low; kings found it useful to keep wives and sons uncertain about the succession and thus dependent on them; highborn wives with ability had the greatest difficulty in accepting their comparatively low status; every new marriage was a threat to the possible succession of sons already born; sons and mothers were tied closely together because a mother's status depended on her son's, and typically a mother thus became an advocate of her son's succession;[64] royal women had most influence after their husbands' deaths, particularly in a disputed succession.

Reference to these Frankish parallels helps to free us from the dangers of the kind of personality-ridden analysis that has so often weakened previous treatments of royal Macedonian women. For instance, in the light of Frankish and other comparative material, it seems less appropriate to see the actions of Eurydice in the succession of her sons and of Olympias in support of her son and grandson solely in terms of their personality traits and more appropriate to consider their actions in terms of their position in polygamous marriages.

MARRIAGE

Although the marriages of royal women, whether a king's bride, daughter, or sister, did not become public extravaganzas until late in the reign of Philip II (see chap. 8), they can never have been typical of marriages generally contracted in Macedonian society and would always have been affected and sometimes determined by dynastic and political concerns.[65] In any event, we have no information about ordinary Macedonian marriages, age at marriage for men and women, identity of the persons involved in contracting marriages, or general cultural expectations and understanding of the institution. As always, we should be hesitant to assume that Athenian or southern Greek marriage practices are applicable to Macedonia in general, let alone to royal marriage. Many of the royal brides and their fathers were neither Macedonian nor Greek, and may have brought their own cultural expectations to marriage arrangements. Moreover, merely the fact that a number of Macedonian kings were polygamous while classical Greeks were monogamous inevitably alters the nature of their marriages in fundamental ways.

Greenwalt concluded that Argead males generally married in their early twenties and that women married somewhat earlier, in their late teens.[66] Well-known exceptions to these generalizations (Alexander, who first married close to the age of thirty [see ROXANE], and Adea Eurydice, who married in her mid-teens [see ADEA EURYDICE]) occurred for political reasons. In comparison to the Athenian pattern, the royal Macedonian pattern was older brides and younger grooms. Greenwalt argues that the Athenian age pattern for marriage derived primarily from economic concerns, whereas Argead age patterns for marriage reflect both the need for the stability offered by the early production of a male heir and the varying foreign policy requirements of monarchs. In the Argead period, the emphasis seems to have been on producing numerous heirs, probably because (quite apart from high infant and childhood mortality) so many kings died fairly young and royal successions were generally problematic. Although it is possible that some male Argeads married before they took the throne, more typically they married soon after.

Royal Macedonian marriages are commonly referred to as "marriage alliances," a terminology that I will adopt because it indicates—correctly I believe—that virtually all royal marriages were contracted, at least in part, for political and dynastic reasons.[67] Waldemar Heckel has argued that scholars have overestimated the political nature of royal and elite Macedonian marriages.[68] His cautions are salutary but somewhat overstated. Although he is correct to point to the alacrity with which Macedonian nobles abandoned the ties created by marriage in the service of self-interest, this fact does not demonstrate that the marriages were not contracted for political reasons but merely that they might be abandoned if the political situation changed. Given the pragmatic attitude toward marriage in the ancient world and the likelihood that royal marriages were contracted for political reasons as well as to produce heirs, we should doubt assertions that any royal marriage was contracted for emotional reasons alone and avoid any understanding of royal marriages that assumes that they were primarily emotional and personal in character.[69] These marriages were alliances.

We should remind ourselves, however, that the term "marriage alliance" tends to blur at least four important issues involved in royal marriages. First, whatever the diplomatic benefit of the "alliance," most marriages were also contracted so that the couples would beget children, particularly future rulers.

A second complication arises in terms of marriages in which the primary purpose was political. What was the purpose of "marriage alliances"? Our ignorance about the exact dates and circumstances of many royal marriages (as well as the identity of their initiators) makes it difficult to deal with this issue, but it is seems clear that some marriage alliances were contracted for short-term benefit and others for more lasting concerns.[70] What does it mean for a young woman to move from one family to another? Is she intended to become her birth family's ambassador to the family of her husband, or is she more like a party favor given at the time of a peace treaty or some other alliance and, once given, soon forgotten (see STRATONICE for a good early example)?[71]

STRATONICE 1

Stratonice was the sister of Perdiccas II, who gave her in marriage ca. 429/8 to Seuthes, an important officer of Sitalces, Seuthes' uncle and the Odrysian king of Thrace (Thuc. 2.101.6). Perdiccas arranged the marriage as part of his successful attempt to negotiate an end to the Thracian invasion of Macedonia. Seuthes, persuaded by the offer of Stratonice as well as by a substantial sum of money, convinced his uncle to agree to the departure of Thracian troops.[72] The marriage, similar to that of Gygaea 1, is another example of an early Argead marriage alliance, one that helped to enable the reigning Argead to move from a position of weakness to one of strength.

A third problem occurs: Does the "alliance" empower the giver or the receiver of the bride? Although my use of the words *giver* and *receiver* implies that Argead women, like women elsewhere in the Hellenic world, did not generally make their own decisions about whom they would marry, this is a generalization and did not apply to all marriages involving royal women. Royal marriages initiated by either the brides themselves or their mothers became more common in the Hellenistic period but may

WOMEN AND MONARCHY IN MACEDONIA

well have occurred earlier. That some women exercised the initiative in marriage should be kept in mind when we consider the more or less universal, although often unstated, assumption that the women involved in marriage alliances were always passive pawns in the alliance of two families. Doubtless, this was often or even typically the case, but it is incorrect to believe that it was always so. We know of examples from the late fourth century and the Hellenistic period (CLEOPATRA 2; LANASSA; ARSINOE; STRATONICE 3) in which women functioned as independent players rather than pawns, and this situation may not have been unique to the later and somewhat better documented period.

Fourth, significant differences probably existed between the marriages of kings and the marriages of their daughters and sisters, but we lack the detailed information required to discern real patterns here. It could be the case, for example, that a king's daughters were more likely to marry Macedonians and a king's sons to marry foreign princesses. It would be nice to know if marriages within the ruling dynasty (the marriage of cousins or others Argead by blood; the marriage of a royal widow to her husband's successor, as happened in the case of Cleopatra 1) were common or rare.[73] To put it another way, did the Argead dynasty spread itself out by a series of marriages connecting it to the ruling elite, or did it narrow itself to consolidate royal power and limit the number of possible contestants in succession struggles? I will argue that in Argead times the tendency was to broaden the dynasty, not only through royal polygamy but also through other marriages involving the reigning dynasty, but that this pattern changed by the beginning of the Antigonid period.

CLEOPATRA 1

Cleopatra was, in all likelihood, the wife of both Perdiccas II and his son, her stepson, Archelaus.[74] She had one son by Perdiccas. According to Plato, after the death of Perdiccas, Archelaus eliminated his uncle Alcetas, Alcetas' son, and Cleopatra's son, a seven-year-old, whom Archelaus supposedly pushed down a well. Archelaus told Cleopatra that the boy fell down the well chasing a goose (Pl. *Grg.* 471a–c; Aristid. 45.55).

Aristotle (*Pol.* 1311b15) refers to a wife of Archelaus named Cleopatra by whom he had a son.[75] Was the same woman married to both father and son? Hammond argued that the duplication of the name for the wife of father and son was mere coincidence, the consequence of the fact that it was a common Macedonian name for women,[76] but there is little evidence that it was particularly common, especially so early in Macedonian history.[77] The name has subsequent Argead and royal associations,[78] but cannot be considered common in the fifth century.

Aristotle also reports that Archelaus had two daughters, one married to the king of Elimea during the war against Sirras and Arrabaeus and the other to Amyntas (*Pol.* 1311b),[79] all in an effort to win support for the succession of Archelaus' son by Cleopatra. Both the diction of the Aristotle passage and the implied age of the daughters make it unlikely that Cleopatra, rather than some earlier wife, was their mother.

Cleopatra's place and family of origin are unknown, although something about her background seems to have made Archelaus feel the need to eliminate her much younger son and, if I am right, to marry her himself and have a son by her. John Whitehorne's speculation that Cleopatra was Lyncestian, the sister or daughter of Arrhibaeus, is not impossible.[80] But it is difficult to see why, if that were true, her status and thus her son's status would have threatened Archelaus sometime soon after 413. It is more likely that she was Macedonian, perhaps Argead.[81] Hammond rejected the possibility that Amyntas married his father's stepmother, partly because he considered such a marriage "pointless."[82] But at least one Macedonian king married the widow of his predecessor and mother of the supposed heir (see CHRYSEIS), and such marriages have early medieval parallels, not to mention Homeric ones. The attractions of marrying a royal widow are not entirely clear but could involve considerations of both a practical sort (attention to the influence of Cleopatra or her family or access to the heir for purposes of easy elimination) and a symbolic one.

If this first historical Cleopatra was the wife of both Perdiccas II and his son Archelaus, then hers was a tragic life, not atypical of the lives of better-attested royal women in subsequent periods. Cleopatra bore two sons to two kings, and both were brutally eliminated when mere children by older rivals for the throne. Nothing demonstrates that Cleopatra had any independent power or influence, although Archelaus' tale of accidental death implies that an explanation was owed Cleopatra. If Cleopatra was anything other than a pawn in the games of others, we do not know it.

Many of the issues I have raised about royal marriages are unanswerable or open to only impressionistic solution because of the state of our evidence. However, even if we cannot be sure which circumstances best apply in a given situation, it is worthwhile to be aware of the range of possibilities that may have affected individual kings.

ROYAL POLYGAMY, ROYAL SUCCESSION, AND WIFELY COMPETITION

Around the world, polygamy has been practiced in many forms and circumstances.[83] Macedonian kings often were polygamous. Polygamous marriages are well attested for Alexander the Great and many of the first generation of Hellenistic kings, the Successors. General opinion now holds that Philip was polygamous on an unprecedented scale, ultimately taking seven wives.[84]

There is little specific evidence on the marriages of Argead rulers before Philip II and certainly no direct evidence on their polygamy, but a number of factors make it likely that earlier rulers were polygamous, or could be if they chose.[85] It is difficult, for instance, to account for various aspects of the struggles for succession between Amyntas III's sons by Gygaea and Philip II, his youngest son by Eurydice, if one does not assume that Amyntas was married to both women and fathering children by them in the same period.[86] Perdiccas II may also have been married to more than one woman at the same time.[87] It is striking that neither Philip nor Alexander were criticized for initiating the practice of polygamy or simply for being polygamous. The absence of such criticism strongly suggests that Philip and his son were perpetuating a royal custom, not initiating it.[88] As I have noted, the role of women in the families of Greek tyrants and the role of royal Macedonian women were often similar. It is well known that many tyrants practiced polygamy; their practice tends to confirm the likelihood that earlier Argeads were also polygamous.

Patterns of succession during the Argead period also support the conclusion that many Argead rulers practiced polygamy. Greenwalt has argued persuasively that the lack of a clear succession pattern within the Argead clan and the existence of royal polygamy are not coincidental. He believed that the practice of polygamy tended to create a messy inheritance pattern by generating numerous potential heirs and concluded that Macedonian monarchy benefited from the stability created by critical marriage alliances but suffered from the destabilizing effects of competing claimants to the throne.[89] When many wives produced many sons by the same king (or earlier kings), no clear pattern of succession was established for choosing among rival Argeads.[90] Given the low life expectancy of Argead rulers, a kind of faux primogeniture tended to develop simply because, at best, a man's oldest son might be just old enough to hold onto the throne, but the rejection and murder of minor heirs make it clear that no hard and fast principle of primogeniture was followed.

Attempts to demonstrate the existence of other rules for royal succession are unconvincing.[91] The truth seems to be each succession was situationally determined. A number of factors, many of them quite possibly unknown to us, contributed to the successful succession of a given Argead: the preference of the last monarch; support from powerful groups within the dynasty and the elite; the perceived personal competence of the candidate; support from powers outside Macedonia proper; and the status and influence of the mother of the heir or her family as compared to that of rival candidates.[92] This situation endured, in effect, until the combined effect of Alexander the Great's postponement of marriage until his late twenties and his comparatively early death suddenly produced a succession crisis that was the reverse of those previously experienced: too few instead of too many eligible male heirs.

Although available evidence, particularly the succession pattern, suggests that royal polygamy in Macedonia predated Philip II, it was hardly a uniform or universal custom. The practice of polygamy within the Argead dynasty demonstrably varied considerably between the comparatively modest polygamy of Amyntas III and the much more conspicuous polygamy of his son Philip II. It may well be that a number of Argead kings chose to be monogamous or died too young to marry more than once.[93] Certainly a royal harem never became a symbol of royal power in Macedonia, as it did in many Near Eastern monarchies.

As it is likely that a number of Macedonian kings were polygamous, it is necessary to assess the advantages and disadvantages of this custom. A polygamous king is likely to produce more children than a monogamous king. Monarchies that practice polygamy therefore prioritize the production of heirs; rivalries and conflicts arising from the production of more numerous heirs are, by implication, preferable to the crisis an absence of heirs would produce. Such a preference suits the often-embattled situation of the Argead dynasty in the years before Philip II.

Polygamy did not always produce the desired goal of numerous heirs, however. The general pattern of the Argead period before Alexander was that of numerous and competing heirs, but this was not always the case. The fertility of women in polygamous marriages is about one-third lower than that of women in monogamous marriages, for a variety of reasons, including decreased frequency of sexual activity between husbands and individual wives and the consequences of probable menstrual synchrony of multiple wives.[94] The fertility of individual male Argeads and individual royal wives might differ: Amyntas III (see chap. 2) fathered six sons and one daughter by only two wives, whereas his son Philip produced only two sons and four daughters by seven wives. Factors other than low fertility might limit the production of children: parental absence;[95] conscious reluctance to father children by certain wives;[96] death of wives in childbirth;[97] the deaths of royal children in infancy; and the early and violent deaths of Argead rulers. Reflection on the numerous uncertainties and risks involved in producing an adequate number of male heirs helps to explain why, throughout the Argead period, the benefits of polygamy apparently outweighed the risks.

In addition to maximizing the production of heirs, royal polygamy could give rulers greater flexibility in making and retaining alliances both internal and external. A polygamous king does not reject earlier wives but simply acquires additional ones. Such a king is not compelled to offend the family of a first wife and thus jeopardize the alliance her marriage commemorated when he needs to form further alliances. Philip II certainly exploited this advantage of polygamy to a remarkable degree.

Perhaps the most important aspect of royal Macedonian polygamy affecting royal women is the absence of a clearly defined chief wife. It is not simply that there was no title for chief wife or queen (see below) but that the absence of a system that institutionalized a given royal son as heir designate (e.g., Prince of Wales) meant that no woman had permanent status as mother of the designated heir. This is not to say that, at a given period, there was not a dominant women at court (evidence from other polygamous situations suggests that some women would establish their dominance)[98] but rather to recognize that such dominance was extremely fluid, easily lost, and situationally determined. The introduction of additional wives and the birth of additional royal children could always subvert the existing pattern of dominance and would always have been threatening.

Thus, in the course of her life, a royal wife might begin her career in obscurity, possibly overshadowed by the king's mother and earlier wives, especially if they had already produced children; move toward dominance with the inevitable death of the king's mother, the birth of a son or sons of her own, or the death or disability of rival heirs; establish dominance when her husband began to treat her son as heir; suddenly lose dominance when the king seemed to prefer another heir; but just as quickly regain dominance with the death of her husband and her son's succession to the throne. Such was the career of Olympias,[99] whose life is much better attested than that of any other Argead woman, but it is probably illustrative of the generally uncertain and competitive situation of royal wives. Olympias' husband's mother, Eurydice, may have experienced similar fluctuations in dominance (see EURYDICE 1).

As the example of Olympias suggests, production of sons seems to have been the single most important factor in a woman's status in Macedonian polygamy but certainly not the only one, especially if other sons by other wives were available. Another possible factor was the woman's family. Greenwalt has argued that the rank and political importance of a royal woman's family were probably influential in situations in which multiple heirs were available.[100]

Still another possible factor was nationality. Greenwalt has suggested that the nationality of the royal wife may have limited or increased her rank.[101] As many kings' mothers were not Macedonian, a mother of foreign nationality cannot have been an automatic bar to succession. The truth may be that ordinary Macedonians did not resent foreign wives, at least so long as they were European, but that the elite did, not because of their ethnicity but because of their royal birth and thus superior status. The greater evidence for resentment of Persian wives and children by them speaks to racist feelings about Asians and Asian culture. Whatever their nationality, foreign wives would always have been at a disadvantage because they lacked a local power base, as the tensions at the end of Philip II's reign may confirm.

Moreover, it is possible, although unprovable, that a woman's personal qualities affected her status within a polygamous marriage. I mean

WOMEN AND MONARCHY IN MACEDONIA

by this, not so much how good her personal relationship with her husband was as whether she had the ability to be an effective and energetic advocate of her son and his interests. The polygamy of the Macedonian kings guaranteed that the Macedonian court was an extremely uncertain and competitive place, a testing ground for rival heirs and their mothers in which the lucky, the ruthless, and the most able might hope to succeed. The agonistic values of this society would only have intensified the situation.[102] The mother of a royal son might acquire allies among the other wives and the female relatives of the king.

Whereas popular imagination (and frequently scholarly reconstruction as well) assumes that women within a polygamous marriage would automatically be competitive, evidence from other polygamous societies suggests a more complex and varied picture. On the one hand, judging by other polygamous cultures, the patrilineal nature of Macedonian descent patterns coupled with the apparent tendency of royal polygamy to function as a symbol of unique royal status probably increased tension and competition among wives and their children.[103] The fluidity of the status of Macedonian royal wives and sons would have intensified this tendency.

However, because competition in polygamous marriages tends to decline and coalitions tend to develop as the number of wives increases,[104] there is no reason to assume that all of the seven wives of Philip II competed against each other. Alliances between wives would be particularly likely if wives' interests were not antagonistic: the mother of a daughter or a childless wife might easily combine forces with the mother of a son. It would hardly be surprising if royal mothers allied themselves with one or more of their sons' wives. It is one thing to deduce that mothers of sons had the best chance of establishing dominance, another to conclude that childless wives and mothers of daughters had no importance at all.[105]

ACCESSIBILITY

It is surprisingly hard to tie even well-known royal women to a particular physical place and context and thus not easy to determine to what degree they did or did not share in the comparative seclusion of middle- and upper-class citizen women of Athens and other Greek cities in the classical period.

At present no archaeological evidence confirms the existence of separate women's quarters in Macedonian palaces.[106] Archaeologists believe that they have found fourth-century examples of the *andron* (male dining room) in the palace at Vergina and elsewhere in Macedonia.[107] Archaeological evidence, of course, simply indicates the existence of rooms set up for the use of dining couches, but literary evidence indicates that royal women would not have been present at symposia held in the *andron*.[108] Both the bride and Olympias are absent from accounts of the party after Cleopatra's wedding (see CLEOPATRA 3). Only courtesans appear in accounts of drinking parties in the reign of Alexander. This information, however, tells us only where royal women were not.

Even if we assume that royal women lived in women's quarters, however subdivided, such an assumption hardly requires that we believe they were secluded from the rest of the Macedonian court. Did Macedonian royal women, like so many royal women in Homer, move in and out of the world of men and often appear, however veiled and escorted, in their husbands' or sons' courts? Could they be visited in their quarters by trusted advisers?[109] Surely they appeared at public ceremonies and festivals, as ordinary women did in southern Greece (see below on the religious role of royal women).

We know that some royal women appeared in front of armies (see OLYMPIAS; CYNNANE; ADEA EURYDICE) and on other public occasions,[110] but perhaps more important is the obvious fact that royal women knew many people at court and elsewhere and maintained communication with many people, both far away and close at hand.[111] It is possible but unlikely that virtually all this communication was secondhand, through letters or messengers. In some way a number of royal women were able, apparently as a matter of course, to obtain excellent intelligence about foreign and domestic matters.[112]

To what degree we should connect the fact that royal women seem to have been well informed on a variety of issues to their personal literacy is unclear. In cultures still heavily oral in nature, literacy is not fundamental to knowledge, and this is even more the case for those with the wealth and leisure to be read to. Philip II's mother, Eurydice, learned to read, but rather late in life (Plut. *Mor.* 14b–c). As her background is partly Illyrian (see EURYDICE 1), it is difficult to judge whether she was typical of other royal women. Correspondence of Olympias, Cleopatra, and Adea Eurydice once existed; thus it seems reasonable to conclude that the Hellenized women of the court, particularly by the later fourth century, were literate.[113] The role of many of these women in court intrigue suggests that problems with confidentiality alone would require that they be literate.[114] Whether literate or not, Olympias the Aeacid and her daughter Cleopatra would have known Homer's and other major works, perhaps especially the plays of Euripides.[115]

OCCUPATIONS

It seems obvious that initially and perhaps ordinarily the primary tasks of royal women, like those of other women around the Mediterranean, were domestic, involving household management, care and supervision of children and perhaps other members of the household, and, probably, religious ritual (see below). How household management might have been shaped by royal polygamy during the Argead period is difficult to say. Since we do not know for certain that women had separate quarters, we cannot tell whether all royal wives lived in a common area, perhaps divided into separate apartments for each woman and her children, or whether each woman had an entirely separate household. The former seems the likelier alternative, but whether children would have been raised in common is another matter, equally unknown.

It is reasonable to picture royal wives in the fifth century as usually little more than glorified housewives, possibly performing many domestic tasks themselves, much as royal Homeric women sometimes did, and, like them, with the help of only a few slaves.[116] There is, however, little direct evidence to support this surmise.[117]

By the mid- and late fourth century, the lifestyle of the Macedonian court had grown considerably more luxurious. The grand size of Macedonian palaces was unequaled by any other domestic structures in the Greek world.[118] It is impossible to imagine such large households run only by the wives and daughters of kings; there must have been extensive staff as well, whether free or slave.[119] Fourth-century Macedonian burials indicate considerable change in the material standards of the elite, and the conquests of Philip and Alexander are almost certain to have provided a plentiful supply of slaves to the royal household. Moreover, the fairly constant political activities of Olympias and her contemporaries make it difficult to believe that she or other royal women did much regular domestic work themselves. Women in this period may have done fine work in cloth, but much of what the men of the family wore may well have been purchased or produced by those the women of the household supervised.[120] Royal women by the fourth century should be pictured, primarily, as managers of a large and complex domestic enterprise.

Further evidence confirms the conclusion that we should think of fourth-century royal women as primarily supervisors of large households. Athenaeus (14.359 f.) preserves reference to a letter from Olympias urging Alexander to buy a slave she owns who has special skills in cooking for ritual purposes. The story of the murder of Cleopatra in Sardis suggests a large household of female attendants surrounding her (Diod. 20.37.5). She apparently also patronized a court musician (Paus. 1.44.6).

Much the same applies to the role of royal women in the care of children: they seem to have been supervisors of child care rather than primarily personal providers. We know that Alexander had a nurse[121] and that Olympias did not personally control his early education, although those who did may have been chosen with her in mind.[122] Alexander and Olympias are generally assumed to have been closer than Alexander and his father, but this assumption, if correct, relates at least in part to the way polygamy and succession patterns in Macedonia tended to create mother-son alliances, and may have little to do with emotional closeness (see below). Doubtless royal women played a greater part in the upbringing of their daughters,[123] but even this distinction can be exaggerated. When Cleopatra, the widowed daughter of Philip II, went off to Asia to pursue her marital fortunes, she left her still young children behind and never saw them again.

Royal women often acted independently in domestic and family matters. The evidence is somewhat indirect, but it seems clear that they could own, or at the very least control, considerable property.[124] Royal women do not always have male guardians, although they sometimes seem to. On the one hand, Philip II seems to act like a *kurios* to his daughters, arranging marriages for them, and Alexander tried to arrange a marriage for his sister Cynnane (Arr. 1.5.4–5), even though Cynnane apparently did not want to marry (Polyaen. 8.60). On the other hand, Cleopatra does not seem to have had a male guardian after the death of Alexander; she and her mother try to broker several marriage alliances together; and her last and fatal act was an attempt to marry Ptolemy (Diod.

19.11). Similarly, Cynnane tried to arrange the marriage of her daughter and Philip Arrhidaeus after the death of Alexander (Polyaen. 8.60; Arr. *FGrH* 156, F 9.22). Although Olympias' cousin and nephew, Aeacides, does seem to act in her interest, it is doubtful that he can be considered either Olympias' or Cleopatra's guardian, particularly since Olympias proceeds without him when his army forces him back.[125] Even when a *kurios* seems to be present, he does not always exercise much control.[126]

Clearly royal women also pursued occupations outside the household. Some royal women acquired military training and maintained readiness. Many must have spent much time keeping informed about politics and intrigue. Some traveled for family and religious purposes.[127]

MOTHER-CHILD RELATIONSHIPS: ROYAL DAUGHTERS AND THE DYNASTY
With no clear pattern of succession and royal polygamy at the Macedonian court, it is axiomatic that a mother and her son (and to some degree daughters)[128] had a common cause—the succession of the son as king—and that this common cause put them in a position that was to some degree necessarily antagonistic to the son's father, the king. Even in the happiest, stablest, and most well defined relationship between a king and his apparent heir, there was increasing tension as the former aged and the latter reached majority.[129] Although the royal father might choose another son as heir, the royal mother derived her primary status through her son's ability to succeed to the throne. Royal mothers and sons were natural allies, royal fathers and sons natural enemies. Affection or the lack of it might color or add force to these tensions, but these alliances and antagonisms have a practical aspect, quite apart from emotion. It is simplistic, for instance, to read the close relationship between Alexander and Olympias or the more distant one between Alexander and Philip exclusively in personal and emotional terms. Alexander's mother could be depended on to do all that she could to ensure his succession, whereas his father could not. Alexander's father might even act to prevent Alexander's succession. These were the practical realities of Alexander's early life.

The need for such an alliance intensified if the Argead son had not yet reached majority at the time of his father's death. The mother was then responsible for her son's survival and ultimate ability to reach the throne.

In such an extreme situation, a mother's advocacy of a royal son might determine his survival or spell her own destruction as well as her son's.

It is unwise to assume that the relationship ceased to be close and mutually supportive after the young Argead reached the throne. Admittedly, his relationship with his mother became more complex, particularly as he acquired wives and children. The mother of a king was clearly an important person, but her interests and those of her son were no longer identical. Nonetheless, a royal mother remained the person a king could count on most in a world of intrigue and competition.

Relationships between royal mothers and daughters typically would have been more intimate (presumably the mother was the main companion of the daughter until marriage) and less political, defined by the presumption that sooner or later the daughter would leave for a court or household of her own. For royal wives without sons, though, the relationship might remain close. It is clear that royal widows acted as their daughters' guardians in marriage arrangements and not impossible that, much as among the Roman elite,[130] royal mothers were often consulted about their daughters' marriages even when their husbands were alive.

It is difficult to generalize about royal daughters and their continuing relationship with the dynasty after marriage. As we have already seen, some such women may have been dynastic pawns sent out for the sake of ephemeral political gain and then forgotten. Others may have continued to act as ambassadors for their clan and, in some degree, to identify with the family of their birth. Widowed royal daughters clearly did so. We know that Alexander's relationship with his full sister, Cleopatra, was comparatively close, but we cannot really know whether this situation was typical or peculiar to her lengthy widowhood and her public role in her husband's kingdom and perhaps in Macedonia in Alexander's prolonged absence. Given the predominance of polygamy in the Argead period and the consequent broad and inclusive public presentation of the dynasty, it seems likely that royal daughters and their husbands and descendants played a role in royal politics.

NAMES
No title for royal women existed during the Argead period; one did not develop until the end of the fourth century. And the kings themselves did

not begin to use titles until the reign of Alexander (see n. 13). In the rare instances when wives and daughters of kings appear in documentary evidence, their personal names and patronymics but no titles are used and there are no references to their spouses.[131] The personal names of royal women sometimes had dynastic significance and may have had a function somewhat similar to the titles for royal women that developed in the post-Argead period.

There are two fairly well attested cases in which royal women changed their names at significant moments in their careers. Plutarch (*Mor.* 401a–b) reports that Alexander's mother was known by three names in addition to Olympias, the one she is generally known by; Justin (9.7.13) is also aware that Olympias was not the only name by which she was known.[132] Adea, the daughter of Philip II's daughter Cynnane, took the name "Eurydice" when she married Arrhidaeus (Arr. *FGrH* 156, F 9.23); her husband had already changed his own name when he became co-king (Arr. *FGrH* 156, F 1.1; Diod. 18.2.4). These are the only reasonably certain examples of this practice, because in both cases ancient sources directly state that a woman was known by more than one name. (There are two other, much less certain cases.)[133]

In addition to changing royal women's names on significant occasions, there was also the custom of choosing for a royal woman a name that referred to the accomplishments of a royal male. Philip II named one of his daughters Thessalonice (in memory of his Thessalian military success) and another Europa (in commemoration of his conquest of the Greek peninsula);[134] "Olympias," if not the original name of Alexander's mother, may be another example of this phenomenon (recalling Philip's Olympic victory), thus linking the practice of name changing to significant naming.[135]

A third practice related to the naming of royal women may have had dynastic significance. In addition to the choice of names for royal women that alluded to specific events or accomplishments, even conventional names of both male and female Argeads may have been chosen with some concern for political significance, by referring to appropriate predecessors.[136] For instance, "Eurydice," while hardly a throne name,[137] may well have a particularly strong allusive quality, recalling the memory of Philip II's mother.

All three of these sometimes interlocking habits involving naming of royal women seem to have died with the Argeads. As these practices in effect gave women a semipublic status by reflecting on the actions or status of male or even female relatives, it may be no accident that the custom seems to have come to an end about the time titles for royal women developed. One practice may not have replaced the other, but certainly the use of titles quickly overshadowed the choice of significant names.[138] The transition clearly relates to a change in the nature of monarchy; the earlier practice reflects an understanding of monarchy as both personal and dynastic, the later an understanding of monarchy as an office. In each case, however, women appear to be a part, a branch, of monarchy.

PIETY AND PATRONAGE

From the time of Philip II's mother, Eurydice (and probably earlier), royal women dedicated statues and other offerings at sanctuaries and were generally prominent in cult activities. Eurydice made dedications in association with the Muses (Plut. *Mor.* 14b–c) and to the goddess Eucleia.[139] Olympias, according to Plutarch (*Alex.* 2.2), met Philip at the Samothracian mysteries. She made an offering to the Athenian goddess Hygeia (Hyp. *Eux.* 19) and grand offerings at Delphi (*SIG* I 252N.5 ff.), and her fondness for the Dionysiac mysteries is well known (Plut. *Alex.* 2.5–6). It is distinctly possible that royal women played a role in what amounted to a dynastic cult; a letter attributed to Olympias certainly seems to imply this.[140] Hellenistic royal women like Arsinoe would continue and expand the traditional religious activity of Argead women, a role that in many ways was that of women in ordinary families but on a much grander scale.[141]

Despite the indirect and fragmentary nature of our evidence for the Argead period, it also seems clear that royal women could furnish patronage of various kinds. Some of this patronage seems fairly private, but even private patronage (e.g., Cleopatra's provision of the tomb for a musician) depended in some degree on a woman's ability to control and distribute wealth. But other patronage was either overtly political (e.g., Olympias' ability to protect, at least for a time, Macedonian "draft dodgers" in Curt. 7.1.37 or her daughter Cleopatra's apparent success in protecting Dionysius of Heracleia from her brother's anger in Memnon *FGrH* 434, F 4.37) or fraught with political implications (e.g., Olympias'

WOMEN AND MONARCHY IN MACEDONIA

splendid offerings at Delphi from her son's booty or the gift of grain by Cleopatra to needy Corinth; see OLYMPIAS; CLEOPATRA 2).

FAMILY, COURT, AND MONARCHY

Given the scarcity of evidence, attempting to discuss the construction of gender at the Macedonian court may seem absurdly optimistic. Discussions of the formation of gender roles generally focus on periods and cultures with infinitely more abundant primary evidence than Argead Macedonia. Certainly, it is impossible to speak of gender roles in ancient Macedonian society in general because we know nothing of the lives of ordinary women and little more of the lives of men.[142] But there is just enough evidence on the elite (royal and aristocratic)[143] to raise the issue for men and, I think, for women too. What follows is brief and tentative, because of the limitations of our evidence and particularly because much of our material is filtered through Greek sources with rigid expectations, different from those of Macedonians, about the roles of men and women. However sketchy my conclusions remain, it is important to recognize that there were expectations and judgments made about the behavior of men and women, even if we cannot be certain what they were.

Males in the Macedonian elite were expected to be intensely, even violently, competitive about virtually everything but especially about war, hunting, and politics. A man who had not hunted and killed a boar without a net was compelled to eat while sitting rather than reclining as adult males did (Ath. 18a), and a man who had not yet killed an enemy in battle was marked out by special dress (Arist. *Pol.* 1324b). Squabbles about hunting kills might lead to attempts at regicide (Arr. 4.10.1–14.4).[144] Prowess and daring in warfare was absolutely necessary; the many wounds of Philip and Alexander demonstrate how fundamental this expectation was, even when fulfilling it risked political stability.[145] Symposia, not the comparatively genteel Athenian sort but violent and sometimes lethal affairs, had a nearly constitutional function in Macedonia and were frequent arenas in which political and personal conflicts were vented.[146] Agonistic Homeric values frequently led to competition, even or especially between father and son, and sometimes to violence. Much of this competition, whether over hunting, warfare, drinking, or politics, had a sexual edge; Catherine Mortensen rightly points out that in Macedonia sexual relationships between males in the elite were not limited, as they generally were in Athens, to the young and very young; middle-aged kings had lovers, and the conflicts and jealousies arising from their sexual relationships with men were elements in assassination plots and in competition at court in general.[147]

Expectations for women were different, of course, but not perhaps as different as is often assumed because of the insidious Athenocentricity of much scholarship. The absence of royal women from symposia suggests some degree of sexual segregation. Physical aggression by women was also often condemned, although it is easy to exaggerate the extent of this condemnation.[148] Nonetheless, exactly because of the expectation that they should look out for family interest, women in the elite had to be well informed about public affairs; it was part of being a good mother, daughter, and wife. In defense of and on behalf of family interests, women moved into public areas and activities. Although only a few female members of the elite went into battle, more risked their lives and sometimes paid with them.[149] Our sources consistently admire physical bravery in royal women, often noting that such actions demonstrate their worthiness to be the wives or daughters of kings (Diod. 19.11.6–7, 51.5–6; Just. 14.6.11–12). Aggression, so long as it could be justified by goals deemed appropriate, was expected in some circumstances.

The intense competition that is such a marked feature of expectations for Macedonian males is very much a feature of expectations for elite women too.[150] Much of this competitiveness happens in the context of family advocacy, but it is competition nonetheless. Wives jockeyed for position for themselves and their sons against other wives and their progeny;[151] mothers competed with other women and clans in arranging the best marriages for their sons and daughters.[152] Indeed, the intensity of this competition is confirmed by the frequency with which death and the risk of death is associated with it.[153]

It seems, then, that women were expected to be and to act like men, only less so. The great and nearly impenetrable divide between men and women and expectations about them that characterized Athenian society is not present in Argead Macedonia at least in the elite. The public/private dichotomy that characterized Greek culture to the south was not present to the same degree. In Macedonia elite women moved back and forth between the private and public realms because public life was defined not by the polis but by the royal clan.

Women, in other words, were not excluded from *basileia* in Macedonia but formed part of it because they were part of the clan. Several passages in our sources support this conclusion in a very direct way. In one anecdote Alexander refuses to take some supposed sexual peccadillo of his sister, Cleopatra, seriously because he says she deserves some enjoyment out of her *basileia* (Plut. *Mor.* 818b–c).[154] Plutarch (*Alex.* 9.3) objects to the court of Philip II, complaining that the *basileia* was contaminated by the women's quarters.[155] Diodorus (19.11.5) reports that Olympias considered Adea Eurydice worthy of greater punishment than her husband because the young woman kept saying that *basileia* belonged to her more than to Olympias. Then there are the passages in which Olympias and other royal women are perceived as containers of dynastic *axioma* or in which they are admired because they act, usually courageously, in a way that is worthy of their male relatives (Diod. 19.11.6–7, 51.5–6; Just. 14.6.11; Arr. *FGrH* 156, F 11.40). It is as though royal women are seen as translucent vessels of a kind of dynastic entity and, because of this perception, they can sometimes function, by their own choice or that of others, as vehicles of continuity.

Admittedly, in the ordinary course of things, being part of *basileia* in Macedonia meant little to royal women. They functioned discreetly, only occasionally and peripherally moving into public areas, largely playing the conventional role of women in many ancient Mediterranean societies, but always keeping a weather eye on the welfare of their sons and daughters and thus their own status. In moments of crisis, however, royal women could become the reserve troops of the dynasty—dynastic understudies who, thanks to a critical scarcity of adult male Argeads or at least of those supportive of their sons, suddenly took dynastic center stage. Such a crisis might never come, but royal women had to be prepared and informed for such a contingency, and a surprising number of them took sudden and decisive action when the dynastic spotlight suddenly turned on them.[156]

Significantly, because Greeks associated both polygamy and powerful women with barbarian societies, they condemned the role of royal women in Macedonian monarchy, and Greek sources tended to treat the role of women in this monarchy as problematic, even pathological. In fact, it could be both or neither. The fundamental point here is that "women" and "politics" were not mutually exclusive categories; women were part of the political structure of ancient Macedonia, part of *basileia*.

CHAPTER TWO

Eurydice and the Reigns of
Amyntas III, Alexander II,
and Perdiccas III

The period of the reigns of Amyntas III (393–370) and his two older
sons, Alexander II (370/69–367) and Perdiccas III (365–359), was
one of great instability, both internal and external. The dynastic troubles
that had begun with the assassination of Archelaus in 399 periodically recurred. In this period Macedonia showed little sign of the greatness that
Philip II, the last of Amyntas III's sons to reign, would so brilliantly realize. Not coincidentally, it was during this era of weakness and strife that
royal women first became prominent in Macedonian affairs.

Amyntas III, although hardly a great king, demonstrated considerable survival skills. His most notable achievements (other than fathering
Philip II) were that he became king at all, that his reign was long by
Argead standards, and that he, unlike many Argead rulers, died old and
probably of natural causes. Amyntas, son of Arrhidaeus, was a great-
grandson of Alexander I, but his branch of the royal family had not produced a king in subsequent generations. Amyntas reached the throne
partly by benefiting from the murderous rivalries of other Argeads and
partly by his elimination of competitors (Diod. 14.89.2). Soon after becoming king, Amyntas was driven from his kingdom by an Illyrian invasion that may have (briefly) put another Argead on the throne. Amyntas
regained the throne, however, thanks to the assistance of various outside
powers as well as his own bribes to the Illyrians. Throughout the rest of
his long reign, Amyntas maintained friendly relations with the upper
Macedonian kingdoms of Elimiotis and Lyncestis and managed to play
more powerful Greek states off against each other with sufficient success
to keep Macedonia comparatively safe.

When Amyntas III died, he was succeeded by his son Alexander II, but Ptolemy Alorites, probably another Argead,[1] soon murdered young Alexander (Diod. 15.71.1; Plut. *Pel.* 26–27). Ptolemy then supposedly served as regent for Amyntas' remaining sons. During this regency he was confronted with yet another Argead rival, a certain Pausanias, who led a Thracian-backed invasion. Perdiccas III avenged his brother's murder by murdering Ptolemy and taking the throne (Diod. 16.2.1). Already weakened by struggles against Athens, young Perdiccas III confronted the Illyrian ruler Bardylis and died, along with four thousand of his men, in a disastrous battle against the Illyrians (Diod. 16.2.4).[2] During this moment of crisis, his brother Philip II took control of the kingdom.

As we have seen, little evidence about royal women before the reign of Amyntas III survives, other than scattered references to the marriages of kings and their daughters. We have nothing to prove whether royal women were more than dynastic tokens before Amyntas.

Our knowledge of the role of royal women changes dramatically with the women of the family of Amyntas III, although the change may not have happened until late in his reign and in the reigns of two elder sons. Indeed, the change applies only to some of the women of his dynasty; his daughter Eurynoe seems to have functioned only as the traditional dynastic pawn.

EURYNOE

Justin, the only source who mentions Eurynoe directly and by name, says that she was Amyntas III's daughter by Eurydice (Just. 7.4.5; see EURYDICE 1). He claims that she prevented her mother and her husband (whom Justin does not name but who is sometimes thought to be Ptolemy Alorites), who was also her mother's lover, from assassinating her father the king by revealing to her father both their affair and their plot to kill Amyntas and replace him with Eurynoe's duplicitous husband (Just. 7.4.7). Eurynoe is not referred to again by Justin or any other source.

Nearly all the "information" about Eurynoe mentioned by Justin is dubious or, at the very least, uncertain. Justin never names Eurynoe's husband. Diodorus refers to Ptolemy as the brother, not the brother-in-law, of Eurydice's sons by Amyntas (Diod. 15.71.1, 77.5), as does Marsyas (*ap.* Ath. 14.629d). Plutarch, while discussing Ptolemy, does not refer to any relationship to the house of Amyntas III (*Pel.* 26–27), and the near-contemporary Aeschines (2.29) terms him an *epitropos* (guardian or regent) but mentions no other relationship to the house of Amyntas.[3] Granted that Justin's entire narrative scenario (Eurydice the would-be murderess of her husband and murderer of her two sons) is often doubted, and with good reason,[4] we may wonder whether Eurynoe actually did marry Ptolemy.

There is nothing innately implausible, however, about a marriage between Amyntas's only daughter and Ptolemy, who is usually supposed to be an Argead himself, probably a member of another branch of the royal house,[5] one that Amyntas wished to conciliate. If it is indeed correct that Ptolemy married Eurydice at some point after the death of Amyntas III (schol. at Aeschin. 2.26), then it seems likely that Eurynoe (who is not referred to again) was already dead, probably of natural causes.[6] Ptolemy's apparent later role as regent for Eurynoe's brother Perdiccas[7] might also confirm a marriage to Eurynoe. Uncles are frequently regents. Ptolemy had a son, possibly by Eurynoe, named Philoxenus who was sent to Thebes as a hostage ca. 368 (Plut. *Pel.* 27).[8]

Literary, inscriptional, and archaeological evidence indicates that one of Amyntas III's wives, Eurydice (mother of Alexander II, Perdiccas III, Eurynoe, and Philip II), played a public role in Macedonian life and acted aggressively in the political arena. Eurydice's political career marks a turning point in Macedonian history; she is the first royal woman we know of who took political action and successfully exerted political influence.[9] For the rest of the fourth century some royal women took an increasingly active public role, particularly in succession politics. Then almost as suddenly as the political role of royal women became more prominent at the beginning of the century, by the time the Antigonid dynasty established its hold over Macedonia early in the third century, the political role of royal women began to decline dramatically, if not cease altogether.

EURYDICE 1

Much remains uncertain about Eurydice's life, and this uncertainty has generated controversy. Let us begin, therefore, with what little is certain. Eurydice was the daughter of Sirras[10] and a granddaughter of Arrabaeus of Lyncestis (Strab. 326c). She married Amyntas III, and they had a daughter (see EURYNOE) and three sons, each of whom, in apparent birth order, became kings: Alexander II, Perdiccas III, and Philip II (Just. 7.4.5). At some point in her career, perhaps around the middle of the fourth century, Eurydice dedicated two statues to the cult of Eucleia at Vergina.[11] Some time after the deaths of her husband, Amyntas, and her son Alexander II, Eurydice sought and obtained the help of the Athenian general Iphicrates to preserve the throne for her two younger sons. Iphicrates defeated the invasion of the pretender Pausanias that had threatened her sons' succession (Aeschin. 2.28–29).

Everything else about the life of Eurydice is disputed, beginning with her ethnicity. Although we now know that her father was Sirras, we do not know who Sirras was or where he came from. Sirras has been identified as either a Lyncestian or an Illyrian.[12] Two ancient sources call Eurydice an Illyrian (*Suda* s.v. "Karanos"; Lib. *Vit. Dem.* 9) and a third, a passage preserved in Plutarch's essays (*Mor.* 14c),[13] probably does so as well.[14]

Such an ethnic designation could refer to her general line of descent and not specifically to Sirras. For example, Athenaeus (560 f.) refers to Cynnane as "the Illyrian," even though Philip II was her father. He does so, almost certainly, because he is discussing her Illyrian role as a woman warrior. Although one would expect the designation of a woman's ethnicity to depend on her father's, Cynnane's example shows that this was not always so. Given the current state of the evidence, it seems reasonable to conclude that Eurydice had both Illyrian and Lyncestian (through her grandfather) blood and that, though her father may well have been an Illyrian allied with the Lyncestians, his ethnicity remains uncertain. Theories about Eurydice's career that depend on either identification of Sirras' ethnicity should therefore be treated with some caution. Lack of certainty about Eurydice's ancestry is unfortunate, because her ethnicity may have been an important factor in her career and that of her sons.[15]

As with many royal women, we can only estimate the dates of Eurydice's birth and marriage. Since Eurydice's eldest son, Alexander, took the throne in 370/69, he must have been born by 388 at the latest. Eurydice must therefore have been married to Amyntas by roughly 390. Whether she was Illyrian, Lyncestian, or some combination of the two, her marriage may well have occurred in the aftermath of the Illyrian invasion of 393/2.[16]

All this information would suggest a birthdate for Eurydice no later than 404 and probably no earlier than 410.[17]

Eurydice's husband, Amyntas, was probably polygamous. Justin tells us that Eurydice was not Amyntas III's only wife. He reports that Amyntas also had three sons by Gygaea (Just. 7.4.5; see GYGAEA 2). None of Gygaea's sons became king, and all were ultimately eliminated by Philip II on the grounds that they threatened his throne.[18] Justin does not say which woman was the earlier wife of Amyntas, but he names Eurydice and her sons first and calls Eurydice's son Alexander the eldest of Amyntas III's sons (Just. 7.4.8), as does Diodorus (16.2.4). Once one recognizes the strong possibility that Amyntas was polygamous, there seems no reason to assume that he repudiated either of his known wives. The two marriages may have overlapped for a number of years.[19]

At some point during Amyntas' reign, Eurydice seems to have become the dominant wife. Whether this development was immediate or gradual, connected to her family and relations, to her higher status, to the ages of her sons, or to some combination of all these factors, cannot be determined.[20]

Our sources preserve two differing traditions about Eurydice's career. Justin tells a lurid dynastic saga, focused on Eurydice, dealing with the very end of the reign of Amyntas III and the reigns of Alexander II and Perdiccas III. According to Justin, Eurydice and her son-in-law conspired to kill Amyntas, marry, and give the throne to the son-in-law, but Eurydice's daughter Eurynoe foiled the plot by revealing it to Amyntas, who died, apparently shortly thereafter, of natural causes (7.4.7–8). Justin also claims that Eurydice, spared from punishment by Amyntas because of their common children, nonetheless conspired to kill both her elder sons, Alexander II and Perdiccas III. Driven by her lust, she was willing to murder her sons to put her lover on the throne (7.5.4–9).

Virtually all of the remaining ancient evidence tells a different and generally contradictory tale about the same period, one focused not on Eurydice but on someone named Ptolemy. As we shall see, Ptolemy's identity is not certain, and it is even possible that the sources refer to two different men with the same name.

Diodorus (15.71.1) reports that Ptolemy, Amyntas' son and Alexander's *adelphos* (brother), killed Alexander and ruled as king. A passage in Athenaeus (14.629d), taken from the Macedonian historian Marsyas, confirms this report. Marsyas said that Alexander was killed by Ptolemy's men during a festival. Plutarch's life of Pelopidas (*Pel.* 26–27) offers further confirmation. According to Plutarch, Ptolemy killed Alexander despite an earlier settlement between them worked out by Pelopidas. Pelopidas then forced Ptolemy to agree merely to be regent for Alexander's two younger brothers.

Aside from these different traditions with two different villains on whom the troubles of Macedonia are blamed in the 360s, two other pieces of evidence are relevant to the consideration of Eurydice's life. The scholiast for Aeschines 2.29 claims that Eurydice later married Ptolemy of Alorus. This piece of information, itself of dubious worth, often leads to the assumption that Ptolemy Alorites was the sinister son-in-law, Ptolemy son of Amyntas, of Justin's narrative. If it is true that Eurydice married Ptolemy Alorites (it is suspicious that no other source mentions this) and that Ptolemy Alorites was identical with Ptolemy son of Amyntas,[21] such a marriage would not necessarily have been of her choosing.

Widowed royal wives sometimes married their husbands' successors, particularly if the successors were regents for the widows' sons; the motivation for such marriages is unclear (see Chryseis; Cleopatra 1). Since Ptolemy, Amyntas' son, certainly murdered Alexander II and Eurydice certainly acted to ensure the succession of her remaining sons (see below), it is unlikely that Eurydice voluntarily married her eldest son's murderer[22] but possible if she believed that such a marriage might aid the interests of her remaining sons.[23]

Much more significant information is conveyed in a speech by Aeschines, paraphrasing a speech he made to Philip ca. 346, which alluded to events in the 360s (Aeschin. 2.26–29). Aeschines says that after the deaths of Amyntas and Alexander, when neither Perdiccas nor Philip was of age and the pretender Pausanias was attracting support in Macedonia, their mother, Eurydice, asked the Athenian general Iphicrates, their father's adoptive son, to protect the throne for the two boys and that Iphicrates in fact drove out Pausanias. In the next sentence Aeschines alludes in an unflattering manner to the *epitropos* Ptolemy.

Although Aeschines' description demonstrates some rhetorical exaggeration (Aeschines seems to have lowered the ages of Eurydice's two remaining sons and to have ignored Philip's absence in Thebes to make the scene he describes more pathetic and more vivid),[24] there is no reason to doubt the general truth of the story. Whereas it is possible that Aeschines omitted any reference to Ptolemy for fear of offending Philip and that Eury-dice acted under the command of the regent and her alleged husband, Aeschines clearly expected Philip to agree with his picture of Eurydice as the loyal defender of her sons. No evidence demonstrates that Ptolemy had any role in this incident or suggests that anyone other than Eurydice would have had influence with Iphicrates.[25] Even if Eurydice was prompted by Ptolemy, her successful intervention in political and military affairs re-mains remarkably bold and without known precedent, an extraordinary act for a royal woman.

Scholars used to combine the two distinctly separate stories about the Argeads in the 360s, take the scholiast at his word, and picture Eurydice as a ruthless murderess of her own children, driven by power and lust. More recent work, particularly that of Mortensen,[26] has blamed the "bad Eurydice" story on hostility going back to propaganda generated by the sons of Gy-gaea[27] and on sexual stereotyping. Sexual stereotyping of women with po-litical power doubtless contributed to the enduring popularity of the hostile tradition. Recent scholars have noted the many implausibilities in Justin's narrative and have preferred the near-contemporary evidence of Aeschines. The Plutarch passage that cites Eurydice as a good model in the education of children (Plut. *Mor.* 14c) has been taken as further proof that Eurydice was not a child-murderer.

Eurydice took the unprecedented step of seeking international help when she believed the succession of her remaining sons was in jeopardy, and her attempt was successful. If Eurydice was indeed half-Illyrian, her un-usual assertiveness, much like that of the daughter and granddaughter of the Illyrian Audata, could be tied to the role of women in Illyrian culture (see AUDATA; CYNNANE; ADEA EURYDICE).

No more literary evidence survives about Eurydice, who would have been in her mid-forties at the time of Philip's accession, but recently dis-covered archaeological and inscriptional evidence is relevant to our under-standing of her career. At Vergina in 1982 Manolis Andronicos uncovered a statue base inscribed "Eurydika Sirra Eukleiai [Eurydice, daughter of Sirras, to Eucleia]" in association with a temple to Eucleia. In 1990 a second ver-sion of the Eurydice inscription to Eucleia was found at the Eucleia temple site.[28]

The date and historical context of these inscriptions and the small tem-ple with which they were associated is uncertain. Andronicos and Chrys-

soula Saatsoglou-Paliadeli dated them to the mid-fourth century and believed that Eurydice's dedications were part of the commemoration of
Philip's great victory at Chaeroneia in 338 (see above), but their dating has
rightly been questioned.[29] Other than these inscriptions, the incident described in Aeschines ca. 368/7 is the last known reference to Eurydice. Although it is possible that this woman born late in the fifth century survived
until at least 338, it is unlikely. No narrative source refers to her continued
existence during the entire period of her son's reign. Aeschines' account of
Eurydice's intervention with Iphicrates makes it even more difficult to believe that she was still alive in 346. At 2.28 Aeschines, attempting to support his account of the incident, insists that he recounts it as all who were
present say. Had Eurydice been alive in 346, the date at which Aeschines
delivered the original speech, he would have referred to her, not bystanders,
to confirm the truth of his statements.

Andronicos' association of the inscriptions and temple with Chaeroneia
also seems unconvincing, other difficulties apart. Chaeroneia was not
Philip's only victory, and Eurydice's dedication could have celebrated some
earlier success, for instance, his critical defeat of the Illyrians at the beginning of his reign.[30]

One wonders, though, whether a royal woman would be so deeply involved in the commemoration of a military victory of any sort and whether
it is appropriate to connect the cult to military success. The cult of Eucleia,
a personification of good repute, is otherwise unknown in Macedonia and
somewhat obscure elsewhere. In Athens a temple to Eucleia Eunomia was
indeed a memorial to victory at Marathon (Paus. 1.14.5), but Eucleia cults
elsewhere in Greece were connected to Artemis and, located near or in a
marketplace, often received the offerings of those about to be married. In
Locris and Boeotia Eucleia Artemis was believed to be a daughter of Heracles (Plut. *Arist.* 20.5–6). Borza has argued that this Heraclid Eucleia and her
association with marriage and marketplace is more appropriate for Eurydice's cult.[31]

Even if we assume that Eurydice's dedication was to Eucleia Artemis, the
date remains uncertain and is more likely to have come in the reigns of one
of her sons than in that of her husband.[32] Eurydice may have funded the construction of the temple.[33] If the Eucleia cult at Vergina is connected to Artemis
and marriage offerings, then we may have an early Argead prototype for the
Hellenistic role of royal women as religious patrons, particularly for women.

The inscription by Eurydice preserved in Plutarch (*Mor.* 14c), as now emended (see above), also seems to support this view. Here Eurydice makes a dedication *polietisi* (to or for citizen women) and perhaps to the Muses, grateful for her recently acquired education.[34]

Andronicos also believed that the large Macedonian tomb (the Tomb of the Throne) that was discovered in 1987 near the Rhomaios tomb at Vergina, which contained a remarkable painted throne, belonged to Eurydice. A fragment of a panathenaic amphora found near the tomb has been dated to 344/3, but nothing connects the tomb to Eurydice specifically.[35] We must either reject the reading of the Aeschines passage as signifying that Eurydice was dead by 346 or conclude that the Tomb of the Throne did not belong to Eurydice. It is more likely that Eurydice had died by the early 340s.

Not only did Eurydice intervene in a public and aggressive way on behalf of her sons, playing dynastic politics with some skill, but her dedications around Vergina also speak to a new public role for Argead women. It is also noteworthy that her role and prominence seem to have been greatest not in the reign of her husband but in those of her sons and in their minorities. The remarkably hostile tradition preserved in Justin is testimony to how unusual and threatening her actions were. Nonetheless, Eurydice succeeded in her goals. All the remaining rulers of the Argead dynasty were her descendants.

Eurydice was not the only wife of Amyntas III. He was also married to Gygaea 2. Since Amyntas was middle-aged when he assumed the throne, he probably had married before becoming king,[36] but such an early marriage need not have been to either Gygaea or Eurydice. After all, the only reason we know that Gygaea existed is that she bore sons who lived to adulthood. Amyntas' son Perdiccas II apparently had a wife, but no reference to the marriage or the name of the wife survives.[37] In any event, Eurydice's prominence needs to be understood in the context of Amyntas III's other marriage, which also produced three sons.

Gygaea 2
Justin (7.4.5) reports that, in addition to the three sons and one daughter Amyntas III had by Eurydice (see Eurydice 1), he had three sons by Gygaea:

Archelaus, Arrhidaeus, and Menelaus. He is the only source to mention Gygaea by name and to refer to her and her sons again. Justin (8.3.10) later recounts that Philip attacked Olynthus because it had sheltered two of his half-brothers after he had murdered the third and explains that these were sons of his stepmother (*noverca*) whom he wished to eliminate because they had a claim on the throne. Philip succeeded in doing so (Just. 8.3.11). Despite its lack of corroboration, no one has doubted Justin's testimony, probably because sources for Amyntas' reign of are generally so poor and because the information he provides seems plausible.

Scholars have assumed that Gygaea was an Argead, primarily because the only other Gygaea known (see GYGAEA 1) was an Argead.[38] As we know so few female names,[39] at least for the early Macedonian period, it is difficult to say whether "Gygaea" was such a rare name that it was likely that anyone who held it was an Argead. In the absence of information to the contrary, the assumption seems reasonable.

Less reasonable is the equally common belief that Gygaea was the first wife of Amyntas III.[40] Two ancient sources call Alexander II the eldest of Amyntas III's sons (Diod. 16.2.4; Just. 7.4.8),[41] and another refers to Alexander as Philip's oldest brother (Aeschin. 2.26).[42] Assuming that Justin lists both sets of brothers in the order of their births, Amyntas apparently did not follow the usual custom of naming his eldest son (whether Alexander or Archelaus) after his own father, so the names of his sons offer no help in determining which marriage was earlier. That Gygaea's sons made no attempt to claim the throne until the 350s strongly suggests that they were younger than Eurydice's sons, not older.[43] Amyntas may have married both women within a short time, much as Philip II seems to have done with several of his wives.[44] It seems especially unlikely that, having produced three sons by Gygaea before becoming king, Amyntas not only married Eurydice shortly after taking the throne, but rejected Gygaea and her three sons at a time when Eurydice had no sons.[45]

The evidence suggests that Amyntas married Eurydice before Gygaea, but perhaps only shortly before. Although no ancient source explicitly says that Amyntas, like his son Philip II, was polygamous, the evidence strongly suggests that he was. Justin's (8.3.10) reference to Gygaea as Philip's *noverca* is particularly striking, when combined with the apparently younger ages of

Amyntas' sons by Gygaea and with Eurydice's survival well past the death of Amyntas.[46] His marriage to Eurydice, whatever her ethnicity, was probably arranged to cope with external problems (see EURYDICE 1), whereas his marriage to Gygaea may have been meant to conciliate internal factions, especially if she were indeed a member of another branch of the Argead clan. Indeed, Amyntas' modest political polygamy may have been a model for his son Philip's much more spectacular polygamy.[47]

At some point Eurydice and her sons established dominance over Gygaea and her sons. The failure of the supposedly Argead Gygaea's sons to compete successfully with those of Eurydice requires explanation, although other, apparently more popular Argead claimants were available.[48] If Gygaea was not an Argead but simply a member of the Macedonian elite, Eurydice's status may have been perceived as higher and her sons thus preferred,[49] but it is more probable that the first two of Eurydice's sons were sufficiently older than Gygaea's sons to render competition unlikely. By the time of Philip, Eurydice's line had acquired more royal authority because both of Philip's older brothers had already been kings.[50] Gygaea may also have died much younger than Eurydice, thus eliminating the possibility of success that a powerful mother-advocate like Eurydice could convey to her sons.

Why, beginning with Eurydice, did royal women often become aggressive public figures? Certainly no one factor will explain the phenomenon. Much of the literary and epigraphic evidence about Eurydice has been preserved because of the spectacular career of her youngest son; Philip's success lies behind a precipitate improvement in the quality of source material from ancient Macedonia. This improvement in our information base may slightly exaggerate the degree of change suggested by Eurydice's career. Nonetheless, for the first time events in the life of a royal woman were also central to the political history of Macedonia in that period. Eurydice herself was, however, the most important factor in the change. Her Illyrian roots, her connection to a society in which women in the elite played an important and even a military role, help to explain her unprecedented actions. Desperate circumstance—the death of her husband and assassination of her eldest son—may have forced her to alter the traditional role of a royal Macedonian woman to ensure the survival and succession of her remaining sons. Moreover, her character and personality may have been inclined to boldness and innovation.

The decisions and policies of various royal males also contributed to the change. The new role of royal women, something that happened largely after the death of Amyntas III, reflects a new development in the nature of Macedonian monarchy. The public presentation of the monarchy increasingly involved the women as well as the men of the clan. Monarchs, hoping to improve dynastic stability, began to publicize royal women. The growing wealth and power of the royal dynasty during and after the reign of Philip II increasingly separated it from the rest of the elite. This elevation of the royal family included women, partly because kings chose to emphasize the specialness of the royal family. Within the broad group of the royal clan, kings stressed the currently dominant nuclear family and its immediate ascendants and descendants (see below).

Eurydice's sons would triumph after years of nasty and sometimes bloody dynastic politics with not only Gygaea's sons, but other Argead opponents as well. Whether because of the order of their marriages, the greater status or political importance of Eurydice, or the greater age of her sons, she became the dominant wife of Amyntas. Ironically, her victory may not have been final until well after the death of her husband (see EURYDICE 1; GYGAEA 1).

During the reigns of Eurydice's sons there had been two dynastic murders and assorted pretenders, and, in all probability, the rumor campaign preserved by Justin had already begun to develop. Dynastic shoring up would have been in order, particularly a kind that emphasized the respectability of the king's mother and held her up as a model for the women of her kingdom. If Eurydice's ethnicity were an issue—we do not know that it was—then the unapologetic inscriptional references to her father may have been intended to flaunt what could not be denied. The Eucleia cult could even have had a kind of dynastic association; women so often symbolized family and continuity of family that such a possibility should not be ignored.

Elements in Eurydice's career tend to reappear in the lives of other fourth-century royal women: accusations of scandal involving the abuse of power and sexuality; participation in cults as a means to entrench a woman and her heirs; and participation in succession politics, particularly by widowed royal mothers. Thus, for reasons associated with the troubles and uncertainties of the Argead clan in the 360s, the king's mother became more prominent, more part of the public role of the monarchy. In the royal family of Macedonia, the good mother had become the mother-advocate, a symbol of family renown and a model for ordinary women. Eurydice's youngest and most successful son would begin to confirm and even expand the public role for royal women his mother had first assumed in a period of crisis, without displaying interest in encouraging independent action by any of the women of his family.

CHAPTER THREE

Royal Women and Philip II

Philip (359–336) was Macedonia's greatest ruler. When he took the throne after his brother and four thousand other Macedonians had been massacred in a battle against the Illyrians, he faced numerous foreign threats and a variety of Argead pretenders. He coped with the immediate crisis through a combination of bribes and diplomacy and used the time he had thereby bought himself to build a new national army.

Within a year, using his new model army, he decisively defeated the Illyrians and began to incorporate the principalities of upper Macedonia into his kingdom. The result was an expanded army and aristocracy. Philip then moved against Athenian interests and colonies on the northwestern Aegean coast. His military success brought him new allies, rich mines, and many new recruits for the ruling class.

Philip soon annexed Thessaly (352). Temporarily at peace with Athens, he led a successful campaign against the Phocians, experienced additional victories against the Illyrians and Thracians, and continued to expand his sphere of influence in southern Greece. Athenian concern over Philip's success led to renewed war in the northern Aegean (340), and in 338 at Chaeroneia in central Greece he confronted a combined Theban and Athenian army and inflicted a decisive defeat.

Philip was now master of the Greek peninsula. Despite his external success, during the last two years of Philip's reign, his court was troubled by domestic strife resulting from conflicts between the rival claims of two of his wives. It is possible that this strife may have led, directly or indirectly, to his assassination (see below). He and his "allies" met at Corinth in 337: a league was formed with Philip as its head. It effectively set up Macedonian domination of southern Greece. At Corinth Philip proclaimed war against the Persian empire, and a preliminary expedition was sent to Asia Minor, but Philip did not survive to lead the expedition he had planned. He was assassinated in Macedonia in 336, during the celebration of his daughter Cleopatra's wedding, and it was his young son Alexander who led the joint Graeco-Macedonian expedition to Asia Minor in spring 334.[1]

Such was the career of the man who masterminded Macedonia's rapid transformation from a backwater of the Hellenic world into its leading power. The reign of Philip was notorious because of his many marriages, but it was not generally a period in which royal women acted as independent agents.

ROYAL MARRIAGE FOR POLITICAL ADVANTAGE

The main source of information on Philip's marriages is a famous passage in Athenaeus' *Deipnosophistai* (13.557b–e)[2] that preserves a fragment of Satyrus' life of Philip II.[3] The passage includes a generalization about the relationship between Philip's marriages and his wars. It lists in what may or may not be chronological order the wives of Philip and the children he had by each. It also includes some related material about events at Philip's court.[4] The text and my purposefully literal translation follows:

Φίλιππος δ᾽ ὁ Μακεδὼν οὐκ ἐπήγετο μὲν εἰς τοὺς
πολέμους γυναῖκας,ὥσπερ Δαρεῖος ὁ ὑπ᾽ Ἀλεξάνδρου
καταλυθείς, ὃς περὶ τ᾽ν ὅλων πολεμ᾽ν τριακοσίας ἑξήκοντα
περιήγετο παλλακάς, ὡς ἱστορεῖ Δικαίαρχος ἐν τρίτῳ περὶ τοῦ
τῆς Ἑλλάδος Βίου· ὁ δὲ Φίλιππος αἰεὶ κατὰ πόλεμον ἐγάμει.
ἐν ἔτεσι γοῦν εἴκοσι καὶ δυσὶν οἷς ἐβασίλευεν, ὥς φησι
Σάτυρος ἐν τῷ περὶ τοῦ Βίου αὐτοῦ, Αὐδάταν Ἰλλυρίδα γήμας
ἔσχεν ἐξ αὐτῆς θυγατέρα Κύνναν· ἔγημεν δὲ καὶ Φίλαν
ἀδελφὴν Δέρδα καὶ Μαχάτα. οἰκειώσασθαι δὲ θέλων καὶ τὸ
Θετταλ᾽ν ἔθνος ἐπαιδοποιήσατο ἐκ δύο Θετταλίδων γυναικ᾽ν,
ὧν ἡ μὲν ἦν Φεραία Νικησίπολις, ἥτις αὐτῷ ἐγέννησε
Θετταλονίκην, ἡ δὲ Λαρισαία Φίλιννα, ἐξ ἧς Ἀρριδαῖον
ἐτέκνωσε. προσεκτήσατο δὲ καὶ τὴν Μολοττ᾽ν βασιλείαν
γήμας Ὀλυμπιάδα, ἐξ ἧς ἔσχεν Ἀλέξανδρον καὶ Κλεοπάτραν.
καὶ τὴν Θρᾴκην δὲ ὅτε εἷλεν, ἧκε πρὸς αὐτὸν Κοθήλας ὁ τ᾽ν
Θρᾳκ᾽ν βασιλεὺς ἄγων Μήδαν τὴν θυγατέρα καὶ δ᾽ρα πολλά.
γήμας δὲ καὶ ταύτην ἐπεισήγαγεν τῇ Ὀλυμπιάδι. ἐπὶ πάσαις
δ᾽ ἔγημε Κλεοπάτραν ἐρασθεὶς τὴν Ἱπποστράτου μὲν ἀδελφήν,

Ἀττάλου δὲ ἀδελφιδῆν· καὶ ταύτην ἐπεισάγων τῇ Ὀλυμπιάδι ἅπαντα τὸν βίον τὸν ἑαυτοῦ συνέχεεν. εὐθέως γὰρ ἐν αὐτοῖς τοῖς γάμοις ὁ μὲν Ἄτταλος ᾿ νῦν μέντοι γνήσιοι, ἔφη, καὶ οὐ νόθοι βασιλεῖς γεννηθήσονται. καὶ ὁ Ἀλέξανδρος ἀκούσας ἔβαλεν ᾗ μετὰ χεῖρας εἶχεν κύλικι τὸν Ἄτταλον, ἔπειτα κἀκεῖνος αὐτὸν τῷ ποτηρίῳ. καὶ μετὰ ταῦτα Ὀλυμπιὰς μὲν εἰς Μολοττοὺς ἔφυγεν, Ἀλέξανδρος δ᾿ εἰς Ἰλλυριούς· καὶ ἡ Κλεοπάτρα δ᾿ ἐγέννησε τῷ Φιλίππῳ θυγατέρα τὴν κληθεῖσαν Εὐρώπην.

Philip of the Macedonians did not lead women into war, as did Darius (the one deposed by Alexander), who, throughout the whole campaign, led about three hundred concubines, as Dicaearchus records in the third book of his History of Greece. *But Philip always married in connection to a war. Anyway, in the twenty-two years in which he reigned, as Satyrus says in his* Life *of him, Philip, having married Audata an Illyrian woman, had by her a daughter Cynnane and he also married Phila the sister of Derdas and Machatas. Wishing to govern the Thessalian nation as well,5 he begot children by two Thessalian women, of whom one was a Pheraean, Nicesipolis, who bore to him Thessalonice, the other the Larissan Philinna by whom he fathered Arrhidaeus. And, in addition, he also gained the kingdom of the Molossians, having married Olympias, by whom he had Alexander and Cleopatra. And when he conquered Thrace, Cothelas, the king of the Thracians came over to him, bringing his daughter Meda and many gifts. Having married her also, he brought her in beside Olympias. In addition to all of these, having conceived a passion for her, he married Cleopatra, the sister of Hippostratus as well as the niece of Attalus. And, having brought her in beside Olympias, he afflicted everything in his whole life, for right away, during the actual wedding festivities, Attalus said, "Now, at any rate, genuine not bastard kings will be born." And Alexander, having heard this, threw the cup which he held in his hands at Attalus and thereupon he threw his cup at Alexander. And after these things, Olympias went into exile among the Molossians and Alexander among the Illyrians and Cleopatra bore a daughter to Philip called Europa.*

The above passage has been the focus of endless scholarly debate,[6] much of it occasioned by misunderstanding of the meaning and context of the statement that Philip always married *kata polemon*. Athenaeus, not

Satyrus, is clearly the author of this generalization,[7] itself a continuation of the opposition Athenaeus had already created between the actions of Darius and Philip in terms of women and war. Athenaeus forced the extension of the opposition, trying to relate it to Philip's marriages, by the dubious means of asserting some sort of connection between Philip's marriages and wars, despite the fact that the passage that follows does not seem to demonstrate such a connection. This artificial or even false connection between two unrelated topics is typical of Athenaeus. What little organization the thirteenth book of Athenaeus has is largely by loose association. His transitional statement has as much intellectual credibility as the mindless "segues" heard today on television news shows.[8]

What does marrying *kata polemon* mean? It has often been read as though Athenaeus had said *meta polemon* (after a war)[9] and, so understood, has occasioned numerous earnest attempts to connect each marriage to certain wars and dates. Athenaeus's diction, however, is vague and allows for a number of possibilities, only one of which would be a marriage made at the conclusion of a war. His phrase could refer to a marriage made at the beginning of a war or at any time during the course of a war; to a marriage made in an attempt to prevent a war; and to a marriage made after a war was over, perhaps when hostilities had subsided. Athenaeus' phrase, in short, is hardly an appropriate or precise tool for arriving at firm dates for any of Philip's marriages and certainly not for reaching conclusions about his policies, whereabouts, or actions.

The seven marriages listed do not seem to demonstrate the truth of Athenaeus' *kata polemon* assertion, and, more surprisingly, he seems to make no effort to make them do so.[10] For example, there is no reference to Philip's Illyrian wars in terms of his marriage to Audata, even though this is the first marriage mentioned. For some of the marriages (e.g., Phila or Cleopatra) it is likely that no connection to a war was possible.

There are probably two reasons for this disparity between Athenaeus' assertion and his support. First, what follows his assertion may be either a quotation, perhaps with omissions, or a paraphrase from Satyrus[11] and thus heeds Satyrus' agenda, not that of Athenaeus. This would explain the listing of the children Philip had by each wife, even though this information is irrelevant to Athenaeus' generalization. It would also account for the fact that the scant information provided about the circumstances of some of the marriages has nothing to do with wars.[12]

Second, Athenaeus' analysis is harebrained. The list and its explanations offer little direct connection to wars but frequently suggest that the marriages made for political gain, for reasons of state. In the Hellenic world, war so often was identical with foreign policy that it is not surprising that Athenaeus subsumes one category in the other. We, however, should not make the same mistake.

In the light of these problems, what value does the Athenaeus passage have? It is indeed an accurate and complete list of Philip's wives and his children, possibly excepting some who died very young.[13] It clearly describes Philip as polygamous, not serially monogamous. Nothing in the passage suggests that any of these women were less than wives (Athenaeus' statement alone makes that clear: this is a list of Philip's marriages)[14] or that there was any formal distinction in their status.[15] The trouble Cleopatra's marriage caused is linked directly to Attalus' interpretation of her marriage, not to the marriage itself. This is confirmed by Athenaeus applying the same verb to both Meda and Cleopatra; the action, the status, is the same, but the interpretation is different.

Scholars have disagreed about whether the list preserved in Athenaeus is chronological. The position of the two Thessalian women on the list, in particular, has led many to conclude that the list does not preserve the order in which Philip married these women.[16] Neither Athenaeus nor Satyrus directly asserts that the list is chronological. The diction of the passage makes it clear that the order of the last three (Olympias, Meda, and Cleopatra) is chronological because Philip is said to *epeisagein* (bring in beside) Olympias first Meda and then Cleopatra. Athenaeus/Satyrus may have chosen this verb, not used earlier in the passage, simply on stylistic grounds, for the sake of word variation,[17] but his choice has the effect of asserting the order in which these three women were married.[18]

What about the women listed before Olympias? Are they too listed in chronological order? Nothing in the diction of the passage helps to answer this question, but it is likely that Satyrus would have listed the wives in chronological order—likely but hardly certain—*if he knew the order of the marriages*. It is not clear that he did.[19] The obscurity of Argead rulers before Philip should make one question whether he did. We know nothing, for instance, about the marriages of his older brothers; the existence of his son Amyntas indicates that Perdiccas III married, but when or to whom is unknown. General scholarly opinion has Philip marrying at least four and possibly five women by the end of 357. In those early years, even Philip was yet another shadowy and possibly ephemeral Macedonian ruler and the women he married, so close together, in whatever order, much more so. Royal marriages were not yet the grand state affairs that Philip and subsequent Hellenistic rulers would make them (see below and chap. 8).

Satyrus may have avoided overtly chronological references in the early portion of the list because he was not able make them. He may simply have known that Philip married most of these women within a short time. His willingness to use *epeisagein* twice in a row toward the end of the passage suggests that more than a desire for verbal variation motivated his diction; he felt surer of his ground about the last three women. If we assume that Satyrus meant his list to reflect the order in which Philip married these women, it appears that Satyrus thought that Philip had married *both* Thessalian women before he married Olympias, but he may have been wrong.

Satyrus intended his list to be in chronological order, but the early part may not have been. Satyrus' list need not be rejected out of hand but taken with a grain of salt. It can more appropriately be used to see the big picture, less appropriately to argue for the date or order of the early marriages. My intent, therefore, while discussing each marriage briefly, is to look for the overall pattern and intent in the marriages of Philip and not to spend much time on the specifics, particularly the dates, of each one. Such specificity would imply a certainty our evidence simply cannot generate.

As I have noted, virtually all attempts to date Philip's marriages have him marrying four to five women within the first two years of his reign (ca. 359–357), although a few believe that he married his fifth wife somewhat later (ca. 353–352; see NICESIPOLIS). Then, according to most views, there is a long lull until 342 or perhaps 339 (see MEDA). Philip's last marriage, to Cleopatra, as well as the marriages he arranged for his two daughters and tried to arrange for his son Arrhidaeus, seem to fall within the last two years or even less of his reign (338–336; see below). This pattern strongly suggests that Philip's marriage policy had three stages: first, he stabilized his Macedonian base through numerous marriages; then, once secure, he avoided further alliances for a number of years; finally, on the eve of his great expedition, he again involved himself in a number of marriage alliances, primarily to stabilize the dynasty before his departure.

Philip unified Macedonia as it had never been before. He was also polygamous on a scale never seen before in Macedonia. This is not a coincidence: Philip used royal marriages both to build internal stability and to extend Macedonia's power. At least in the early years of his reign, Philip made royal polygamy a fundamental support of his external and internal policy. While I have argued that earlier Argead kings were sometimes polygamous, Philip's polygamy differed dramatically from the comparatively modest practices of his predecessors who seem to have taken the occasional second wife. Philip married seven women, five in a short time. His marriage policy should be understood, therefore, as an aspect of his general policy of centralization and consolidation of power. Quite apart from the political alliances and compromises these marriages commemorated, his wives, like elite women elsewhere, functioned as vehicles for the display of family wealth and power. Philip instigated a quantum leap in the display of Argead wealth and power by possessing so many women at once.[20]

These first marriages were arranged not only to create unity. Philip had followed two earlier full brothers to the throne, each having met the kind of violent end so typical of Macedonian rulers. Although there were rivals from other branches of the royal house and even troubles caused by Philip's half-brothers, initially Philip's only heir was his brother Perdiccas' infant son. Philip had good reason to see the danger of such a scarcity of heirs. He married many women quickly to produce many heirs. The marriages did produce a number of children quickly, but they did not continue to do so. In those first years Philip could have had no way of knowing that his first five marriages would not continue to produce crops of royal children.

Let us look briefly at the first five marriages. Philip's marriage to Audata clearly related to his attempt to cope with that traditional Macedonian problem, the Illyrians. The marriage is more likely to have come after his victory against them than before (see AUDATA). It was not the first such royal Macedonian-Illyrian marriage (See EURYDICE 1).

AUDATA

Audata the Illyrian is the first-mentioned wife of Philip II on the famous list of Philip's wives and children preserved in Athenaeus (557c), which also notes that she had a daughter, Cynnane, by him (see CYNNANE). No ancient source provides a patronymic for Audata or names any male relative. It is usually assumed that she was closely related to Bardylis,[21] the Illyrian leader who inflicted

the disastrous defeat on Perdiccas in 359 (Diod. 16.2.4–6) that brought Philip
II to the throne and on whom Philip II, in turn, inflicted an even greater defeat
in 358 (Diod. 16.4.3–7). She may have been a relative of Philip's mother.[22] Although it is possible that Philip married her before his successful confrontation
with Bardylis and that Bardylis's puzzling failure to follow up his success
against Perdiccas is explained by such a marriage alliance,[23] it is far more likely
that the marriage occurred after Philip's victory against the Illyrians.[24]

Nothing more is said about Audata by any ancient source directly, but
a number of sources report that her daughter, Cynnane fought in battle and
trained her daughter Adea Eurydice to fight in battle (Ath. 560 f.; Polyaen.
8.60; Arr. FGrH 156, F 9.22–23; see CYNNANE; ADEA EURYDICE). Given that
Macedonian women did not ordinarily engage directly in warfare whereas
Illyrian women apparently did,[25] it seems very likely that Audata trained
Cynnane in military matters, just as we know Cynnane trained her own
daughter. If so, then Audata, despite the absence of further reference to her
in the sources, probably lived into her daughter's teens and may still have
been alive at the time of her daughter's marriage to Philip's nephew Amyntas.[26] Audata seems not only to have maintained an Illyrian identity in a
Macedonian context but also to have passed that somewhat alien identity
on to her daughter and granddaughter.[27]

The only other point of significance about Audata's career is the possibility that she, like other royal women, changed her name, probably at the
time of her marriage. The evidence for this is much poorer than that for
her granddaughter's name change, Philip Arrhidaeus', or Olympias'.
Athenaeus/Satyrus, as we have seen, calls her Audata (Ath. 557c), an Illyrian name, but Photius' summary of Arrian (FGrH 156, F 9.22) calls Cynnane's mother Eurydice, the name of Philip's part-Illyrian mother, the name
her own granddaughter would one day assume. Calling her "Eurydice"
could easily be a mistake of either Arrian or Photius,[28] but it could signify
that Philip chose to change his Illyrian wife's name to something more
Greek, or it could speak to his filial piety or simply to a desire to indicate
that her status had changed.[29] The quality of the evidence does not permit
any certainty on the matter of a change in her name.[30]

Marrying Phila, apparently a member of the upper Macedonian royal
house of Elimeia, obviously contributed to Philip's efforts to unify Mace-

donia internally by bringing the princely families of upper Macedonia under his control (see PHILA 1). Judging by the prominence of Phila's family in the rest of his reign and Alexander's, this marriage functioned, probably as it was intended, to tie the once-independent upland dynasties to the central king by providing benefits to its members. He would not marry another Macedonian until the last years of his reign.

PHILA 1

Phila's name appears second on Athenaeus' list of Philip II's wives (Ath. 557c). She is identified not by a patronymic but by the names of her brothers, Derdas and Machatas. It is usually assumed that Phila was a member of the upper Macedonian royal house of Elimeia, probably a daughter of Derdas II.[31] If so, Phila's marriage would have been the third alliance between the Argeads and her house.[32] The marriage (although its date and its place in the chronology of Philip's marriages are not entirely clear) may have been connected to Philip's annexation of Elimeia.[33]

One of Phila's brothers, Derdas, seems to have gone into exile and was later taken captive by Philip at Olynthus (Theopomp. ap. Ath. 436c), but the other brother, Machatas, was probably the father of Harpalus, Alexander's longtime friend and notorious treasurer. Members of Phila's family were prominent in the reigns of Philip II and Alexander; the family seems to have declined after Harpalus' disastrous fall.[34]

There is no other reference to Phila preserved in our sources. She may have died soon after her marriage, but there is no evidence that she did. The childless Phila (no child is ascribed to her in the list preserved in Athenaeus) probably remained at court, perhaps for many years, sunk in the royal obscurity common to childless wives of kings.[35]

The apparent prosperity and success of most of her family in that period suggest that she was not discarded and may have retained status and respect despite her failure to produce children.[36] Wives who produced children, particularly heirs, would have had more prestige, but this does not mean that Phila had no status at all. It would have been natural for her to attempt to advance her nephews as she had no children of her own and her position (until the last years of his reign) as Philip's only Macedonian wife may have enabled her to retain influence. It is also possible, however, that the prominence of her family, the importance of remaining close to those members

of the Elimeiote dynasty willing to work within the Argead framework, is sufficient explanation for their favored position under Philip and his son. Phila
may have borne children who did not survive to adulthood. If so, her status could have varied over the course of Philip's reign.

The placement of the two Thessalian women on Athenaeus' list has generated the greatest doubts about its chronology, particularly the placement
of Nicesipolis (see NICESIPOLIS). Satyrus may have discussed the two women
together and out of order, but it seems more likely that he did not and that
Philip married both Thessalians early in his reign. That Philip married two
Thessalians indicates the importance of Thessaly to his military and political base. Nicesipolis' daughter, apparently named to commemorate a Thessalian victory of Philip's, was born much later than her other half siblings
(with the exception of Cleopatra's baby), but this does not necessitate a
later date for the marriage (see below and THESSALONICE).

NICESIPOLIS

The list of Philip II's wives (Satyr. ap. Ath. 557d) includes Nicesipolis of
Pherae. The passage notes that Nicesipolis had a daughter, Thessalonice, by
Philip. Since the Satyrus/Athenaeus passage puts Philip's relationships to
both Nicesipolis and another Thessalian, Philinna, in the context of a political alliance (he is said to have had children by these women in order to
lay claim to the Thessalian people), both Nicesipolis and Philinna should
be considered wives of Philip, not concubines. Stephanus Byzantinus (s.v.
"Thessalonice") explicitly states that Philip married Nicesipolis.[37] If anything,
this conclusion is more obvious in the case of Nicesipolis than Philinna.
Whereas the sources preserve a number of slurs referring to Philinna's birth,
there are no such references to Nicesipolis. Stephanus cites Lucius the Tarraian for the fact that she was wellborn and the niece of Jason of Pherae
(Steph. Byz. s.v. "Thessalonice").[38]

Stephanus also relates that Nicesipolis died twenty days after the birth
of her daughter and that Philip named his daughter after his victory in Thessaly (Steph. Byz. s.v. "Thessalonice").[39] The date of Nicesipolis' marriage to
Philip is uncertain. It is often assumed that Philip could not have married her
before 353 or 352 because she was a Pheraean,[40] but, just as the list implies,

Philip may well have married both Nicesipolis and Philinna quite early in his reign, before his marriage to Olympias in 357.[41] Thessalonice could have been born some years after the marriage (see THESSALONICE).

Philip may have arranged both Thessalian marriages early on to conciliate rival factions in Thessaly. (We should not assume that these marriages all succeeded in achieving the goals for which they may have been contracted; continuing difficulties with Pherae need not mean there was no Pheraean marriage.)[42] In any event, as Philinna's son Arrhidaeus was old enough to marry by the end of Philip's reign, his mother must have been married to Philip by roughly 357 (see PHILINNA).

PHILINNA

Philinna, a Thessalian from Larissa, bore Philip II a son, Arrhidaeus, later called Philip (Satyr. ap. Ath. 557c; usually referred to as Philip Arrhidaeus). A number of ancient sources consider Philinna anything but respectable. Plutarch (*Alex.* 77.5) calls her an obscure and common woman. Justin (9.8.2) terms her a dancing girl (*saltatrix*) and a Larissan whore (*scortum*) (13.2.11). Athenaeus (13.578a) preserves a fragment of Ptolemy, son of Agesarchus, that also speaks of her as a dancing girl and includes her on a list of notorious royal mistresses.

Athenaeus' list (13.557c) paints a different picture of Philinna and her connection to Philip. It seems to categorize Philinna as a wife, not as a mistress or a concubine,[43] and certainly puts her relationship to Philip in a political context. Athenaeus has Philip claiming the Thessalian nation by begetting children by two Thessalian women.

Although it is difficult to see why sleeping with a Thessalian whore would have endeared Philip to the Thessalians, whom he certainly wanted to conciliate, it seems reasonable to conclude that Philinna came from a respectable family, perhaps even the distinguished Aleuadae, and was a wife of Philip, not a mistress.[44] Philinna was apparently a widow with a young son at the time of her marriage to Philip.[45] The negative tradition about her probably derives from assorted layers of propaganda in the period after the death of Alexander, from the fact that she was not from a royal dynasty, and from Greek misunderstanding of polygamy.[46]

The exact date of Philinna's marriage and therefore the date of the birth of her son are unknown, but, in the light of Arrhidaeus' planned marriage to the daughter of Pixodarus in spring 336, the marriage must have occurred soon after Philip took the throne, probably in 358 or 357.[47] It is not certain, therefore, whether Arrhidaeus was older or younger than his half brother Alexander.[48] Nothing more is heard of Philinna.

Since Alexander was born in June 356, Philip must have married Olympias no later than the end of 357 (see OLYMPIAS). The benefits of marrying a Molossian princess are obvious, though not as extensive as those claimed by Satyrus and not necessarily greater than those to be gained by connections in Thessaly. This marriage did not immediately become Philip's most important one simply because Alexander ultimately became Philip's heir.

OLYMPIAS: PART 1

Olympias, the mother of Alexander the Great, was the best known of Philip's seven wives. Her father was Neoptolemus, ruler of the Molossians (Diod. 19.51.1; Just. 7.6.10, 17.3.14). Her family, the Aeacids, Hellenized since the days of her great-grandfather, claimed descent from Pyrrhus, son of Achilles, and Helenus, son of Priam (Plut. *Alex.* 2, *Pyrrh.* 1; Paus. 1.11.1). Her mother's identity and ethnicity are unknown.[49] She had two siblings: a sister, Troas, ultimately the wife of their uncle Arybbas (Just. 7.6.11) and a brother, Alexander, later ruler of the Molossians and husband of Olympias' daughter (Diod. 16.72.2; Just. 7. 6.10–11).[50]

Women in the Molossian-Epirote culture may have had more legal rights and a more prominent role in the family than elsewhere in the Hellenic world. If so, Olympias's expectations about her role and what constituted appropriate behavior for a woman, royal or otherwise, may have been somewhat different from those of southern Greeks and perhaps also Macedonians.[51] She may have passed this expectation of a wider role on to her daughter Cleopatra (see CLEOPATRA 2), whose own Epirote experience would have reinforced it.

Olympias, like other royal Macedonian women, may have been known by other names at various periods in her life. Plutarch (*Mor.* 401) observes that nicknames often caused real names to be obscured and claims that Alexander's mother, Polyxena, was later called Myrtale, Olympias, and Stratonice. Justin (2.7.13) claims that Myrtale was the name Olympias was known by as a child. Various theories have been developed to interpret the contradictory testimony of these two authors;[52] it is likely that Olympias was known by different names (or at least by additional names) at various periods in her life. The significant naming of royal women along with the changing of their names reflect their comparatively public status and indicates that these names functioned as quasi-titles.

Since Alexander was born in 356, Olympias was probably born between 375 and 371.[53] Plutarch's tale of a love match between Olympias and Philip, born out of a chance meeting at the mysteries of Samothrace (*Alex.* 2.1–2), should be rejected as fiction.[54] Olympias' uncle Arybbas (her father was dead by this period and Arybbas was king) arranged the marriage to Philip as a political alliance, similar to many and perhaps all of the other marriages Philip contracted. The marriage could and in many ways did unite the Molossians and Macedonians, two northern semi-Hellenized peoples with a common border and a common problem, the Illyrian menace. The placement of Philip's marriage to Olympias relative to his other early marriages is unclear (see above). Olympias bore Philip two children, both of whom were born early in her marriage: Alexander III (the Great), in 356, and Cleopatra, soon after (see CLEOPATRA 2).

Little is known of Olympias' activities, role, and status during the reign of her husband. Caution should be used in assessing the little evidence our sources offer. A variety of factors—the subsequent alleged propaganda campaign of Cassander, the hostility of Hellenic culture toward politically active women, the probable resentment of various Macedonian aristocrats of her prominence in the reign of her son and later—have created an extremely negative tradition about her in the sources. Much of the extant information derives from suspect anecdotal material. In addition, Alexander's later importance and Olympias' later prominence may have led ancient authors to exaggerate her role during Philip's reign, and this exaggeration may have been increased by Greek writers' assumption that she was Philip's only wife or that she was, in some formal sense, his chief wife.[55]

Philip had fathered another son (Arrhidaeus, or Philip Arrhidaeus) by another wife, a son close to Alexander in age, so it is not clear at what point Olympias began to be accorded the status appropriate to the mother of the youth Philip was treating as his heir. In Philip's reign there is no evidence for a title or other indication that any of Philip's wives was somehow the chief wife or uniquely queen. Untidy Macedonian succession patterns do not suggest that Philip's choice of heir would have been immediately obvious, particularly because the two boys were close in age.

Arrhidaeus suffered from a disability, probably mental, which kept him from being regarded as able to rule in his own right. Plutarch, who blames Arrhidaeus' condition on a poisoning attempt by Olympias (*Alex.* 77.5), implies that Arrhidaeus had reached late childhood or perhaps even early adolescence before his condition became obvious. The veracity of his report and its implications are uncertain.[56]

At some date in Philip's reign, certainly by Alexander's early teens, Olympias was probably considered Philip's most important wife, primarily because of her son's growing importance. This status was not formal and likely varied throughout her marriage.[57]

There is no evidence that Olympias exerted any influence over her husband (although she may well have), and there is virtually no evidence on the nature of her relationship with her husband during their more than twenty-year marriage. Philip's treatment of Olympias' brother, Alexander, could indicate that she had political influence with Philip. Philip first brought his brother-in-law to his court and subsequently, having ousted Arybbas from the Molossian throne, replaced him with Olympias' young brother. Although it is likely that Olympias approved of Philip's actions, and may have advocated them, Philip, desirous of a close yet dominant relationship with his Molossian neighbors, might easily have followed such a policy whether married to Olympias or not.[58]

Tradition says that Alexander and his mother were close throughout their lives and implies that he and his father were competitive and less close. In this case tradition is probably correct, although not necessarily for sentimental or emotional reasons. The mother's role as advocate for her son's succession has already been noted. Philip's frequent absences on campaigns and the inherent element of competition built into the roles of adult king and near-adult heir would have distanced him from Alexander. Reading further psychological truths into these relationships or even assuming that they primarily involved real affection or personal animosity is dangerous, both because the innately political nature of dynamics in a royal family adds the element of political utility to whatever emotional forces are at work and because our own under-

WOMEN AND MONARCHY IN MACEDONIA

standing of the nature of family—feelings and relations between husbands and wives and parents and children—differs profoundly from that of fourth-century Greece and even more from that of the Macedonian dynasty.[59]

What we actually know about Olympias during the years from 357 until the time of her husband's murder (and events immediately preceding it) in 336 is modest indeed. One of her son's early tutors, Leonidas, was a relative of Olympias (Plut. *Alex.* 5.4). Philip probably selected the tutor, but it was a choice bound to flatter Olympias and her family. Leonidas could even have been Olympias' nominee.[60]

The sources portray Olympias as fond of religion in general and Dionysiac and other mystery cults in particular (Plut. *Alex.* 2; Ath. 12.560 f., 14.659 f.). Disallowing the obviously spurious and ex post facto stories about Alexander's birth and the divine snake[61] and sifting out the more lurid assumptions about the nature of her activities in these cults, Olympias was indeed active in religious matters and particularly devoted to Dionysiac cults. In this she resembled other women of the Macedonian royal family (who seem often to take prominent roles in religious activities), women of the Hellenic and Hellenized world in general (who often played important roles in family and even civic cults and who were said to be especially fond of Dionysiac and other mystery cults), much of the Macedonian and northern Greek population among whom Dionysiac cults were popular and omnipresent in cultural objects, and, of course, her own son. Surviving information makes it difficult to judge whether Olympias was unusually intense in her religious devotion or simply better known for it because of her high public profile.[62]

It is often claimed that relations between Philip and Olympias deteriorated toward the end of Philip's reign, but the truth is that we know virtually nothing about their relations at any period. Plutarch (*Alex.* 9.3) says that Olympias, whom he characterizes as a troublemaker, made the bad situation of royal polygamy, with its involvement of women in public affairs, worse by exacerbating the already difficult dealings of royal father and son. His remarks precede his account of the troubled last years of Philip's reign and seem to refer only to them. If anything, Plutarch implies that Olympias and Philip never got along and, in sense, never could because of the nature of polygamy. Earlier passages, supposedly dealing with the end of sexual relations between Philip and Olympias but actually supporting Alexander's subsequent claims to divine parenthood (Plut. *Alex.* 2.4, 3.1) deserve no credence.[63]

Whatever the nature of personal dealings between Philip and Olympias, their public relationship and Olympias' status were dramatically affected by Philip's last marriage to a young Macedonian woman named Cleopatra (see CLEOPATRA 3), a marriage that occurred within a year or so of Philip's great victory at Chaeroneia in 338 and in the context of his planning for the Graeco-Macedonian invasion of the Persian empire. Philip's last marriage disturbed the delicate balance of succession politics. Whatever Philip's motivation for this last marriage, Alexander came to perceive it as a threat to his status when the new bride's guardian proposed a toast that brought into question Alexander's legitimacy as heir to the throne (Plut. *Alex.* 9.4–5; Satyr. ap. Ath. 13.557d; see CLEOPATRA 3 and below). Alexander, taking his mother with him and leaving Olympias with her brother in Molossia, went into exile, to Philip's hereditary foes, the Illyrians (Plut. *Alex.* 9.4–5; Ath. 13.557d; Just. 9.7.5–7).

The public quarrel between royal father and royal son was quickly settled (Plut. *Alex.* 9.6; Just. 9.7.6), and Alexander returned to court. It is not certain whether Olympias returned as well, although it seems likely that her return was a necessary part of the formal reconciliation and that she must have been present by the time of her daughter's marriage.[64] Plutarch (*Alex.* 10.1–3) alone recounts a tale that implies that relations between Philip and Alexander continued to be tense despite the formal reconciliation. At the urging of his mother and friends, Alexander attempted to replace his brother, Arrhidaeus, as prospective groom in a marriage alliance with Pixodarus, satrap of Caria. Philip exploded with anger when Alexander's activities were exposed.

Philip's arrangement of the marriage of Olympias' daughter to Olympias' brother—the wedding celebrations were the actual context for Philip's murder—has been misread by some as an indication that Olympias was being replaced by her daughter. Others have rightly seen it as part of the formal reconciliation between father and son, intended to reaffirm the status and importance of Alexander's Molossian heritage.[65]

Philip II was assassinated in late summer or early fall 336 by a young Macedonian noble named Pausanias with a well-known personal grievance (his sense that Philip, his former lover, had betrayed him by failing to punish those who had raped him), but much speculation in both ancient (Plut. *Alex.* 10.4; Just. 9.6.4–7.14) and modern times assigned ultimate responsibility to Olympias and/or Alexander. Our sources for the event are poor (Diod. 16.93–94; Plut. *Alex.* 10.4; Just. 9.6.4–7.14; Arist. *Pol.* 1311b; *POxy.* 1798), and no certainty on the matter is possible.

Assassination theories and scholarship abound (see below for further discussion). Olympias and her son undeniably benefited by Philip's death. Relations between Philip and Alexander were clearly troubled in the period after Chaeroneia. Others, however, also benefited from his demise (e.g., the Persians), and at least some of these ran less risk by involving themselves in an assassination plot than either Olympias or Alexander did. The involvement of mother and son is possible but far from certain. Further judgments about Olympias' actions cannot depend on such uncertain evidence. Her contemporaries wondered about her involvement, but few, if any, can have known the truth. (See chaps. 4 and 5 for parts 2 and 3 of OLYMPIAS.)

Many years passed before Philip married again. By 355 or so Philip had five wives and probably four children (two boys, two girls), as well as a potential heir in his nephew Amyntas. (He may have had other children who did not survive long enough for us to hear of but whose existence could have given Philip further, if ultimately false, comfort about the succession.) By this point in his reign he had also moved from the defensive to the offensive in terms of power politics. He was still a young man with many more campaigns and, it must have seemed, many more sons in him. At this stage Philip may have seen further marriages and wives as destabilizing, and he probably felt no more need for them.

It is not possible to date the beginning of Philip's interest in a campaign against Persia—the idea was older than Philip—or to choose a moment after which Philip thought less about Greece and more about Asia. The process was probably incremental, with pleasant possibilities gradually becoming probabilities. It is in the nature of conquerors such as Philip and his son that they combine long-term goals, possibly quite vague, with an interest simply in what lies over the next hill and that they demonstrate an ability to juggle and sometimes combine such concerns.[66] A wife taken from a friendly but defeated tribe around the Danube would have obvious benefits even if Philip did not invade Asia but greater ones if he planned to.

His marriage to Meda may have been a wild card, the consequence of her father's offer, which Philip felt he could not turn down, but it was more likely the first sign of another change in his marriage policy (see MEDA). By 342 or 341, both his dynastic and his foreign policy needs had changed again. He had produced no more children except for Thessa-

Ionice and, most important, no more sons who survived. By this date, Arrhidaeus' deficiencies would have emerged, so that Philip was aware that he had only one son who was a viable heir.[67] The king was a generation older, much wounded, and likely to be more concerned about the future. Philip's growing interest in a Persian campaign may have combined with his dynastic worries.

MEDA

Meda appears only on the list of the wives of Philip II in Athenaeus (557d). The passage refers to Meda's father as Cothelas, a king of the Thracians, and provides this context for the marriage: after Philip had taken Thrace, Cothelas went over to him, bringing with him his daughter and a considerable dowry. No mention is made of children of hers by Philip, and no other reference to Meda exists. Cothelas was actually king of the Getae, a seminomadic people who inhabited the region between Thrace and the Danube.[68] There is no consensus on the specific political circumstance of the marriage and thus the exact date.[69]

Because of the lack of further reference to Meda, it is often assumed that she died soon after her marriage. Nonetheless, she could have remained at court for many years, childless and inconspicuous. Repudiation is unlikely, because it would have negatively affected Philip's apparent alliance with her father.[70]

Hammond has considered her a good candidate for the identity of the woman buried in the antechamber of Tomb II at Vergina,[71] but this is unlikely to be correct (see chap. 9). Meda lived and died in obscurity, both a trophy for Philip's conquests and a hostage to ensure her father's good behavior.

Philip's victory at Chaeroneia coupled with the planned invasion generated a flurry of royal Macedonian weddings, marriages clearly intended to create more Argead heirs, quite possibly because Philip intended to take both his sons and his nephew with him on the Asian campaign. Within about a year, Philip arranged marriages for his two elder daughters and took yet another bride himself. All three marriages seem to have to do with dynastic and internal concerns rather than with foreign affairs, even though one of them appears to relate to foreign affairs as well. In addition, he planned a foreign marriage for Arrhidaeus, though the marriage never happened.

WOMEN AND MONARCHY IN MACEDONIA

Philip had his daughter by Audata, Cynnane, marry his brother's son, Amyntas. The marriage, obviously intended to consolidate the dynasty, clearly marked Amyntas as a secondary heir. It may have occurred before Philip's marriage to Cleopatra, or it may not (see below and ADEA EURYDICE). If it happened after Philip's marriage, this marriage could also have contributed to Alexander's troubled dealings with his father (see below).

CYNNANE PART 1

Cynnane[72] was the daughter of Philip II and his Illyrian wife, Audata (see AU-DATA). Because of the controversy surrounding the order and date of the marriages of Philip II, we can only estimate her date of birth, but it probably fell well after 358 or 357 (see below).

Cynnane's mother taught her to be a warrior, and she fought in Philip's campaigns against the Illyrians. In one of these battles, she not only defeated the enemy but also confronted and killed their queen (Polyaen. 8.60). Cynnane would later pass the military training and tradition she had received from her mother on to her own daughter, Adea Eurydice (Polyaen. 8.60; see ADEA EURYDICE).[73] Cynnane had a monarchical tradition strikingly different from that of Macedonia. This tradition permitted royal women not only to embrace military activity but also to pursue political goals through military institutions, primarily through the army. Teuta, a third-century B.C. Illyrian ruler, acted as regent for her stepson and attacked and defeated many Greek powers before being forced to submit to Rome (Polyb. 2.2–12). Women generally played a larger and less secluded role in Illyrian than in Hellenic society.[74]

Philip arranged Cynnane's marriage to his nephew Amyntas, son of Perdiccas III (Polyaen. 8.60; Arr. FGrH 156, F 9.22).[75] Most scholars assume that the marriage of Cynnane and Amyntas occurred late in Philip's reign, probably between 338 and 336, because Polyaenus (8.60.4) says that Amyntas' murder followed swiftly on his marriage. If Cynnane were born in 358, she could have married as early as ca. 343,[76] and would have been a rather elderly bride any time after about 340 (even granted the evidence that suggests that female Argeads may sometimes have married later than Greek women in general, in their late rather than early teens).[77] A birthdate in the mid- to late 350s makes more sense for a woman who is likely to have married well after 340.[78] What little we know about Amyntas also suggests a marriage date of 338–336.[79] Amyntas' marriage to his cousin Cynnane suggests that Philip was treating Amyntas as his heir, next in line after Alexander.[80]

If Cynnane did indeed marry her royal cousin in the last year or year and a half of her father's reign, then the marriage could have seemed threatening to Alexander, coming in the context of the troubled aftermath of Philip's marriage to Cleopatra and Alexander's apparent insecurity about his succession. Amyntas' marriage could have had much the same effect on Alexander as Arrhidaeus' projected marriage to Pixodarus' daughter: he may have taken it as a warning from Philip that other heirs were possible.[81] As with Arrhidaeus' projected marriage, the marriage to Cynnane was the first public recognition that Philip had given Amyntas. Although Philip probably hoped that the marriage, like the others he had arranged, would generate more Argead heirs, he created an alternative branch to the Argead family tree, a branch that would cause difficulties for the rest of his family and whose existence contributed to the end of the dynasty (see chap. 5).

While Cynnane's subsequent career confirms the picture created by the story of her warlike exploits against the Illyrians and thus enables us to conclude that she was a brave, capable, and audacious woman, our much more limited information about her husband has led some to conclude that he was "innocuous," perhaps a pawn in his ambitious wife's plans.[82] This view of Cynnane's husband depends heavily on the absence of information about him and on the fact that he did nothing to assert himself throughout Philip's reign. Given his age, Amyntas could only have entertained thoughts of taking the throne himself toward the end of Philip's reign, and that period was, of course, the most successful and stable of Philip's reign. If Amyntas had ambitions to recover the throne for his branch of the family, he was better advised to wait for the opportunity that Philip's departure for Asia would bring.[83]

Whether or not Philip was enamored of Cleopatra, Attalus' ward, he certainly intended the marriage to produce more heirs before his long absence on the Asian campaign. In fact, Cleopatra had only one child, Europa, who was murdered while still an infant.

Ironically, Philip may have chosen a wife from Attalus's family to avoid the divisiveness that would ensue if he took a bride from the families of either Parmenio or Antipater, the two greatest generals in the

WOMEN AND MONARCHY IN MACEDONIA

kingdom. Choosing Attalus' niece may have seemed a way to avoid controversy. If such was Philip's intent, he failed.

Although there are no references to Attalus before Cleopatra's wedding, can we reasonably assume that the prominent role Attalus played in the last year of Philip's reign and the beginning of Alexander's was solely the consequence of Cleopatra's marriage?[84] Several factors suggest that Attalus had status apart from that as Cleopatra's guardian. First, Attalus' famous toast at the wedding banquet and the events it precipitated are suggestive of Attalus's status. Although Attalus put an interpretation on the marriage that Philip did not (so far as we know), Philip was unwilling to correct it. Instead he sided with Attalus against his own son, the apparent heir, in a very public manner.[85]

Second, there is Philip's puzzling reaction to the rape of his former lover, Pausanias. The rape, part of a vendetta engineered by Attalus and, according to Plutarch (*Alex.* 10.4), Cleopatra, went unpunished by Philip.[86] This led to Philip's assassination.[87]

Third, Philip appointed Attalus, along with Parmenio and perhaps Amyntas, to lead the advance Macedonian expedition in Asia.[88] Attalus was sufficiently popular with his troops in Asia (Diod. 17.2.4–3.2, 5.2) that, even after the death of Philip, Alexander had to proceed gingerly to arrange his elimination,[89] as well as that of other family members with important positions.[90] Diodorus (17.2.3–4), at least, understood Attalus to be a threat to Alexander's throne, possibly because Cleopatra and Attalus had Argead blood (see CLEOPATRA 3).

It is difficult to ascribe the remarkable degree of influence Attalus exercised to Cleopatra's marriage alone. Twice Philip sided with him in disputes in which the king's self-interest should have led him to the other side. Heckel rightly speaks of Philip's "almost deferential treatment of Attalus."[91] Diodorus (16.93.7) describes Attalus as a courtier and a person who had great influence with Philip[92] and explains that Philip did not wish to punish Attalus for the rape because of his relationship to him[93] and because of his current military service (16.93.8). Only at this point does Diodorus (16.93.9) refer to Attalus' relationship to Cleopatra, the marriage, and the Asian command. Attalus seems already to have been important and influential. His niece's royal marriage simply offered further advantage. His military appointment suggests that Philip placed considerable faith in his skills and that Attalus had the experience to engender that faith. Being the honorary father of the bride would hardly be recommendation enough.[94] Even if Cleopatra had immediately borne a son, years would have passed before he could threaten his older rival, Alexander. The relatives of Philip's other Macedonian wife, Phila, do not seem to have enjoyed anything like Attalus' clout.[95] It is also dangerous to exaggerate his power, however.[96]

CLEOPATRA 3

Cleopatra, a Macedonian aristocrat and Attalus', niece,[97] was Philip II's last bride (Ath. 557d, 560c; Diod. 16.93.9; Plut. *Alex.* 9.4; Arr. 3.6.5; Just. 9.5.8–9). She married him after Chaeroneia, probably in late summer or early fall 337,[98] and bore him a daughter named Europa (Ath. 557e) shortly before her husband's murder by Pausanias (Diod. 17.2.3), in late summer or early fall 336.[99] Sometime after Philip's death but before Alexander's departure for Asia, Olympias had Cleopatra and her baby killed (see below; chap. 4). The marriage to Cleopatra precipitated a quarrel between Philip and his apparent heir, Olympias' son, Alexander. This quarrel disrupted the Macedonian court in the last year of Philip's reign. Tremendous disagreement persists over why the marriage had the consequences it did and how extensive these consequences were.[100] This disagreement, in turn, has generated disputes over many aspects of Cleopatra's background and the context and chronology of events in her short career.

Plutarch (*Alex.* 9.4) tells us that Cleopatra was a *parthenos* (maiden) at the time of her marriage and that Philip became enamored of her despite, or perhaps because of, her youth. This information makes it likely that she was no more than eighteen at the time of her marriage in 337, possibly as much as four years younger. A birthdate between 355 and 351 seems reasonable. The date of her death is controversial (see below), but she may have died only a year after her marriage and cannot have lived longer than a year and a half after that event, if Plutarch's testimony that Alexander had not yet left for Asia at the time of her murder is correct (Plut. *Alex.* 10.4).[101] If my estimates are reasonable, Cleopatra was less than twenty when she died. If so, she was too young at the time of her death to have been the woman whose remains lie in the antechamber of Tomb II at Vergina (see chap. 9).

Both Plutarch (*Alex.* 9.4) and Athenaeus (557d) say that Philip's *eros* motivated the marriage that proved so divisive. Since Athenaeus himself says that Philip always married in connection to a war (557b) and Plutarch's similar assertion about the motivation of Philip's marriage to Olympias (Plut. *Alex.* 2.1) has rarely been taken seriously, many have and looked instead for political motivation for a marriage that had undeniable political consequences. Others, however, impressed by the entirely negative political repercussions of Philip's last marriage, have concluded that only an irrational explanation will suffice for a choice so patently troublesome.[102]

Both interpretations of the motivation for the marriage suffer from being based on events after the marriage, and thus both tend to read the past from the future. In 337 Philip, about to leave on his great Asian expedition and in need of heirs, arranged a number of royal marriages. Concern about the succession seems unsurprising and appropriate.[103]

Given that he had probably decided to marry again, does his choice of bride indicate that he was driven only by erotic impulses, unaffected by political concerns? Certainly not. These motives are not mutually exclusive, as the example of Henry VIII and Anne Boleyn demonstrates. Although most of Philip's wives had been foreign, the eve of his departure for Asia probably did not seem like the moment to select another foreign wife. The king probably returned from the meeting of the League of Corinth determined to marry yet again and to marry a Macedonian. He may have already fixed on the family of the bride. Perhaps, as our sources suggest, he was also attracted by young Cleopatra and saw no reason not to marry her.

Who was Cleopatra? Her father and her brother Hippostratus were apparently dead by the time of her marriage, and her uncle Attalus served as her guardian.[104]

Another factor in this complicated equation is the possibility that Cleopatra may have had Argead blood, probably through an earlier king's daughter. Her name hints at an Argead connection.[105] If Cleopatra could claim some royal blood, her attractiveness as a bride is further explained, and perhaps the reaction of Alexander and Olympias to what on the surface appear to be Attalus' inflated ambitions for children born to her.[106]

This marriage proved unexpectedly explosive. Philip had intended it to provide more male heirs and perhaps to please his erotic needs. Certainly he did not mean to disrupt Macedonia just as his great invasion loomed. One important reason why the marriage to Cleopatra was so divisive was that Attalus made it so by his interpretation of it at the wedding feast and by his treatment of Pausanias.[107] The marriage may also have precipitated a collapse of the balance of power at court between Antipater and Parmenio. Parmenio and Attalus are linked both by the marriage of Parmenio's daughter to Attalus[108] and by their joint command. Parmenio had to involve himself in Attalus' death to remain in a position of power after the Philip's death.[109]

The sources suggest that Olympias killed Cleopatra and her baby soon after Philip's murder (Just. 9.7.12; Paus. 8.7.5; Plut. *Alex.* 10.7). Despite the chronological uncertainties of the period immediately after the assassination, there seems to be no reason to reject this implication. Cleopatra and Europa were probably murdered before Attalus was eliminated.[110] These murders were pragmatic, although possibly vengeful as well, and not without precedent. Olympias chose to force Cleopatra to kill herself, in recognition of a status they shared to some degree (see chap. 4).[111]

Cleopatra is so named in all our extant sources but one, Arrian. Arrian (3.6.5), in a flashback in his main narrative, refers to a person who can only be the woman otherwise known as Cleopatra, as "Eurydice." Is Arrian's "Eurydice" simply a mistake,[112] or is it evidence for another example of name changing at critical moments by members, especially female members, of the royal family? Is "Eurydice" a new name the bride took at the time of her marriage,[113] or is the name by which this young woman is generally known the new one and "Eurydice" her earlier name?[114] Granted the existence of other, more certain cases of name changing, it is impossible to deny this possibility, but the evidence in this case is much less compelling than that for Adea Eurydice and Philip Arrhidaeus (Diod. 18.2.4; Arr. *FGrH* 156, F 1.19, 23), or Olympias (Plut. *Mor.* 401a–b; Just. 9.7.12).

We know nothing of Cleopatra as an individual. She may have been an innocent pawn in the struggles of older and more powerful figures such as her uncle and Olympias, or she may have been a much tougher and more ambitious figure. If she was indeed involved in the plot against Pausanias as Plutarch (*Alex.* 10.4) claimed, the latter is the more likely probability. Her pregnancy would hardly have prevented her from being consulted. As Roxane's murder of Stateira and her sister demonstrates (see ROXANE), pregnancy did not prevent dynastic vindictiveness.[115] There is no evidence of a literary tradition hostile to Cleopatra.[116] Plutarch's inclusion of Cleopatra may be less literal than it appears, however. He may be treating Attalus and Cleopatra as a dynastic unit but may not have information about her personal participation in the "punishment" of Pausanias. Her death and daughter's remain pathetic testimony to the violence of dynastic confrontations in

WOMEN AND MONARCHY IN MACEDONIA

Macedonia whether or not the last wife of Philip was as ruthless as his best-known one.

The final marriage Philip successfully arranged was that of his daughter by Olympias, Cleopatra, to Olympias' brother Alexander, now the Molossian ruler (Diod. 16.91.4–93.2; Just. 9.6.1–3). Philip was murdered at these wedding festivities. This marriage was ostensibly a foreign alliance, confirmation of the Molossian tie initiated a generation before and compensation to Alexander of Epirus for Philip's apparent slight to Alexander's sister (because Alexander did not want to go to war with Philip does not mean that he was happy about the offense to his clan). The marriage, however, was primarily intended to solve the domestic mess created by Attalus' insult to the Macedonian Alexander at Philip's wedding to Cleopatra.[117] Whatever Attalus said at the wedding banquet, Alexander's ability to succeed had been questioned and his mother's lineage somehow insulted (thus the departure of mother and son from court). Making a grand state affair of marrying Olympias' brother to Olympias' daughter was meant to smooth over these dynastic upsets by stressing the prestige of those seemingly slighted (see below for other purposes). Philip would have been comparatively uninterested in any children produced by the marriage but very concerned that dynastic stability be regenerated. In this sense, the marriage resembles that of Amyntas and Cynnane.

CLEOPATRA 2: PART 1
Cleopatra was the child of Philip II and Olympias and thus Alexander the Great's only full sister (Satyr. ap. Ath. 13.557d). She was probably born a year or two after her brother, in 355 or 354.[118] We have no information about her until the period of her marriage to her uncle, now ruler of Molossia, Alexander of Epirus. Philip arranged the marriage and planned to make it the occasion for an international display of Macedonian wealth and power on the eve of the great Persian expedition (Diod. 16.91.4–93.2; Just. 9.6.1–3; also see chap. 8 below).

Philip intended Cleopatra's marriage to mollify Alexander of Epirus, Olympias, and her son Alexander in the wake of the insults offered to them by Attalus at the time of Philip's last marriage to Attalus's ward, another Cleopatra. Justin (9.7.7) claims that Olympias tried to convince her brother, to whom she had fled, to make war on Philip but that Philip's marriage offer prevented this. Alexander of Epirus had been placed on the throne by his royal brother-in-law and was thus not in an easy position. It seems likely that Olympias returned to Macedonia for her daughter's wedding.[119]

The wedding, in fall 336, instead of easing the tensions between these two royal families and providing a showcase for the newly imperial Macedonia, was overshadowed by the assassination of Philip II, who was struck down during the public festivities after the wedding.[120] Philip's arrangements for his daughter's wedding were unprecedented. He had not accorded this kind of international attention to the marriage of Cynnane (another, probably older daughter) to his nephew Amyntas, son of Perdiccas III, perhaps because he wished to deemphasize Cynnane's marriage to his alternate heir (see CYNNANE). The status of Olympias and Alexander's status as an heir also help to explain Philip's emphasis on Cleopatra. (See chaps. 4 and 5 for parts 2 and 3 of the life of Cleopatra.)

Philip involved himself in plans for another royal marriage in this same period, but the marriage did not take place. Negotiations were proceeding for a marriage between his mentally limited son, Arrhidaeus, and the daughter of a friendly western satrap, Pixodarus, but these negotiations were interrupted when Alexander interjected himself as a rival bridegroom (Plut. *Alex*.10.1–3). Alexander apparently saw this marriage alliance as a threat to his position as heir. Philip may have viewed the marriage as another opportunity to create more Argeads, should they be needed.[121]

OTHER USES FOR ROYAL WOMEN

Important developments relating to women and Macedonian monarchy occurred during Philip's reign, but only a brief mention is necessary here (see chap. 8 for further discussion). Two of Philip's innovations generated royal traditions that lasted well into the Hellenistic period, probably because both reflect the changes in monarchy begun by Philip and perpetuated by Alexander and Hellenistic rulers.

WOMEN AND MONARCHY IN MACEDONIA

Having centralized his royal authority to an unprecedented degree and transformed his backward kingdom into the greatest Hellenic power, Philip stood out from the rest of the Macedonian elite more than any of his predecessors. In addition, he needed to display his power in a comprehensible and effective way to Greeks to the south, peoples still unused to and hostile to monarchy. Especially toward the end of his reign, Philip showed interest in elevating the status of the monarchy. The problems generated by his accomplishments provide the context for his innovative use of royal women.

Shortly after his victory at Chaeroneia, Philip arranged the construction of the Philippeum at Olympia, an ambiguous structure in which stood five chryselephantine statues: Philip, Philip's father and mother, Alexander, and Olympias. The victor at Chaeroneia presented to the general Greek public an image of the monarchy that was dynastic rather than personal and that alluded to the divinity of all its members, including women. The presence of the women's statues in the Philippeum signified that Philip had made women part of the public presentation of the monarchy (see chap. 8). His choice of names for two of his daughters (see THESSALONICE; EUROPA) and perhaps some of his wives (see AUDATA; OLYMPIAS; CLEOPATRA 3) is another example of the same choice; their names mirrored the prestige and accomplishments of the males.[122] Similarly, Philip chose to turn his daughter Cleopatra's wedding into an international affair, a kind of festival of Macedonian monarchy and power.

EUROPA

Europa was the daughter of Philip by his last wife, Cleopatra, Attalus' ward (Ath. 557d; see CLEOPATRA 3). Europa was probably Cleopatra's only child. Satyrus/Athenaeus mentions only her, but Pausanias (8.7.7) recounts that Cleopatra was killed along with a male infant, and Justin, although reporting that the murdered baby was female (9.7.12), also knows of a son Caranus (11.2.3), possibly a son of Cleopatra's. A number of factors suggest that Satyrus should be valued over Pausanias and Justin.[123]

Europa was born only a few days before her father's murder (Diod. 17.2.3) and was probably murdered, along with her mother, by Olympias (Just. 9.7.12; Paus. 8.7.5)[124] not long after Philip's assassination. Although revenge may have played a role in these murders, Olympias' motivation was primarily dynastic (see chap. 4).

Alexander's role in the murder is uncertain. Pausanias and Justin (9.7.12) mention only Olympias in terms of the crime. Plutarch (*Alex.* 10.4) refers to Olympias' savagery to Cleopatra (he does not say that she killed her, nor does he mention the baby) and says that it was committed in Alexander's absence and that Alexander scolded his mother about it. Justin (12.6.14–15) seems to hold Alexander himself responsible for the murder of Cleopatra, probably because he understood it to be something Olympias did with Alexander's approval. If Cleopatra was buried in the antechamber of Tomb II at Vergina (see chap. 9), no traces of Europa's remains have been found with those of the woman.

To this grisly tale of dynastic infanticide we must append a brief discussion of the name of this ill-fated baby. Like her much older half-sister, Thessalonice, her father named her after one of his military triumphs. Philip seems to have borrowed from farther south the habit of giving politically significant names to women,[125] particularly daughters, in his clan. His interest in giving wives and daughters names of significance is in keeping with his general tendency to emphasize the dynastic nature of his power and to include women in the public portrayal of the dynasty.

Philip's innovations, however, relate to his conscious manipulation of the public image of Macedonian monarchy and power—to appearance, not to reality. As we have seen, in polygamous marriages one woman tends to become dominant. Although Philip rapidly acquired four or five wives, two of whom quickly had sons, Philip's mother, Eurydice, may have remained the dominant woman at court for some time, if she lived long into her son's reign (see EURYDICE 1). Olympias's and Philinna's sons were roughly the same age; their status may originally have been similar. By the late 340s, however, Alexander seems to have been treated as Philip's heir, and that surely meant that Olympias had become the dominant woman at court; Eurydice must have been dead or dying and Arrhidaeus' incapacities must have become obvious. But Olympias and her son's dominance was situational rather than institutional.[126]

Did individual royal women play independent roles in public or private court life during most of Philip's reign? We do not have evidence to clearly demonstrate that they did; this is not to say that one of them did not, just that we cannot prove it.

At the time of Philip's assassination by Pausanias in 336, although royal women were increasingly part of the public presentation of the Macedonian monarchy, any role they played in politics in Macedonia was muted, possibly confined to disputed successions. Royal women appeared to be pawns in power marriages and remained extremely vulnerable to changes in status, no matter how prestigious their marriages and how many children they bore. Some may have been powerful behind the scenes, but none in front. We cannot tell whether a royal marriage enhanced not only the power of a woman's clan but also her own. Did the circumstance of these still-shadowy royal women lead to the murder of Philip?

ROYAL WOMEN, MARRIAGE, AND
THE ASSASSINATION OF PHILIP

In an indirect way Philip's assassination indisputably related to royal polygamy and the situation of royal women. Pausanias killed Philip because he had failed to act to right a grievous wrong done Pausanias, even though Philip had been Pausanias's lover (a relationship that seems to have brought the expectation of favors). The king failed to act because the wrong had been done by Attalus, the guardian of Philip's latest wife, Cleopatra (Diod. 16.93.8–9),[127] and perhaps with the knowledge and cooperation of Cleopatra herself (Plut. *Alex.* 10.4). In this case the influence achieved by the clan of a royal wife was considerable, even if Attalus' own standing contributed to his influence with the king as well.

If Olympias conspired with Pausanias to kill her husband, the involvement of royal women in Philip's assassination was more direct. If she did, was it out of personal jealousy, because she feared that if she did not act Alexander would never reach the throne, or because she wanted her son to become king immediately, which would enhance her standing?

These questions will doubtless continue to worry scholars, because our evidence on the assassination of Philip is too poor to permit anything like certainty. My limited purpose here is to consider what the period of the assassination tells us about royal women in Philip's reign.[128]

Although a public reconciliation was fairly rapidly effected, private feelings may well have remained distinctly more hostile. The Pixodarus affair (Plut. *Alex.* 10.1–3) showed that Alexander continued to feel threatened. If his cousin Amyntas married Cynnane about this time, Alexander and his mother may have seen both projected marriages as indications that his position in the succession was jeopardized, particularly because we hear of no such arrangements for him. They may have been right.[129]

The upsets at Philip's court were well known to the Hellenic world, which was doubtless intrigued and perhaps titillated by the oddity (to Greeks) of a political world in which women and marriage played so large a role (Ath. 13.557b–e, 560c; Plut. *Alex.* 9.3–6). The stress Philip put on his daughter Cleopatra's marriage relates, among other things, to his need to calm public talk about the troubled court and succession (Diod. 16.91.4–92.5). Given the notoriety of his family problems, it is not surprising that some people blamed Olympias, with or without her son, for the death of Philip (Plut. *Alex.* 10.4; Just. 9.7.1–14).

Olympias could have been involved. Her role in subsequent deaths demonstrates that in some circumstances she was capable of murder (Just. 9.7.12, 14.5.1–10; Diod. 19.11.2–9; Paus. 8.7.5, 1.11.2–4). She had opportunity.[130] Obviously, Olympias and her son benefited by Philip's death in 336, not only because of what happened but also because of what did not happen. Alexander was not prevented from becoming king, and Olympias was not denied the enviable role of mother of the king. That they acquired this status in 336, instead of years later, meant that Alexander, not his father, led the glorious expedition to Asia and that Olympias immediately began to exercise much more influence than she had before.

Olympias had the capacity for murder and the means, and she clearly benefited from the murder. Did she have motivation? Yes. Her motivation was not sexual jealousy, however, although it is so often and so absurdly ascribed to her. Olympias was the fourth or fifth wife of a man notorious for his sexual relationships with men and women. It is difficult to see why Olympias, after twenty years of marriage to the enthusiastically polygamous Philip, would have been sexually jealous of Cleopatra. Arguments that Olympias' sexual jealousy led her to murder forget the very different nature of marriage in the ancient world, the reality of polygamy, and assume circumstances similar to those of modern marriage.[131] Her desire to secure her son's immediate succession was a powerful motive. Later in her life Olympias killed a number of people in

WOMEN AND MONARCHY IN MACEDONIA

an attempt to do the same for her grandson (see OLYMPIAS).

While we cannot deny that Olympias may have been involved, we cannot prove that she was, nor can we ignore the obvious evidence that a number of other people had equally good reasons, possibly better, to assassinate Philip.[132] Pausanias had strong motivation, and may well have acted alone. Various Greek powers had every reason to offer support to Pausanias, who demonstrated some desire to survive his crime and would therefore have needed a safe place. The assassination of those perceived to be tyrants had a long and honorable history in the Hellenic world; Pausanias might have been welcomed in Athens or Thebes as a hero. The Persians, the most obvious beneficiaries of Philip's sudden death, would have been better able to offer safe haven to his assassin than any Greek power. Various possible Macedonian factions, some of whom certainly showed interest in the throne after the death of Philip, might have played a role in bringing it about. We will probably never know whether Pausanias acted alone. If he did not, Olympias is no more and arguably less plausible as a conspirator than a number of other possibilities. If she and her son were indeed involved, then their motivation would have sprung from the fact that in Macedonia polygamy was combined with the absence of a clear succession pattern.

CHAPTER FOUR

Royal Women and
Alexander the Great

Alexander III, son of Philip II, succeeded his father as king of Macedonia (336–323) and as the leader of the joint Graeco-Macedonian invasion of Persia his father had planned. Alexander left Macedonia in 334 and, though he conquered the Persian Empire and marched his army to the borders of modern India, he never returned to his homeland. In Alexander's absence, his father's old general, Antipater, controlled the Macedonian army (about half of it remained at home) and exercised general control over Macedonia and the Greek peninsula (see below).

As Alexander moved east, he gradually attempted to change the nature of Macedonian monarchy, claiming for himself divine sonship and (probably) divinity itself and borrowing many of the customs, symbols, and institutions of Persian monarchy. He was transforming himself from a Macedonian into an Asian ruler, with a power base more Asian than European. His Macedonian officers and troops resisted these innovations in the direction of absolute monarchy. His progression eastward was marked by a series of confrontations, assassination plots, murders, and executions. When he returned from India, Alexander, rather than return to the Greek peninsula, set up a seemingly permanent base at the ancient city of Babylon. He died in Babylon on June 10, 323. His death (almost certainly of natural causes) precipitated a struggle among his surviving generals (known as the Successors or Diadochi) for control of his empire, a struggle that would lead to the end of the Argead dynasty (see chap. 5).[1]

The women of Alexander's family achieved greater prominence in the reign of Alexander than in that of his father. Accidental events as well as Alexander's policies contributed to this development. Alexander did not, however, categorically reject Philip II's practices with regard to royal women. At first he seemed to turn Philip's policies upside down, but in later years he appeared to pattern his actions on those of his father.

Superficially, Alexander's marriage policy did not resemble Philip's. Whereas Philip married seven times, largely early in his reign, Alexander married only three times, quite late in his reign. By the time Alexander made his first marriage, many of his greatest conquests were already complete, his major alliances already made. Even after he began to take wives, he acquired several important allies without the benefit of marriage alliance (the Indian ruler, Porus, for instance). Nonetheless, those marriages Alexander did contract share the apparent goal of most of Philip's, unity: Alexander's greater willingness to establish marriage alliances toward the end of his reign may also mean that sufficient time had passed since the trauma of his father's last marriage to enable Alexander to see marriages as something more than sources of trouble and instability.

Both father and son applied the same kind of marriage policy to their female relatives that they employed for their own marriages. Philip's fondness for using marriage as a device meant to create or maintain political alliances was not limited to his own marriages. Alexander, in contrast, demonstrated no more interest in arranging marriages for his female family members than he showed in arranging his own. Alexander used royal women (not only the members of his own family but those of other dynasties as well) for political aims best characterized as consolidationist rather than unificatory (rather than create or commemorate a new unity, he intended women to maintain or intensify an existing unity). The roles he assigned royal women often related to continuity with the past, with the maintenance of tradition, and with elevation of the status of the monarchy through elevation of the dynasty. Such uses of royal women were not unknown to Philip, but they did not have the importance for his reign and policies that marriage alliances did.

Thus the policies of father and son relating to royal women did not differ in kind, but they differed considerably in emphasis. Profound differences in the events of the two reigns tended to intensify this distinction. In contrast to Philip's frequent but relatively brief absences on campaigns at a near distance, Alexander's absence was long—permanent as it proved—and extreme in terms of distance. His absence gave what became permanent importance to the women of his family.

Another unique aspect of Alexander's reign (and the period immediately following it) highlighted the women of his family: the scarcity of male Argeads. Whereas most Argead monarchs, coping with the consequences of generations of royal polygamy, suffered from the difficulties created by a plethora of eligible heirs, claimants, or pretenders, as Alexander's reign went on, Macedonia began to experience the reverse of these difficulties. Alexander himself did much to bring about this scarcity of adult male Argeads (and even male children). He eliminated other contenders, most notably his cousin Amyntas,[2] at the beginning of his reign and avoided marriage and thus the possibility of the creation of legitimate heirs until nearly ten years after he took the throne. We cannot hold Alexander entirely responsible for the absence of male Argeads, however. For a man with seven wives, Philip had not had many children, let alone sons. Indeed, unless his son Arrhidaeus' problems became evident very late, it is surprising that Philip did not marry more often in the hope of producing more male heirs; as the youngest brother of three, all of whom lived long enough to reign, he had reason for concern about his own low production of heirs. The truth is that, even if Alexander had married at the beginning of his reign and immediately produced a healthy and capable son, such a boy would have been too young to constitute a mature political presence, even at the end of his father's reign.

Let us begin our consideration of the role and uses of royal women during Alexander's reign by looking at areas other than marital policy and focusing on the women of his own family. Alexander chose to stress the roles of his mother and full sister, Cleopatra, and all but ignored the other women of his immediate family: virtually no reference to his two half-sisters and his great-niece survives (see THESSALONICE; ADEA EURYDICE). We hear of Cynnane only because Alexander attempted to arrange her departure from court.[3] Soon after her son came to the throne, Olympias probably killed Alexander's baby half-sister, Europa, as well as the infant's mother, Philip's last wife, Cleopatra. Alexander may well have been involved in these dynastic murders, as he certainly was in others (see OLYMPIAS: PART 2; CLEOPATRA 3; EUROPA).

As opposed to the women purposely kept obscure, Alexander made his mother, Olympias, and his sister, Cleopatra, now the widow of the Molossian king Alexander, his official family. He indicated this intention by many public gestures. Much as Philip and his father, Amyntas, had attempted to narrow the official royal family to the descendants of Amyntas by Eurydice, Alexander demonstrably narrowed his formal family to Olympias and Cleopatra.

OLYMPIAS: PART 2

Olympias played a much more public role in Macedonian affairs during her son's reign than she had during her husband's. Whereas it is impossible to demonstrate that Olympias tried to exert political influence over Philip, our sources make it clear that she often attempted to influence her son. What is less clear is whether these attempts were successful.

Olympias' new prominence derived in part from two important facts. First, Alexander did not marry until relatively late and then only Asian women. Second, his absence from 334 on meant that for the rest of his reign the only members of the dynasty in residence in Macedonia were women, and, of these, his mother remained the most prominent. Indeed, as the years passed Olympias came to stand for the dynasty, both in formal matters and in the minds of many of the people of Macedonia and the Greek peninsula.

Necessarily identical in the years before Alexander came to the throne (his accession was all-important), the aims of mother and son may now have varied to some degree, and distance and differing experience may have exacerbated these differences. Nonetheless, son and mother inevitably continued to share much common political ground. In the cutthroat world of Macedonian power politics, each had more reason to trust the other than virtually anyone else. If Alexander died or was weakened, Olympias might lose everything; if Olympias was weakened, and especially if she was *seriously* compromised, Alexander lost his most dependable advocate and source of information. Ties of affection may well have bound mother and son, but the ties of self-interest were also considerable. For these reasons, Alexander singled out his mother and full sister as his official family.

After the death of Philip, a number of Alexander's enemies were eliminated, among them Attalus, guardian of Philip's last bride, Cleopatra (Just. 11.5.1). In one passage (9.7.12) Justin blames the murder of Cleopatra, along with an infant she bore Philip, on Olympias, but in another he implies that Alexander was responsible (12.6.14). No other major Alexander narrative mentions the murder directly, although the second-century A.D. geographer Pausanias (8.7.7) also blames it on Olympias. A passage in Plutarch, which may or may not refer to the murder, has Alexander reproaching his mother for treating Cleopatra savagely (Plut. *Alex.* 10.4). The sources imply that this murder occurred soon after Philip's death. If Olympias, with or without Alexander's complicity, did indeed kill Cleopatra, her motivation, although very likely including revenge, was probably similar to Alexander's in effecting the other murders (Attalus, Amyntas, the sons of Aeropus) of the period: removing dynastic rivals and possible complications.[4]

After Alexander's departure, our literary tradition refers to an apparently voluminous correspondence between Alexander and Olympias (see below). He sent booty home to her, and she apparently made splendid dedications at Delphi taken from this booty (Plut. *Alex.* 25.4; *SIG* I 252N. 5 ff.). In 333 she made offerings in Athens to the goddess Hygieia, probably on her son's behalf (Hyp. *Eux.* 19).

But Olympias' role between 334 and 323 encompassed much more than that of a devoted and doting mother. There can be no doubt that she played a public role in affairs of state, both external and internal. What is much less clear is to what degree her role was authorized by her son and to what degree she used the opportunity of her son's long absence for her own aggrandizement. Nor is it easy to clarify her physical location, position, power, and authority vis-à-vis both her daughter, Cleopatra, and Antipater, Alexander's general.

Certainly, the evidence of her location is ambiguous. Pausanias (1.11.2) and Livy (8.24.17) place Olympias in Epirus by the time of her brother's death or soon after, and a speech of Hyperides (*Eux.* 25) seems to imply that she was there was about 330. Yet other evidence suggests that Cleopatra continued to exercise power as a regent in Epirus for some time after the probable return of her mother to Epirus, at least as late as 330 (see CLEOPATRA 2: PART 2).

The nature of her position in this period is problematic. Olympias appears on a list of recipients of grain from Cyrene, twice in fact (*SEG* IX 2); this inscription may date to 333/2.[5] Olympias and Cleopatra are listed in the Cyrene inscription by name only, whereas all the other names on the list belong to states. On the basis of parallel male usage it has been argued that mother and daughter were functioning as heads of state.[6] Olympias was assumed by Athenian politicians to have had a role in Macedonian public policy (Hyp. *Eux.* 19–20) and possibly Molossian too (Hyp. *Eux.* 25). When Harpalus, Alexander's treasurer, absconded with treasury moneys to Athens, not only Antipater and Philoxenus but Olympias as well (Diod. 17.108.7) demanded his extradition.[7] Thus the evidence indicates that Olympias had a position of some authority during her son's reign, although whether her power was based in Macedonia or Molossia or both is not certain.

The most suggestive information about the position and authority of Olympias and her daughter is a curious passage in Plutarch (*Alex.* 68.3) asserting that in the troubled later years of Alexander's reign (ca. 325/4 seems to be implied)[8] Olympias and Cleopatra formed a faction against Antipater and shared Alexander's *arche* (rule), Cleopatra taking Macedonia and Olympias Epirus. Plutarch has Alexander (apparently indifferent to any trouble this caused Antipater) approve his mother's more sensible choice of Epirus on the grounds that Macedonians could not bear to be ruled by a woman.[9]

The evidence certainly suggests that both Olympias and her daughter exercised considerable public power in Epirus and Macedonia, and to some degree in the entire peninsula. It seems likely that at least some of the time they shared this power. Extant evidence confirms only concerted efforts by mother and daughter and offers not a single example of conflict (see below).[10]

The sources indicate that Olympias tried to influence her son's policy by means of epistolary attacks on various figures at Alexander's court. Unfortunately, the authenticity of any of the correspondence preserved in the sources is doubtful.[11] Virtually all the references to Olympias tend to discredit her and to assert that Alexander was not swayed by his mother, no matter how often she attempted to exert influence over him (Plut. *Alex.* 39.7).[12]

Often the idea seems to be that Olympias warned her son against individuals or groups she considered dangerous to his interests, people like Amyntas, one of the sons of Andromenes, implicated but found innocent of complicity in the "conspiracy" of Philotas (Curt. 7.1.36–40),[13] or Alexander the Lyncestian, ultimately found guilty of conspiring against Alexander and executed (Diod. 17. 32.1–2). Plutarch (*Alex.* 39.5) says that Olympias warned Alexander about the amount of wealth and thus power he was supposedly distributing to friends. In some sense all the men she is supposed to have accused (including Hephaestion and Antipater; see below) did prove dangerous to the stability of her son's rule.[14]

The substance of the attacks, aside from indicating hostile relations between Olympias and the other parties, is often unclear, but generally the "correspondence" depicts Olympias as jealous of others close to Alexander. Diodorus (17.114.3) says that when Olympias criticized Hephaestion (Alexander's best friend and probable lover) in her letters to Alexander, Hephaestion dared to write back to scold her, and Plutarch claims that Alexander let him read one of her letters, although he usually kept her letters secret from others (*Alex.* 39.5; *Mor.* 180d, 333a, 340a). Plutarch blames her troubles with Hephaestion on jealousy. After all, Craterus (Plut. *Alex.* 47.5–7) and Eumenes (Plut. *Eum.* 2.1–2.4–5) also envied him and, perhaps for the same reason, his influence with the king.

Although most of these rivalries appear to be petty and, whether genuine or not, typical enough of the extremely competitive Macedonian court, the best known of them, the rivalry with Antipater, had greater significance. The specifics of their quarrel are unknown, but it appears that each accused the other of taking too much power. It is likely that this quarrel was at least in part the result of the vague, undefined nature of Olympias' position and authority.

Diodorus reports that Olympias left Macedonia because of her quarrels with Antipater (18.49.4; see also Paus. 1.11.3, in apparent contradiction to the Plutarch passage discussed above).[15] Her efforts against Antipater were ultimately successful and led to his "demotion" (Diod. 17.118.1; see also Arr. 7.12.5–7). Plutarch (*Alex.* 39.7) implies that it was actually Antipater's complaints about Olympias, rather than hers about him, that wore away at Alexander. If, as it appears, Olympias had claimed for many years that Antipater was exceeding his powers and could not be trusted and Alexander ultimately came to interpret Antipater's actions, rightly or wrongly, in the same fashion, it is difficult to see how Olympias's influence can be denied.[16]

The frequent assertions that Alexander ignored or rejected much of his mother's advice may be based on Plutarch's genuine views, or on subsequent tradition about her, or on a public image that required the king to act like a conventional Greek male and deny the role that many Greeks suspected women of the royal family played in politics. Olympias' struggles with Antipater, and perhaps those with others, may also mean that Macedonian nobles, ever desirous of limiting the power of the monarchy, found it safer to attack the mother of the king than the king.

Cleopatra's marriage to her uncle Alexander quickly produced two children, Cadmeia and Neoptolemus (Plut. *Pyrrh.* 5.5). Then, about the same time his nephew embarked on his eastern expedition, Alexander of Epirus departed on his fatal expedition to Italy.[17]

It is likely that Cleopatra acted as regent in Molossia from the time her husband departed until some date well after his death in winter 331/30. Aeschines (3.242), ca. 331, mentions an Athenian embassy delegated to carry condolences to her. The embassy may simply have been a polite and politic gesture, but it may indicate a recognition of some sort of official status. She shipped grain to Corinth in 333/2, or more likely somewhat earlier (Lycurg. *Leoc.* 26),[18] and in 330 she appeared as *thearodoch* (an official who receives envoys sent to consult oracles or present offerings) for, probably, the new Epirote alliance (SEG XXIII 198).[19] Like her mother, she also appears on a list (*SEG* IX 2) of those who received grain, apparently in famine time, from Cyrene (see OLYMPIAS: PART 2 for the significance of her appearance on the list). Thus Cleopatra, like her brother, seems to have assumed the rule of a country when she was not (or barely) out of her teens.

Although this evidence suggests that as late as 330, Cleopatra had considerable control over affairs of state in Epirus, she may not have exercised this control alone. Olympias had returned to Epirus (see OLYMPIAS: PART 2). Although the grain lists on which mother and daughter appear do not connect them to any state and thus cannot clarify their respective responsibilities, Plutarch (*Alex.* 68.3) says that Cleopatra and Olympias shared Alexander's rule, Cleopatra taking Macedonia and Olympias her homeland. It is likely that mother and daughter shared the rule of Molossia for several years and that, toward the end of Alexander's reign, Cleopatra returned alone to Macedonia. Olympias and Cleopatra probably worked in concert, just as they did after Alexander's death.[20]

Cleopatra's relationship with Alexander could have been close. He sent her some war spoils from Gaza, in addition to those he sent to Olympias (Plut. *Alex.* 25.4). Cleopatra was able to intercede with her brother on behalf of the tyrant of Heracleia (Memnon *FGrH* 434, F 4.37). Dionysius of Heracleia would not have appealed to her had she not been reputed to be influential with her brother. Her activities as provider and recipient of grain may mean that she was cooperating with her brother's eastern Mediterranean activities. Macedonian and Epirote rulers had been act-ing in concert for about a generation by this period.[21] This evidence may seem slight, but compared to the absolute lack of evidence connecting Alexander to his two half-sisters (other than his abortive early attempt to marry off the widowed Cynnane; see CYNNANE), it implies that he was much closer to Cleopatra and that he accorded her higher status.

Cleopatra did not remarry during her brother's reign. Other than the failed attempt to marry off Cynnane, Alexander displayed no interest in hav-ing any of his sisters marry and little interest in getting married himself until comparatively late in his reign. Plutarch (*Mor.* 818b–c) preserves an anecdote that implies that Alexander encouraged Cleopatra to take lovers rather than remarry, much as Charlemagne later did with his daughters.[22] In Plutarch's tale, when informed that his sister is carrying on an affair with a handsome youth, Alexander expressed approval and implied that it was, in a sense, a privilege of participation in *basileia*.[23] What Cleopatra's view of Alexander's marriage policy may have been is unknown, but an obvious consequence of his reluctance to arrange marriages for his sisters was that she, at least, was able to maintain a degree of independence and power that she probably could not have maintained if married.

The position of Olympias and Cleopatra was anything but static: Alexander's reign saw change and increasing insecurity because of his deteriorating relationship with Antipater and with his own troops as well as problems maintaining Macedonian dominance of the Greek peninsula. The women's prominence increased as the reign proceeded, thanks to a variety of factors. The longer Alexander was gone, the more his mother or sister were, for Macedonians, the royal family and the king's representatives in a way that Antipater could never be. As rela-tions between Alexander and Antipater worsened (or at least became more distant), the king had more reason to place his trust in these royal women (whose security was tied to his) than in the old man. Changes in the nature of Macedonian monarchy, begun by Philip and in-creased dramatically by Alexander, tended to elevate and accentuate the royal family and diminish the importance of nonroyal members of the Macedonian elite. In addition, the death of his sister Cleopatra's husband so soon after her marriage offered her opportunity for political action that would probably not have been available to the wife of a reigning Molossian ruler.

For Alexander, Olympias and Cleopatra were the royal Macedonian equivalent of the "folks back home," and he used them to create an image of cozy, more or less domestic piety for the Macedonian and Greek public. In doing so, Alexander was probably simply stressing or modestly extending the traditional role of royal Macedonian women, who, like other Hellenic women, were frequently associated with family piety and religion in general.

And yet Olympias and her daughter demonstrably attempted to play a less traditional political role as well as a traditional domestic one. They did so with mixed success. Until recently the usual view of their political activities was that Alexander allotted them no duties whatsoever and that Antipater was Alexander's sole legitimate representative, that Alexander paid no attention to his mother's attempts to influence him, and that such attempts constituted nonlegitimate "interference" with Antipater's entirely legitimate and thus appropriate action. Hammond has launched a series of arguments successfully attacking this view, but also—mistakenly—maintaining something like the reverse, that Olympias and later Cleopatra held an office quite distinct from that of Antipater. Hammond believes that while Cleopatra acted as regent in Epirus, Olympias remained in Macedonia until 324, exercising some sort of official position involving nonmilitary duties and religious matters, a position he identifies as *prostasia* (leadership).[24] He also believes that only in 324 did Olympias return to Epirus, essentially exchanging positions with her daughter and becoming regent of Epirus as Cleopatra took up *prostasia* in Macedonia.[25]

Yet the sources permit interpretations of the position of Alexander's mother and full sister different from those of Hammond, whose description of the roles of Olympias and Cleopatra as *prostasia* depends on his reading of Macedonian political institutions. Hammond believes that in Alexander's time the Macedonians had a clearly defined (if unwritten) "constitution" and thus looks for an office to assign those who seem to be exercising political power. There is evidence, as we have seen, for the political authority of both Olympias and Cleopatra but none to indicate that either held a particular office or that authority was defined by office in the Argead period. The role of Olympias and Cleopatra can be categorized as neither illegitimate and unofficial nor the reverse. Such categorization does not apply.

There can be no doubt that Olympias and her daughter attempted to influence Alexander's decisions and policies and that each was successful at times. The obvious implication of the incident involving Dionysius of Heracleia (Memnon *FGrH* 434, F 4.37) is that Cleopatra was widely believed to exercise influence with her brother. A great body of anecdotal material survives which tends to picture Olympias attempting to influence her son but failing to do so. Plutarch (*Alex*. 39.7) explicitly insists that Alexander did not allow his mother to participate in public or military affairs. Most of this anecdotal material should be regarded with considerable skepticism for a variety of reasons, not the least of which is that some of the same sources that deny Olympias's influence with Alexander contain stories that, in fact, demonstrate its existence (e.g., Arr. 7.12.6–7; Plut. *Alex*. 39.7). The sources do fairly consistently claim, however, that she sought to aggrandize her own role and that she suspected that other figures at court used their influence with her son to further their own interests, perhaps at his expense (see OLYMPIAS: PART 2).

This general anecdotal tradition emphasizes Olympias's conflict with Antipater (Arr. 5.12.5–7; Diod. 17.118.1; Just. 12.14.3; Plut. *Alex*. 39.7, *Mor*. 180d). Supposedly both Olympias and Alexander used their communications with Alexander to attack the other, with what success, in each case, remains unclear. A careful reading of the sources suggests that Antipater's influence was originally greater than Olympias's (thus her departure, under whatever circumstances and at whatever date, for her homeland)[26] but that as Alexander's dealings with Antipater grew more tense, perhaps even hostile, Olympias's influence grew and Antipater's credibility diminished. Olympias did not always get what she wanted, but those who doubt that she played an important role in Antipater's removal from office and summons to Babylon (the significance of which, although not clear, cannot easily be seen as other than negative) have a weak case.[27]

If Arrian's (7.12.6–7) description of the basis of the quarrel between Antipater and Olympias is accurate (each asserted that the other was assuming more power and status than was rightful), neither her position nor Antipater's (let alone the line between their respective responsibilities) can have been spelled out in any detail. This very lack of definition was at least one reason for their rivalry. Plutarch's tale (*Alex.* 68.3) about the joint political action of Olympias and Cleopatra against Antipater and Alexander's refusal to interfere suggests that he preferred this lack of definition and used it and the ambitions of Olympias and Antipater for his own ends, ends that varied over the course of his reign.[28]

Thus, as the years passed, Alexander's "official family" (Olympias and Cleopatra) tended to represent the monarchy and the dynasty in Alexander's lengthening absence. This development derived both from decisions of Alexander and from their own quite independent actions. Alexander's increasing suspicions of others and the growing resentment of his changes in the monarchy could easily have led him to place greater trust in the views of his mother and sister. Whatever his personal feelings about them, he and they knew that self-interest alone required interest in his survival and success.

Alexander also consciously used the women of other dynasties to further his goals. One instance of this tendency relates to Ada,[29] a member of the family of Carian dynasts. She had been ousted from rule by her brother Pixodarus. Her demotion was perpetuated by another male member of the dynasty, working with the Persian king. When Alexander arrived in Caria, Ada (who had fortified herself in a citadel) went over to his side; Alexander responded by making her ruler of Caria again, and she adopted him as her son (Arr. 1.23.7–8). Plutarch (*Alex.* 22.4, 22.5) reports that he called her mother and that she, just as his real mother supposedly did, tried to arrange various comforts and luxuries for her "son." Despite the more independent role of women in the Carian monarchy (they were more directly tied to the determination of succession than in Epirus or Macedonia and were able to rule or co-rule), Alexander once more was able to use a quasi-familial role to entrench himself and establish his legitimacy and piety.

Alexander's preference for and manipulation of the role of royal son and brother rather than the more typical one of father and husband is even more evident in his treatment of the women of the family of Darius, who came into his hands after Darius' defeat at Issus in 333. Alexander treated all the members of Darius' nuclear family with compassion and gallantry: their fears that Darius had died (he had, in fact, escaped from the scene of his defeat) were calmed (Plut. *Alex.* 21.1–3; Arr. 2.12.3–8; Just. 11.9.12–16; Curt. 3.12.26; Diod. 17.37.3–6).[30] Darius' mother, Sisygambis, was, much more than Ada, treated like a second Olympias.[31] Before one of them became his wife in 324, his daughters were treated like sisters for whom Alexander was responsible,[32] and Alexander was affectionate to Darius' six-year-old son.[33] But, above all, the stories insist that Alexander respected the chastity of Darius' wife, Stateira, although she was supposedly a great beauty. When she died, he arranged a magnificent funeral for her at which he was the chief and dramatically demonstrative mourner (see STATEIRA 1).

Evaluating the significance of Alexander's treatment of the royal Persian women proves no easy task. The rapturous enthusiasm of the sources for Alexander's self-restraint in not raping Stateira now seems cloying at best and possibly unjustified. Yet it does seem to be true that Alexander, always an admirer of sexual self-restraint, did not personally (Barsine aside) exercise the brutal control over captive women, sexual and otherwise, typical of other ancient conquerors.[34] Indeed, our sources stress on Alexander's sexual *sophrosyne* (moderation) was almost certainly created, at least in part, to deal with contemporary incredulity that Alexander had not had sexual dealings with Stateira (see STATEIRA 1; n. 1).

STATEIRA 1

Stateira, the wife of Darius III, was captured after the battle of Issus, along with her two daughters and young son and her mother (nothing is known of her before this date). All surviving accounts stress Alexander's unusually humane treatment of Darius' family. Some sources maintain that Alexander, in company with Hephaestion, visited the royal women in person shortly after their capture, while others claim that Alexander merely dispatched Leonnatus when he heard the royal women grieving over the supposed death of Darius. Plutarch (*Alex.* 22.3) even has Alexander boast that he never saw Stateira, despite her being considered the most beautiful woman in Asia.

Rhetorical embroidering on the general theme of Alexander's self-restraint in not raping Stateira is a major focus of narratives of Alexander's treatment of the Persian royal women. This universal admiration for Alexander's respect for Stateira's chastity, however, is somewhat questionable in the light of our knowledge, admittedly fragmentary, of her death. An awkward feature relating to this event survives. Two sources (Plut. *Alex.* 30.1; Just.

11.12.6) report that she died in childbirth,[35] and all imply that she died in 331, about two years after her capture. Since Stateira had not been in Darius' presence since November 333, the ugly possibility arises that Alexander had impregnated her. This worry is often dispelled by doubting that she died in childbirth or arguing that the dating of her death is wrong and that she in fact died relatively soon after her capture.[36]

Although one cannot reject either of these possibilities out of hand—clearly either or both could be true—neither can one reasonably leap to the conclusion that either or both are correct. If Alexander did not have sexual relations with Stateira, his restraint would not have been caused by his consistent respect for Persian women's sexual chastity. His relationship with Barsine demonstrates that this was not the case (see BARSINE). Alexander's supposed resistance to Stateira's beauty should more reasonably be attributed to political factors. Fear of alienating the Persian elite and fear of offending the xenophobic Macedonians could have made him circumspect. Whatever the case, the problem with each of these political explanations is that at times Alexander risked both such possibilities (e.g., the burning of Persepolis and the attempt to introduce to the Macedonian court the Persian ceremony of *proskynesis*, a gesture recognizing the social superiority of the person for whom it is performed).

Still, a sexual relationship with Stateira seems at least possible, if unlikely. One could argue that just as Alexander's relationship with Barsine was not merely sexual but political as well, so also with Stateira. In each situation Alexander allied himself to members of the Asian elite without, at least yet, legitimizing the alliance. At the same time, by his sexual possession of these women, he made a statement unlikely to be lost on either Persians or Macedonians.[37] Or one might surmise that Alexander intended to marry Stateira in the end, and only her premature death made him choose her daughter instead.[38] Marrying the wife of the man he had conquered, especially if she was a member of the defeated dynasty, would be less surprising than simply having a sexual relationship with her. Raping Stateira would seem to be the sexual equivalent of the burning of Persepolis, but then Alexander did burn Persepolis.

The evidence does not permit certainty about whether Alexander left Stateira unmolested or whether she suffered the fate of so many captured women and died miscarrying a child of Alexander's. Nonetheless, it is likely that Alexander did not have a sexual relationship with Darius' wife.

The evidence does permit us to conclude, however, that the nearly obsessive emphasis of the surviving sources on Alexander's sexual respect for Stateira—an emphasis that may well go back to Callisthenes—speaks to a perceived problem and derives from an ancient attempt, by means of counterpropaganda, to combat the rumors already current. Many, including Darius, suspected that Alexander had made Stateira his mistress and the endless anecdotes praising Alexander for his restraint with respect to Stateira were created to eliminate that suspicion.

But it is not simply differences between our attitudes and values and those of antiquity that make analysis of Alexander's treatment of the Persian women difficult. Conscious artifice on Alexander's part, a bit of ancient propaganda and image making, shaped his approach to them. One aspect of this antique "airbrushing" of Alexander's role is obvious enough: Greek literary tradition consistently portrayed the royal women of the Achaemenid dynasty as powerful and influential figures, particularly in matters related to the succession to the throne. Whatever the Achaemenid reality, Greeks and Macedonians would have believed that Persian royal women were important symbols of the monarchy and thus had great potential as symbols of continuity and vehicles of legitimization. Alexander's treatment of the three generations of the women of Darius' family leaves no doubt that such was certainly his supposition.[39]

The most problematic aspect of the story of Alexander and the Persian women is not its purpose but rather its nature. Despite the obvious opportunity to establish continuity and legitimacy by marrying and the many precedents from his father's reign, Alexander was only willing to be father to the royal daughters and son to the queen mother. Not until 324, nine years after they had passed into his control, did Alexander marry one of Darius' daughters, three years after he had taken his rather obscure first wife. Even then, the emphasis at Susa was not specifically on Alexander's marriage to Darius' daughter but on mass marriages in general.

Some of this surprising focus on Alexander as father, brother, or son rather than husband derives from the forces that shaped Alexander's marriage policy for himself and others in his control (see below). But his elaborate courtly dealings with Sisygambis and her granddaughters and his self-conscious reluctance or perhaps even refusal to have any dealings

with Darius' wife must also relate to his preference for the role of royal
son and brother. He may have found these roles more comfortable and
useful and less controversial than that of husband. Diodorus says that
both Sisygambis (17.38.1) and Olympias (19.11.2, 51.6) had *axioma* (dig-
nity, distinction). These formidable women, similar particularly in their
tough-minded deaths, were somehow able to sum up, to stand for, their
respective dynasties at critical moments. Alexander seemed singularly
sensitive to this potential in royal women, particularly royal mothers.
Moreover, he was adept at manipulating it for his own ends.

A less prominent aspect of the role of royal women during the reign
of Alexander was marriage alliances. He married late and less frequently
than his father, but he did marry, and all his marriages (and arguably his
one certain heterosexual liaison) were politically inspired. Questions
about his marriage policy occur. Why was Alexander reluctant to have
himself and other members of his family marry? Why did the marriages
he arranged come late in his reign, and why did he return to the policies
of his father?

Alexander's marriage policy is not much discussed, but when it is,
the discussion usually begins with the story in Diodorus (17.16.2) that recounts that Parmenio and Antipater advised Alexander to delay his departure for Asia until he married and produced an heir and that
Alexander, on heroic grounds (it would be a shameful delay of military
action for the sake of domestic concerns), refused to take the advice. As
I have observed, this anecdote is probably not historical (see chap. 1).
Nonetheless, Alexander did postpone marriage, not just in 334 but again
and again until 327. This delay need not mean that he was entirely unconcerned with the need for an heir but certainly implies that he did not
judge the succession a priority. Typically, two reasons have been suggested for Alexander's failure to marry and for his comparative disin-
terest in the succession.

One explanation, Alexander's supposed lack of sexual interest in
women, should be dismissed.[40] His relationships with Barsine and Bagoas
and his possible relationships with *hetairai* prove that Alexander, while
not a particularly sexual person, had sexual desires and, at least occasionally, acted on them.[41] Like his father, although hardly on the same
scale, he apparently found members of both sexes attractive. In this orientation, of course, he resembled many other Greek and Macedonian

males.[42] More important, the ancient world viewed marriage as not primarily a sexual relationship but as the means for creating legitimate heirs.[43] Since Alexander did marry three times and impregnate two women, however belatedly, it seems clear that, enthusiastic or not, he was able to do the male Macedonian equivalent of the Victorian bride's injunction to "think of England."[44]

The more compelling explanation for Alexander's long lack of interest in marriage has been based on an analysis of his personality found in both ancient and modern writers: his obsession with the heroic code, with individual achievement, and with his attempt to surpass the deeds of the great heroes consumed him and made him unconcerned about what came after him.[45] It would be foolhardy to deny the truth of this analysis of Alexander's character and motivation and yet nearly equally so to insist that Alexander's Homeric absorption in personal achievement is the sole explanation for his marriage policy.

His motivation was complex, both politically and personally. The careers of his three sisters during the period of his reign demonstrate that Alexander's reluctance to arrange royal marriages was more than personal. Aside from his unsuccessful attempt to marry Cynnane to Langarus, he is known to have shown no interest at all in arranging marriages for his sisters. Thessalonice's marriage was put off astonishingly late; at least his other two sisters were widows with children.[46]

Alexander's attempt to arrange a marriage for himself with the daughter of Pixodarus even before he became king (Plut. *Alex.* 10.3) is another sign that his lack of enthusiasm about marriage for most of his reign cannot reasonably be attributed to an overly strong commitment to the heroic code. Even in his early youth, when an occasion like the Pixodarus alliance arose that suggested that a marriage offered some benefit, he was eager enough, even disastrously so. Fearful that the marriage Philip was arranging with Pixodarus' daughter and Alexander's half brother, Arrhidaeus, indicated that Alexander himself had fallen out of favor with his father, the young man interjected himself into negotiations as an alternate bridegroom, only to cause the collapse of the alliance and to infuriate his father. (Some have doubted the veracity of the Pixodarus incident, but their arguments are not persuasive.)[47]

One reason Alexander delayed marrying may simply be that he, like most other people, changed a great deal between twenty and thirty. The youth of twenty entirely concentrated on military success, and the immediate prospects of victory may well have made him unconcerned about what seemed the distant future, but the man of nearly thirty who married Roxane may have been more able to take the future seriously and, of course, the less glamorous nature of his campaigns in that period made at least this particular marriage more advantageous (see below).

As his marriages were politically motivated, it would be wise to look to factors political rather than personal, or at least primarily personal, to explain his prolonged bachelorhood. Alexander's experience of trouble and uncertainty at Philip's court because of Philip's many marriages and heirs (a situation that anecdote says Alexander resented; Plut. *Mor.* 178 f.) initially led him to see marriages as more likely to cause than solve problems. Outsiders considered Philip's many alliances dangerous and the cause of the tensions of Philip's last years (Plut. *Alex.* 9.3–5). What had been an effective tool in Philip's centralization of Macedonia early in his reign may well have been interpreted by his son, coming to maturity at the end of the reign, as a political ploy whose potential for divisiveness was at least as great as its potential for benefit.

At least until the troubles of the Bactrian and Sogdian campaign, Alexander judged his political needs to fall primarily under the heading of consolidation and found that his female relatives (and adopted ones) could help to consolidate an already unified monarchy but feared that choosing any bride would prove divisive. How would Antipater have reacted had the king married a daughter of Parmenio, or, for that matter, how would Parmenio have felt had Alexander married one of Antipater's many daughters?[48] Apparently Alexander believed marriages for his sisters had the same potential for divisiveness.

A historical parallel may provide clarification. Despite many differences in the nature of the two monarchies—political values, marriage customs, and capacities of individual rulers—some striking similarities exist between the situation of Alexander the Great and his reactions to his father's policies and that of Elizabeth I of England and her reactions to the policies of her father. Not only were Henry VIII and Philip II men of rather similar temperament who belong to the short list of great rulers whose successors and children equaled or perhaps surpassed their own achievements, but both were also notoriously many-wived kings whose marriages caused their heirs much pain, both political and personal.

Elizabeth's solution is well known. Rather than marry and thus divide her subjects, she temporized and never married, instead using her unmarried state as a kind of political icon.[49] After her death, and to some degree before it, England felt the consequences of her dynastic irresponsibility or temporizing. Alexander's reaction is curiously similar, allowing for the differences in culture, gender, and time. He too temporized, feared to choose a spouse from among his subjects, and yet knew that foreign brides might cause even more problems. In place of Elizabeth's royal virginity, we have Alexander's sexual self-restraint, his *sophrosyne*. Both solutions emphasized the specialness, even uniqueness of the royal personage. Alexander did marry in the end but, because he married Eastern women whom he knew his Macedonian subjects would never accept, it was as if he had not married at all. Like Elizabeth, Alexander was a great temporizer about dynastic and other matters, and like Elizabeth's England, Macedonia paid a heavy price for that temporizing, a price that, as in England, involved the end of a great dynasty.

Let us turn to the specifics of Alexander's marriage politics, keeping in mind the forces that shaped his early years on the throne. As we have seen, shortly after he arrived in Asia, Alexander came into control of the women of the family of Darius, but he did not take an Achaemenid bride until 324. At the same time the royal Persian women passed into Alexander's control, so did Barsine, daughter of the satrap Artabazus by a sister of the famous Greek mercenary generals Mentor and Memnon. Artabazus, with his entire family, spent many years in the court of Philip. Yet at the time of Barsine's capture, her father continued to be one of Darius' most dogged supporters. Alexander began a sexual relationship with Barsine (Plut. *Alex.* 21.4) that endured until at least 327 (Diod. 20.20.1), when she bore him a son called Heracles.

The relationship with Barsine may constitute Alexander's first efforts at incorporating his "Persianizing" policy into dynastic, marital, and sexual relations as well as court ceremony and appointment of officials. Alexander never married Barsine, but, at least until 327, their relationship was obviously not perceived as dishonorable by her family; indeed, it may have been the incentive that helped to bring Artabazus to change sides once his personal duty to Darius was ended by that monarch's death. Alexander's marriage to Roxane in 327, which took place in roughly the same time frame as the birth of Barsine's son, altered the situation.

Barsine[50] was the daughter of Artabazus (Plut. *Alex.* 21.4; *Eum.* 1.3), a Persian satrap and grandson of a king.[51] Artabazus married a sister of the Rhodian mercenary captains Mentor and Memnon (Diod. 16.52.4; Dem. 23.154, 157), probably about 362 B.C., though possibly earlier.[52] The marriage proved an extremely successful and useful alliance. A connection to able Greek mercenaries could only prove helpful to an ambitious western satrap.[53] Barsine is likely to have been a product of this supposedly remarkably fertile marriage (Diod. 16.53.3 claims that Artabazus's Greek wife gave him eleven sons and ten daughters).[54]

Barsine was probably born in 357 or 356, about the same time as Alexander.[55] Barsine's father rebelled against the Persian king Artaxerxes III and, using various Greek mercenary forces, was initially successful against the armies of the king.[56] But in the end he was compelled to go into exile at the court of Philip II of Macedonia, taking with him his wife and children and his younger brother-in-law, Memnon. Artabazus became the guest-friend of Philip (Diod. 16.52.3; Curt. 6.5.2–3).

The sojourn of the clan of Artabazus in Macedonia lasted about ten years, from 352 to 342 (Diod. 16.52.3–4). Barsine grew up at Philip's court. Not surprisingly, Plutarch (*Alex.* 21.4) reports that she had a Greek *paideia* (education, training), although it is unclear whether *paideia* in this context refers to formal education or simply means that she was brought up like a Greek girl.[57] Barsine, the daughter of a Rhodian and a woman who came to maturity in Macedonia in the midst of a large and polyglot family, must have known Greek. Moreover, Barsine may well have known Alexander as a child.[58] Even the narrowly defined sexual roles for men and women in Athens permitted very young girls and boys to play together, and the Macedonian court was considerably more open (see chap. 1). Two children both living in the palace and about the same age almost certainly knew each other. Doubtless Barsine would have known the women of Alexander's family.

Barsine's background was eclectic and cosmopolitan. She was born into the very highest Persian nobility, into that now quite Hellenized group of satrapal families that had dominated Asia Minor for more than a century. Yet she was also related to the Greek mercenary adventurers whom her satrapal relatives increasingly used to fight their frequent battles among themselves and against their kings.[59] The rest of her life would continue to reflect this rich cultural mixture, a mixture that in the end would cause her death.

In 342 the elder of Artabazus' brothers-in-law, Mentor, having recently regained favor with Artaxerxes, managed to persuade the king to recall his brother and brother-in-law and their respective families (Diod. 16.52.3–4). Several of Barsine's brothers achieved high positions, and Mentor was now commander in chief of the coast of Asia Minor. Barsine married her much older uncle. This marriage, certainly meant to reconfirm the ties of loyalty that bound Artabazus to these two brothers, must have been quite brief, because Mentor apparently died not long after the reconciliation.[60] Barsine had one child from the marriage, a daughter old enough to marry Nearchus at the Susa weddings in 324 (Arr. 7.4.6).

Probably soon after she was widowed, Barsine married her younger uncle, Memnon (Plut. *Alex.* 21.4), also an adept military leader.[61] From this marriage too would come one child, a son too young to fight in the struggle against Alexander (Curt. 3.13.14). After the capture of Miletus, Memnon sent his wife and children to Darius, partly, says Diodorus, to ensure their safety and partly to encourage the king to appoint him supreme commander of the western coast, as his brother had been, by providing the king with hostages for Memnon's good behavior (Diod. 17.23.5–6). After some success, Memnon also died suddenly and Barsine was a widow a second time (Diod. 17.29.4). Apparently she remained in the charge of Darius and, along with many of the wives and children of the high nobility and royal family, was captured at Damascus by Parmenio after the battle of Issus. The Graeco-Persian clan of Artabazus and the Rhodian mercenaries remained tightly knit. Curtius reports that along with Barsine, the wife of her brother Pharnabazus (who had succeeded his uncle, at least in part, in his command),[62] a son of Pharnabazus, three daughters of Mentor (probably stepdaughters of Barsine),[63] and Barsine's son by Memnon were all captured together (Curt. 3.13.14).

Sometime after her capture, probably in 332 or 331, Barsine, already twice widowed and a mother of two and now in her middle twenties, became involved in a relationship with Alexander the Great (Plut. *Alex.* 21.4; *Eum.* 1.3). The relationship was certainly sexual, as Plutarch's diction suggests and the birth of a son makes certain (Paus. 9.7.2; Lycoph. *Alex.* 801–4; Plut. *Eum.* 1.3; Diod. 20.20.1; Curt. 10.6.11; Just. 13.2.7).[64] The son, Heracles, was born about 327 (Diod. 20.20.1),[65] long after the relationship with Alexander had apparently begun.

Historians usually describe the relationship between Barsine and Alexander as an affair, not a marriage.[66] They do so with good reason. Plutarch describes their relationship in terms referring to sexual intercourse rather than marriage. The rejection of Heracles as an heir at the time of his father's death and the general neglect that he received from the Successors until after the death of his half-brother, Roxane's son (see BARSINE: PART 2), all speak to the fact that the younger son by Roxane was automatically preferred to Barsine's child. In contrast, Alexander's relationship with Roxane is clearly described as a marriage (Arr. 4.19.5; Plut. *Alex.* 47.4; Curt. 8.4.25).

While there can be no doubt that Macedonians universally gave Roxane's son preference over Barsine's, a number of factors suggest that Alexander's relationship with Barsine, if less important than his relationship with Roxane, was something more substantial, perhaps more formal and more political, than is usually understood. About a year passed between the beginning of Barsine's relationship with Alexander and the time at which her father, after the death of Darius whom he had loyally followed to the end, went over to Alexander with all his kin (Curt. 6.5.1–5; Arr. 3.23.7).[67] Nonetheless, Alexander was already claiming to be legitimate ruler of the Persian Empire and already interested in winning over the Persian elite.[68] Alexander had personal ties with Artabazus (Curt. 6.5.2). Once Artabazus and his tight-knit family made their allegiance to Alexander, they received important appointments. Alexander would have hesitated to do anything to offend Artabazus, and the clan would have been unlikely to swallow an insult. Whatever Alexander's relationship to Barsine, it must have been one that her family found acceptable for the most powerful surviving Persian satrapal family.[69]

Other evidence suggests that Alexander's relationship with Barsine was something more than a brief, sexual one. It is certain that the sexual relationship continued for a number of years because Heracles was born in 327 (Diod. 20.20.1), or, if Justin (15.2.3) is right, as late as 324. Barsine's son's name also seems pointedly meaningful because it not only recalls Alexander's personal emulation of Heracles but also refers to the Argeads' supposed Heraclid ancestry.[70]

Plutarch (*Eum.* 1.3) notes that Eumenes and Ptolemy both married sisters of Barsine. Not only does he describe these women as Barsine's sisters rather than Artabazus' daughters, but he also explains that the marriage was a sign to Macedonian troops of Eumenes' high status with the king because it meant that the king had considered him worthy of relationship in marriage. Plutarch then mentions Barsine and Heracles. Scholars have usually assumed that ties between Alexander and Barsine were cut in 327, after Heracles' birth and Alexander's marriage to Roxane,[71] but the passage in Plutarch clearly implies that whether or not the sexual relationship persisted, Barsine continued to be regarded as having high status. One wonders whether the universal assumption that Barsine and Heracles had long been in Pergamum is correct. We know only that Justin, (13.2.7) reports they were there at the time of Alexander's death and that Diodorus (20.20.1), in describing the events of 309, says that Heracles had been brought up in Pergamum.

One aspect of Plutarch's account of Alexander's relationship with Barsine is puzzling (*Alex.* 21.4–5). Plutarch says that Alexander respected the chastity of the women who became captives, except for Barsine, and that Barsine was the only woman with whom he had sexual relations before marriage. He goes on to say, citing Aristobulus as his source, that Alexander was persuaded to initiate this relationship with Barsine by Parmenio, who noted her high birth and beauty (her Greek *paideia* and good disposition are also mentioned favorably).

Much about the passage is dubious. Whether or not Parmenio and Antipater had earlier advised Alexander to marry, it is likely enough that the old general would want Alexander to marry because he was concerned about the succession. But, as we have seen, Plutarch's language makes it clear that Parmenio was suggesting only a sexual relationship, not marriage. One doubts that Parmenio cared about Alexander's sex life enough to find young women for him who could not produce legitimate heirs. The relationship between Alexander and Parmenio is never pictured as intimate but perhaps as even antagonistic.[72] More important, the reference to Parmenio's advice does not inspire trust. The sources for Alexander's reign preserve a series of anecdotes recounting occasions on which Parmenio gives advice that Alexander, nearly always correctly, rejects. Many attribute this body of anecdotes to attempts to blacken Parmenio's name after his murder by Alexander.[73] Plutarch's story is probably fiction.

Within a brief period in 327, three events occurred: the birth of Alexander's son by Barsine; Alexander's marriage to Roxane; and Artabazus' retirement, supposedly because of old age. The order of the first two events is not clear, but certainly the third came after Roxane's marriage.[74] Age may have been only an excuse; Artabazus may have been reacting to the marriage of Roxane.[75] Other members of Barsine's family, however, continued to hold high position in Alexander's court,[76] and, as we have seen, Barsine still had status as late as 324.

It is difficult to assess this conflicting and uncertain evidence, particularly because of the many cultural cross-currents affecting our surviving sources. Barsine and her father may have had one view of her relationship with Alexander, Alexander another, and the Macedonians yet another. Recent work on royal women in the Persian monarchy has suggested that there was a distinction between married and unmarried women of the king and that those married to the king had to be Achaemenids, or at least Persians; from these women were born legitimate sons. Women of foreign descent could not be married to the king and could not produce legitimate sons. They should perhaps be called "women of the king," not wives (too high a status), but not concubines (too low and unrespectable a status).[77]

Barsine and her family would probably have understood her status as a woman of the king, a respectable and formal role. If so, then the marriage to Roxane, also an Asian and thus as "foreign" from a Macedonian position as Barsine (not to mention the somewhat lower status of the family of Roxane), may have insulted Artabazus because it placed his daughter in a diminished role. Artabazus' family was wise in the ways of power. It chose not to confront the king about his preferential treatment of Roxane but to retain its status. This policy does not mean that the family was happy with the implied change in Barsine's status. (See chap. 5 for part 2 of the life of Barsine.)

The marriage to Roxane, daughter of a Bactrian chieftain, comes as a surprise in the context of Alexander's reign (see ROXANE: PART 1). It is very like many of Philip's marriages,[78] arranged to symbolize or generate peace between combatants, not a marriage intended to have long-term political consequences or one created primarily to produce heirs. Why did Alexander, after so many years of temporizing, so suddenly marry the daughter of a comparatively obscure chieftain?

The answer to this question has three parts. First, Alexander married Roxane because he needed to: the campaigns in Bactria and Sogdiana were going badly, and the resistance of the provincial elite was intense. His marriage had the obvious beneficial local effect that he intended; Roxane's father and others came over to him.[79] Second, Alexander married an Eastern woman at this time, despite Macedonian resentment, because he was more willing than earlier to ignore or suppress Macedonian resentment to his many changes in Macedonian monarchy and particularly to his adaptation and adoption of Eastern ways.[80] Third, by 327 he may also have been somewhat more concerned about producing an heir than he previously had been. For years Alexander had been inventing a new sort of monarchy, and he may finally have become interested in having someone to whom he could pass on his invention.

ROXANE: PART 1

Roxane,[81] a daughter of the Bactrian noble Oxyartes,[82] became the first wife of Alexander the Great early in spring 327.[83] The immediate circumstances surrounding her marriage to the Macedonian conqueror are obscured by conflicting and confusing information in our sources,[84] but it seems most likely that Roxane, along with her other sisters and her mother, came into Alexander's hands before her father, a former follower of the Persian pretender Bessus and a participant in the Sogdian/Bactrian revolt against Alexander, had surrendered to him. Alexander's possession of Roxane and treatment of her (no sexual relations but royal attention) probably precipitated her father's surrender.[85] Roxane's marriage to Alexander, whether according to Macedonian custom as Curtius (8.4.27) asserted or Persian as some have claimed,[86] ended his nearly ten years as a royal bachelor.

Both ancient and modern writers have speculated about Alexander's motives for marrying Roxane. Most ancient sources claim that Alexander fell in love with her, more or less at first sight, because of her great beauty and impressive demeanor (Arr. 4.19.5; Plut. *Alex.* 47.4, *Mor.* 332c, 338d; Curt. 8.4.24–26), but modern writers, as well as some ancient ones (Plut. *Alex.* 47.4), have concluded that he was motivated by policy as well.[87]

The revolt of Bactria and Sogdiana had presented Alexander with great military and political problems that long had caused upset and were not easily resolved. Resistance to Macedonian conquest proved deep-seated and fairly successful. After initial conciliatory attempts, Alexander had employed brutal yet ultimately unsuccessful repression against this provincial resistance. Only recently had he returned to his earlier more conciliatory policy.[88] Thus marriage to the daughter of a prominent and still-rebellious member of the provincial elite could convey both conciliation and legitimacy. Its immediate result, Oxyartes' surrender and diplomatic involvement in ending the last of the revolt (Arr. 4.20.4, 21.6–9; Curt. 8.2.19–33), explains its more general consequence, appeasement of the Bactrian and Sogdian elite.

One can only conclude that the benefits the marriage brought outweighed, at least in Alexander's judgment, the disadvantages it also entailed. Alexander's particular military excellence was his ability to adjust to new circumstances, to innovate when previous practice no longer suited present problems. In many ways this judgment applies to Alexander's abilities in general. The marriage to Roxane represents, in terms of marriage policy, yet another example of Alexander the improviser. He needed something to conciliate remaining resisters and (paradoxically) symbolize his victory; marrying Roxane served to do both. If the marriage alienated many Macedonians or infuriated Artabazus (and it may have done both; see BARSINE), then one can only conclude that Alexander was more concerned about Bactrian rebels than about Macedonian sentiments or Persian satraps already committed to him. It may also matter that Alexander was no longer such a very young king and was perhaps more inclined to think in terms of the relatively distant future, if only on the modest scale implied by his marriage to Roxane.

Certainly Roxane played no prominent or public role during the rest of Alexander's reign, or, indeed, in the period after his death. She probably followed him to India, and she may have borne a child there who died shortly after birth (Metz Epit. 70).[89] There is no reason to conclude that Alexander and Roxane had no sexual relationship until the last year of his life.[90] Although Persian kings typically took the women of their family with them on campaign, Macedonian rulers did not (Satyr. ap. Ath. 557b). One can think of only one reason why Alexander, contrary to custom, would have taken his only legitimate wife with him to India. Had he simply intended to imitate Persian custom and reject Macedonian, then he would surely have taken all the Persian royal women instead of leaving them behind in Susa.

In 324 Alexander took two new wives, the daughters of the last Persian kings (STATEIRA 2; PARYSATIS). The sources say nothing about how Alexander's later marriages affected Roxane's status, although they likely had a negative effect. Curtius (8.4.25) implies that Roxane's comparatively modest status compared to the daughters of Darius was a problem, even at the time of her wedding. Roxane's subsequent supposed murder of Darius' daughters (see below) confirms the idea that she saw them as a threat. (See chap. 5 for part two of the life of Roxane.)

Finally, in 324, some nine years after he could have, Alexander married Darius' eldest daughter, Stateira, and he may also have married a woman from the rival branch of the Achaemenid dynasty, Parysatis, daughter of Ochus (Arr. 7.4.4; see STATEIRA 2 and PARYSATIS below). The context for the wedding (or weddings) was unique, the mass weddings at Susa. The surviving accounts of these mass weddings and the elaborate pomp and ceremony surrounding them certainly convey the sense that this event was artifice, an elaborate contrivance by Alexander meant to display and convince—but convince them of exactly what remains somewhat unclear.[91]

STATEIRA 2

Stateira,[92] the eldest daughter of Darius III and his wife (another Stateira),[93] became the second wife of the man who defeated her father and seized his empire, Alexander the Great. After Darius' defeat at Issus, Alexander's army captured Stateira and most of the rest of her family: her grandmother Sisygambis,[94] her mother, her young brother, and her sister.[95] At the time of their capture in November 333, Stateira and her sister were both of marriageable age (Curt. 3.11.24; Diod. 17.36.2).

Whereas the treatment of most of the Persian women captured by Alexander's army was terrible and typical of that allotted captives in ancient warfare (Diod. 17.35.5–6), Alexander singled out the women of Darius' family, not only sparing them the horrors meted out to their female compatriots but allowing them to retain the superficial and ceremonial signs of their status and treating them in a manner intended to seem familial.[96] The focus of Alexander's attention was not Stateira and her sister, or her mother, but her grandmother Sisygambis.

After their capture, Stateira and the rest of her family lived in insulated and yet apparently secure luxury. At some point between the time of their capture and 331, her mother died of natural causes, perhaps in childbirth (see STATEIRA 1). Sisygambis, the younger Stateira's grandmother, clearly replaced her mother as the guardian and primary parent of Darius' children. During (roughly) this same period, Darius involved his daughter Stateira in his diplomatic negotiations with Alexander. Many problems surround the evidence on Darius' correspondence with Alexander and the nature and number of his offers to Alexander and Alexander's counteroffers, but it appears that Darius first tried to ransom his family members and, perhaps

WOMEN AND MONARCHY IN MACEDONIA

when that failed, offered a daughter (apparently Stateira) in marriage to Alexander, along with control of an area of his empire that was already in Alexander's power. In all accounts Alexander rejects Darius' offer. Arrian (2.25.3) says that Alexander also stated that if he wanted to marry Darius' daughter, he would, whether or not Darius agreed.[97]

Then in 330 Alexander left the Persian royal family, including Stateira, behind in Susa (until this point they had apparently followed the king's campaign, much as they had Darius'), having arranged that they all be taught the Greek language (Diod. 17.67.1). No explanation of Alexander's motivation in arranging this education is offered by any ancient source. It must signify that he intended to continue to use the royal family as symbols whose significance varied according to his needs, but it may well signify more. It is difficult to see why Alexander would have wanted Darius' daughters to learn Greek unless he intended them to marry Greek speakers, and he could not allow them to marry just any courtier. As early as 330 Alexander may already have decided to marry at least one of Darius' daughters.[98]

Alexander was in no rush to marry either Stateira or her sister, although he obviously could have done so as early as 333. Instead, he began his relationship with Barsine about the same time and in 327 married Roxane (see above). He did not marry Stateira until 324, nearly ten years after she had come under his control. Their marriage was part of the grandiose wedding festival at Susa, an event now usually interpreted as the final act of his conquest.[99] (See below for discussion of the timing of this marriage.)

Alexander's death almost immediately brought Stateira's own. Plutarch (*Alex.* 77.4) reports that after the death of Alexander, Roxane, pregnant but still very jealous of her Achaemenid co-wife, arranged the secret murder of Stateira and her recently widowed sister as well as the concealment of the crime, and he reveals that Perdiccas was either actively or passively involved. No ancient source asserts that Stateira was pregnant, but Roxane must have feared that she was or that she could claim that she was. Perdiccas had his own reasons for preferring Roxane to Stateira (see ROXANE: PART 2).[100]

Stateira's feelings and ambitions remain unknown. Her career testifies to the critical importance of royal women in Persian monarchy in Greek eyes (see chap. 1) and her death demonstrates that only Alexander had any genuine interest in attempting to create continuity with Achaemenid monarchical tradition and that interest died with him.

PARYSATIS

Parysatis, the youngest daughter of Artaxerxes Ochus, survived her father's murder and, with her mother and sisters, lived on into the reign of Darius III. She, her sisters, and her mother were all captured after the battle of Issus (Curt. 3.13.12–13). As they were part of the large contingent of wives and children of the Persian elite captured by Parmenio at Damascus (3.13.6, 12–13), Parysatis and her family had probably remained at court after her father's downfall. She and her family, like the other royal family, that of Darius III, may have remained at Susa while Alexander was in India.[101]

Arrian alone preserves Aristobulus' report that at Susa in 324 Alexander married not only the daughter of Darius but also Parysatis, the youngest daughter of Ochus (Aristob. FGrH 139, F 52). His testimony has generally been accepted, primarily because the marriage seems to make so much sense. Alexander, having finally decided to risk the tensions marriage into the Achaemenid dynasty inevitably would cause (see above), sensibly decided to tidy up all dynastic loose ends by marrying women from both branches of the royal family. As a veteran of Macedonian dynastic infighting, Alexander is likely to have seen the advantage in dealing with both branches of the dynasty.[102]

Nothing further is heard of Parysatis. Although it is correct that only two references to her are preserved in ancient sources and that her life was truly obscure, it seems peculiar that a wife of Alexander, especially an Achaemenid, would have been ignored by the Successors and by Roxane. A number of factors suggest that Plutarch (Alex. 77.4) wrongly reported that it was Stateira's sister, Drypetis,[103] the widow of Hephaestion, whom Roxane murdered along with Stateira and that Roxane's second victim was actually Parysatis, daughter of Ochus.

It is certainly possible that Plutarch could have made such an error. The sources are riddled with confusion involving the names of various Persian royal women and members of the elite. The confusion is not surprising. Many female names recurred frequently within the royal family and among the elite. Like Macedonian royal women, some of them may have had different names at different times in their lives.[104] These women seem to have lived in seclusion during the reign of Alexander, thus increasing the possibility that Macedonians and Greeks would confuse them, or at least their names.

More important, Parysatis makes more sense as a murder victim than Stateira's sister. Roxane had little motive (with Perdiccas' connivance) to

WOMEN AND MONARCHY IN MACEDONIA

murder Drypetis[105] but compelling reasons to eliminate both Achaemenid wives of Alexander before either could claim to be pregnant or make other trouble for Roxane and her supporters. Had Roxane murdered Stateira but saved Parysatis, she could have inadvertently given Parysatis an importance she did not have previously. Just as it had made sense for Alexander to marry women from both branches of the Achaemenid line, so it made sense for Roxane to murder both women, not just one.

Moreover, it would not make sense to murder Drypetis. She could not claim to be pregnant by Alexander. She might have been a good choice of wife for a member of the Persian elite attempting to take advantage of Alexander's unexpected demise, but Persian or Asian wives were not appealing to Macedonian generals in 323, and a woman under their control could not rush off to wed a Persian rebel.

The meaning of Alexander's Achaemenid marriage is straightforward, particularly if he married Parysatis as well as Stateira: the unequal inclusion of Persian tradition in his new monarchy and the possibility of the birth of a half-Argead, half-Achaemenid heir. Granted that both young women had been in Alexander's control for many years and that the Greek instruction he arranged for Stateira seems to imply that he intended to marry her at some future date, one wants to know not only why Alexander married Stateira but also why he had not married her before 324.

As early as 333, marriage to Stateira offered numerous advantages. Not only would Alexander acquire a legitimate wife able to produce heirs, but he would also significantly increase the strength of his claims to legitimate rule of the Persian Empire. As I have noted, Alexander's treatment of Stateira's mother and grandmother demonstrates that he was well aware of the significance Greek literary tradition accorded Persian royal women. Marriage to the wife or daughter of a conquered leader has often been seen as an essential part of a successful conquest.[106] Arguably, a man able to produce half-Achaemenid heirs would have a much better chance of winning over the Persian elite.

Despite these potential advantages, Alexander did not think it safe or effective to attempt a marriage alliance with the Achaemenids before 324. All the surviving accounts of Alexander's reign preserve numerous references to the growing resentment of Macedonians, both ordinary soldiers and aristocrats, to Alexander's Persianizing policy in all its forms. His marriage to Roxane, in itself not popular, was not nearly as threatening as his marriage to Stateira would be: it looked and was so much like that of many of his father's marriages, an alliance of a relatively temporary sort made with a relatively unknown leader to end a campaign. There can be no doubt that the Macedonians would dislike Alexander's marriage to an Achaemenid even more. Justin (12.10.9–10) says directly that Alexander used the mass marriages at Susa to mitigate his own marriage, which Justin terms a *crimen* (crime or fault).

The context in which Alexander's Achaemenid marriage alliances occur (the "mutiny" at Opis, with all it implications for a changing of the guard, the arrival of the Epigonoi, the departure of Macedonian troops) implies that so long as Alexander perceived Macedonians as central to his power, he dared not marry an Achaemenid. Alexander simply could not afford to marry Stateira until 324 when, in many ways, he showed himself willing to demonstrate to the Macedonians that they were no longer central. Only when he had truly changed the base of his power did he proceed with the marriages that he must have long intended. His marriage to Stateira is part of his rejection of Macedonia, one of many signs that he had become an Asian ruler. Whatever his earlier claims to legitimacy, the marriage to Stateira suggests that only in 324 did he seriously and consistently attempt to rule his empire as the successor to the Achaemenids.[107]

Postponing the marriage changed its implication to some degree. A marriage to a daughter of Darius in the 330s would have been a statement of the reality of Alexander's conquest, but by 324 it functioned as a symbol for continuity rather than the already completed conquest. The halfway measure of his relationship with Barsine was no longer necessary. It is no wonder that Roxane was worried about these women and any children they might produce: Alexander had made them the future (see ROXANE).

By the time of Alexander's death, his private circumstances resembled those of his father's much more than in his early years. He integrated his unificatory and consolidationist policies with regard to royal women. His marriages and heirs (or potential heirs) united his new conquests, his Eastern realms. His mother and sister, standing in for his presence, watched out for royal interests in the areas his father had cen-

WOMEN AND MONARCHY IN MACEDONIA

tralized and conquered. Whatever the significance of Alexander's summons of Antipater to Babylon and his replacement by Craterus, this dual decision was possible only because Alexander had, in his mother and full sister, representatives of his personal interests on the scene at home. In Asia he had Sisygambis, whose actions after his death tell us that she had reached the conclusion that the fate of her family was tied to Alexander's survival.[108]

Like Philip, Alexander used royal women both to unify the areas he controlled and to consolidate power and institutions, but, unlike his father, Alexander's preference was for the latter over the former. He found royal mothers more useful and less troublesome than royal wives. Some blame for the struggles of the Successors in the years after his death and for the demise of the dynasty must certainly be assigned to his policies, but the only way Alexander could have secured the succession to his throne was by living longer; marrying and begetting earlier would not have been enough. Moreover, a son none of the elite would accept as ruler did no good; perhaps Alexander married as late as he did because only late in his reign did he believe that the political context existed for the acceptance of any son of his by any woman, Macedonian or Asian.

CHAPTER FIVE

Olympias, Cleopatra, Cynnane, Adea Eurydice, and the End of the Argead Dynasty (323–308)

The sudden death of Alexander the Great in June 323 plunged the Macedonians and the empire they had conquered into more than forty years (323–280) of confusion during which his generals, the Successors or Diadochi (e.g., Ptolemy, Antigonus, Seleucus, Perdiccas, Leonnatus, Lysimachus, Craterus), struggled over the fruits of Macedonian conquest.[1] Ultimately, they and their descendants created three great kingdoms, ruled by three different dynasties, and these powerful monarchies dominated the rest of the Hellenistic period (280–31). Even before the death of Alexander, there had been signs of trouble in his empire: a renewed threat of rebellion on the Greek mainland and the possibility that Antipater, ordered to hand over his position in Macedonia but unresponsive to the order, might also rebel, taking with him much of the Macedonian army. These troubles, however, were modest compared to the crisis precipitated by Alexander's death.

Alexander had no male heir in any meaningful sense. Roxane was pregnant and delivered a son, Alexander IV, a month or two after the king's death, but it would be many years before he could rule. Barsine had an illegitimate son by Alexander, but young Heracles was only a few years older than his half brother. The only adult male Argead was Arrhidaeus, Alexander's mentally limited half brother. In the days after Alexander's death, the army and Alexander's generals championed opposing solutions to the succession crisis: the generals supported Perdiccas as regent for Roxane's child, assuming it was a boy, but the army wanted Arrhidaeus. The result of this confrontation was an unworkable compromise: there were two kings (the infant Alexander IV and Arrhidaeus, now called Philip Arrhidaeus), neither of them competent to rule in his own right, and Perdiccas was regent. Once this unhappy solution had been reached, those generals present in Babylon divided up the empire.

Then the wars began. Some able officers of Alexander's, such as Craterus and Leonnatus, were eliminated very early; others of the young men who had marched out to Asia with Alexander in 334, such as Lysimachus and Seleucus, died old and violently, on the field of battle or at the hand of an assassin.

Nearly halfway through this confusing and poorly documented period, the last of the male Argeads was eliminated (ca. 309 or 308), and soon after (from ca. 306 on) Alexander's former generals began to take the title *basileus*, or king.[2] Early in the period of the Successors, royal women played a critical and sometimes central role in events, but gradually, they, like Alexander's sons, were murdered. By ca. 308, only one, Thessalonice, remained. Ultimately she too would die by violence (see chap. 6; THESSALONICE).

Scholarship for this period has blamed the demise of the dynasty that had ruled Macedonia from its historical beginnings on the actions of several royal women, most notably Olympias and Adea Eurydice, daughter of Philip II and wife of Philip Arrhidaeus.[3] Scholars have wrongly characterized the actions of these women as interference, driven only by revenge.[4]

Behind the notions of both interference and revenge lie a series of tacit and thus unexamined assumptions. If individuals are to be blamed for the end of the dynasty, it must be demonstrated that the dynasty failed because of their actions. Such a demonstration is impossible: given the scarcity of viable males, the Argead dynasty was all but doomed by the time Alexander the Great died. Based on the record of royal succession in Macedonia, the elite of Macedonia must have known from the time of Alexander's death on that only the remotest chance would allow the dynasty to survive, at least through the male line.

Child heirs to the throne had not succeeded in Macedonia. Neither of the two available children was close to adulthood at the time of Alexander's death, and neither had the kind of powerful uncle/guardian figure who might have given his succession a genuine chance. The mental state of the available adult, Arrhidaeus, invited manipulation by others. Since the period after Alexander was marked by chronic military activity, real power proved to be tied directly to military success. Alexander's young sons, his limited half brother, and the women of his family were all excluded from significant military activity and thus military success. The deck was stacked against what was left of the dynasty.

A number of incidents, many involving royal women, attest that loyalty to the dynasty persisted among the general population, both soldier and civilian.[5] Even among the elite some loyalty to the dynasty survived.[6] Mere sentimental attachment to the dynasty was not enough, however, to maintain it.[7] Those most likely to be deeply committed to the survival of the dynasty, its surviving members, were those most without the means to perpetuate it. "Blame," even if taken primarily in a causal rather than a moral sense, is not a concept applicable to the choices of those Argeads who survived Alexander's death.

And yet "blame," when applied to royal women in this period, has indeed often had a moral edge, perhaps because Olympias and to some degree the other women of the dynasty acted in ways very different from the traditional image of women in the ancient world, if not quite so different from the reality of royal female action in Macedonia and Epirus. Olympias, Cynnane, and Adea Eurydice were ruthless women, capable and sometimes guilty of brutality. This said, one must then note that the men of this period were at least equally ruthless and brutal.[8] Although Macedonian struggles for the succession had always been violent and often murderous—regicide and attempted regicide were common—[9] the first forty years after Alexander's death were ones in which violence, treachery, and atrocity escalated. The period can be understood as an accelerated, more intense version of previous historical patterns of political violence.

A number of factors intensified the violence in Macedonian politics. Previous struggles for the throne, however violent, had generally been limited to the Argeads. As the years passed, hopes for the continuance of the Argead dynasty faded. When various Macedonian generals moved to establish dynasties of their own, the number of combatants in the struggle for legitimacy and succession increased dramatically. Violence limited to the royal clan no longer seemed practical when successful violence might bring legitimacy to a new ruling family.

Attribution of motive for this increased violence is a complex task.

WOMEN AND MONARCHY IN MACEDONIA

The wars of the Successors were civil wars of a sort and civil wars are notoriously nasty, perhaps because of the frequency of occasions on which a victor might feel betrayed by recently defeated opponents. Many violent acts of the Successors could have been committed either because of practical benefit for the perpetrators (elimination of competitors) or to avenge perceived wrongs.

It seems reasonable to attribute particularly nasty manners of death to vengeance (e.g., Diod. 19.44.1). Those murders or other acts of violence that seem gratuitous in practical political terms (e.g., Diod. 18.37.2, 47.3) as well as those acts apparently publicly proclaimed by the agent to be revenge (Diod. 19.11.8) can also be categorized as acts of vengeance. Conversely, when the sources insist that the murder was committed reluctantly and the murderer may have gone out of his or her way to give an honorable burial to the victim, then it seems reasonable to rule out revenge (Plut. *Eum.* 7.8, 19.2). Revenge may well have been a frequent motive for violent acts in the period of the Successors, but simply assuming that it was a motive for a particular action suggests that we know more than we usually do about the goals of individuals. In any event, revenge had a much better public image, even propaganda value, in antiquity than it has had in post-Christian times. The perpetrator of vengeance, therefore, might have been admired as a person committed to justice rather than condemned as a savage.

Although political violence certainly worsened in the age of the Successors, the Argead dynasty had always acted with violent divisiveness. Claimants to the throne typically met on the battlefield or became involved in plots against each other. Royal polygamy and the uncertain succession pattern lay behind the internecine squabbles of the Argeads (see chap. 1). Admittedly, the actions of Olympias, Cynnane, and Adea Eurydice were also divisive, but their behavior indicates how little different their goals and standards were from those of Macedonian males. Moreover, their bitter struggles recognized political reality: once or if Alexander IV reached maturity, there would be no need for an incompetent adult king and the fiction of dual kingship would come to an end. The continuing survival of each nonruling king compromised the specialness of the other and the security of his supporters. Sooner or later, one of the kings would have to be eliminated.

Before Alexander's death, as I have observed, women of the Argead clan had occasionally played a role in succession politics, often as mothers supporting sons as heirs. The unprecedented scarcity of adult male Argeads after Alexander's death caused royal women to play a greater and more aggressive role in succession politics. This expanded role was not, primarily, the traditional one of advocate for male children but more often that of royal bride or agent for a royal bride. The reason for this change was that the mothers of Alexander's two sons were Asian women ignored in the Macedonian homeland and by most Successors and thus largely excluded from the political arena.[10] European Argead women, however, could offer themselves, or those they were responsible for, as potential sources of Argead blood and half-Argead heirs. In the case of Olympias, this situation may have been accidental (her half-Asian grandson was not available to her until very late in her life), but it is nonetheless true.

The implication is obvious: the women acted on the assumption that the dynasty had little or no chance through the male line but that a connection through the female line might prove attractive to many of the generals. Alexander's full sister and his mother may not have been indifferent to the survival of Alexander IV, but they certainly took action that was not dependent on his survival. Had they been deeply committed to the survival of the dynasty through the male line, they would surely have paid more attention to Alexander's other son, Heracles.[11]

The Successors apparently shared the view that there was little hope for the survival of the dynasty. Not long after Alexander's death, his generals began to perform various kinglike acts.[12] Diodorus consistently represents the various generals, as a group and individually, as aiming at the *basileia* soon after Alexander's death, and he frequently reports that generals accused their rivals of desire for the *basileia*.[13] The consistency with which Diodorus advances this assertion probably means that this was the interpretation of Hieronymus, universally regarded as Diodorus' primary source for this period. Hieronymus may have been writing with the benefit of hindsight, but his judgment, usually informed and intelligent, should not be ignored. Long before the assumption of the royal title by the first of the Successors in 306/5,[14] the actions of the Successors suggest that they had begun to work their way toward the establishment of new dynasties. Those within and with-

WOMEN AND MONARCHY IN MACEDONIA

out the dynasty indicated soon after Alexander's death that they did not realistically expect the dynasty to endure much longer, particularly through the male line.

If one terms the public actions of royal women "interference," then one obviously assumes that they acted without legitimacy. Such an assumption is dubious. Monarchy in Macedonia involved the rule of the Argead clan; it was not an office, something from which women could be excluded (see chap. 1). Whatever small concern had existed for constitutional issues (as opposed to ill-defined political habits and traditions) and well-defined offices before the death of Alexander diminished to near-nonexistence afterward. Once the first of the regents, Perdiccas, had been murdered, the legitimacy of all following regents is extremely questionable.[15] Various of the Successors proved happy to use claims of illegitimacy against their enemies, but there is little reason to consider such charges as anything other than propaganda, easily abandoned when participants switched sides, as they so often did.[16] Moreover, if we understand Macedonian monarchy not in constitutional terms but as a matter of blood and the reign of a family, then as male Argeads became scarce, legitimacy necessarily reposed in the surviving women of the dynasty.

Bearing in mind these general trends, a consideration of the situation and probable self-interest of each the most active royal women in the period after Alexander's death should be clarifying.

OLYMPIAS: PART 3

In 323 Olympias had long been resident in her Molossian homeland, and she would remain there until 317. In Molossia she was physically remote from the fray precipitated by Alexander's death. Nonetheless, her son's death was a personal and political disaster. It is no wonder that she believed, probably wrongly, that her enemy Antipater and his sons were responsible for the death of her previously unvanquished son (Diod. 19.11.8–9; Plut. *Alex.* 77.1–3). Personal grief aside, for the first time in her life she faced physical danger (her continued existence benefited none of the Successors, and her demise might have pleased a number of them), and her actions suggest that she was aware of this unpleasant truth. Soon after Alexander's death she sought help from her own Aeacid dynasty and from a possible husband for her daughter, the widowed Cleopatra.

Cleopatra pursued a marriage to Leonnatus (Plut. *Eum.* 3.5), probably at Olympias' urging, but his death prevented this plan. Aeacides, Olympias' cousin and nephew, returned from exile and became ruler of the Molossians. Whether he returned at her bidding or on his own, he consistently acted in Olympias' interests.[17] Olympias sent Cleopatra to Sardis (where most of the Macedonian army, Perdiccas the regent, and the kings were located) in the hope of preventing Perdiccas' marriage to one of Antipater's daughters, but this plan also failed and Cleopatra was effectively confined to Sardis by Antigonus (see CLEOPATRA 2: PART 3). Olympias, lacking control of either her daughter or her grandson, was stymied, although still safe enough with Aeacides in Epirus.

Olympias' opportunity for renewed power and influence came with the death of the hated Antipater in 319 and his replacement as regent by Polyperchon (Diod. 18.48.4). If Olympias was born sometime between 375 and 371, in 319 she was an old woman by ancient standards. Even if she was in good health (and we know nothing about this), she cannot have been certain that she would live long enough to secure her grandson Alexander IV's position as sole ruler of Macedonia in his own right (let alone the rest of his father's empire). The child was about four years old and surely needed to reach the age of eighteen (ca. 305) to have a reasonable chance of ruling in his own right, but by that time Olympias, if still alive, would be seventy or close to it.

From the moment Olympias heard of her son's death and the birth of Alexander IV, she must have known that the chances of her grandson surviving long enough to be more than a figurehead were slender indeed and that if she took an active role as Alexander IV's advocate, she lost what little security her relatively remote base in Epirus and her cousin's protection offered. Diodorus (18.58.3–4, 19.35.6) makes it clear that she was quite conscious of the danger of becoming her grandson's supporter, yet she did so. She risked her life and lost it in an attempt to ensure her grandson's survival and ultimate rule.

This selfless goal was doubtless not her sole motivation. During her son's career, she sought to increase and entrench her power and influence. These motives remained powerful, possibly increased by her relative obscurity in the years since her son's death but also possibly lessened by the inescapable approach of her own death. Ancient culture, especially ancient elite culture, tended to put less emphasis on the individual and more on the family and its preservation over the generations than does our own.

WOMEN AND MONARCHY IN MACEDONIA

Shortly after Polyperchon became regent, he asked Olympias to return to Macedonia, take over responsibility for her grandson, and also take on some more general role (Diod. 18.57.2, 48.4; and see below).[18] Olympias refused Polyperchon's offer at least once and possibly twice (Diod. 18.48.4, 57.2). Neither Diodorus nor Justin tells us when she finally accepted Polyperchon, or on what terms. Diodorus (18.58.2–3) speaks of a letter Olympias sent Eumenes (Alexander's secretary and the only Greek Successor) asking him for advice about whether to return to Macedonia. Polyperchon's offer is not mentioned specifically, but it appears to be the reason for her letter.[19] Diodorus explains Olympias' reluctance in terms of her distrust of her grandson's supposed guardians, whom she believed really wanted the *basileia* for themselves. Eumenes gives her sensible advice: wait until it is clear if Polyperchon or Cassander wins the war that had developed between them. During this time Alexander IV as well as Philip Arrhidaeus remained with Polyperchon. Olympias had yet to meet Alexander IV.[20]

Given the political acumen and caution displayed in her dealings with Polyperchon and Eumenes, Olympias' abrupt departure for Macedonia and acceptance of Polyperchon's offer in fall 317 require more explanation than those who paint Olympias as a politically incompetent harpy tend to recognize. The immediate cause of her departure was either the knowledge that Adea Eurydice was now allied with her old enemy and Antipater's son, Cassander, and had made him regent or the realization (or suspicion) that something like that was imminent. But the fundamental cause of Olympias' apparent reversal of policy was apparently her perception that the political fiction created at Babylon—two joint kings from different branches of the royal family that had been rivals for more than a generation—must someday be exploded and replaced by a return to unified monarchy. Naturally, she hoped that Alexander IV would become that single ruler. Time was on the side of Olympias and Alexander IV, if only the young king could survive to adulthood (see ADEA EURYDICE).

Olympias came back to Macedonia with her grandson, her nephew Aeacides,[21] and some Epirote forces as well as some of Polyperchon's. Judging by subsequent events, apparently the Macedonians did not perceive her as an invader. Adea Eurydice and her husband met the invaders at Euia on the Epirote-Macedonia border. Duris (ap. Ath. 560 f.) called the encounter the first war between women and claimed that Olympias went to battle to the beat of a drum, like a Bacchant, and that Adea Eurydice was equipped as a Macedonian soldier.[22] There may not have been a real battle since the Macedonian army immediately went over to Olympias and the royal husband and wife were soon captured. After treating the royal pair cruelly, Olympias caused the deaths of both. She also killed one of Cassander's brothers, dishonored the tomb of another, Iolaus, and brought about the deaths of one hundred supporters of Cassander. Diodorus (19.11.9) notes that Olympias' actions caused some Macedonians to dislike her (see further below).

Olympias has been universally condemned for these actions, on both moral and political grounds. Polyperchon has usually been judged incompetent because he chose to involve himself with her.[23] Neither of these assessments has merit. The view that Olympias failed because she misjudged the political situation is difficult to support. She had limited options, and time was a factor in pursuing them, as we have seen. The deaths of Adea Eurydice and Philip Arrhidaeus were a necessity, however heated the reaction. Left alive, Philip Arrhidaeus might become the tool of virtually any faction. Adea Eurydice presented a real threat to Olympias and her grandson not only because of her position relative to her husband but also because she could produce a child who was both Argead and, perhaps, the son of one of Alexander's generals.

More problematic is the slaughter of the reported one hundred supporters of Cassander. Here the risk was more equal to the benefit that might result. Though these deaths had their advantages as preemptive strikes against Olympias' enemy, they also held out the possibilities of alienating public opinion (as they apparently did in part) and of failure (as they certainly did). Opposition remained. The elimination of Cassander's followers was risky in political terms, with disadvantages as well as advantages. Even if the murder of these people constituted a political misjudgment, the more important point is that Olympias, her forces, and her allies failed not because of alleged or real political blunders but because of military blunders.

There were a series of military blunders. Polyperchon certainly bears some responsibility, but so must Olympias, who either believed that she had military skills sufficient to handle the situation or put her trust in men and in plans that she should not have.

When in spring 315 Olympias surrendered to Cassander on a promise

WOMEN AND MONARCHY IN MACEDONIA

of personal safety,[24] her fate was sealed (Diod. 19.50.5; Just. 14.6.5). It proved difficult to find someone to kill Olympias (confirming that her failures were primarily military, not political), but Cassander was finally able to do so by manipulating the families of those she had killed (Diod. 19.51.2–6; Just. 14.6.6–12).[25] The narratives of Justin and Diodorus make it clear that Olympias stayed wily to the end. Had she succeeded in appearing at her trial, as she wished, she might have survived.[26] Her last acts and death resemble those of her associate and friend Eumenes. Both continued to scheme and plot to the end and faced death with resolve (Diod. 19.43.1–9), and both, arguably, lacked the stable military base necessary to survive in the cutthroat age of the Successors.

Of Alexander's three sisters, two, Cleopatra and Cynnane (see CLEOPATRA, below), took immediate action to enter into the struggles made inevitable by Alexander's death. The third and youngest, Thessalonice (see THESSALONICE), did nothing, probably because she was under Olympias' control.

CLEOPATRA 2: PART 3

Cleopatra was in Macedonia when her brother died. Alexander's death placed Cleopatra and her mother in danger at the same time that it signaled a decline in their power and influence. In response, as well as in keeping with their past behavior, they continued to act as a political unit as long as possible. Cleopatra was Olympias' most immediate hope for guaranteeing survival and continuing influence. And, because of their shared goals, Olympias was probably one of the few whom Cleopatra could trust. Moreover, Cleopatra, in her early thirties, could still produce a child, a grandson of Philip and a nephew of Alexander.

Soon after Alexander's death, Cleopatra, probably with her mother's aid, attempted to stabilize her position by marrying one of her brother's generals, Leonnatus. Plutarch associates the marriage with Leonnatus's plan to rule Macedonia (Plut. *Eum.* 3.5). Antipater had already offered a daughter of his to Leonnatus (Diod. 18.12.1), and so Cleopatra's interest in Leonnatus appears to be part of the continuing rivalry between her family and that of Antipater. Although this rivalry is usually associated solely with Olympias, it should not be viewed in such narrow terms. As we have seen, Plutarch (*Alex.* 68.3) says that Olympias and Cleopatra formed a faction against Antipater. It was Cleopatra who had been dealing most recently with Antipater in Macedonia. Cleopatra would soon confront him again. Their rivalry was also part of the pattern of competing marriage alliances that developed after Alexander's death (see below).

Antipater's offer of a daughter in marriage to Leonnatus probably dates to fall 323 and Cleopatra's offer of herself as bride to late winter or early spring 323/2; Antipater's offer occurs in the context of his actions immediately after Alexander's death, whereas Cleopatra's seem to come as a reaction to Antipater's.[27] Marriage to Leonnatus offered several advantages to Cleopatra. He had been a close associate of Alexander's, and he was probably known to Cleopatra and connected through Philip II's mother to the royal house.[28] He was physically closer to Cleopatra than some of the better-known Successors. Leonnatus' defeat and death in battle in spring 322 (Diod. 18.15.3–4) put an end to Cleopatra's first plan.

The Leonnatus episode suggests several things. Cleopatra was interested in the rule of Macedonia, apparently quite apart from any claim Alexander IV had on it. She saw the clan of Antipater as a threat to continued Argead rule in Macedonia. She may have felt the immediate need of the physical protection of a Macedonian general other than Antipater.

R. Malcolm Errington has argued that Cleopatra's initiative to Leonnatus demonstrates her unimportance because she had to take the first step rather than wait for offers.[29] His argument, however, contains a series of unargued and dubious assumptions. She may have put herself in a stronger position by initiating marriage negotiations. As far as we know, whenever Cleopatra showed interest in one of the generals, he responded. Rather than show her weakness, Cleopatra's initiative in marital matters demonstrated her prestige. Moreover, the generals had to be more cautious than Cleopatra about marriage: anyone who made her an offer had to think of the military consequences, whereas she had to worry about the military consequences if she did *not* marry.

When Leonnatus died in battle, Cleopatra and Olympias turned to Perdiccas as a likely husband for Cleopatra. Like Leonnatus, the regent Perdiccas was related to the royal house and a close associate of Alexander's. Indeed, on his deathbed Alexander apparently gave him the royal signet ring.[30] Cleopatra set off for Sardis in Asia Minor (where much of the Macedonian army, the regent, and the kings were encamped) and arrived in late spring or early summer, about the same time that Nicaea, one of Antipater's many daughters, arrived with the same marital intent (Diod. 18.23.1–3; Arr. *FGrH* 156, F 9.21). Like her earlier attempted match, this new effort appears to have arisen as a response to the threat of a marriage alliance of Antipater's, a response possibly encouraged by Eumenes' efforts. But Perdiccas, who had asked for Nicaea in the period immediately after Alexander's death (when he was more in need of Antipater's support), could not yet risk offending the old general. Perhaps Perdiccas would have been willing to become polygamous as the Argeads had done (certainly the Successors would later practice polygamy), but Antipater would not be happy with having his daughter so clearly ranked second. So, despite his desire to marry Cleopatra as part of an attempt to control Alexander's kingdom, Perdiccas temporized, supposedly planning to reject Nicaea and marry Cleopatra as soon as he dared (Diod. 18.23.3, 25.3; Just. 13.6.4–8). When Antipater and Craterus learned of Perdiccas' plans (Diod. 18.25.3; Arr. *FGrH* 156, F 26), hostilities against Perdiccas began. In late spring 320, Perdiccas, having suffered a series of military and political defeats, was assassinated by his own officers (Diod. 18.33–36.5; Plut. *Eum.* 5–7; Arr. *FGrH.* 156, F 26–27).[31]

Cleopatra's departure for Sardis was extremely risky, the first of two critical decisions that would ultimately put her in the hands of her enemies and lead, many years later, to her death. It would appear that she was willing to jeopardize her life in an attempt to regain lost personal power.[32] Her actions were probably not motivated by concern for the future of the dynasty as a whole, even if Olympias supported her. Neither Cleopatra nor her mother had any contact with Alexander IV as yet, and he, in any event, had already been recognized as king. Cleopatra's marriage to Perdiccas might have made Alexander IV even less necessary to her.

The murder of Cynnane, shortly after Cleopatra's arrival in Sardis, would certainly have made her aware of the lethal risk she was running, had she not been aware initially. But, rather than return home when her ambitions were not immediately gratified, Cleopatra stayed on, after Perdiccas's marriage to Nicaea, accepting gifts sent through Eumenes from a somewhat two-faced Perdiccas, who supposedly planned to desert Nicaea in the end and marry Cleopatra (Arr. *FGrH* 156, F 26).

Cleopatra remained in Sardis even after the death of Perdiccas, probably to keep close to the marriage market[33] but obviously in danger. Many of

Perdiccas' associates, including his sister, were killed, and others, like Eumenes, under sentence of death, survived only as outlaws (Diod. 18.37.1–2). Eumenes, Cleopatra's sponsor and advocate in her dealings with Perdiccas, now appeared in Sardis, hoping to win favor with her by confronting Antipater there (Plut. *Eum.* 8.4) and probably planning to use her prestige to regain some kind of legitimacy (Just. 14.1.7–8). She persuaded him to depart.

Plutarch (*Eum.* 8.4) thought Cleopatra persuaded Eumenes to leave because she feared that Antipater would somehow blame her if he did not. Arrian (*FGrH* 156, F 11.40) claims it was because she feared, not Antipater's blame, but that of the Macedonian people if it appeared she had encouraged war between Eumenes and the nearby forces of Antipater. Given the history of Antipater's dealings with her and the rest of her family, not to mention the confrontation that immediately followed, Arrian's interpretation is certainly more likely than Plutarch's. Cleopatra may also have doubted Eumenes' ability to defeat Antipater.[34]

Antipater, having marched east, soon arrived in Sardis and, despite Cleopatra's moderate actions, reproached her for her *philia* (friendship) with Perdiccas and Eumenes. According to Arrian, she defended herself more strongly than was the custom among women and accused Antipater in turn of many things. Arrian (*FGrH* 156, F 11.40) claims that Cleopatra and Antipater ultimately parted peacefully, but his statement means little, unless Arrian interpreted Antipater's failure to murder Cleopatra as a peaceful parting. Because of the uproar Cynnane's death precipitated and his very recent troubles with Adea Eurydice (see ADEA EURYDICE), Antipater probably did not dare to eliminate Cleopatra yet. One wonders if their confrontation occurred before the troops or in private.[35] He may have had vague plans for her, most likely marriage to Cassander.[36]

Cleopatra's decisions to stay in Sardis and to send Eumenes away were fateful. She was never able to leave. From this period she stayed on, through the deaths of her mother and Eumenes (winter 317/6), the marriage of her half sister Thessalonice (spring 316), and the deaths of her two nephews (ca. 310–309). The sources do not mention her during this long period. The usual view has been that in these roughly twelve years she was the prisoner of Antigonus, probably entrusted to him by Antipater at the time of his return to Macedonia,[37] but the truth is probably more complex.

Certainly Cleopatra did not stay in Sardis because of any quarrel with her mother or because Olympias lost interest in her daughter's affairs after the return of the kings to Macedonia.[38] There is no evidence either for conflict between mother and daughter or for the assumption that Cleopatra never acted independently. As mother and daughter spent long periods in different countries with communication possible only with long delays, some independence was inescapable. Olympias' name is not mentioned in terms of Cleopatra's projected marriage to Leonnatus, although it is mentioned in relation to her marriage to Perdiccas. It could be true that Olympias, once in control of her grandson or at least within range of being so, may have placed greater emphasis on him and his fate, but she cannot be described as neglecting Cleopatra if Cleopatra was no longer a free agent.[39]

Diodorus' description of the events that precipitated the end of Cleopatra's long stay in Sardis is revealing. He says that she *quarreled* with Antigonus and having a preference for Ptolemy, attempted to leave Sardis to join him. The governor of Sardis, having been commanded by Antigonus to watch her closely, was able to stop her. Antigonus ordered him to arrange, secretly, for her murder but blamed her death on certain women and gave Cleopatra a royal burial (Diod. 20.37.3–6). Diodorus' testimony implies that Cleopatra and Antigonus had a previous arrangement, but an unequal one, based on the disadvantages to him of being known as her murderer and the advantage to be gained from preventing any of the other Successors from marrying her.

Cleopatra may have preserved her life for a number of years by tacitly accepting a situation in which she could not marry or remove herself from Antigonus' watchful eye. It may be significant that even at the time she began her long exile in Sardis she would have been reaching the end of her childbearing years. Sometime in that period she would probably have reached menopause.[40] It was increasingly unlikely that she could bear a child who would be a grandson of Philip II and a nephew of Alexander the Great. Marriage, by this stage, could offer her only the chance to be a kind of royal figurehead, a token of legitimacy rather than the chance to be a royal mother, a role likely to give her more power. Cleopatra may have had no other, or at least no better, options than to accept remaining in Sardis. Her sudden attempt to escape to Ptolemy strongly suggests that the deaths of her nephews had made her, quite rightly, fear for her own life and attempt to escape.[41]

What little evidence survives demonstrates that, like her mother, Cleopatra was a brave woman, full of resolve and capable of real daring. Assessing her skills at political analysis is more difficult and likely to lead to oversimplification. Her failure to accept Eumenes' protection led to her virtual incarceration in Sardis for her remaining years. When she made her choice, she believed that she would not be checkmated in this manner, but she was wrong. Perhaps she hoped that the Macedonian troops, already unruly through Adea Eurydice's efforts, would support her as they sometimes had Adea Eurydice or that she would be able to play off Antipater's interests against those of Antigonus. Whatever her reading of the situation, she miscalculated.

However, the concern Arrian attributes to her about popular sentiment among the Macedonians was perfectly justified, and attaching herself to Eumenes might well have led to the results she feared. In a very real sense, by 320, exposed as she was in Sardis, she had no good choices left. Her critical decision was her initial one to accept danger in return for the hope of royal power. That was a decision that many male Argeads and several other female Argeads had embraced again and again over the years.

Her final act, her attempt to escape Antigonus and try to reach Ptolemy, rather than the impulsive act of an unrealistic and romantic middle-aged woman, actually demonstrates her hardheaded political acumen. She realized that killing Argeads was no longer dangerous and that eliminating her would simplify matters for virtually all the remaining Successors. Ptolemy, having constructed his legitimacy around her brother, was a logical port in this storm.

That none of the Successors married her, although Diodorus (20.37.4) tells us that at one time or another virtually all of them entertained the idea, speaks to their lack of interest in genuine continuity with the Argead past. Cleopatra would have been a worthy heir to Argead tradition—tough, daring, and willing to venture all for power—and that is precisely why she was killed rather than married.[42]

Cynnane's clever response to the death of Alexander suggests that she had a good understanding of the popularity of the royal house, including its women, among the army. She planned to manipulate this loyalty to achieve the victory of her branch of the Argead house over the aims of the rival branch, headed by Olympias.

After Alexander's murder of her husband, Amyntas, Cynnane was kept in obscurity throughout her half brother's reign. She had only one child by Amyntas, a daughter, Adea, later called Eurydice (see ADEA EURYDICE). Soon after Amyntas' death,[43] Alexander planned that his half sister would take another husband, Langarus, but Langarus died before the marriage could happen (Arr. 1.5.4–5).[44] Polyaenus (8.60) reports that Cynnane did not wish to marry again, but the fact that she did not is more likely the result of Alexander's reluctance to involve himself or the women of his family in marriage alliances (see chap. 4).[45]

We hear nothing more of Cynnane in the years of her brother's reign, except that she was, according to Polyaenus (8.60), training her daughter in military skills. Cynnane may well have resented Alexander, her husband's murderer.

Cynnane was slower to react to the news of Alexander's death than her half sister, Cleopatra (see CLEOPATRA 2: PART 3), for several reasons. Cynnane was a more obscure and even exotic figure to whom the thoughts of the Successors would not as naturally or rapidly turn. The rivalry of Cleopatra and her mother with Antipater's clan tended to force Cleopatra into the marriage market sooner. Cynnane's options were more limited and less obvious than Cleopatra's.

When Cynnane reacted, instead of searching for a husband to provide political and military support as Cleopatra did, she took the military and political initiative into her own hands. Cynnane, like Cleopatra, also sought to arrange a marriage, but a marriage with a very different purpose than those projected by Cleopatra.

Cynnane's plan was extraordinarily bold and intelligent, although it pitted her directly against her two most obvious enemies, the families of Antipater and Olympias. Cynnane responded to the possibilities opened up by the news that the army had forced the aristocrats to accept Arrhidaeus[46] as co-king with the as-yet-unborn child of Roxane. She cunningly devised a scheme that would put herself and her daughter, currently dynastic outsiders, in the very center of power. She hoped to bring about the marriage of her very young daughter to Arrhidaeus (Polyaen. 8.60; Arr. FGrH 156, F 9.22). She raised an army, managed to defeat Antipater's attempt (he was perhaps more wary because of Cleopatra's earlier departure) to prevent her from leaving Macedonia, and crossed to Asia. Although this daring plan ultimately proved fatal to Cynnane, it succeeded in its object and was brilliantly conceived.[47]

The marriage Cynnane desired for her daughter, however incongruous in personal terms, was nearly ideal for a woman who wanted real and independent power for herself and her daughter. The wife of Arrhidaeus, unlike ambitious royal women whose power came through the minority of a son who was first heir and later king, would never have to worry about her political pawn growing up. Arrhidaeus was, apparently, a permanent minor, an ideal tool. Even if his wife were not officially regent, she might be able to choose or influence those who were, and his mere presence could legitimize activities quite possibly of his wife's design.

The marriage conveyed other benefits and suggests the possibility of additional motives. This marriage could have produced an Argead heir free of the Asian blood that so many Macedonians disliked and distrusted, a son who could restore the descendants of Perdiccas III to rule and thus avenge the death of Amyntas. The army was much more committed to the Argead dynasty than to the aristocracy. In subsequent years the army was often the decisive factor in political events. It could very possibly have preferred such a child to Alexander's son. Cynnane and her daughter, because of their warrior training and tradition, seemed ideally suited to manipulate the feelings of the Macedonian army.

Even before she had to deal with Antipater's attempts to short-circuit her designs or the subsequent troubles she encountered in Asia, Cynnane must have known what great peril surrounded this enterprise. We know of no Macedonian generals who supported her (though Antigonus and others later exploited Cynnane's fate for their own interests). Indeed, faction-ridden though Macedonian power politics was at this stage, Cynnane's plan tended to threaten virtually all existing factions.

Although Cynnane's exertions on behalf of her daughter clearly parallel those of Olympias and her daughter in the same period, some important differences should be noted. Olympias and Cleopatra attempted to manipulate events in the indirect way royal women had done for some time, whereas Cynnane and Adea Eurydice subverted the traditional political roles for women in Macedonian society. They conducted military actions themselves and put little or no trust in male assistance.

Confronted with the threat posed by Cynnane's dynastic ambitions,

WOMEN AND MONARCHY IN MACEDONIA

Perdiccas, the regent, sent out his brother Alcetas to prevent her from joining the main army. Alcetas foolishly tried to eliminate the threat by murdering Cynnane in front of his army.[48] Instead of thwarting Cynnane's plans, Alcetas' crime brought them to fruition. The army rebelled and forced him to arrange the marriage for which Cynnane had given her life (Polyaen. 8.60; Arr. FGrH 156, F 9.23).[49] If Cynnane had desired a safe and long life, then her Asian expedition was "ill-advised,"[50] but it is unlikely that this was her goal. She seems knowingly to have embraced the dangers of her policy.

In the period from the death of Alexander to that of Antipater, an immediate interest in marriage alliances manifested itself. Antipater initiated the pattern, very soon after Alexander's death, by attempting to arrange a series of marriages between his many daughters and various of Alexander's generals.[51] Some marriage alliances developed as a response to the network of marriage alliances Antipater attempted to create; these seem to be part of the general tendency for women from both branches of the royal family to oppose Antipater and be opposed by him (see below; also see CYNNANE; CLEOPATRA 2; ADEA EURYDICE). Others were intended to combat the ambitions of the rival branch of the royal family. The general response of the Macedonian elite to the crisis and insecurity created by Alexander's death was to pursue new security through new and often conflicting ties of marriage.

The city of Sardis in Asia Minor, where the regent and most of the Macedonian army were located, became the focus for this war of weddings. The brisk marriage market at Sardis would seem funny, were it not that many of its consequences were tragic. Since Cleopatra and Antipater's daughter, Nicaea, arrived in Sardis about the same time (Diod. 18.23.1–3), Antipater must have sent Nicaea to marry Perdiccas about the same time that Olympias dispatched Cleopatra for the same end (Arr. FGrH 156, F 9.21). Fearing to offend Antipater before his position was stronger, Perdiccas married Nicaea, as he had promised, but kept Cleopatra on a secret string (Diod. 18.23.3, 5.3; Just. 13.6.4–8). Shortly after the arrival of Perdiccas' rival brides, Cynnane and her daughter, Adea, appeared, also with marriage in mind—but marriage to Philip Arrhidaeus, the girl's half uncle, who was now co-king with Roxane's child. As we have seen, Cynnane's end run around Antipater and the rest of the elite proved at once fatal and successful: Cynnane died, but the army, mutinous at the murder of the daughter of Philip and sister of Alexander, forced the marriage of Adea (who now took the name of Philip's mother, Eurydice) to the mentally limited king (Polyaen. 8.69; Arr. *FGrH* 156, F 9.23).

ADEA EURYDICE

Adea Eurydice (initially simply Adea) was the daughter of Cynnane, Philip II's daughter by the Illyrian princess Audata (see CYNNANE; AUDATA), and Amyntas,[52] son of Perdiccas III, the elder brother of Philip II. Philip II arranged the marriage of Cynnane and Amyntas toward the end of his reign. Their only daughter was probably born between 338 and 335 (Polyaen. 8.60; Arr. *FGrH* 156, F 9.22).[53]

Adea Eurydice was doubly an Argead, uniting the lines of Philip II and Perdiccas III. It is possible that Adea Eurydice's father was briefly king as an infant (Just. 7.5.9–10).[54] After the death of Philip II, Amyntas seems to have made an attempt to take the throne and Alexander had him killed (Curt. 6.9.17,10.24; Plut. *Mor.* 327c; Arr. *FGrH* 156, F 9.22).

As we have seen, the part-Illyrian Cynnane trained her daughter in the military arts (Polyaen. 8.60; Duris ap. *Ath.* 560 f.). Cynnane raised an army and reached Asia and the Macedonian army there. Her intention was to force the marriage of her daughter to Arrhidaeus (hereafter called Philip Arrhidaeus).[55] The murder of Cynnane ensured the success of her plan. The troops rebelled and forced her murderers to allow the marriage of the two Argeads (Arr. *FGrH* 156, F 9.22–23).

Adea (who now took the name Eurydice)[56] was catapulted at an early age into the center of the struggle for power that followed the death of Alexander, and at that very moment she was deprived of her mother and mentor. Adea Eurydice proved to be as daring and bold as her mother. Taking up where her mother had left off, she began to try to woo the now extremely unpredictable Macedonian army away from the various generals in charge. Apparently, she viewed the confusion after the murder of Perdiccas as her own opportunity to assert her authority against the king's new and possibly temporary guardians.[57]

The three surviving sources give very different views of the events that followed and of Adea Eurydice's role in them. These differences are too often glossed over.[58] According to Diodorus (18.39.1–4), after the army and the kings and their *epimeletai* (managers/regents/guardians), Peithon and Arrhidaeus, arrived at Triparadeisus, Adea Eurydice began to interfere and oppose their plans. The *epimeletai* summoned an assembly. When they saw that the Macedonians were paying increasing attention to her commands, they resigned.[59] The Macedonians then chose Antipater as *epimeletes autokrator* (supreme manager). When Antipater arrived a few days later, he found Adea Eurydice trying to create discord and to alienate the Macedonians from him. There was great upset in the army. An assembly was called, and Antipater, after speaking to the crowd, halted the tumult and somehow frightened Adea Eurydice into silence.

Arrian's narrative (*FGrH* 156, F 9.30–33) offers quite a different picture of the situation. Adea Eurydice did not permit the temporary regents (Peithon and Arrhidaeus) to do anything without her approval, and at first they did not speak against her. Later they opposed her participation in any public action on the grounds that this was their area of concern until the arrival of Antigonus and Antipater. When these two arrived, sovereignty was given to Antipater. The army asked Antipater for back pay, but he answered that he could not pay them immediately. Adea Eurydice was aware of the army's anger against Antipater and used it to begin unrest. She spoke in assembly against him, supported by her secretary, Asclepiodorus, and also by Attalus,[60] and Antipater scarcely escaped slaughter. Responding to Antipater's call for assistance, Antigonus and Seleucus spoke in opposition to the crowd and thus put themselves in danger. After Antipater escaped death, he went to his own camp, summoned his officers, and, with difficulty, was able to halt further upset and take over rule.

Polyaenus' version (4.6.4) of these events differs markedly from the other two because it omits all mention of Adea Eurydice. Instead, it focuses on Antigonus, who risks his own life to save Antipater and is treated with respect by the army.

The accounts of Arrian and Diodorus dealing with these events are somewhat confusing, and the events themselves must have been chaotic. Adea Eurydice apparently attempted to gain control of the army and nearly did. To do so, she was quite willing to bring about the deaths of several generals, including Antipater. Although Diodorus does not say, surely the only thing that would have frightened Adea Eurydice into submitting to Antipater was a death threat. Diodorus' account is much more flattering to Antipater than the other two accounts, which emphasize the role of other generals and make the degree of danger to all the leaders much clearer.

This near-toppling of a leader with as much authority as Antipater possessed was a remarkable beginning for a girl probably still in her teens. Like her mother, Adea Eurydice tended to pursue power through the army. Her popularity (as well as her mother's) with the army seems comparable to that of Philip Arrhidaeus; the army was more loyal to the Argead dynasty, including women, than to the elite. Its loyalty had limits, however, or Antipater could not have suppressed Adea Eurydice, much as he did Cleopatra.

From the start, the sources say, Adea Eurydice, rather than her husband, initiated action and policy. Adea Eurydice's marriage put her in a unique situation. Philip Arrhidaeus seems to have been treated as a permanent minor. Although her position might seem more advantageous than that of a widowed royal mother because her "minor" would never reach adulthood and independence, in actuality Adea Eurydice was in a weaker position exactly because Arrhidaeus would never be able to stand alone. After all, the power and influence of a royal mother ultimately derived from the fact that her son sooner or later would become an independent ruler.

Adea Eurydice's marriage was unusual in another respect. She was an Argead, and she had married Philip Arrhidaeus because of her royal lineage. Her membership in the royal clan meant that if Adea Eurydice did not soon produce an heir, she was as vulnerable as Alexander's sisters to forced marriage or captivity at the hands of one of the Successors. Had she produced a son soon after her marriage, he would have been close in age to Alexander IV and thus a relatively viable contender for the throne, but the longer her marriage lasted without the birth of a child, especially a son, the more precarious her position became.[61]

The aged Antipater (see OLYMPIAS; CLEOPATRA 2; CYNNANE) had consistently opposed the power of Argead women. His death in 319 (of natural causes) was therefore an opportunity for Olympias and Adea Eurydice particularly, because none of the remaining Macedonian males had his unrivaled authority.

Adea Eurydice and her husband had returned to Macedonia with Antipater shortly before his death. Polyperchon now replaced Antipater as regent (Diod. 18.48.4). Alexander IV and his mother, Roxane, had come to Macedonia with Adea Eurydice and Philip Arrhidaeus. The return of the kings coupled with the death of Antipater seem to have precipitated a final confrontation between the two surviving branches of the royal family, a confrontation that became fatal for both.

Adea Eurydice's long-term policy would have been increasingly shaped by her failure to produce an heir at the same time Alexander IV was growing toward maturity. At some point during the period in which Olympias was contemplating Polyperchon's offer of a return to power (roughly 319–317; see OLYMPIAS), Adea Eurydice and her husband left the physical presence of Polyperchon and began to reside in Macedonia. Much as her mother had managed an end run around Antipater, Adea Eurydice could have engineered her and her husband's escape from Polyperchon, perhaps with the aid of some troops she had won over. Although this would suit what we know of her character, such a colorful episode, if it occurred, would most likely be mentioned by our sources. It is more probable that she somehow persuaded Polyperchon to let them go or even that he decided that they were expendable. His subsequent gullibility with Cassander in the matter of Heracles suggests that he might have been guilty of such stupidity.[62]

Once free of Polyperchon's control and back in Macedonia, Adea Eurydice apparently made overtures toward Cassander, enemy of Polyperchon and Olympias. Cassander seems to have made a brief expedition to Macedonia while Polyperchon was in the south,[63] and their relationship may have been established then.[64] Justin (14.5.1–2) says that Adea Eurydice's turn to Cassander was prompted by the knowledge that Polyperchon had asked Olympias to return to Macedonia, but Diodorus (19.11.1) may be closer to the truth when he says that Eurydice's subsequent moves were motivated by the knowledge that Olympias had not only received Polyperchon's offer but was actually preparing to return. However, Olympias, who had delayed her acceptance, may have been prompted to go forward by the news of Adea Eurydice's departure for Macedonia. Either way, the ambitious women's mutual fears may have prompted each to take action.

The formal nature of Adea Eurydice's relationship with Cassander is not clear. Diodorus (19.11.1) implies that she assumed the regency herself and simply asked Cassander for help while trying to win over prominent Macedonians. Justin (14.5.2–3) suggests that, writing in the name of her husband, she offered both the regency and the generalship to Cassander. It seems unlikely that Adea Eurydice had any authority either to assume the regency herself or to name someone else to it, and it is not certain that her husband had such a power; formalities were unlikely to be her concern, however.[65]

The political relationship between Adea Eurydice and Cassander is, if anything, less clear than the formal one. Diodorus says that she asked Cassander to help as soon as possible, in keeping with his statement that she believed that Olympias and company were about to arrive, but Cassander clearly did not return when asked, although the danger must have been obvious enough. He did not return until he knew the consequences of Olympias' invasion. Odder yet, Diodorus reports that when Olympias, Polyperchon, and Aeacides and their forces arrived at the Macedonian frontier, they found that Adea Eurydice and her husband had not waited for Cassander but had come out to meet them with an army. Justin reports that Cassander departed for a campaign in Greece and returned when he heard of trouble in Macedonia; this sequence of events makes more sense since Justin's narrative puts the alliance with Cassander earlier, when Olympias' return to Macedonia had simply been requested by Polyperchon but she had not yet decided to accept his offer.

The understanding between Cassander and Adea Eurydice does not seem to have been a close alliance but rather one of convenience in which neither party trusted the other. Why else was Cassander so slow to return and Adea Eurydice so willing to encounter the enemy army without him? He may not have been terribly concerned with the survival of Adea Eurydice and her husband,[66] and she may have feared that she would be forced to marry him, just as her aunt Thessalonice was soon made to do.

When Olympias returned to Macedonia, her nephew Aeacides, king of Molossia, Molossian troops, Polyperchon, and some Macedonian troops came with her. Adea Eurydice, with her husband, met them at the borders with a Macedonian force. Duris (ap. Ath. 13.560 f.) says that Eurydice wore the armor of a Macedonian infantryman into battle. It is likely that she planned to fight, as her mother had. She may have had contempt for Polyperchon's and Aeacides' military skill. Her failure against them, after all, was political, not military. Despite Adea Eurydice's efforts to persuade and bribe them, the Macedonian army immediately went over to Olympias, because of her prestige as the wife of Philip and mother of Alexander. Philip Arrhidaeus and then Adea Eurydice were captured (Diod. 19.11.1–3; Just. 14.5.8–10).

Olympias first walled up the royal pair. Then Philip Arrhidaeus was executed and Adea Eurydice told to kill herself but given the choice of the noose, the sword, or hemlock (Diod. 19.11.5–7; Ael. *VH* 13.36). According to Diodorus, Adea Eurydice died a noble death, much resembling a scene from tragedy, calling down vengeance on her murderer.[67] The forced suicide of Adea Eurydice and the murder of her husband made Olympias unpopular with some but not all Macedonians (Diod. 19.11.5–9). Cassander did accept the role of avenger, however, and as he began to take over the rule of Macedonia, he was careful to bury Adea Eurydice, Philip Arrhidaeus, and Cynnane with royal splendor at Aegae (Diod. 19.52.5; Diyll. *FGrH* 73, F 1).[68]

Adea Eurydice and Olympias had few options and acted exactly as male Argeads had for generations, attempting to eliminate rival branches of the dynasty. Unwittingly, they set in motion the series of events that ultimately made the murder of young Alexander IV possible and left no other male Argeads available.

The double kingship of Philip Arrhidaeus and Alexander IV was a fiction that could never have lasted. Had Olympias and Adea Eurydice not, in effect, eliminated each other, one or several of the Successors would have done much the same.[69] Nevertheless, Adea Eurydice reacted to her circumstances with courage and considerable intelligence. If one can fault her, it would be for her failure to wait for Cassander and his troops, but even here there are many unknowns that may have limited her options, as I have tried to suggest. She may have feared and distrusted Cassander as much as she did Olympias and Polyperchon.

The overt militarism of Adea Eurydice and her mother worked no better in the long run than the more political maneuvering of Olympias and her daughter. In all periods of Macedonian history, the ability to command troops was critical, but this was especially so in the period of the Successors. Even Adea Eurydice, because she was a woman, could not maintain long-term control over a Macedonian army. As we have seen, in the end her popularity with Macedonian troops counted for less than the authority of the old general Antipater. Moreover, as the events at the time of Olympias's invasion suggest, Macedonians tended to see Olympias's branch of the Argead family as more legitimate than that of Adea Eurydice (Diod. 19.11.1, 5–7; Just. 14.5.8–10). Adea Eurydice's career is striking because of the degree to which she seems to have pursued goals and use means to achieve them identical to those of males in the Macedonian court but telling in that she failed to achieve those goals because she was a woman.

The murder of Perdiccas changed things for both Cleopatra and young Adea Eurydice. As we have seen, Adea Eurydice nearly succeeded in taking over the army in the insecure period after Perdiccas' death, but Antipater won out in the end. For Cleopatra, Perdiccas' death was a disaster from which she never recovered. She had lost her chance for independent action and spent many years in Sardis under the control of or at least in fear of Antigonus.

The death of another regent, Antipater, always the opponent of the ambitions of the women of the Argead house, brought renewed opportunities for these women, particularly because none of the guardians or regents after Antipater had his authority or his broad support. Polyperchon replaced Antipater as *epimeletes* of the king and *strategos autokrator* (supreme commander), and Antipater's son Cassander was second in authority (Diod. 18.48.4).[70]

Up to this point, Polyperchon had shown himself to be merely competent militarily in relatively subordinate positions. He would prove to be incompetent—unsuccessful in the field and often unable to command the loyalty of his troops. Although Polyperchon's persistent military failures were the immediate cause of the collapse of the dynasty, his political policies must also be addressed because they directly involved royal women.

Wheras Polyperchon's lack of military talent is undeniable, it is less certain that he was equally inept politically. Errington has argued that Polyperchon's political ineptitude equaled or surpassed his obvious failings as general, primarily because he believes that Polyperchon precipitated his own political undoing by reversing Antipater's policy both in Greece (by rejecting support for the oligarchies) and in Macedonia (by aligning himself with Olympias and therefore against the clan and following of Antipater).[71] Hammond has taken a more forgiving view: he assumes that Polyperchon was reacting to Cassander's machinations rather than precipitating them.[72] Diodorus' narrative (18.49.1–4, 18.54.1–57.4) supports Hammond. Judging by his subsequent career, Polyperchon's weakness in matters political had more to do with lack of resolve than with inability to intrigue or to build consensus.[73]

What was the nature of the new regent's offer to Olympias? Diodorus (18.49.4) first says that Polyperchon offered her the *epimeleia* (care or custody) of her grandson Alexander IV and *basilike prostasia* (royal superin-

WOMEN AND MONARCHY IN MACEDONIA

tendence) if she returned to Macedonia. Since Olympias did not accept his offer at once, Polyperchon asked again, after his reversal of Macedonian policy in Greece; on this second occasion she was simply requested to return to Macedonia to take up the *epimeleia* of her grandson until he came of age (18.57.2). Diodorus refers to the position offered Olympias by Polyperchon on a third occasion (18.65.1), in reference to Olympias's demand that Nicanor, the garrison commander of Munychia who was loyal to Cassander, restore it to the Athenians: Nicanor had heard that Polyperchon and the kings were about to return Olympias to Macedonia and grant her the *epimeleia* of Alexander IV and her former *apodoche* (favor) and *time* (honor).[74]

The meaning of Polyperchon's offers is uncertain. Something about the offer involved *basileia,* or rule. Diodorus says that Polyperchon invaded Macedonia to restore Olympias and Alexander IV to *basileia* (19.11.2) and that Adea Eurydice had claimed that *basileia* belonged to her rather than to Olympias (19.11.5). We can agree that *epimeleia* meant something like commission or charge over someone or something and that *prostasia* signified leadership or perhaps protection and that both terms are often used by ancient authors to refer to the powers of those who stood in the place of the king, but it is not clear that either term refers to a specific office or to clearly defined powers.[75]

It seems best to conclude that *prostasia* was a general term like *hegemonia* (command) or *arche* (rule or command). Why else was there the need to add the qualifying adjective *basilike* (royal), as Diodorus does? In offering *prostasia* to Olympias, Polyperchon was offering undefined power and position, as much as she could get and as little as he would allow. Olympias' claim to legitimacy derived from who she was, not from any title. It was, after all, because of who she was that Polyperchon had made his offer. Despite the vagueness of Polyperchon's offer, any reckoning would seem to mean that Olympias was offered greater power and prestige than any royal woman before her.

Nonetheless, Olympias rejected whatever combination of powers, hoped for and real, Polyperchon was promising for some time. On Eumenes' advice, she initially temporized but in the end did not follow his policy of caution. In early fall 317 she returned to Macedonia, in the company of her nephew Aeacides, now king of Molossia, and his army, Polyperchon and his forces, and her grandson and daughter-in-law Roxane (Diod. 19.11.2).[76] Polyperchon's deteriorating situation may have contributed to her decision, but it is likely that Olympias' reversal of policy had more to do with Adea Eurydice.

The structure of the alliance Olympias joined is as unclear as that of Adea Eurydice.[77] In Diodorus's account the army is led by Aeacides and Polyperchon, but its purpose is to restore Olympias with her grandson to *basileia*. In Justin (14.5.8), there is absolutely no mention of Polyperchon, only Aeacides, and Olympias, not her nephew, is clearly in charge. Duris (ap. Ath. 560 f.) also seems to portray Olympias as the one in charge. Diodorus (19.11.2) says that when the two armies, one Macedonian and the other partially Macedonian, encountered each other, Adea Eurydice and Philip Arrhidaeus's army changed sides, impressed by the *axioma* of Olympias and their memories of the benefits of her son's rule. Justin's (14.5.10) account stresses the memory of her husband as the decisive factor. All the sources make Olympias's reputation the crucial factor in the army's about-face, and none mentions her legal position or Adea Eurydice's.

Then, as so often happened after a round in the wars of the Successors, the victors eliminated the leaders of the defeated party. Justin (14.5.10) simply records matter-of-factly that Olympias ordered the death of Adea Eurydice and Philip Arrhidaeus (14.5.10). Trouble, he says (14.6.1), came because of the *caedes* (slaughter) she also arranged, in a manner *muliebri magis quam regio* (more feminine than royal), a reference, apparently, to the deaths of supporters of Cassander mentioned in Diodorus. This, claims Justin, turned *favor* (approval) into *odium* (hatred).

Diodorus's (19.11.3–9) account of events after Olympias' bloodless victory is much more dramatic and should be read with caution. He describes ill treatment of the royal couple that began to turn public opinion against Olympias. Olympias then ordered the king stabbed to death by Thracians and offered Adea Eurydice a choice of suicide methods (c.f. Ael. *VH* 13.36). Diodorus includes a playlike and very implausible death scene for Adea Eurydice and stresses the idea that Olympias's elimination of Adea Eurydice meant that she deserved her own equally unpleasant death. Diodorus believed that the distinction between husband and wife in manner of death was intended to indicate that Olympias was more vengeful to Adea Eurydice because she claimed that the *basileia* belonged to her, not Olympias.[78] He then adds much more specific detail about the "caedes" of Justin. Olympias killed Cassander's brother Nicanor and overturned the tomb of his brother Iolaus (who she believed poisoned Alexander), claiming that she did so in vengeance for her son's death. She also had one hundred important Macedonian supporters of Cassander. Diodorus concludes this section with the doubtless apocryphal deathbed warning of Antipater against the rule of women.

Seen in practical terms, what had been virtually inevitable from June 323 had finally happened: one of the two Argead factions had eliminated the other. Our sources are poor, but it is likely that Olympias simply had the royal pair killed and did not bother with a "trial." Considerations like those that led Alexander to prefer murder to a trial for Parmenio are likely to have led to her decision: she was not certain how the assembly would react. Adea Eurydice had already demonstrated considerable skill as an orator, and Olympias probably preferred not to chance giving her another opportunity.[79]

The elimination of Adea Eurydice and Philip Arrhidaeus does not seem to have significant long-term consequences, although modern historians have often considered these "atrocities" of Olympias decisive in her own destruction and the end of the dynasty. Such a judgment cannot be supported by the sources. Let us begin by eliminating the moralistic aspect of modern treatments of these events. Although Olympias' brutal treatment of Cassander's followers doubtless cost her some support among neutral Macedonians, had her military efforts been successful, it might also have spared her further resistance to her rule in Macedonia. Certainly there was nothing unique about Olympias' slaughter of some one hundred of Cassander's supporters; his own forces were responsible for a similar slaughter of five hundred soon after (Diod. 19.63.2), and this was but one of many mass murders.[80]

The deaths ordered by Olympias all happened in early fall 317. Events and chronology become much less clear after this. According to Diodorus (19.35.1), Cassander immediately gave up his siege of Tegea and headed north. He was able to circumvent the Aetolian (allies of Olympias and Polyperchon) blockade of Thermopylae by using sea transport.

What happened next is quite puzzling, even allowing for Polyperchon's talent for failure. It is difficult to understand what Olympias, Polyperchon, and the rest planned to do, given that they must have known Cassander would return as soon as he heard what had happened. Obviously, whatever they planned failed, but it is hard to discern any plan, however unsuccessful.

Polyperchon seems to have taken a relatively peripheral role from the first, even though he had initiated this whole series of events. Troops sent by Olympias to prevent the passage of Cassander's forces into Macedonia via various passes failed to achieve their goal. Olympias' men got to the passes after Cassander's troops had already taken possession of them (Diod. 19.35.3). The faithful Aeacides, prevented from aiding Olympias by another force sent by Cassander to prevent passage, then experienced a rebellion and was deposed in favor of an alliance with Cassander (19.36.2–4). Cassander approached Olympias with his main force, and she, accompanied by a large noncombatant court, was besieged over the winter of 317–316 and into the spring.[81] Before she retreated to this stronghold, however, Diodorus (19.35.4) says that she appointed Aristonous her *strategos* and ordered him to carry on the war. The officer Cassander dispatched to deal with Polyperchon and his army in Perrhaebeia managed to bribe away most of Polyperchon's troops (Diod. 19.36.6).

One can attribute much of Cassander's success to his own competence and acumen and to the lack of same in his opponents, but what happened remains confusing. Cassander's enemies may have counted on his being unable to reach Macedonia with force before the spring, and their ineptitude may derive in part from surprise. Even if this were the case, Polyperchon's position on the sidelines and the paradoxical situation of Olympias (on the one hand, she seems not to have expected to be personally involved in military activity—e.g., her female court—and on the other, she, a woman with no known military experience or training, was dispatching troops)[82] remain unexplained, as do other questions. Why is Aristonous *strategos*? Does that mean Polyperchon no longer held that position? Given Diodorus' account of Olympias' orders, why do we find Aristonous in Amphipolis instead of defending Olympias?

And, finally, once Olympias was surrounded and knew of her danger, why did she stay on at Pydna when she was able to escape by sea for some time after the siege began (Diod. 19.35.6)? Diodorus says that she was waiting for help by sea from many Greeks and Macedonians, but which ones? She may not have yet known of Aeacides' failures (they may not yet have happened), and Polyperchon's final loss of face (Diodorus characterizes his assistance as Olympias' last hope) came somewhat later (19.36.6). Yet Olympias seems to have persisted even past these events. It may be significant that even when she surrendered, Aristonous wanted to hold on because, according to Diodorus (19.50.8), he had a recent victory against Cassander's forces and did not yet know of Eumenes' death.

The explanation not only for Olympias's persistence (as well as that of Aristonous) but also for the apparent lack of clear chain of command in the forces opposing Cassander may have something to do with Eumenes. Both Polyperchon and Olympias had asked Eumenes to come to Macedonia to aid them and Alexander IV (Diod. 18.57.3; Nep. *Eum.* 6.4). By the time matters had grown so grave in Macedonia, they had grown equally so for Eumenes,[83] but neither Olympias nor Aristonous, both under siege, may have known. They may have hoped that Eumenes, so much more competent and trustworthy[84] than Polyperchon, would somehow remove himself from his Asian affairs and come to their rescue, or at the very least send help.[85]

By the time she surrendered, Olympias must have known she had little hope of survival, despite Cassander's supposed promises of personal safety (Diod. 19.50.5). Although he simply arranged the murder of Aristonous (Diod. 19.51.1) and Monimus, Olympias' other loyal commander,[86] Cassander, perhaps after an abortive attempt to eliminate Olympias by deception, apparently tried to legitimize his inevitable killing of Olympias by means of a trial.[87] The assembly, almost certainly made up of the men who had just conducted the siege for Cassander, not surprisingly condemned Olympias to death (Diod. 19.51.2) but then proved surprisingly unwilling to kill her. Cassander had forbidden her to appear in front of the assembly to defend herself. Diodorus (19.51.3–4) says that Cassander prevented her appearance[88] because he feared that the Macedonians might change their minds because of Olympias' *axioma*.

As the assembly refused to carry out its own sentence, Cassander turned to two hundred chosen soldiers, but they also refused to kill Olympias because of her *axioma*. In the end he had the relatives of those of his supporters whom Olympias had murdered kill her (Diod. 19.51.5). Curiously, the same relatives had to be persuaded by Cassander to lodge the charges against Olympias in the assembly (Diod. 19.51.1; Just. 14.6.6), and Diodorus (19.51.5) notes that they agreed to kill her not only for vengeance but also to win Cassander's favor. The details of the "trial" suggest that, even at this late date, Olympias was far from universally condemned.[89]

Cassander had reason to attempt (an attempt he then may have aborted) a public trial, although Olympias, in a similar situation, had preferred murder to the uncertainty of the assembly's verdict. The reason for the divergence in their behavior in similar circumstances has little to do with who was more brutal or more law-abiding but much to do with self-interest. Whereas Olympias had much to lose and little to gain from a public trial whose verdict was uncertain, Cassander had more to lose if he failed to involve the assembly in a public condemnation of Olympias and relatively little to risk as long as he was able to prevent her from appearing or speaking.

Why did Olympias and her supporters lose? The answer should be obvious from Diodorus' narrative. She did not lose because she killed Adea Eurydice and Philip Arrhidaeus or Cassander's supporters but quite simply because she was defeated by Cassander's forces. Diodorus's account of the gradual decline of her support in Greece and Macedonia attributes it neither to the popularity of Cassander nor to dislike of Olympias. His narrative consistently attributes the process to Cassander's military success (and his clever manipulation of that success). Diodorus reports that, as it became increasingly evident that Cassander would win, people feared being on the losing side. Diodorus frequently notes that they changed sides reluctantly, something confirmed, at least for the Macedonians, by the difficulty Cassander had in getting her killed and by Diodorus' references to her *axioma*.[90]

Cassander consistently demonstrated himself to be a competent commander who also had competent underlings who followed him loyally,[91] and Polyperchon equally consistently proved himself the opposite. (Aeacides was loyal but unable to offer meaningful assistance.) Winning in the agonistic cultures of Greece and Macedonia had always had something of a moral force, but in the chaotic times after Alexander's death, military victory determined all and little else mattered. Olympias' forces lost and Cassander's won and that is the end of the matter; events in Macedonia in the late fourth century in no sense resembled a morality play.

Whatever slender chance there had been for the survival of the Argead house died with Olympias and Eumenes. As soon as Cassander

WOMEN AND MONARCHY IN MACEDONIA

had eliminated the problem of Olympias, he married Thessalonice, a daughter of Philip's (see Thessalonice), founded a city named after himself, secluded young Alexander IV and his mother under guard at Amphipolis, and buried Adea Eurydice, Philip Arrhidaeus, and Cynnane according to royal custom (Diod. 19.52.1–5; Just. 14.6.13).

Diodorus claims that Cassander had begun to hope for the *basileia* of the Macedonians (Diod. 19.52.1) and that he had already decided to kill Alexander IV and Roxane in order that there would be no successor to the *basileia*. But he wanted to test popular opinion before he proceeded. So, for the time being, says Diodorus (19.52.4), Cassander treated the youth like a private citizen. Diodorus (19.52.5) explains Cassander's actions during this transitional period on the grounds that he was already conducting himself in a royal manner. One can only speculate about Cassander's long-term plans for murder, but Alexander IV's isolation at Amphipolis seems sinister. It is difficult to ascribe Diodorus's judgment on Cassander's ultimate intentions to pro-Antigonid propaganda.[92] There is nothing implausible in Diodorus's view given that Cassander murdered the youth in the end and had his half brother killed as well. Certainly Cassander had constructed a situation that would make it increasingly easy for him to remove the young Argead and take the throne: Diodorus (19.52.1) rightly puts Cassander's marriage to Thessalonice in terms of his desire to be related to the old ruling house. It gave him more claim to legitimacy than his dubious and uncertain appointment by Adea Eurydice.

Alexander IV lived on in what were probably grim circumstances until sometime after the conclusion of a treaty making very temporary peace among the rival generals Ptolemy, Cassander, Lysimachus, and Antigonus (Diod. 19.105.1). According to the terms of the treaty, which recognized Cassander as *strategos* of Europe, he and probably the other three would retain their positions until Alexander's son came of age. The wording of this treaty has been seen as precipitating the murder of the young king, but his entry into adolescence and the imminence of adulthood would surely have had the same effect.

The exact date of the murder, which all sources indicate was concealed for some time, is uncertain.[93] Diodorus (19.105.2) says that Cassander, seeing that Alexander IV was nearing adulthood and that there was talk in Macedonia about giving him his ancestral kingdom, sent orders that the head of the guard kill Roxane and her son and conceal the bodies (see ROXANE: PART 2). Diodorus (19.105.2–4) observes that this double murder relieved the other Successors of their fear that they would have to yield the areas they controlled, areas that were becoming, in effect, their kingdoms (see also Just. 15.2.5; Paus. 9.7.2).[94]

ROXANE: PART 2

Roxane was with her husband, Alexander, at the time of his death in Babylon in June 323. She was either six months (Curt. 10.6.9) or eight months (Just. 13.2.5) pregnant. Many Macedonian aristocrats wanted no real successor to Alexander; ordinary Macedonian soldiers preferred Philip's other son, Arrhidaeus. Nearchus' attempt to champion Heracles, Alexander's son by Barsine, Nearchus' mother-in-law, met with no support. Perdiccas, now recognized as regent, persuaded all parties to await the birth of Roxane's child and, if it proved a boy, to recognize the infant as king as well. Roxane's child was a son, Alexander IV. A bizarre double kingship, in which neither king was competent, was now created.[95]

Relatively little attention has been paid to Perdiccas' surprising commitment to Roxane's unborn child. It probably derived from the fact that it would be a long time before the child could assume real power,[96] but this alone is not an adequate explanation. He may also have been influenced by the fact that Alexander had married Roxane as well as by the convenient coincidence that Roxane was there and under his control whereas Barsine was far away. A story, told only in Plutarch (*Alex.* 77.4), may be suggestive. Plutarch reports that Roxane, with Perdiccas' connivance, arranged the secret murder of Stateira, daughter of Darius and Alexander's second wife, as well as that of Stateira's sister (see PARYSATIS). Plutarch offers extreme jealousy as Roxane's motivation for this double murder but does not expand on this comment. The daughter of the last ruler of the Persian Empire had greater prestige than Roxane. We do not know that Stateira was pregnant, but Roxane may have felt that it was not worth taking any chances. Further mention of this incident in other sources would be reassuring, particularly because it so resembles stereotypical portrayals of Persian royal women in Greek literary tradition.[97] Nevertheless, Plutarch's account is probably true (see STATEIRA 2; PARYSATIS). Perdiccas' participation, active or passive, speaks again to his intense involvement in assuring that Roxane's child was recognized as king. It would be useful to know more.

146 WOMEN AND MONARCHY IN MACEDONIA

From this point on, Roxane and her child were in the power of a succession of regents. After the elimination of Perdiccas, she passed into the control of Antipater, who brought her and her child to Macedonia (Diod. 18.39.7). After Antipater's death, the new regent, Polyperchon, invited Olympias, grandmother of Alexander IV, to return to Macedonia from her native Epirus and take charge of the child king (see OLYMPIAS). Polyperchon's offer speaks volumes about Roxane's powerlessness and insignificance in the period of the Successors. She was all but invisible to Greeks and Macedonians and could convey none of the prestige and power that Olympias or Adea Eurydice could.[98]

When Adea Eurydice (see ADEA EURYDICE) and Philip Arrhidaeus went over to Cassander (Just. 14.5.1–4), Olympias, working in concert with Polyperchon, defeated Adea Eurydice and her husband and forced their deaths. Alexander IV was now sole ruler, if in name only (Diod. 19.11.2; Just. 14.5.8–10).

Cassander soon returned to Macedonia. Olympias, along with a large retinue, including Roxane and Alexander IV, retired to Pydna to withstand a siege (Diod. 19.35.5). During this period of Olympias' brief dominance, a betrothal or perhaps even a marriage between two royal children, Alexander IV and young Deidameia, daughter of Aeacides, was apparently arranged (Plut. *Pyrrh.* 4.2; see OLYMPIAS). Olympias, finally compelled to surrender by Cassander, was soon killed and Roxane and her son now passed into the hands of yet another regent, the most ruthless yet, Cassander (Diod. 19.50–51; Just. 15.6.13).

Diodorus asserts that after this victory in 316, Cassander now began to hope to take over rule, not just care, of the Macedonian kingdom. He decided to somehow remove Roxane and her son (19.52.1–4). But, given the uncertainty of Macedonian sentiment at the time, Cassander temporized by sending Roxane and young Alexander IV to the citadel of Amphipolis under a guard commanded by a trusted adherent of his, Glaucias. Cassander deprived the boy king of his royal pages[99] and any other sign of his royal status and ordered that he be treated like a private citizen, not like a king (Diod. 19.52.4–5).

Roxane and her son spent some quiet but not necessarily pleasant years at Amphipolis. Either the treaty of 311 that Cassander and some of the other Successors concluded (Diod. 19.105.1)[100] or, more likely, the near-adulthood of Alexander IV caused his murder. According to Diodorus (19.105.2–4),

Cassander, seeing that Alexander, now about fourteen, was growing up and that Macedonians were beginning to say that he should be released and allowed to rule his ancestral kingdom, ordered the trusty Glaucias to murder mother and son, conceal the bodies, and let no one know of the crime (Just. 15.2.5; Paus. 9.7.2). The date of the murders of Roxane and her son is uncertain, but they were probably killed in 310 (before Cassander's murders of Barsine and her son by Alexander).[101] Only later did the murders become known, and later yet outside Macedonia.[102]

Roxane's career was pathetic. Throughout her adult life she was in the power of a Macedonian male, often one indifferent or even hostile to her welfare and that of her son. Her father, having benefited from her marriage, continued his career more or less unaffected by the struggles of the Successors while his daughter lived on, apparently unconnected to her family, in the alien West.[103] Roxane may have murdered Stateira and her sister, although, if this is the case, it is the sole aggressive act of an otherwise passive life.

The murder of Alexander IV (ca. 311–309) made the nearly forgotten Heracles, Barsine's son, suddenly important (see BARSINE: PART 2). The candidacy of Heracles for kingship and his murder (ca. late 309), along with that of his mother, came about because of the revived ambitions of Polyperchon. He had spent the years since his disastrously unsuccessful attempt to gain control of Macedonia through Olympias and Alexander IV in obscurity in the Peloponnesus. He now decided to make another try for major political power by using Heracles to oust Cassander as the ruler of Macedonia. Polyperchon's new efforts to regain power were surprisingly successful at first. He made an alliance for aid with the Aetolians, gathered support among Macedonian enemies of Cassander and those still committed to the idea of an Argead king, and put together a large army and a considerable war chest. He marched to the borders of Macedonia where he met Cassander and his army. The support for Heracles was considerable, and Cassander could have been in serious trouble, as Diodorus' narrative (20.20.2–4, 28.1) makes clear.[104]

At this critical moment Cassander demonstrated the savvy that had helped him, along with considerable military skill, not only to gain control over the kingdom but also to maintain it during this very unstable period. He seems to have had considerable insight into Polyperchon's

WOMEN AND MONARCHY IN MACEDONIA

character. Cassander now suggested that Polyperchon change sides, support him, and gain some sort of overlordship in the Peloponnesus by abandoning Heracles. On the brink of victory, Polyperchon once more revealed the incompetence and stupidity that characterized his conduct during most of his career (perhaps failure of nerve had something to do with his decision as well). Unbelievably, Cassander successfully persuaded him to kill Heracles and Barsine, and Polyperchon sank back into deserved obscurity.

The fate of Roxane, like that of Barsine, demonstrates how complete was Graeco-Macedonian contempt for Asian culture. Other royal women might take advantage of the uncertainties of the period to pursue their own goals, but such options were never open to Roxane or Barsine.

BARSINE: PART 2

By the time of Alexander's death in 323, Barsine and her son were settled in Pergamum, perhaps on a family estate.[105] There they probably remained until their fatal summons to Macedonia by Polyperchon in 309.[106]

After the death of Alexander left the monarchy vacant, Perdiccas and most of the Macedonian aristocracy preferred solutions involving either a committee of its members or a regency for Roxane's not-yet-born son. Nearchus, however, who had married Barsine's daughter at Susa (Arr. 7.4.6), put forward Barsine's son Heracles as his father's successor (Curt. 10.6.10–12). His suggestion was rejected both by the aristocracy and by the ordinary troops, who would at first accept neither of Alexander's sons by Asian women and would ultimately force the officers to accept the mentally limited but non-Asian Arrhidaeus as co-king with Roxane's son.[107]

By 309 Heracles was nearing adulthood. His obscurity might seem surprising, given the scarcity of male Argeads, but his lengthy and quiet sojourn in Pergamum makes sense. The army had already demonstrated its disapproval of Heracles. The Successors were interested in the surviving members of the family of Alexander and Philip only to the degree that any of them might serve their self-interest.[108] Why champion another man's son when it was increasingly apparent that one's own sons might become kings?[109] Any Macedonian aristocrats still genuinely loyal to Alexander would surely prefer his legitimate son.

Everything changed when Cassander murdered the now-maturing

Alexander IV and his mother, Roxane (Diod. 19.105.2–4). Heracles was now the only male Argead left[110] and therefore a serious candidate for the throne. Diodorus' narrative makes it clear that the Macedonians were now interested in this son of Alexander's and that Cassander feared their interest.[111] Polyperchon asked Heracles (and probably his mother) to come to him (Diod. 20.20.1–2). Cassander's army showed signs of going over to Polyperchon and Heracles because of continuing loyalty to the Argeads, but Polyperchon, at Cassander's urging, killed both Heracles and Barsine (Diod. 20.28.2–4).

The evidence tells us nothing of the character of Barsine. We know of no action that may reasonably be assumed to be her own doing other than her return with her son to Macedonia. A lifetime in the courts of Asia and Macedonia cannot have left her unacquainted with the dangers inherent in a return to Macedonia. Perhaps her son, at seventeen more or less an adult, persuaded her to take the risk with him and she loyally followed him, as she had her father, her husbands, and her lover. Perhaps Barsine, the child of two able, ambitious, and daring families, embraced danger in pursuit of power and glory when finally given a chance to make a decision. Whether a pawn in the deadly political games of Macedonia and Asia or a would-be player come late to the table, Barsine, as well as her son, died because none of the Successors wanted to perpetuate Argead rule and because she and her son were neither Eastern nor Western, neither legitimate nor entirely excluded from possible succession.

Cassander's motivation for the murder of Alexander's two sons and their mothers should be connected to the increasing age of the two young men. Diodorus' narrative makes it clear that considerable feeling for retaining an Argead on the throne remained (19.105.2; 20.20.2–4, 28.1). Various versions of the specifics of the murders of the youths survive, but all accounts describe them as secret murders, not public executions. According to Diodorus, Cassander saw Heracles as a serious threat, a threat he was able to eliminate only because Polyperchon's gullibility led him to murder the very young man whom he had introduced to Macedonia in order to return himself to power.

The Successors, whatever their more specific ambitions, wanted no genuine continuity with the Argead past, although they found false or artificial ones occasionally useful. As infants and boys, the sons of Alexander had some utility as pawns, but once they neared manhood, their murders or at least attempted murders were inevitable.

The female Argead line fared little better. We shall turn to Thessalonice's fate in the next chapter, but Cleopatra, Alexander's full sister, was murdered at the command of Antigonus, probably soon after the death of Heracles. The precipitant, as we have seen, was almost certainly the deaths of her nephews. Her murder, like that of her nephews, involved a cover-up (Diod. 20.37.3–6).

What did her murder mean? Diodorus (20.37.4) says that all the Successors wanted to marry Cleopatra in order to gain rule over the whole Macedonian empire. When one considers that Cleopatra spent many years (ca. 320–308) under the control of the general most often credited with a desire to acquire control of her brother's entire empire and that neither he nor his son married her, the conclusion is obvious. For the Successors, with the exception of Cassander's unique situation, Argeads were unnecessary. Royal women, brought into prominence by the scarcity of males in the royal house, briefly took or tried to take positions of power in the transitional period after the death of Alexander the Great, primarily by functioning as vehicles of legitimacy. They were unable to sustain their power, partly because it was not in the interests of the other Successors for them to do so but primarily because they lacked the military might and success to do so.

Olympias and Cynnane and their daughters demonstrated that they shared with male Macedonians virtually identical standards for behavior, including a willingness to commit brutal and violent acts (see chap. 1). Their failure to *achieve* dynastic dominance, rather than their struggle to *establish* it, caused the end of the dynasty. Little distinguished their aims from those of Philip II in the early years of his reign when he defeated a series of Argead contenders, including some of his half brothers. The difference lies in their success. Both Philip's actions and those of Olympias and Adea Eurydice could be characterized as "divisive" and "destructive" of the unity of the royal house, but no one thinks of Philip II in those terms because *he* won and ended the division by his victory.

This dynasty came to an end not because its last adult members, all women, acted divisively—the history of the dynasty was one of violent divisiveness—but because the women were unable, either by themselves or through male representatives, to defeat the rival generals militarily. They lost, and the generals won. Having won despite rather long-lasting sentiment for retaining the Argead dynasty on the throne, each general, after a suitable discreet interval, was able to claim *basileia* for himself and to take the title *basileus*.

CHAPTER SIX

Royal Women in Transition: The Antipatrids and the Descent to Chaos (316–277)

Although Alexander the Great's sons survived a few years longer (see chap. 5), the end of the Argead dynasty came with Cassander's defeat and the execution of Olympias in spring 316. From that moment on, Cassander, son of Antipater, ruled Macedonia, although he did not use a royal title for many years.

At first the transition to a new ruling dynasty seemed to be smooth, but Antipatrid power rapidly and spectacularly disintegrated within a few years of Cassander's death as the line of Antipater self-destructed. As a consequence, whereas the other two great monarchies of the Hellenistic period had well-established and stable dynasties by the beginning of the third century, Macedonia itself, the old homeland, endured another generation of confusion and near-collapse before Antigonus Gonatas stabilized the kingdom ca. 277 and put the Antigonids on the throne, a position his family would retain until centuries later when the Roman conquest abolished Macedonian monarchy.

This transitional period is poorly documented, particularly after the departure of the last of Cassander's sons (Antipater, named after his famous paternal grandfather), ca. 294. Demetrius Poliorcetes killed one of Cassander's sons and drove the other into exile, but Demetrius himself reigned as king only briefly before he was humiliated and forced out of the kingdom in about 288. Pyrrhus (king of Molossia and son of Olympias' cousin Aeacides) and Lysimachus (another of Alexander's old generals) split the kingdom after Poliorcetes' humiliation, but neither was based in Macedonia, each seeing his Macedonian territory as part of a larger empire. Lysimachus ultimately forced Pyrrhus out of Macedonia, but first his own family began a murderous internal struggle and then he was defeated and killed in battle in 281 by another of Alexander's now-elderly generals, Seleucus. Seleucus did not live to rule his old homeland, however; soon after his victory against Lysimachus, he was murdered by his supposed ally, Ptolemy Ceraunus, disinherited son of Ptolemy, king of Egypt.

Ceraunus's murder of Seleucus set the stage for the real nadir of the troubles of the kingdom. Ceraunus was able to establish some kind of control over areas of Lysimachus' former kingdom, including at least part of Macedonia, although he had various rivals to contend with. However, he was killed in battle against marauding Celtic tribes (probably in summer 280), and then about three years passed during which there was either no king at all or only ephemeral ones. Only then (ca. 277) was Antigonus Gonatas able, gradually, to retrieve Macedonia from complete chaos.[1]

The role of royal women during this period of increasing disorder was somewhat more limited than that of their counterparts at the very end of the Argead dynasty, but it is clear that they continued to play a part in the political strife of the day and to be prominent in the public presentation of monarchy. The dynastic insecurity of Macedonia in this era was more or less a guarantee for the continuing importance of royal women: where possible, they would function as symbols of continuity; where innovation was undeniable, they helped to generate legitimacy for families not previously royal. This role for royal women would change with the coming of Antigonus Gonatas, but this painful transitional period was the last one in Macedonian history in which royal women were an important aspect of Macedonian monarchy.[2]

For practical purposes, Cassander began a new royal dynasty in 316, although he did not murder Alexander IV for another six or seven years (concealing it for some additional period), did not arrange the murder of Heracles for another year, and postponed taking a royal title until a later period than did the other Successors.[3] Diodorus (19.52.1) rightly concludes that the actions Cassander took as he gained power in Macedonia in 316 mean that from the start his intention was almost certainly kingship.[4] As Diodorus notes, Cassander's marriage to the Argead Thessalonice makes this clear.

Cassander apparently intended to build his new dynasty on the basis of his own considerable military and political competence, the memory of his father Antipater's long administration of the country, and his Argead marriage, a marriage that produced three sons, half Antipatrid, half Argead. Cassander's policies demonstrate that he did virtually everything one might reasonably expect that the founder of a new dynasty might do to build respect and acceptance for his family's rule and yet maintain continuity with the past. With caution and political savvy, he built what certainly appeared to a solid base for his new dynasty. This task was accomplished with the help of a number of able assistants, some family members and some not.[5] His wife, Thessalonice, was a particularly important part, if only in a formal way, of the dynastic base he so carefully constructed.

THESSALONICE

Thessalonice, a daughter of Philip II by Nicesipolis of Pherae (Ath. 11.784c, 13.557c), became the wife of the first non-Argead ruler of Macedonia, Cassander. Her mother may have been a relative of Jason of Pherae and was certainly wellborn (Steph. Byz. s.v. "Thessalonice"), despite assertions to the contrary. Nicesipolis died about three weeks after her daughter's birth (Steph. Byz. s.v. "Thessalonice"; see NICESIPOLIS) and so did not play any significant role in public life.

Although there is general agreement that Thessalonice was named in commemoration of a Thessalian victory of Philip's (Steph. Byz. s.v. "Thessalonice"), uncertainty remains about both the date of Philip's marriage to Nicesipolis and about the approximate date of his daughter's birth (see NICESIPOLIS and chap. 3).

A birthdate of 352/1 would make her a remarkably old spinster at the time of her marriage ca. 316.[6] That her father arranged no marriage for her but did so for his other two daughters strongly suggests that she was not old enough to marry during Philip's reign. That she produced three children, apparently in rapid succession, soon after her marriage also argues for a comparatively late date for her birth, given the rapid decline in fertility that women experience after thirty. Thessalonice is likely to have been born toward the end of the 340s.[7]

We know nothing of her life from the time of her birth until her appearance in Olympias's entourage, along with other royal female kin, at the siege of Pydna in 317/16 (Diod. 19.35.5). Olympias probably brought her up.[8] A passage in Plutarch (Mor. 141c) generally supposed to refer to Nicesipolis suggests friendly relations between Olympias and Nicesipolis. After the death of Nicesipolis, Olympias could only profit from the control of a second king's daughter in addition to her own daughter. It is difficult to imagine where else Thessalonice could have grown up than in the household of Olympias, unless possibly in that of her half sister, Cleopatra. Thessalonice most likely followed her stepmother to seclusion in Molossia and returned to Macedonia with her. After Olympias' defeat and death at the hands of Cassander, he immediately married Thessalonice (Just. 14.6.13; Diod. 19.52.1–2; Heidel. Epit. *FGrH* 155, F 2.4).

Thessalonice was remarkably old for an Argead bride. She was probably about thirty, but could have been as old as thirty-five. Although no sources offer an explanation for her prolonged spinsterhood, there were probably several contributing factors. Philip did not arrange a marriage for her because of her youth (her older sisters' marriages, after all, were arranged only at the very end of Philip's reign). Alexander, in keeping with his general marriage policy, chose not to make a marriage for her during his reign even though she had certainly reached marriageable age (see chap. 4).

Olympias proved no more interested in finding a husband for Thessalonice. In the period immediately after Alexander's death, when Olympias and Cleopatra seem to have acted in concert in matters related to her possible marriage plans, Olympias would not have wanted to compromise her daughter's prospects by allowing another daughter of Philip's to enter the competitive market for marriage alliances. Once Cleopatra either removed herself from the marriage market or was perhaps removed by Antigonus in about 320 (see CLEOPATRA 2: PART 3), Olympias may have feared to arrange a marriage for Thessalonice because it could have weakened her daughter's or her grandson's position.[9] We have no information about whether Thessalonice resented the postponement of her marriage. If she did, she may have blamed Olympias, but because Olympias was probably the only mother she had known, perhaps not.

Cassander's brutal elimination of Olympias meant that Thessalonice passed from the control of one powerful individual to that of another. We know nothing of her attitude toward Cassander and her marriage. Antigonus, Cassander's enemy, claimed that Cassander had forced the marriage (Diod. 19.61.2), and it is certainly possible, even likely, that Thessalonice, brought up in Olympias' court and a survivor of the rigors of Cassander's siege of Pydna, may have been a reluctant bride. Ordinarily, remaining unmarried and childless in this culture would have been difficult for a woman and limiting for a royal woman, but the careers of her two half sisters certainly made the dangers of marriage politics obvious enough. Neither of them seemed eager to marry until Alexander's death, but both were widows with children (see CYNNANE; CLEOPATRA 2).[10] It is possible that Thessalonice would have preferred unmarried seclusion.

Whatever her preferences, what Thessalonice got from Cassander was, in fact, married seclusion. She bore three sons to Cassander (apparently in rapid succession; see below), and her husband founded a city named after her, as well as one named after himself (Dion. Hal. 1.49.4; Strab. 7, frs. 21, 24; Steph. Byz. s.v. "Thessalonice"; Heidel. Epit. *FGrH* 155, F 2.4).

Cassander's reasons for marrying her almost certainly account for her continued personal obscurity. He was moving toward monarchy himself, and marriage to a daughter of Philip II meant that he could claim continuity with the past, produce half-Argead heirs by her, and, as uncle by marriage, act as guardian to Alexander IV.[11] The creation of the city of Thessaloniki, apparently the first city in the Hellenic world named after a royal woman, was entirely in keeping with Cassander's policies. It emphasized in a unique way his connection to the Argead past without giving his wife any real power (see chap. 8). Cassander seems to have been careful to keep her from direct public attention, doubtless afraid that she might use it to acquire the power and influence sometimes exercised by other women of her family.

Shortly before her death, Thessalonice emerged from the royal obscurity in which, whether by chance or preference or both, she had led most of her life. The occasion for this transformation was one that usually brought new power and prominence to a royal woman. The death of her husband, followed rapidly by the death of her eldest son, Philip, left Thessalonice a royal widow with young sons. Tragedy soon followed: relatively soon after the death of her son Philip, Thessalonice was murdered by her son Antipater (Diod. 21.7.1; Plut. *Demetr.* 36.1; Just. 16.1.1–4; Paus. 9.7.3–4). Her other son, Alexander, sought help from Pyrrhus and Demetrius, only to be murdered in turn by Demetrius (Diod. 21.7.1; Plut. *Demetr.* 36.6, *Pyrrh.* 6.1–7.1; Just. 16.1.9). Antipater sought help from his father-in-law, Lysimachus, but Lysimachus had him murdered instead (Porph. *FGrH* 260, F 3.5; Just. 16.2.4; Euseb. *Chron.* 1.232). It is important to understand that Thessalonice was not regent. Instead, the sources refer to a kind of shared kingship, whose origin is unknown (see below). A consideration of the ages, comparative and absolute, of Thessalonice's surviving sons is relevant to understanding both the murder and the shared kingship that preceded it. Plutarch (*Pyrrh.* 6.2) says that Antipater was Cassander's second son and thus the elder of the two surviving brothers, but Porphyry (*FGrH* 260, F. 3.5) says that he was the younger. Karl Julius Beloch argued that Antipater must have been the elder brother because of his name (i.e., his name commemorated his paternal grandfather) and because he does not seem to have appreciated the shared title, as he would have had he been the younger brother.[12] Perhaps. Another possibility is that the young men were twins and Antipater was the elder of the pair. Cassander, desperate for heirs, may have risked raising twins, fearing the absence of male heirs more than the possible troubles inherent in royal twins. None of Thessalonice's children could have been born before late 316, and the younger two, even if they were twins, cannot have been born sooner than late 315 or early 314.

The last of the Argeads died, either because Thessalonice attempted to exercise control over the succession and her political inexperience made her death possible or because she attempted to maintain harmony in a dangerous situation, one possibly not of her own contriving (see below for further discussion). Whichever alternative is the truth, she died because she was an Argead, her murder demonstrating that even her own son had little interest in continuity with the Argead past, much like the rest of the Successors. The *axioma* of her Argead blood was an inconvenience to him. Ironically, Thessalonice's murder almost certainly precipitated the collapse of the Antipatrid dynasty as well.

During her marriage to Cassander, Thessalonice is not known to have had any political role of an active sort, but her passive role was critical to Cassander's path to kingship: she was the Argead mother of his sons. To highlight the importance of his Argead marriage, Cassander did the unprecedented: about the same time that he founded an eponymous city (as Philip, Alexander, and many of the Successors would do), Cassander also made an eponymous foundation in his wife's name. Through this act he suggested a kind of legitimacy through continuity with the past without directly asserting that continuity. Similar motivation probably lies behind another unusual choice of Cassander's. Thessalonice seems to have been his only wife. Although a number of the Successors practiced polygamy,[13] Cassander chose not to.

WOMEN AND MONARCHY IN MACEDONIA

Within a few years of Cassander's death, all that he had accomplished was negated, the last rulers of his dynasty were eliminated in humiliating fashion, and subsequent attempts to reestablish the dynasty were entirely unsuccessful.[14] The surprisingly rapid collapse of the Antipatrid dynasty deserves more attention than it has so far received.[15]

The death of Cassander was followed within about four months by the death of the eldest son of Cassander, Philip IV. Both men were probably victims of consumption.[16] It is quite likely that at the end of his life Cassander was not only aware that he was dying of consumption[17] but also that his oldest son had the disease. Young Philip's symptoms were probably obvious before his father's death, possibly well before.[18] The marriage patterns of his younger sons also support the idea that in his last days Cassander realized that not only his own but also Philip's death was imminent. Philip, his heir and briefly his successor, had no wife we know of, yet both his younger sons, although decidedly younger than royal grooms would usually have been,[19] were married. Antipater was married to Eurydice, daughter of Lysimachus, and Alexander married Lysandra, daughter of Ptolemy (see EURYDICE; LYSANDRA). Although the dates of both these marriages are uncertain, it is much more likely that Cassander arranged these marriages than that either Thessalonice or his sons themselves did so. Both brides were daughters of Cassander's sisters, making him the likely sponsor of the marriages.[20] Neither Thessalonice nor her sons had the international experience or prestige to make such alliances accessible to them. Thessalonice herself had no obvious incentive to arrange marriages for them so early, because as long as her sons had no wives, her own position was more powerful. Although there can be no certainty, it is likely that Cassander, sensible of the dangers ahead for his family, did the best he could for the two sons he believed might survive him longer than his heir, to shore up the base of the dynasty he had founded.

EURYDICE 2

Eurydice, daughter of Lysimachus, married Cassander's second son, Antipater. It is not clear at what date the marriage occurred and, more important, who arranged it. Justin (16.1.7) implies that the marriage already existed when Antipater fled to Lysimachus, whereas Eusebius (*Chron.* 232) might be taken to imply that the marriage took place after Antipater's flight. A number of factors, most notably Lysimachus preoccupation with the Getae, make it unlikely that the marriage alliance was arranged after Antipater had gone into exile.[21]

If, as seems likely, Cassander arranged this marriage, the daughter of Lysimachus would have been an appropriate choice for him. She was the child of his own sister Nicaea, and Lysimachus had long been his ally.[22] If Antipater himself created the connection to Lysimachus, its context could have been his search for support in his struggle with his brother. Indeed, it could have been his first move in response to having to share the kingship with his brother, something he resented.

Whatever the initial reasons for the alliance, young Antipater certainly used it to seek protection and possibly support when, after he murdered his own mother, his struggles with his brother worsened. Lysimachus arranged a reconciliation between the two brothers (Just. 16.1.7–8; c.f. Plut. *Pyrrh.* 6.3–4), but that was made meaningless when Demetrius murdered Alexander and had himself proclaimed king (Just. 16.1.18). Lysimachus, busy with another war, handed over to Demetrius that part of Macedonia that had been in Antipater's control (Just. 16.1.19). When Antipater protested his father-in-law's treatment, Lysimachus had him killed and Eurydice, his own daughter, imprisoned, apparently because she had supported her husband rather than her father (Just. 16.2.4; Euseb. *Chron.* 1.232).[23]

What little we know of young Eurydice suggests that she was a woman of some determination. The circumstances that led to her imprisonment speak to the complex nature of marriage alliances. Her father saw her not only as his political pawn but also as someone whom he expected to represent him and his interests and not her husband's.[24] We do not know why Eurydice maintained her loyalty to her husband at a time when it was expedient to abandon it. She may have seen more power for herself in a possible resurgence of her husband's claim to Macedonian rule than in supporting her father. She may have been fonder of her husband than her father. Nothing further is known of her.

Lysandra

Lysandra was the wife of young Alexander V as well as his first cousin. She was the daughter of Alexander V's paternal aunt Eurydice by Ptolemy I. Lysandra's marriage to Alexander V is mentioned in only one ancient source (Euseb. *Chron.* 1.232),[25] and the passage offers no suggestion about the date. Thus, as with the marriage of Alexander's brother Antipater to Lysimachus' daughter Eurydice (see EURYDICE 2), various deductions about the significance of the marriage are possible, depending on the date one assumes for it.

As we have seen, Cassander is more likely than either his wife or his son to have been the one who arranged this marriage, as well as the marriage of Alexander's brother. Certainly, Alexander V could have contacted Ptolemy, perhaps early in the period of his struggle with his brother.[26] Ptolemy may have initiated the marriage alliance, whatever the date.[27]

Regardless of who initiated it, the marriage seems to have done little to benefit Alexander V. Ptolemy I did not come to his son-in-law's aid. Pyrrhus did, of course, at a heavy price for Alexander (Plut. *Pyrrh.* 6.2). It is possible that Ptolemy may have influenced Pyrrhus to "assist" Alexander, but self-interest could also have been Pyrrhus' sole motivation.[28]

We hear of no children of Lysandra's by Alexander V and know nothing of her activities during her husband's brief reign or at the time of his murder by Demetrius. Although some have doubted it, she must also be the Lysandra, daughter of Ptolemy, who also married Agathocles, son of Lysimachus, and fled as a widow with children to the court of Seleucus.[29] This uncertainty about her identity suggests the general obscurity of her career. Macurdy rightly compared her and her sister-in-law Eurydice to the pawn-like role of kings' daughters in fifth-century Macedonia.[30] Lysandra functioned as a royal token, not as an independent agent.

The deaths of her husband and eldest son propelled Thessalonice from the shadows of court life into the center of the political stage; this central position somehow precipitated her murder by her son, Antipater, and contributed to the collapse of the dynasty. Our sources are so poor and fragmentary for this period that it is difficult to reconstruct the sequence of events, let alone their motivation.[31] Nonetheless, it seems clear that, after the brief reign of Philip IV, Thessalonice was not regent for her younger sons. No ancient source says she was regent, but this is often assumed.[32] Indeed, no woman had held such a position in Macedonia previously.[33] While we do not know with certainty either the ages of Thessalonice's remaining sons or which was older, either or both could have been about eighteen by the time of Philip's death (see THESSA-

LONICE). If both were in their later teens, why posit a regency for which there is no evidence?

Instead of speaking of a regency, the sources refer to shared rule by the remaining two sons. Eusebius (*Chron.* 1.231) mentions no regency, and Justin (16.1.2) explicitly states that after the death of Cassander Macedonia was divided between the brothers. Whether this division refers to shared kingship or to an actual geographic split in the kingdom is uncertain.[34] Shared kingship, although unusual, had precedents in Macedonian history.[35]

In the light of the negative nature of the precedents for dual kingship and the peculiar vulnerability of a new dynasty, why did dual monarchy reassert itself at this critical moment? The sources offer no explanation, but most scholars hold that Cassander's widow instigated dual rule.[36] As daughter of Philip, half sister of Alexander, and widow of Cassander, Thessalonice doubtless had great *axioma* in Macedonia, but it is unlikely she had the power, especially on her own, to instigate a dual monarchy. The sources say that Antipater believed that she somehow favored or was better disposed to his brother Alexander and that this perception drove him to murder her (Just. 16.1.2–4; Paus. 9.7.3). What this favor of hers consisted of we do not know. She may have wanted her younger son (if Alexander really was the younger) to be sole king, or she may have wanted, for whatever reason, to maintain the dual kingship, whereas Antipater wanted to rule alone. Justin's (16.1.4) insistence that no blame could be attached to her actions better suits the latter alternative.

Three other, more plausible explanations for the dual monarchy exist. The Macedonian elite may have divided its support between the two brothers. As they were so close in age and equally inexperienced, the absence of a marked preference is not surprising. Outside influence, one or more of the Successors, may have been behind the division of the kingdom. Certainly it would not have been the first time outsiders attempted to influence Macedonian succession.[37]

But if it is correct that Cassander arranged *two* marriages, those of his younger sons, then it is more likely that the dual kingship of his younger sons was also his idea, just as it may have been the policy of Alexander I. Otherwise, given that both sons were younger than was generally the case for royal grooms,[38] he would surely have arranged only one marriage. It may at first seem unlikely that the canny Cassander, let alone any king, would purposely set up such a division of the kingdom, but he may have if either he or elements of the court feared that either or both of the surviving sons would also develop consumption.[39]

Thessalonice became involved in the struggle for the succession. Her involvement somehow led to her murder by Antipater. Three sources offer direct testimony about the motivation for this murder. Justin (16.1.2) observes that, in the context of their dual kingship, Antipater perceived that his mother "propensior fuisse pro Alexandro videbatur" (seemed to be more favorably disposed to Alexander). Justin somewhat cryptically adds that in this matter, "nullum maternae fraudis vestigium fuit" (there was no trace of maternal wrongdoing; Just. 16.1.2–4). Pausanias (9.7.3) resembles Justin in claiming that the murder happened because Thessalonice showed more favor to Alexander. Diodorus (21.7.1) says that Antipater acted out of jealousy but does not explain from what the jealousy derived. The other extant sources do not provide any explanation of motive for the crime but put it in the context of the struggle between the brothers (Plut. *Demetr.* 36.1, *Pyrrh.* 6.2; Porph. *FGrH* 260, F 3.5; Just. 16.1.2–4).

Thessalonice was a political neophyte, and her inexperience easily could have led to risky policies. Whether she initiated the dual kingship or simply supported a policy her husband had initiated, her commitment to its maintenance apparently contributed to her death. Antipater murdered his mother because of her influence, her ability to support his brother, whether this influence derived from being a royal wife or the daughter of Philip II, or both.

Thessalonice, however, may just as easily have been the victim of violence that was at least as much domestic as political. Had Antipater's motives been strictly political, it would have made more sense for him to murder his brother, not his mother. She could hardly support a dead man. Generally, the Successors tried to conceal their more heinous crimes (e.g., the murders of Cleopatra, daughter of Philip, or of Alexander IV and Roxane) out of concern for public opinion. Antipater, however, apparently made no attempt to conceal matricide, a crime that was unprecedented even in the violent and murderous period after Alexander's death. Such openness about so horrific an act suggests that it was inspired by strong emotion at least as much as it was by politics.

Thessalonice is the last royal Macedonian woman who was, of a certainty, murdered for reasons that were clearly at least partially political, just as she is the last royal woman, other than Arsinoe, for whom there is evidence of political activity and influence while she was married to a king of Macedonia. Her death is all the more ironic if it happened, at least in part, because she was a dutiful widow, not because she personally wished to play a more active political role.

The elimination of Antipater's sons, as well as the subsequent failure of remaining Antipatrids to reassert their rule, may be tied to the unprecedented matricide that precipitated their political troubles, particularly because the matricide was a reminder that the Antipatrids had gained their position by murdering some of the last Argeads.[40] After all, the matricide was also the murder of the last Argead by one of the last of the Antipatrids to rule. Whatever the dealings of Pyrrhus and young Antipater's father-in-law, Lysimachus, Antipater died in exile at the hands of his father-in-law and his brother Alexander died by betrayal, at the hands of his successor, Demetrius Poliorcetes.[41]

The brief and ill-conceived reign of Demetrius Poliorcetes (294–288/87) requires only brief discussion. As we have seen, Demetrius achieved the throne by treachery and violence and was recognized as king primarily through coercion, although also because no other more attractive alternative candidate presented himself to the Macedonian elite (Plut. *Demetr.* 37; Just. 16.1.9). Plutarch (*Demetr.* 37.3) attributes Demetrius' success in hanging on to the throne he had seized to his marriage to Antipater's daughter Phila and their nearly grown son. Demetrius was a much married man at the time he took the throne of Macedonia,[42] and during his brief sojourn there he actually acquired yet another wife, Lanassa, but Phila had the greatest *axioma* of his wives and it was this marriage that mattered in Macedonia and gave some semblance of legitimacy to the upstart (see LANASSA). Although Phila was generally known for her political skill and wisdom (Diod. 19.59.3–6), we do not know of any specific political activity on her part while her husband ruled Macedonia (see PHILA 2). The marriage of Demetrius' daughter by Phila, Stratonice, to Seleucus (in 300) was a grand production and a sign of future Hellenistic royal practice (see chap. 8). Stratonice herself seems to have retained a surprising degree of connection to the dynasty of her birth, long after the first of her two Seleucid marriages (see STRATONICE 2). Demetrius' many wives and use of female members of his dynasty to reinforce his individual and dynastic position is imitative of Philip II.

PHILA 2

Phila was Antipater's daughter. Diodorus (18.18.7) says, probably correctly, that she was the eldest of his four daughters, although she may not have been the first to marry.[43] A younger daughter could have married first, or Phila's marriage to Balacrus could date to the same period or predate it. Phila was probably born in about 350 B.C.[44] Diodorus (19.59.5) claims that her famous father valued her advice on matters of importance, even when she was an unmarried girl.

Phila first married Balacrus, a bodyguard of Alexander's and later satrap of Cilicia, and had a son by him of the same name. This first marriage may have happened before 336.[45] Phila's whereabouts during this period, as is so often the case in her career, are uncertain. She may have remained in Macedonia, perhaps with her father, or she may have journeyed to Asia and lived with her husband in his satrapy.[46]

Not long after Balacrus was killed (Diod. 18.22.1), Antipater arranged Phila's marriage to Craterus (Diod. 18.18.7). Phila's second marriage was one part of the great alliance system Antipater attempted to create after the death of Alexander, using his daughters' marriages to bind various Successors more closely to him (see chap. 5).[47] Phila's marriage to the popular Craterus was brief but produced one child, a son named after his famous father.[48]

Even before the widow had received the bones of Craterus, her father arranged yet another marriage, her last, to Demetrius, son of Antigonus (Diod. 19.59.3). Demetrius, considerably younger than Phila, is said to have entered the marriage reluctantly, persuaded by his father's arguments about the political profit it might bring (Plut. *Demetr.* 14.2–3, *Comp. Demetr. et Ant.* 1.3).

Phila did not marry again, but Demetrius married four more times, in addition to his many liaisons with courtesans and especially the famous Lamia.[49] Three of the marriages occurred while Phila was alive and still married to Demetrius; the fourth, although it did not take place until immediately after Phila's death, was planned while she was alive. As Plutarch notes (*Comp. Demetr. et Ant.* 4.1), Demetrius' many marriages followed the custom of the kings of Macedonia begun by Philip and Alexander. Plutarch (*Demetr.* 14.2) claims that Phila enjoyed the greatest *time* (honor) and *axioma* of all Demetrius' wives because she was the daughter of Antipater and the widow of Craterus, but it is not clear that this position in the marital pecking order was formally recognized.[50]

Little is known of Phila's activities in the early years of her marriage to Demetrius. She had two children by him, probably born soon after she married him. Her son, Antigonus Gonatas, was later king of Macedonia (see chap. 7) and her daughter, Stratonice (see STRATONICE 2), was married first to Seleucus and then to his son Antiochus (Plut. *Demetr.* 53.4). During the early period of Phila's marriage to Demetrius, she probably lived in Asia Minor, perhaps in Cilicia. She may not have resided in Macedonia again until her husband became king of her homeland in 294.[51]

Information about Phila becomes more plentiful after 306, when her husband (now also married to the Athenian Eurydice; Plut. *Demetr.* 14.1) took the royal title (Diod. 20.53.2–4; Plut. *Demetr.* 18.1–2). Inscriptions dating to shortly after 306 refer to Phila as *basilissa* (royal woman), the first known occasion on which a royal Macedonian woman is given a title,[52] and in Athens a temple was built to her and she was associated with Aphrodite (see chap. 8; Ath. 6.254a). Evidence confirms that she had a bodyguard of her own and probably a court of her own (see above). She fulfilled the role of the dutiful wife, dispatching royal garments and household goods to her husband while he conducted the siege of Rhodes (Diod. 20.93.4; Plut. *Demetr.* 22.1)). Her husband used her *axioma* to help him shore up the legitimacy of his newly established monarchy. This use of royal women became a model for many subsequent kings who would incorporate the women of their family in many of the public aspects of their rule, particularly in royal cults.

It is unclear how Demetrius' marriage to Deidameia, the sister of Pyrrhus and once betrothed to Alexander IV, may have affected Phila's position or status. Demetrius' marriage to Deidameia was celebrated with great public pomp (Plut. *Demetr.* 32.2). W. W. Tarn long ago suggested that Demetrius chose to send Phila to her brother Cassander, not only to negotiate a truce with Cassander at a critical moment but also to remove Phila from the presence of his new wife and the lavish public ceremonies associated with the new marriage.[53] No ancient evidence confirms Tarn's suggestion; its plausibility depends on whether one deduces that Demetrius found having both women in the same place awkward. We know only that somewhat later (see below) he seems to have kept them apart.[54]

It is difficult to establish Phila's location after the disaster to Antigonid fortunes at the battle of Ipsus in 301. Demetrius and her mother-in-law, with some of Demetrius' children, joined forces in Asia, and sailed to Cyprus (Diod. 21.1.4). Phila may have remained in Asia or she may have returned to Macedonia. The sources are silent.[55]

Despite the great defeat, Demetrius recovered and soon happened into another extraordinarily lucky marriage alliance. Seleucus wanted to marry his daughter by Phila, Stratonice (Plut. *Demetr.* 31.3–4; see STRATONICE 2). Phila was with Demetrius in Syria for the wedding of their daughter (Plut. *Demetr.* 32.1). Not long after, Demetrius sent Phila to Cassander to negotiate an end to the hostilities created by the role of Pleistarchus, another son of Antipater, in Asia Minor in opposition to Demetrius. Just as Phila departed on her diplomatic mission, Demetrius' other important wife, Deidameia, joined him, although she died soon after (Plut. *Demetr.* 32.3). Demetrius' original offer of marriage for Ptolemy's daughter Ptolemaïs dates from this same period (Plut. *Demetr.* 32.3), although the actual marriage did not take place for many years (Plut. *Demetr.* 46.3).

After his murder of Alexander V, Demetrius' recognition as king of the Macedonians seems to have depended less on his military might than on the fact that he was married to the daughter of Antipater and had a nearly grown son by her (Plut. *Demetr.* 37.3). At some point, probably not long before he was forced to flee Macedonia, Demetrius married again. As with Deidameia, he married a woman whose prestige was significant enough to suggest possible competition with Phila. He now married Lanassa, daughter of Agathocles of Sicily and former wife of his rival, Pyrrhus. The new marriage brought with it Corcyra, which Demetrius garrisoned (Plut. *Pyrrh.* 10.5; see LANASSA).

Demetrius' headlong fall from power in Macedonia is well known. Having wasted away his original support in Macedonia and alienated many, he ultimately lost out to the more popular Pyrrhus. Demetrius chose exile, but Phila chose to poison herself rather than flee Macedonia (Plut. *Demetr.* 45.1). Her husband, talented at surviving his own disasters, simply married again, this time his long-contemplated bride Ptolemaïs (Plut. *Demetr.* 46.3). Demetrius lived on for some time in exile, but his personal claim to the throne of Macedonia died with (or at least at the same time as) Phila.

A number of features of the Phila's career remain uncertain and ambiguous. Historians have generally regarded her as a saintlike figure in comparison to her husband and other royal women of the period, and she has been portrayed as a loving and long-suffering wife.[56] Her saintliness is based, primarily, on the famous character sketch of Phila that is preserved in Diodorus (19.59.3–6) yet universally considered to derive from Hieronymus.[57] So far as we know, Phila did not demonstrate the ruthless pursuit of self-interest that characterized so many of the Successors, male and female alike (including her own husband; e.g., Diod. 19.103.5–6), but Hieronymus' tribute to the mother of his patron should perhaps be viewed more critically than it usually has been and treated as something closer to hagiography than history.[58]

Many of Phila's actions would suit those of a woman intent on gaining or sustaining the power of the dynasty for her son and heirs. We know no more of her real motivation than of those of other less supposedly saintly royal women. Perhaps the missing portions of Diodorus' narrative that dealt with Phila's activities at critical moments in her husband's career (referred to by Diodorus at 19.59.6) would have offered clarification.

In any event, the belief that Phila was a long-suffering wife of a womanizing husband has no basis in the sources and appears to depend, like interpretations of Olympias that make her the woman wronged, on the unstated assumption that royal Macedonian marriage was like modern monogamous marriage.[59] As we have seen, Plutarch (*Demetr.* 14.2–3; *Comp. Demetr. et Ant.* 1.3) says that Demetrius was reluctant to marry her because she was older than he, but we have little knowledge of the views of the new widow. Diodorus (20. 93.4) does refer to royal clothing and outfits that Phila eagerly sent to her husband (ca. 304). This passage suggests a dutiful and possibly doting wife but tells us nothing of her views on Demetrius's many other women.

It has simply been assumed that Phila was fundamentally bothered by the many women in his life. Perhaps this assumption is correct, but it is equally possible that Phila did not feel strongly about it, was used to polygamy, and found the many other women around him a relief. Plutarch (*Demetr.* 14.3) does say that he showed little *time* to Phila and his other wives, consorting as he did with so many other women. Such behavior may not have endeared him to any of his wives. Moreover, jealousy is not necessarily the norm in polygamous circumstances. As we have seen, as the mother of his heir and the daughter of Antipater, Phila stood at the top of the list of his wives. Plutarch (*Demetr.* 27.3) reports that the striking favor he showed his *hetaira* Lamia inspired jealousy among his wives, but as he notes that Demetrius' friends were also jealous, this jealousy was not necessarily sexual. Certainly, it was not jealousy of one of Demetrius' other women that drove Phila to suicide. She lost hope and killed herself because her husband had lost status again (Plut. *Demetr.* 45.1).[60]

Another, more significant aspect of Phila's career is that in many ways it stood as a model for the role of royal women in the Hellenistic period (not so much in Macedonia as in the other two great Hellenistic kingdoms).[61] As we have seen, Phila may have been both the first Macedonian royal woman to use and be allotted a title and the first royal woman accorded cult worship while still alive.

Diodorus' (19.59.4–5) tribute to her offers a kind of pattern for royal women. According to Diodorus, Phila was able to play the politics of troop manipulation adeptly without, apparently, the blatant militarism of Adea Eurydice. She was wise and the source of good advice. She was a good patroness, able to make marriages for the deserving poor and able to free the just from unjust accusation. Naturally, she was also a good daughter, wife, and sister. We know that she performed diplomatic tasks. With Phila we have more clearly than with her predecessors the king's wife as intercessor, a personification of the human, accessible side of monarchy and particularly of dynasty.

It is especially striking that this is true even though Phila was not born to a royal family nor, in any of her marriages, did she marry into one. Instead, as the years of her final and lengthy marriage passed, she and her husband's family moved in the direction of monarchy and the creation of a new dynasty, a movement in which she and other royal women played a prominent role.

LANASSA

Lanassa, daughter of the Syracusan king Agathocles, was first married to Pyrrhus, bringing to him as dowry the island of Corcyra. Apparently, Agathocles made an impressive public spectacle when he brought his daughter to her first husband (Plut. *Pyrrh.* 9.1), in keeping with the increasing public pomp surrounding royal marriages in the late fourth and early third century (see chap. 8).[62] Lanassa had one son, Alexander, during her brief marriage to Pyrrhus (Plut. *Pyrrh.* 9.1; Diod. 22.8.2; Just. 23.3.3 confuses him with Pyrrhus' son Helenus).[63]

Lanassa ended her marriage to Pyrrhus and retired to Corcyra. She apparently immediately sought another royal marriage, this time to Demetrius Poliorcetes. Plutarch (*Pyrrh.* 10.5) says that Lanassa broke with Pyrrhus because he showed more favor to his barbarian wives. Demetrius, eager to take advantage of his enemy's misfortune, sailed off to marry Lanassa and garrisoned Corcyra. Some have assumed that Lanassa's rejection of Pyrrhus was done with her father's knowledge and support and perhaps at his instigation.[64] That she did not return to her father in Syracuse, remained in Corcyra, and made the marriage offer to Demetrius herself strongly suggests that by this time she was acting as her father's ally, if a subordinate one, rather than as his pawn. Her second marriage probably dates to 291/0.[65]

Her rejection of Pyrrhus cannot signify a dislike of polygamous marriage as Plutarch (*Pyrrh.* 10.5) tells us that it was Demetrius's inclination to marry that made him a plausible marriage candidate for Lanassa, but it may suggest that a certain uneasiness about royal polygamy in relation to the status of royal women was beginning to grow. If we are to believe Plutarch, the problem for Lanassa was not that Pyrrhus had barbarian wives but that he paid more attention to them than to her (see chap. 8).

The motivation for her rejection of Pyrrhus and preference for Demetrius was surely largely political.[66] Lanassa's *time* was damaged. Her pursuit of a husband of equal status to the one she rejected (Plut. *Pyrrh.* 10.5 specifically says that she chose Demetrius because she wanted a royal marriage) makes this clear. Unlike many of the other early Hellenistic royal brides, Lanassa was not Macedonian and thus not necessarily as accustomed to enduring the stresses involved in royal polygamy.

Some scholars have believed that Lanassa may have received a kind of cult worship at Athens, as Phila apparently did (Demochares and Duris ap. Ath. 6.253c–f).[67] Nothing more is known of Lanassa, who may never have visited Macedonia. If Demetrius followed his pattern of behavior when he was married to Phila and Deidameia at the same time, he may well have kept Lanassa and Phila, wives of comparatively similar rank, apart, and Lanassa may have remained in Corcyra. Perhaps because of the absence of further information about this marriage, some have failed to accept its reality, but this view has not won general acceptance.[68] There is nothing to suggest that Lanassa's marriage to Demetrius was a significant factor in alienating the Macedonians from Demetrius, as Macurdy once supposed.[69] The Macedonians had long experience with royal polygamy, and

Demetrius' many other actions were sufficient to explain the Macedonian's alienation.

Stratonice 2

Stratonice was the daughter of Demetrius Poliorcetes and Phila (see Phila 2). In the period after the battle of Ipsus, Seleucus Nicator, reacting to the developing alliance between Lysimachus and Ptolemy, asked Demetrius for Stratonice's hand in marriage (Plut. *Demetr.* 31.3–4). The wedding was marked by the pomp and festivities customary for royal weddings (32.1–3; see chap. 8). This marriage alliance, the first of many Antigonid/Seleucid matches, took place ca. 300–297 and produced one child, Phila, the future wife of Antigonus Gonatas (see Phila 3).

Some years later, ca. 294/3, Seleucus made the remarkable decision to end his marriage to Stratonice and give her as wife to his son Antiochus. The ancient sources attribute Seleucus' decision to Antiochus' passion for Stratonice and Seleucus' selfless fatherly love (Plut. *Demetr.* 38.1–9; App. *Syr.* 59–61; Lucian *Syr. D.* 17 ff.), but a more practical motivation is likely. Seleucus had no need of more sons, whereas Antiochus did.[70] Stratonice's marriage to Antiochus produced two sons (Seleucus and Antiochus, the future king) and two daughters (Stratonice, the future wife of Demetrius II [see Stratonice 3] and Apama, future wife of Magas of Cyrene).

Unlike royal wives in Macedonia, Stratonice received cult worship.[71] She was once thought to have had a personal relationship with Arsinoe, daughter of Ptolemy, because of an inscription referring to her dedication of a statue of Arsinoe (*OGIS* 14), but the authenticity of the inscription is now in doubt.[72] Stratonice died ca. 254, some years after the death of her second husband.

Ordinarily, there would be little more to say of relevance to Macedonian history and monarchy about the daughter of a Macedonian king who left Macedonia in her youth and became involved in the affairs of another dynasty, but Stratonice's career constitutes a special case. Despite her two Seleucid marriages and Asian residence, a considerable body of evidence, primarily inscriptions from Delphi, suggests that Stratonice thought of herself and portrayed herself publicly as an Antigonid, particularly as the daughter of Demetrius, rather than as the wife of two Seleucid rulers.[74]

Like other Hellenistic queens, Stratonice was an extravagant patron of favored cults, in her case that of Apollo on Delos. While it is certainly true that the Seleucids claimed descent from Apollo, it is difficult to attribute her enthusiastic and long-term patronage of the Delian cults to the dynastic claims of the Seleucids, as she ignores her Seleucid connection in making the dedications. Instead, the inscriptions seem to stress her role as royal daughter, and her emphasis on Delos can more plausibly be linked to her brother's reassertion of Antigonid political claims in this area.[75]

Some have attributed her curious emphasis on her Antigonid identity to personal motives (e.g., on the one hand, antipathy toward her second husband because of his role in her eldest son's death and affection for the dashing Demetrius Poliorcetes;[76] and, on the other, the desire to downplay her Seleucid husbands because of the awkwardness or scandalousness of being married to both father and son and guilt over her supposed betrayal of her father).[77] This suggestion is not implausible, but no evidence supports it. Stratonice's motivation could as easily have been political, perhaps because she had more influence with her brother than with either husband or son. One wonders whether her brother's marriage to her daughter, coming as it did at a critical moment in his own career, was in part her doing.

Thus, although there is no evidence that Stratonice played any role in her husbands' and son's reign other than as wealthy patron of appropriate cults, she does seem to have acted in support of the dynasty of her birth. Brides in dynastic marriage alliances are typically seen as passive pawns moved about by the short-term requirements of two dynasties, and doubtless many were. But Stratonice's career, like that of her mother, Phila, suggests that such women were sometimes lifelong ambassadors from one dynasty to another.

Demetrius frittered away the power he had so brutally acquired and died in obscurity, whereas his able wife Phila preferred suicide to humiliating exile (Plut. *Demetr.* 45.1). Despite his signal failure as king of Macedonia, Demetrius was an important figure in the development of Hellenistic kingship, including a number of aspects related to the role of royal women in monarchy (see further chap. 8).

Following the ignominious departure of Demetrius came a period of more than ten years (ca. 288–ca. 277) in which no one was able to establish himself securely on the throne and there were long periods of anarchy or only local rule. Even Lysimachus, when he drove Pyrrhus out and

WOMEN AND MONARCHY IN MACEDONIA

took control over all of Macedonia ca. 284, kept his court in Thrace. Lysimachus was therefore both more and less than king of Macedonia. His successor, Ptolemy Ceraunus, a son of Ptolemy by Antipater's daughter Eurydice, displaced from the succession in Egypt by his own father, had first fled to Lysimachus' court where his sister Lysandra welcomed him and then apparently joined her in a second flight to the court of Seleucus (Paus. 1.10.4, 16.2).[78] When Seleucus began the invasion of his homeland of Macedonia in the hope of becoming king of Macedonia, Ceraunus accompanied him. Ceraunus, in an act of vicious but brilliant opportunism, suddenly murdered his former benefactor Seleucus and soon claimed rule of Macedonia for himself (Paus. 1.16.2, 10.19.7; Strab. 13.4.1; App. *Syr.* 62–63; Just. 17.2.4–5; Memnon *FGrH* 434, F 8). Hoping to gain the citadel of Cassandreia that was currently in her possession, Ceraunus persuaded Lysimachus's widow, Ceraunus' own half sister Arsinoe, to marry him, only to murder Arsinoe's sons by Lysimachus. After his death in battle (ca. 279), complete anarchy then descended on Macedonia until Antigonus Gonatas was able to assert his power as king ca. 277.

Clearly, there was no regular court and no real king in Macedonia from the time of Demetrius Poliorcetes' departure until his son Gonatas became king. As a consequence, I have generally excluded the women associated with the assortment of men who held power in Macedonia during this chaotic period from this work on the grounds that they are not Macedonian royal women. I include Arsinoe with some hesitation, but do so not so much because she was the wife of a Macedonian king (although Ceraunus seems to fit that description better than Lysimachus) as because the events of her life in this period seem to have had considerable effect on the role of royal women in the Hellenistic period and on issues (e.g., polygamy) related to them. Consequently, I concentrate on her career before her return to Egypt and deal only briefly with the later period of her life.

ARSINOE

Arsinoe,[79] daughter of Ptolemy I, was married to Lysimachus and Ptolemy Ceraunus, both of whom ruled Macedonia briefly, although neither was a Macedonian king in the ordinary sense.

Arsinoe was born ca. 316, to Berenice, the obscure cousin of Ptolemy's first wife, Antipater's daughter Eurydice (Paus. 1.7.8). Berenice's status (and her daughter's), both at the time of her daughter's birth and long after, was ambiguous. Ptolemy seems to have embraced traditional Argead polygamy (Plut. *Pyrrh.* 4.4), so there is no reason to believe that Berenice was ever simply a mistress, but it is less certain whether Eurydice and Berenice had equal status from the beginning or whether Berenice only gradually achieved equality with Eurydice and, ultimately, superiority.

Plutarch (*Pyrrh.* 4.4) reports that ca. 298 Pyrrhus concluded that Berenice had the greatest power, virtue, and understanding of Ptolemy's women, implying that by this period she had gained predominance.[80] Ptolemy may never have rejected his wife Eurydice. Eurydice probably left court when her son, Ceraunus, was supplanted by Berenice's son for the succession, something that may have happened as late as 285.

Arsinoe grew up in a tense, competitive, and faction-ridden court in which Ptolemy's two families were pitted against each other. The total victory of Berenice's faction in 285 did not come until many years after Arsinoe's departure for Macedonia and marriage ca. 300.

Ptolemy arranged a marriage between Arsinoe and the now elderly Lysimachus (king of Thrace only at this point). It was the first of two marriages that Ptolemy and Lysimachus arranged.[81] Arsinoe's marriage to Lysimachus produced three sons: Ptolemy, Lysimachus, and Philip.[82] Lysimachus had been married several times before and had an adult son, Agathocles, by Nicaea, daughter of Antipater. Agathocles was married to one of the daughters of Eurydice, Arsinoe's mother's rival. Thus, in her husband's court, Arsinoe had to cope with a situation not unlike that her mother had confronted in Egypt. Indeed, the struggle at Lysimachus' court seems to have continued into a second generation the struggles of Berenice and Eurydice by pitting their daughters against each other.[83]

Other than that she bore three children, little is known of most of Arsinoe's life during her marriage to Lysimachus. It is not even certain that his wife Nicaea was dead when Arsinoe first came to Lysimachus' court.[84] Lysimachus renamed Ephesus Arsinoea after his young wife ca. 294 (Strab. 14.1.21).[85] Thanks to him, she may have controlled and had the income from three cities.[86] Certainly, she had access to considerable wealth. Arsinoe personally paid for the building of a large structure, the Arsinoeum, at Samothrace, as an offering to the Great Gods there (*OGIS* 15 = *IG* XII 227). The structure was probably built during Arsinoe's marriage to Lysimachus.[87] The financing of such a large public structure by a royal woman is otherwise unknown.[88]

The struggle for the succession at the court of Lysimachus came to a head about 283/2, when Arsinoe's eldest son was nearly of adult age.[89] Initially, it seemed to end in victory for Arsinoe's faction. Agathocles was killed and his wife, Lysandra, and children fled court, taking refuge with Seleucus. Agathocles' death, however, proved destabilizing to Lysimachus' Asian empire, some of which seems to have revolted,[90] and Seleucus took Lysandra's situation as an excuse to invade. When Seleucus and Lysimachus met at the battle of Corupedion in February 281, Lysimachus was defeated and killed in battle. Arsinoe escaped by a hair's breadth, exercising ruthlessness and ingenuity to do so (Polyaen. 8.57).[91]

Controversy surrounds many of the details leading to the demise of Agathocles. Memnon (*FGrH* 434, F 5.6) says that Arsinoe tried to kill Agathocles by poisoning but that, when poison failed, Ptolemy actually did the deed. Justin says that Agathocles was poisoned by Arsinoe (17.1.4).[92] The "truth" about many aspects of the Agathocles affair was probably not known in antiquity and cannot be known now.[93] While scholars have often rejected the Phaedra-like aspect of Arsinoe's motivation (Arsinoe, first enamored of Agathocles, then turned to vengeance when she was rejected; Paus. 1.10.3), they have more often accepted the idea that she, rather than her husband, was the instigator of Agathocles' death.[94]

It is indeed likely that Arsinoe plotted to eliminate Agathocles from the succession (and that her son, Ptolemy, was personally involved in the effort),[95] but it is equally likely that Agathocles and Lysandra were feverishly counterplotting against Arsinoe and her sons, and perhaps against Lysimachus himself.[96] Even if Agathocles remained loyal, Lysimachus' seemingly puzzling preference for his younger son can be explained by his reluctance to begin to yield power to his heir. Choosing his younger son enabled him to postpone this problem.[97]

The decision was his to make, not Arsinoe's. Painting Lysimachus as a doddering dupe to his scheming young wife is wrong. His speed and daring (if overconfidence) in the following campaign hardly suggest a man in his dotage. It is not necessary to conclude that Arsinoe had little or no influence over her husband[98] to believe that he would not have acted against his own self-interest as he judged it.

The hostility of the sources to Arsinoe in particular and powerful women in general obviously complicates this issue. (See chap. 1.) Although it is often implied that Arsinoe's pursuit of the throne for her son was ill-advised and brought destruction down on her family, in fact, neither she nor Agathocles had much choice: one of Lysimachus' sons would be chosen and the other, sooner or later, killed, if not by Lysimachus, by the victorious son.

The ultimate victor at Corupedion, although unable to enjoy success for long, was neither Lysimachus nor his conqueror Seleucus but Ptolemy Ceraunus. Within a few months he turned his attention to his half sister, Arsinoe.

Arsinoe had returned to Macedonia with her three sons and was ensconced in the fortress of Cassandreia, supported by a force of mercenaries. Ceraunus began to try to persuade Arsinoe to marry him (Just. 17.2.6–11). She was naturally suspicious, doubtless recalling their opposing sides in the dynastic struggles in the courts of Ptolemy and Lysimachus and his elimination of Seleucus (Just. 24.2.3–4, 6–7). In the end he persuaded her to marry him, partly by swearing a solemn oath before the gods (Just. 24.2.5–8) and partly by promising that he would adopt her sons and recognize their place in the succession to the Macedonian throne (17.2.8) and that he would not marry another woman or have children by any other woman (Just. 24.2.9). Justin gives somewhat contradictory explanations of Ceraunus' motivation for this marriage offer. Ceraunus' intent was probably sinister from the start.[99] Like the marriage Antigonus Gonatas arranged between Nicaea and his son, the future Demetrius II, this was a trick marriage.[100]

Why did Arsinoe accept Ceraunus' offer? Justin (24.6.7) says she feared her half brother's wrath and thought the marriage would protect her sons, but he implies, probably incorrectly, that she was also motivated by a desire to regain the title *regina* (24.2.9, 3.3; see chap. 8). She may have feared that, without the help of a general with an army, she could not hope to see her eldest son, Ptolemy, placed on the throne.

Ptolemy, insisting that the offer was a trick (Just. 24.2.10), apparently decamped, displaying his mother's knack for survival.[101] Arsinoe, still cautious, arranged for a public wedding celebration outside the city, recognition of her new role in front of the army, and a very public reception of her sons by her new husband within the city, but her caution did not avail. Ceraunus killed her two younger sons in front of her, but allowed her to take refuge at Samothrace (Just. 24.3.1–9; Memnon *FGrH* 434, F 8.7) and, finally, to return to her brother's court.[102] Ceraunus did not long survive his murderous machinations, losing his life in battle (Just. 24.3.10, 5, 6; Memnon *FGrH* 434, F 8.8), but Ptolemy, Lysimachus' son, did survive. His attempts to gain or perhaps regain the throne of Macedonia failed, but he seems to have lived out his later years as a local power in Asia Minor.[103]

WOMEN AND MONARCHY IN MACEDONIA

Did Arsinoe sacrifice her sons' interest, or at least her eldest son's, to her own, as is sometimes suggested?[104] The sources, such as they are, do not say. The truth may have been more complicated and more painful for both mother and surviving son. Arsinoe rightly doubted her young son's ability to acquire the throne on his own but wrongly judged the dependability of her half brother. Her son wrongly gauged his own ability to reach the throne but rightly judged his half uncle's ruthlessness. No further contact with his mother is certain, and no wonder. The actions of both contributed to what neither wanted, the deaths of the two younger sons of Lysimachus.

Shortly after her return to Egypt, Arsinoe found herself involved in a struggle for power between two royal women for the third time in her life. Her brother Ptolemy II's wife seems gradually to have lost out to Arsinoe. Ultimately, Arsinoe married her full brother (the first such royal sibling marriage in the dynasty)[105] and the first wife was sent away. The sources attribute both the rejection of the first wife and the marriage to Arsinoe II to Ptolemy II alone (Paus. 6.7.1; schol. ad. Theoc. 17.128). The scholiast says that Ptolemy II himself discovered that Arsinoe I was conspiring against him, exiled her to Coptos, and married his sister. Despite the testimony of the sources, it is usually assumed that Arsinoe II was behind her brother's exile of his first wife. Even if, as seems likely, she tried to influence her brother to pursue this course, it was his decision, just as Arsinoe's earlier dynastic victory had been Lysimachus' decision.[106]

Arsinoe had no children by her brother and had to recognize his children by his first wife as heirs (Paus. 1.7.3), but she otherwise enjoyed unprecedented status and powers in Egypt.[107] Arsinoe undeniably played a major role in public affairs in Egypt and was given titles and status indicators of remarkable significance.[108] She may have received cult worship in her lifetime,[109] and after her death her cult continued to be popular.

Arsinoe's career highlights the problems of royal polygamy. Her career also epitomizes historiographical difficulties inherent in considering the careers of powerful royal women (see chap. 1), whose power more often came through influence on the main power holder, less often through the ability to wield power directly. Almost in direct proportion to a royal woman's influence, the sources are likely to describe an ambitious woman's actions in more negative terms than similar actions by royal men. Scholarship has often perpetuated this tendency.[110]

Royal women did not yet experience a marked decline in power and influence in Macedonia in this period of transition and chaos. The careers of Arsinoe and Phila resemble the careers of various of their Argead predecessors much more than they do those of subsequent obscure Antigonid wives and daughters (see chap. 7). It is in this period, however, that the first signs of the decline of royal polygamy appeared. It is also in this period that many practices developed which, in Hellenistic monarchies other than Macedonia itself, would institutionalize the power of royal women.

CHAPTER SEVEN

Women and Monarchy in the Antigonid Period (277–168)

Antigonus Gonatas (277–239) restored Macedonia to stability and firmly established his dynasty on the throne through a combination of military success and diplomatic skill. Macedonian impatience and despair at the many years of chaos coupled with Antigonus' victory were the more important reasons for the initial acceptance of his rule, but his ancestry probably also helped to win him support. That Macedonia had once been ruled by an Antigonid (his father, Demetrius Poliorcetes), however briefly and incompetently, may have contributed to the successful establishment of Antigonid rule in Macedonia under the staid son of Poliorcetes and Phila; it may not have been entirely irrelevant that Gonatas was also a grandson of Antipater.

The Antigonid dynasty produced a number of competent if not charismatic rulers but ultimately could not defeat the power of Rome. Antigonus dealt handily with the external threat of invading tribesmen, reestablished Macedonian influence in southern Greece, made the court at Pella once more an intellectual center, and built an alliance with the Seleucid dynasty. Many of these policies would endure for much of the remaining history of independent Macedonia. During the later stages of Antigonus's long reign, his son Demetrius II (239–229) played an important part in Macedonian affairs, probably co-ruling with him. Demetrius became embroiled in Epirote and southern Greek affairs, not always successfully, and died in battle against an Illyrian tribe. Demetrius had one son, Philip V, too young to rule at the time of Demetrius' death. Antigonus Doson, Demetrius' cousin, ruled as regent and then king (229–221). Doson dealt with the barbarians who had killed his cousin and restored Macedonian influence in Greece through careful diplomacy and military action.[1]

From this time on Rome played an increasingly important role in Greek events in general and Macedonian history in particular. Philip V (221–179), now old enough to rule, finally took the throne and maintained Doson's successes in Greece, but the gradual encroachment of Roman influence and his attempts to combat it led to war with Rome and his defeat (197). After this failure, Philip tried to coexist with the Romans, but Roman interference in Macedonian succession doomed this policy. His son Perseus (179–168), the last king of Macedonia, rebuilt Macedonian influence in Greece and abroad, but both Rome and its ally, Eumenes of Pergamum, were threatened by his success. Rome declared war, Perseus was defeated and taken captive, and Macedonia became part of the Roman Empire.

Royal women played a markedly diminished role in the Macedonian monarchy during the Antigonid period. Historians of Macedonia, severely limited by the dearth of evidence for the later period, often presume—perhaps indulging in some degree of wishful thinking—that comparatively little changed in Macedonian monarchy from Argead to Antigonid times. The considerable alteration in the role of women in monarchy suggests that the general presumption of lack of change should be questioned and possibly qualified.

Macurdy first pointed to this dramatic decline in the political importance of royal women. She varied in where she placed the beginning of decline,[2] but it had certainly begun by the time the Antigonid dynasty was firmly established. Some women in the preceding transitional period had exercised demonstrable power and influence, but from the era of Antigonus Gonatas on, none would. Although the scarcity and the poor quality of extant sources for the Antigonid period must raise the possibility that the apparent obscurity of royal women in this period is just that, apparent not real,[3] I shall argue that this obscurity constitutes reality as well as appearance. As we try to understand why Antigonid women became such shadowy figures, we must recall that in this same period the opposite tendency can be observed in the two other great Hellenistic dynasties, particularly that of the Ptolemies. Any explanation for the changed role of women in Antigonid monarchy must therefore cope with the growing distinction between the role of royal women in Macedonia proper and that in the other Hellenistic monarchies, particularly as marriage alliances guaranteed that women moved back and forth between the two quite different circumstances. Indeed, in two cases royal wives who played limited roles in Macedonia, when transplanted to one of the other Hellenistic kingdoms, were able to pursue wider goals with more freedom of action (see STRATONICE 3; LAODICE; and below).

Antigonus Gonatas' approach to the problem of establishing a new dynasty resembles that of his cautious uncle Cassander more than that of his proverbially incautious father. One would expect an appropriate marriage alliance at the beginning of his reign, and that, in fact, happens. Although arranged earlier, Antigonus Gonatas' marriage to his Seleucid niece, Phila, took place only after he took the throne. Middle-aged by the time of his marriage, he had nonetheless not married previously, although he had produced a son by a *hetaira* named Demo, whom he seems to have treated as his heir but who died young (Plut. *Mor.* 119c; Ael. *VH* 3.5). Until he acquired his political base in Macedonia, Antigonus Gonatas probably seemed a poor risk to prospective fathers-in-law.

DEMO

An Athenian *hetaira* named Demo probably bore Antigonus Gonatas a son named Halcyoneus. Athenaeus (13.578a), citing Ptolemy, son of Agesarchus, as his source, says that Demo bore a son of that name to Antigonus (no patronymic or epithet provided).[4] As Antigonus Gonatas is known to have a son named Halcyoneus who led a relief force to Argos against Pyrrhus and brought Pyrrhus' head to his father (Plut. *Pyrrh.* 34.4–6),[5] it is usually assumed that this young man is Demo's son.[6]

As Halcyoneus was old enough to hold a responsible command in the campaign that ended in Pyrrhus' death ca. 272, he must have been born after the turn of the third century, long before Antigonus Gonatas' marriage to Phila.[7] Tarn argues that Halcyoneus was brought up not only as a "prince of the blood" but also as "crown prince."[8] Although there was no such clearly defined position as "crown prince" in Macedonia, Antigonus Gonatas seems to have treated Halcyoneus as his heir. This is unsurprising, given that he long lacked legitimate issue. Even at the time of the campaign against Pyrrhus, Antigonus Gonatas' son by Phila, Demetrius, would have been only a toddler and Antigonus Gonatas would therefore have needed a viable heir until Phila's son matured. Antigonus Gonatas' dealings with his son Halcyoneus seem to have been intimate and domestic.[9]

If Demo truly was a *hetaira*, her status apparently did not bar her son from the succession, although it might have disadvantaged him, had he lived longer (Plut. *Mor.* 119c; Ael. *VH* 3.5), in comparison to a more mature Demetrius. It is significant that Antigonus Gonatas did not marry until his forties and was apparently content (or forced to make do) with a courtesan's son as an heir until he took control of Macedonia. Only then was he a plausible groom for a royal bride and, perhaps, only then did he concern himself with the lineage of his heir.

Antigonus Gonatas' marriage to Phila, his only marriage, produced one child, his heir, the future Demetrius II. Antigonus Gonatas, like Cassander, chose monogamy. It is possible he was reacting, for personal or political reasons or both, against his father's notorious polygamy.[10] Apparently, Antigonus Gonatas preferred the advantages of monogamy, despite the obvious risk he took in having only one heir. His preference for monogamy and apparent willingness to cope with the danger implicit in having only one heir is the typical, although not the universal, pattern for his dynasty.

His marriage, the second between an Antigonid and a Seleucid, looked back to Cassander's marriage to Thessalonice (which it resembled) and forward to a series of Seleucid/Antigonid alliances.[11] The marriage marked a kind of watershed in Macedonian history, in two different respects. On the one hand, it signaled (indeed, was made possible by) the fact that the worst of the troubles of the years after the collapse of Demetrius Poliorcetes' monarchy were at an end. Order, in the shape of a restored monarchy under the restored Antigonid dynasty, could return. On the other hand, it also happens to involve the first of a long line of Antigonid royal wives and daughters who seem, according to extant literary sources, to have been powerless and apolitical (certainly by comparison to royal wives and daughters in the fourth century). Gonatas' wife, Phila, is virtually invisible in literary sources but surprisingly well attested in epigraphic sources.

PHILA 3
Phila, the daughter of Stratonice (see STRATONICE 1) and Seleucus Nicator, married her uncle, Antigonus Gonatas (*Vita Arati*, Westermann 53, 60).[12] Her

WOMEN AND MONARCHY IN MACEDONIA

betrothal had probably been arranged when her half brother, Antiochus, made peace with Antigonus Gonatas, but the wedding did not take place until 277/6 or a bit later, after Antigonus Gonatas' victory over the Celts at Lysimacheia.

Antigonus Gonatas, apparently conscious of the symbolic potential of his wedding, seems to have turned it into an occasion to commemorate the return of a real Macedonian court and court life. Aratus of Soli wrote a wedding hymn for the event (as well as an epigram dedicated to Phila (*Suda* s.v. "Aratos"), and it is possible that the wedding was tied to the initial celebration of the *basileia* festival.[13] The wedding was therefore part of his general program to portray himself and his returned dynasty as traditional and committed to continuity with the Argead past.[14]

Little is known of Phila. She bore Antigonus Gonatas a son, the future Demetrius II, and she lived until at least 246.[15] Her husband took no other wife. A statue of her was erected at Delos, part of the new Antigonid emphasis on the island.[16] Phila had a *temenos* (sacred precinct) at Samos.[17] A recently discovered inscription seems to paint a more activist picture of Phila's role.[18] A Cassandreia inscription seems to suggest not only that Phila had courtiers (not surprising or unprecedented), but also that she and her personal appointees played some role in the administration of the kingdom. The inscription may testify to the ability of the *basilissa* to intercede, to act in the interests of various parties, with her husband.[19]

Literary sources suggest that Phila played no significant political role in her husband's reign. Inscriptions imply that, whatever power Phila had, her role and that of royal women may have become more institutionalized under the Antigonids but, perhaps because more defined, more limited.

Demetrius II succeeded his father, although he reigned much more briefly (239–229).[20] Demetrius II's reign is particularly obscure[21] and the position of royal women within it even more so. Although he may have married as many as four women, it is usually said that Demetrius II was serially monogamous and Demetrius Poliorcetes was the last polygamous Macedonian king. This may have been the case, but we should not assume it was without discussion.[22]

In earlier Macedonian times, polygamy was a strategy Macedonian kings pursued with varying enthusiasm: Philip II was a much more enthusiastic polygamist than either his father or his son. It is not so much that the Argeads were polygamous but that they could be and often were. Polygamy was an important aspect of Macedonian monarchy and intimately connected to the frequent struggles for the succession. However, it did not play the role in Macedonian monarchy that royal polygamy did in the monarchies of Egypt or the Near East where, practiced on a grand scale with harems, it functioned more as a symbol of royal power than as a practical political device.

Although by the end of the fourth century a number of factors made royal polygamy less attractive, monarchy in Macedonia proper was more conservative (consider, for instance, the rejection of royal cult) than in the new Hellenistic monarchies. Nothing automatically prevented the survival of polygamy in Macedonia after its disappearance elsewhere. We should pay attention to the apparent decline in popularity of royal polygamy but not assume its absolute disappearance, especially in Macedonia itself. Even if Antigonus Gonatas or any other Antigonid consciously and publicly rejected polygamy (we have no evidence that they did), nothing would prevent another Antigonid ruler from returning to the practice of Philip and Alexander if he found it convenient to do so. My principle in considering the role of women in Antigonid monarchy has been to examine the surviving evidence for each reign and to note the likelihood that the international preference for royal monogamy affected the Antigonids too.

Demetrius II married at least three and quite possibly four times. Even if Demetrius II ruled with his father before his comparatively short sole reign, the existence of four named wives in itself suggests the possibility of polygamy. His first two marriages happened while his father still reigned and were probably primarily Antigonus Gonatas' doing. Demetrius II's first wife was Stratonice, his half aunt. This marriage created yet another Seleucid/Antigonid tie but produced no sons.

STRATONICE 3

Stratonice, daughter of the elder Stratonice (see STRATONICE 2) and Antiochus I, married Demetrius II while his father, Antigonus Gonatas, was still alive. The marriage, uniting two people already related by blood several times over, follows the tradition of Antigonid/Seleucid marriages and probably took place during the mid-250s.[23] Demetrius was probably much younger than Stratonice. The marriage produced no sons but possibly a daughter, Apamea (see APAMEA 1).

Saying anything further about Stratonice and this marriage alliance becomes difficult. Demetrius II's marriages, their order and duration, are especially obscure. Most scholars have assumed that his marriage to Stratonice, confirming as it did the ties of the two dynasties, was his first. His probable age at the time of this marriage—early twenties—also tends to suggest that it was indeed his first.

Two ancient sources (Just. 28.1.1–4; Agatharchides ap. Joseph. *Ap.* 1.206–8 = *FGrH* 86, F 20) report that Stratonice left Macedonia and her husband to return to her homeland. Justin explicitly states that Stratonice voluntarily ended her marriage; Agatharchides implies it. Agatharchides offers no explanation for Stratonice's motivation, but Justin does. They disagree about the date, either absolute or relative to other events, of her departure as well as its circumstances.

In Syria, according to the account preserved in Josephus, having tried and failed to marry her nephew Seleucus II, Stratonice created a revolt in his absence and was ultimately executed at Seleucia. Agatharchides' account compels us to assign her Syrian intrigues to a period after Seleucus II's accession in 246 but need not lead us to believe that they followed immediately on her departure from Macedonia. One could argue that Agatharchides' account allows for the possibility that Stratonice left Macedonia during the reign of her brother but was not politically active until her nephew's reign. Although possible, this interpretation seems to stretch the sense of the account preserved in Josephus. Quite apart from this difficulty, his account contains an obvious factual impossibility. Josephus says that Stratonice was executed by her nephew in Seleucia, but from the time of his accession, the city was no longer in Seleucid hands.[24] She could not have been executed by that king in that place.

Justin (28.1.1–4) connects Stratonice's departure to Demetrius's marriage to the Epirote princess Phthia. Justin says that she left because of the new marriage. In Justin (28.1.2), Demetrius clearly marries Phthia while he is still married to Stratonice. She considers the situation so insulting that she tries to get her brother to make war on her former husband. Justin's account, like that preserved in Josephus, contains an apparent factual impossibility. On the one hand, Justin (28.1.1–2) terms Demetrius *rex* (king), a position he did not hold, at least not alone, until 239; on the other, the king referred to, Antiochus, was dead by 246.

Despite the conflicting testimony of the sources, some conclusions about Stratonice's career are possible. Demetrius' marriage to Stratonice had produced no son. This failure must have been an increasing worry for Demetrius and his father, particularly since Stratonice was probably significantly older than her husband. One would expect Demetrius to marry again so as to produce an heir.

His marriage to Nicaea, an older, childless woman of lower status than Stratonice, is unlikely to have constituted a threat to Stratonice's position (see NICAEA), but his marriage to an Epirote princess, Phthia, would have been much more disturbing. Phthia's status would have approximated Stratonice's. If Phthia was also the mother of Philip V, as some have argued (see below), Stratonice would no longer have been the royal wife with the greatest prestige. If the mother of Philip V (born ca. 238/7) was yet another woman named Chryseis (see below), Stratonice's status would also decline, both because of her husband's Epirote bride and because another wife had produced a son.

Since both extant accounts contain errors, it is difficult to prefer one to the other.[25] Justin's version, however, has the advantage of providing a plausible explanation for Stratonice's departure, especially if one believes that Phthia was soon pregnant with Philip V. It is less easy to accept Justin's apparent early date for these events, and one could conclude that he has confused his Seleucids and reject this part of his account. Alternatively, one could disconnect Phthia's marriage from the immediate period of Philip V's birth and accept Justin's references to Antiochus and the arguments of those who believe that Demetrius was co-king with his father for a long time.[26]

Stratonice's career provides some significant information about the changing role of royal women in Macedonian monarchy. If my conclusions here are accepted, her career suggests that royal polygamy persisted in Macedonia but that, as the third century went on, royal women increasingly found it unattractive and might reject participation in such a system, when it disadvantaged them.

As Macurdy noted, Stratonice's intrigues in Syria subsequent to her departure from Macedonia, whatever their exact nature and involving whichever male Seleucid, show her to have been a woman of spirit,[27] willing to take risky initiatives. Stratonice's subsequent career demonstrates that the rapid decline in importance of royal women in third-century Macedonia cannot be ascribed to their personalities but to the circumstances in that period in Macedonia. Stratonice abandoned her marriage because the role of an Antigonid wife, particularly a childless one, offered her too little scope.

APAMEA 1

The existence, let alone the name of such a person as Apamea, daughter of Stratonice and Demetrius II, half sister of Philip V, and later wife of Prusias I of Bithynia, has been disputed. The evidence is indeed scant and is further complicated by the probability that there was a second Antigonid Apamea (the daughter of Philip V) who married a second Prusias (see APAMEA 2).

On the whole, ancient evidence seems more likely to support the existence of such a royal woman with such a name than it is to deny it. Polybius (15.22.1), referring to a time well before the marriage of Prusias' son Prusias II to Philip V's daughter, calls Prusias I the relative by marriage of Philip V. This passage, while demonstrating the reality of an earlier marriage alliance, offers no information about the identity of those who had already tied the two dynasties together, although it might be taken to imply that they were close to both Philip V and Prusias I.

Both Strabo (12.4.3) and Hermippus (*FHG* III 51, F 72) state that Prusias I renamed the town of Myrleia Apamea after his wife when Philip V captured it and gave it over to him. Granted that one of Demetrius II's wives was the Seleucid Stratonice (see STRATONICE 2), it was thought that Stratonice had produced a daughter by Demetrius II with an appropriately Seleucid name and that this daughter later married Prusias I.[28] Then doubts were expressed, primarily because of an inscription found at Piraeus naming the mother of Nicomedes II (and thus the wife of Prusias II) as Apamea[29] and because Stephanus Byzantinus (s.v. *Myrleia*), rather than make the wife of Prusias I the epononym of Apamea as Strabo and Hermippus do, instead claims that the city was named by Nicomedes II after his mother, the wife of Prusias II.

Although there can be no certainty, given the poor nature of the evidence, it seems more likely than not that this earlier Antigonid Apamea existed and did marry Prusias I, as F. W. Walbank persuasively argues.[30] Indeed, one might wonder at the oddity of the later Antigonid daughter with the Seleucid name if the earlier example, daughter of a Seleucid princess, did not exist.

Subsequent to his marriage to Stratonice, again arranged by his father, Demetrius married (ca. 245) Nicaea, the widow of their treacherous cousin Alexander, to bring back under Antigonid control the citadel and troops the widow's husband had earlier removed from Antigonid hands.

NICAEA

Nicaea's origins are uncertain. She was probably from a northern elite family, although not from a royal dynasty. Craterus (Antigonus Gonatas' half brother and loyal deputy in Greece, holder of the citadel of Corinth) went to considerable difficulty to import her as a bride for his son Alexander (Livy 35.26.5). After the death of Craterus, his son Alexander rebelled from the control of Antigonus Gonatas.[31] When Alexander subsequently died, rumors suggested that Antigonus had poisoned him (Plut. *Arat.* 17.2). On her husband's death, Nicaea inherited control of the great citadel whose return Antigonus coveted.

Antigonus Gonatas therefore sent his son Demetrius to her to propose a marriage between them. Nicaea agreed but retained control of the fortress. Antigonus Gonatas arrived and celebrated the marriage with the splendid display and spectacle now expected in royal weddings (see chap. 8) but used the festivities to distract Nicaea from her forces on the citadel and managed to trick them into surrendering control to him (Plut. *Arat.* 17.2-5; Polyaen. 4.6.1). The date of these events is not certain but is likely to have been 245 or 244 B.C., about ten years after Demetrius' first marriage, in a period when he still had no known male heirs.[32] Nicaea is not heard from again in connection with Demetrius.

Plutarch's account seems to imply that the marriage happened,[33] but it probably was not consummated. We hear of no children born from it. Although it is unlikely that the Antigonids ever intended the marriage to last, their offer of marriage must have seemed plausible to Nicaea. As her early caution with regard to the citadel demonstrates, she was well aware of how much father and son wanted it back but apparently concluded that it was reasonable that they would offer marriage to get it. Since Plutarch (*Arat.* 17.2) tells us she was older than Demetrius and we know of no children of hers from her earlier Antigonid marriage, she is unlikely to have been expected to produce heirs for Demetrius or to have expected it herself. She found it plausible, as the Antigonids expected, that they would offer a marriage alliance for political, not dynastic, reasons.

Nicaea's motives for accepting Demetrius' suit seem obvious enough, particularly in the light of Plutarch's narrative. She may have wanted physical security (her former husband was, from the Antigonid point of view, a traitor) and an end to ultimate military responsibility for the citadel (nothing suggests she had any personal military experience). She certainly wanted status. Plutarch's account emphasizes the royal nature of the wedding and the splendor of the public celebrations. It is not certain that her former husband had taken the title *basileus*.[34] There is no evidence that she was ever *basilissa*, although her husband's position and her own seem to have been at least quasi-royal,[35] but marriage to the Antigonid heir would certainly have been more prestigious than her first marriage.

Demetrius' "marriage" to Nicaea has often been seen as proof that he was single when it occurred,[36] yet there is no real evidence that this was the case. It is unlikely that Stratonice, his first wife (see STRATONICE 2), had as yet left Macedonia. Nicaea was no threat to her,[37] and there is no evidence that polygamy had entirely yielded to serial monogamy among the Antigonids, or that *basilissa* was a title limited to only one royal wife, if several existed at the same time (see chap. 8). The bait that tempted Nicaea to her disaster was not necessarily being Demetrius' sole wife but rather a more prestigious marriage, a royal marriage, greater physical security, and, perhaps, the remote chance that she might become the mother of a future king.

Demetrius' marriage to Nicaea, therefore, cannot be used to support arguments about the date of the beginning or the end of his other marriages. The Nicaea episode indicates that some women who were either part of the Macedonian elite or married into it continued to have occasional opportunities for the acquisition of power, military or otherwise, as they had in the fourth century but that they proved much less able to capitalize on these opportunities than their predecessors.

As we have seen, Stratonice left Macedonia of her own accord to pursue other ambitions in her homeland, including another royal marriage. Demetrius may have been reluctant to divorce her for fear of offending her family. Agatharchides (*FGrH* 86, F 20) does not specify a motive for Stratonice's departure, but Justin (28.1.1–4) says that she left because of yet another marriage of Demetrius to the Molossian princess Phthia. According to Justin, then, Demetrius planned to be polygamous but Stratonice left rather than accept a polygamous situation that, unlike the marriage to Nicaea, disadvantaged her.

PHTHIA

Phthia was the daughter of Alexander II of Epirus and his half sister, Olympias. On her father's death, her mother, Olympias, offered Phthia to Demetrius II because she, regent for two minor sons, needed help against the onslaughts of the Aetolians. According to Justin (28.1.2), Olympias knowingly committed her daughter to a polygamous marriage because she was desperate for Demetrius' assistance. His acceptance of Olympias' offer, whatever his motivation, apparently precipitated not only the departure of his Seleucid wife, Stratonice, but also the beginning of a war with the Aetolians. Despite Olympias' efforts, the demise of the Aeacid house soon followed.[38]

Little more is known with certainty of Phthia. Her name has been restored to Athenian inscriptions dated to 236/5 and 235/4, both of which refer to her husband as *basileus* and to her as *basilissa* and also mention their children. The name of no other wife of Demetrius II will fit in the spaces to be restored.[39] Phthia's name also appears on several Delian inventories. On the Delian lists, *basilissa* Phthia, the daughter of Alexander, offers a *phiale* (a flat cup or bowl used for drinking or libations).[40] The omission of her husband's name could mean that she made the dedication after his death or before her marriage, but it could mean that, like Stratonice, daughter of Demetrius Poliorcetes, and her many dedications at Delos (see STRATONICE 1), Phthia used the patronymic only, although she was married (see chap. 8).

Scholars have long debated whether Phthia was the mother of Philip V. Philip V was born ca. 238/7 (Polyb. 4.5.3, 24.1). As we have seen, inscriptional evidence demonstrates that Demetrius was married to Phthia by 236/5. Moreover, the reference in the inscription to children of Phthia's[41] suggests that she had married Demetrius several years before, ca. 238/9.[42]

Therefore, Phthia was almost certainly married to Demetrius, father of Philip, at the time of Philip's birth; it is impossible to rule her out of consideration as his mother. As we shall see, however, another woman may well have been his mother (see CHRYSEIS and below).

The difficulty with believing that Phthia was Philip V's mother is basic. Although Demetrius II was almost certainly married to Phthia at the time Philip V was born (238/7), the only ancient evidence about Philip V's mother calls her Chryseis, not Phthia.

CHRYSEIS

A woman named Chryseis had become the wife of Antigonus Doson by ca. 227/6 when she made a generous contribution to the Rhodians after their terrible earthquake (Polyb. 5.89.7). Virtually nothing else about her life is certain.

Three ancient sources say that she was the mother of Philip V and therefore, necessarily, either the wife or mistress (Eusebius' language, however, specifies that Demetrius married her; see below) of Philip's father, Demetrius II. Eusebius (*Chron.* 1. 237–38) says that Demetrius, having married one of his captives and named her Chryseis, had his son Philip by her. After the death of Demetrius, his relative (known to us as Antigonus Doson), already guardian for Philip, was made king by the Macedonians, who made him marry Chryseis (see chap. 1 on marriage of royal widows). Doson promised not to raise any children of his by Chryseis. *Etymologicum Magnum*, s.v. "Doson," says that Doson married Chryseis, the mother of Philip. Syncellus (535.19) says that Philip V was the son of Demetrius and the captive Chryseis.[43] Three other sources say that Doson married the mother of Philip but do not name the woman in question (Plut. *Aem.* 8.2; Just. 28.3.9–10; Paus. 7.7.4).

If we had no other information about Demetrius' marital arrangements and children during this period, we would conclude that Chryseis, Philip V's mother, was wife first to Demetrius II and later to Doson. But Demetrius was almost certainly married to Phthia at the time of Philip V's birth and had children by her (see PHTHIA). Common sense makes some conclusions plausible. Philip's mother, whoever she was, was married to his father. Doson would not have married her had that not been the case.[44] Given the existence of ancient sources that say that Doson married Philip's mother and that Philip's mother's name was Chryseis, that other sources know that Doson married Philip's mother but do not name her, and that no source offers another name for Philip's mother, it is quite likely that Chryseis was indeed his mother. Thus the evidence suggests that Demetrius II was married to Phthia at the time of Philip V's birth but that the name of Philip V's mother, a woman who was almost certainly also the wife of Demetrius, was Chryseis.

There are two possible solutions to this seeming paradox.[45] In recent years, following a suggestion first made by Tarn, many scholars have held that Phthia and Chryseis were the same woman.[46] This is not impossible. In other cases where scholars have concluded that the same royal woman was known by more than one name, however, there has been direct evidence linking the several names and suggesting that they referred to the same person (e.g., Diod. 18.2.4 and *FGrH* 156, F 1.1, 1.9, 1.23; Plut. *Mor.* 401a–b). Cases that lack such direct evidence have generally been disputed, and no ancient source links the two names Phthia and Chryseis. Moreover, the practice of name changing seems to have died out in the late fourth century, as formal titles for royal women developed (see chaps. 1, 8). The possibility that Chryseis and Phthia were the same person cannot be ruled out, but it is not strong.[47]

The alternative solution is obvious. If Demetrius was not married to one woman with two names, then he was married to two women at the same time and one of them, Chryseis, was the biological mother of Philip V and the future wife of Antigonus Doson. In that case, Demetrius was polygamous. Sylvie Le Bohec rightly pointed out how suspiciously convenient for historians the Phthia-Chryseis hypothesis remains,[48] convenient, that is, if one refuses to consider the possibility of polygamy. There has been a consistent tendency in scholarship on Antigonid Macedonia to assume (but never argue) that Macedonian kings had ceased to be polygamous or at least that they had one official *basilissa* (see chap. 8). As a consequence, most scholars have failed to note how strong the evidence is that Demetrius had two wives (at least) during the early 230s and that Doson subsequently married the one who was the mother of the heir. Certainly the burden of proof must remain with those who wish to argue that Phthia and Chryseis were the same person. Whereas we have both literary and inscriptional evidence for each woman's separate existence, we have no evidence that links them.

Demetrius II was polygamous but not on the scale or with the enthusiasm of Philip II or Demetrius Poliorcetes. If the information is correct that Doson, when he married Philip V's mother, whoever she was, had to promise that he would raise no sons of his by her (Porph. *FGrH* 260, F 3; Euseb. *Chron.* 1.238; c.f. Ceraunus' offer to Arsinoe: Just. 24.2.9), then we have further evidence that Antigonid kings found the risk of too many heirs greater than the risk of too few. The primary reason for Demetrius' polygamy is that, having reached his late thirties, he had no heir. Faced with this threat to the succession, he was forced to return to the messy habits of the Argeads and early Successors. The risk of too many heirs was considerable, but the risk of none at all was greater.

The volume of scholarship dealing with the issue of the identity of Philip V's mother is disproportionate to its importance. More important than straightening out this obscure tangle is the obvious message of its obscurity. We know nothing certain about the mother of the greatest of Antigonid rulers, not even so elementary a fact as her identity. Nothing could be more compelling evidence for the decline of the importance of royal women and their role in Macedonian monarchy during the Antigonid period.

The obscurity of royal women is even more marked in the reign of Philip V.[49] Although we know that Philip V had two wives because we know that his two sons, Perseus and Demetrius, had different mothers, we do not know the names of either. No evidence necessitates that he was married to these women simultaneously. Polycrateia, widow of the younger Aratus, *may* have been the mother of Perseus, who is said to have been Argive (Plut. *Arat.* 54.3, *Aem.* 8.7), but we do not know this for certain. Perseus' mother, whoever she was, may have died before Philip married Demetrius' mother. The only serious struggle for the throne between two members of the Antigonid dynasty occurred during the reign of Philip V. Although the two brothers had different mothers and each apparently had support within Macedonia, we hear of no political roles for their mothers or (if one assumes at least one if not both women were dead) their families. Instead, Rome plays the mother's role as advocate for one candidate for the throne over the other.[50]

POLYCRATEIA
Polycrateia, originally the wife of the younger Aratus of Sicyon (Livy 27.31.8), after conducting an affair with Philip V while he was a guest in her husband's house (Plut. *Arat.* 49.1, 51.2–3), was ultimately carried off to Macedonia by

Philip (Livy 33.21.23–24). As Livy narrates the deaths of the Arati before he announces her departure for Macedonia and as he claims that Polycrateia accompanied Philip in the hope of a royal marriage (27.31.8), it is usually assumed that she left after their deaths, ca. 213. The deaths are often attributed to Philip V's skill as a poisoner (Polyb. 8.12.2–6; Plut. *Arat.* 52, 54; Paus. 2.9.4). This is the obviously hostile tradition about Polycrateia.

Beloch suggests that Polycrateia did indeed marry Philip V and that she may have been a member of the Argive house of Polycrates of Argos, influential at the court of Ptolemy Philopater and Ptolemy Epiphanes. He also argues that Polycrateia was the mother of Perseus, last of the Macedonian kings.[51] What little ancient evidence there is about Perseus' parentage is also extremely hostile. According to Plutarch, he was the son of an Argive seamstress, Gnaethaenion, and he was smuggled into court by an unnamed wife of Philip who claimed that he was her son by Philip (Plut. *Arat.* 54.3, *Aem.* 8.7). Livy (39.53.3–4) simply says that Perseus was the son of a *paelex* (concubine) and did not resemble his father (implying that, as Plutarch stated, Perseus was not Philip's biological son).

What to make of a tradition so overtly hostile to Philip V and Perseus and so overtly sympathetic to Roman interests is no easy task.[52] It seems almost certain that Philip married Polycrateia, as Livy implies. The omission of this fact from sources so generally uninterested in royal women is hardly surprising, and the tale in Plutarch about the dubious paternity of Perseus suggests that he, at least, believed that Philip V had a wife who was neither the natural mother of Perseus nor the mother of Demetrius. The veracity of the account of royal adultery is dubious. Hammond could be right to attribute it to a misunderstanding of Macedonian royal polygamy as well as to general hostility to Philip V.[53]

Polycrateia may not have been the mother of Perseus, but it is possible she was. It is difficult to believe that our sources would have missed such a juicy bit of gossip about the parentage of the prince they so loved to hate,[54] but Perseus' somewhat unusual name[55] and the belief that his mother was Argive are suggestive. All the passages denigrating his birth as compared to his rival half brother, Demetrius, could be hostile exaggerations based on the fact that his mother was not Macedonian and not of a royal family.[56]

Why, if he already had a son and if it was contrary to usual Antigonid practice, did Philip V marry again, even if his first wife were dead?

Could his second wife have been more prestigious than his first? Given his other ambitions, one might expect that he would have tried for prestigious brides and marriage alliances, yet that does not seem to have been the case. Perhaps Rome already cast so long a shadow that Philip hesitated to contract an international alliance; perhaps his reading of domestic politics and his concerns with the Greek peninsula lay behind his surprisingly insular marriage policy.[57]

After Philip's son Perseus succeeded him, international marriage alliances certainly became an Antigonid goal. Aside from a possible early marriage to a Bastarnian princess,[58] Perseus was sought in marriage by Seleucus IV for his daughter Laodice and also gave his sister Apamea as a bride to the king of Bithynia (see LADDICE; APAMEA 2). Indeed, these two glamorous marriage alliances (celebrated with as much pomp as the Roman presence permitted) aroused the anger and jealousy of Eumenes of Pergamum and were the cause of his complaints to Rome (Livy 42.12.2–4; App. *Mac.* 11.2). This Seleucid alliance (which probably produced two sons and a daughter) would do no practical good to Perseus in the end[59] but speaks to the grand plans and prestige he had early in his reign. Supposedly, it was the capture of the children of this marriage that led to Perseus' own capture (Plut. *Aem.* 26.2).[60] Laodice apparently lived to wed again and ended her days in other, although equally violent, circumstances. If she played any political role in the desperate struggles of her husband's reign, we do not know it.

LAODICE

Laodice, daughter of Seleucus IV, married Perseus, the last king of Macedonia about 178/7, at her father's request (Livy 42.12.3–4). She was probably his second wife.[61] Treaty bound not to make the trip himself, Perseus arranged for the Rhodian navy, newly outfitted at his expense, to convey his bride to him with great pomp: the king gave each of the sailors on the accompanying ships a golden crown, and a host of dignitaries attended (Polyb. 25.4.8–9; App. *Mac.* 11.2; Livy 42.12.4).

This splendid and yet traditional alliance of two dynasties so often united by marriage in the past nonetheless seemed threatening in the context of the growing power of Rome. Eumenes II complained to the Roman senate about Perseus' two recent marriage alliances,[62] both with royal houses, and of his use of the Rhodian fleet (Livy 42.12.3–4; App. *Mac.* 11.2). In Livy, Eumenes argues to the Romans that Perseus's popularity came in part from anti-Roman sentiment and that Perseus, as evidenced by the two weddings and their good reception internationally, had great authority even among the other kings. In Appian, Eumenes saw both the marriage alliances and the Rhodian arrangement as somehow subversive. The Romans may have seen the marriages as signifying a coalition of kings aligning against them, whereas it actually signified a coalition against Eumenes.[63] The power of Rome and the disruption in Hellenic affairs Rome's growth precipitated were so great that maintaining traditional practice could be interpreted as provocative, and so, in a way, it was.[64] The alliance did Perseus little practical good when war with Rome came.[65]

Laodice apparently had three children by Perseus, two boys and a girl (Plut. *Aem.* 33.4). Probably not long after her marriage, the Delians put up an honorary inscription to her, praising her for her *eusebeia* (piety) to the sanctuary, commemorating a relationship that had become customary between them and the royal women of Macedonia (*IG* XI 4.1074, SIG 639 = *Choix* 70).[66]

But the patterns so long well established among Hellenistic dynasties were shattered by the brutally decisive defeat of Perseus at Pydna. Plutarch (*Aem.* 26.2) preserves a hostile and yet pathetic account of the last days of independence for the Antigonids. Perseus fled with his wife and children to sanctuary on Samothrace, another traditional recipient of royal Macedonian *eusebeia,* but, tricked at every turn, he finally gave himself up to Roman authorities when they contrived to capture his children.[67] Laodice, however, unlike her husband and her children, all of whom marched in the Roman triumph (*Aem.* 33.4), somehow managed to find her way back to the court of the Seleucids.

We do not know why Laodice, after capture by the Romans, was able to return to her homeland while her husband and children were retained in Roman custody. Her separation from her husband and children may have been involuntary, the consequence of Roman reluctance to offend her brother, or it may have been voluntary, particularly given the apparent hopelessness of her husband's situation. Perhaps when her husband turned himself in for the sake of their children, she did not. In most ancient legal systems, a mother had no legal claim on her children, who were seen as the property of her husband. It would have been easier than in modern circumstances, therefore, for a mother to be separated from her children or to separate herself.

Some years later Laodice's brother Demetrius I arranged a new dynastic marriage for her, this time with the king of Cappadocia, Ariarathres V, but her would-be groom backed out of the arrangement when he feared Roman disapproval (Diod. 31.28; Just. 35.1.2). Then, in all probability, she married her brother, and it is her image that appears with his on coins.[68] After her husband's death she and her son were murdered by his regent (Livy, *Epit.* 50). Her murder suggests that she had acquired political power in her homeland and it was necessary to eliminate her.

This last Macedonian royal wife is typical of many such women. Our evidence demonstrates that she, like so many other brides in marriage alliances, functioned several times over as a kind of dynastic token. She may have had ambitions and drives of her own—her survival of the collapse of Antigonid power as well as her murder could suggest that—but there is no evidence to tell us more.

APAMEA 2
Perseus gave his sister in marriage to Prusias II of Bithynia, at Prusias' request, about the same time that Perseus took his Seleucid bride, Laodice (App. *Mith.* 12.1.2; Livy 42.12.3–4). The sources connect this royal alliance to Perseus' great prestige at the time. Although neither Livy nor Appian names this Antigonid bride, it is likely that she was called Apamea. An inscription from Asia Minor but found in Piraeus[69] demonstrates that the name of the mother of Nicomedes II, son of Prusias II, was Apamea. Naming an Antigonid princess after the founding mother of the Seleucid dynasty might seem odd but not perhaps if she had a half aunt of that name (see APAMEA 1). While one ancient author claims that Apamea's son Nicomedes II renamed the city of Myrleia after her (Steph. Byz. s.v. "Myrleia"), two others claim that Prusias I renamed the city after his wife Apamea (Strab. 12.4.3; Hermippus *FHG* III 51, F 72; see APAMEA 1). Perseus derived no long-term benefit from the marriage; certainly his brother-in-law was no help in his final confrontation with Rome (Livy 42.29.3).

The pattern of evidence on royal women throughout the Antigonid period demonstrates that they played a smaller and less public role in Macedonian monarchy than previously.[70] The poor quality and quantity of the sources for most of the Antigonid period could distort this pattern, but the much better documented reigns of Philip V and his son Perseus make it evident that royal women played no significant role in political events, even in circumstances that had enabled them to do so in the past. The mothers of Philip II and of Alexander were powers to be reckoned with, but we cannot be sure even of the name of Philip V's mother. His sons by two different women struggled for power and, again, we do not even know their mother's names, let alone have any reason to believe that they played a role in their sons' succession struggles. At that moment when Antigonid history is best documented, royal women are virtually invisible within Macedonia.

Why did royal women become so much less prominent in Antigonid Macedonia at the very time that they were becoming more important both individually and institutionally elsewhere? Macurdy argued that the decline in political action by royal women was not so much a change as a return to an earlier Argead norm. Her analysis is unfortunately vitiated by the fact that she appeared to equate "political action" by royal women with political rule.[71] Political action by Argead women, as we have seen, covered a broad range of activities, most typically the exercise of influence, but never included rule.

Macurdy also claimed that the power of the last three Argead generations of royal women had been the exception because of "force of circumstances and because of their own strong will and determination to secure it,"[72] implying that chance and personality explained both the power of some Argead women and the lack of it in Antigonid women. Chance and the vagaries of human character, together and separately, may indeed have been factors in the limitation of royal women's role. If, for instance, an unusual number of royal wives happened to die early, some of the decline in prestige and action might be explained. A series of passive, domestically oriented royal wives would certainly have had consequences. The power of even an aggressive woman such as Stratonice, wife of Demetrius II, may have been constrained by the chance that she failed to produce a son.

Yet these factors alone do not provide an adequate explanation for this long-term phenomenon. Although still without a son, Stratonice was able to play a much more active political role outside of Macedonia (see STRATONICE 2). So too, apparently, did Laodice, wife of Perseus (see LAODICE).

　　　　　　　　　　　WOMEN AND MONARCHY IN MACEDONIA

Their Macedonian context rather than their personalities or their ability to produce heirs limited them. Both of these women were murdered after their departure from Macedonia, apparently because of their political influence in Seleucid circles. But, unless one countenances Livy's (42.5.4) slander about Perseus' murder of an anonymous wife, no one bothered to murder a royal wife in Macedonia after Thessalonice. In Antigonid Macedonia, royal wives were too insignificant to be worth murdering.

The same circumstances that in the fourth century produced political prominence for royal women—struggles for the succession, periods with a minor heir to the throne—failed to produce them in Antigonid times. Whoever the mother of Philip V was, she was able to play no role in events. Whoever the mother and whatever the maternal clan of Philip V's son Demetrius, we hear nothing of them. Situations that in the past had created possibilities did not in Antigonid times. The decline in the importance of royal women cannot simply constitute a return to earlier Argead days, because the same circumstances did not produce similar consequences.

Factors more important than chance and personality acted to limit the role of royal women after the establishment of the Antigonid dynasty.[73] This decline in the importance of royal women was directly connected to changes in the nature of Macedonian monarchy, just as the earlier growth in the power and prominence of royal women had been.

A passage in Plutarch suggests one kind of change in Macedonian monarchy. Plutarch (*Demetr.* 3.3–4) pointed out that the Antigonids, unlike the other dynasties, did not indulge in dynastic violence, noting that Philip V's execution of his son Demetrius was the only exception. In the other dynasties, he said, the killing of sons by fathers and the murder of mothers, wives, and especially brothers were so much the norm that they came to be seen as an ordinary part of royal statecraft. The Antigonids avoided dynastic murder by avoiding multiple heirs and multiple wives, let alone the combination of the two; the only Antigonid king who had more than one adult son was the only one who was forced to kill a son because of a contested succession. Demetrius II, the only Antigonid king likely to have been polygamous, experienced some strife because of his multiple wives (i.e., Stratonice's departure and supposed warmongering) but escaped serious trouble because he had only multiple wives, not multiple sons by different wives. The Antigonids did not murder their wives or mothers, because, as we have seen, there was no need to.

The Antigonids, compared to the other dynasties as well as to the Argeads, consistently preferred a narrow public presentation of the monarchy, one that reduced the size of the dynasty by limiting the number of heirs and the public role of royal women. Perhaps because they had to cope with the rule of a country shattered by years of anarchy and destabilized by the end of the Argead dynasty, the Antigonids avoided perceived risk. Like their contemporaries elsewhere, they seemed increasingly inclined to see multiple wives as problematic (see chap. 8), but whereas elsewhere the decline of polygamy tended to elevate the status of the royal wife, it does not seem to have done so in Macedonia proper. Unlike their contemporaries, many Antigonids also saw unacceptable risk in multiple sons. The consequence of both inclinations was to emphasize the person of the king rather than the dynasty.

The narrowing of the public image of the monarchy was not the only change in the nature of Macedonian monarchy that affected the role of royal women. Antigonid monarchy may increasingly have been understood as an office rather than as the dominance of the clan, as it had been in Argead times. Such an understanding of monarchy may have begun to develop in the chaotic period after the departure of Demetrius Poliorcetes and may have solidified when the Antigonids took over. The demise of the Argead clan necessitated that dominion be distinguished from dynasty. The career of Sosthenes, a non-Argead who ran Macedonia but refused a royal title (Just. 24.5.1), demonstrates this development. When Antigonus Gonatas became king, dominion and dynasty had to be consciously reunited, and their relationship was somewhat rationalized in the process. The monarchy had been so closely tied to the only royal family that Macedonia had known that dynasty superseded office in thinking about monarchy. Now that the link between dynasty and monarchy had been broken and dynasty could no longer easily supersede office, Macedonians were more able to see kingship in abstract terms, as an office that any person or family, if appropriately recognized, might hold.[74]

These changes in the nature of monarchy led to a deemphasis on the women of the clan at the same time that some formal aspects of the role of royal women were institutionalized. The virtual disappearance of the interrelated phenomenon of multiple wives and multiple heirs obviated the role of royal mother as succession advocate.[75] By the time an Antigonid succession actually was disputed, the mothers of the rival heirs ap-

WOMEN AND MONARCHY IN MACEDONIA

parently played no part in their struggle and the king himself resolved the dispute, during his own reign.

Monarchy in the Argead period, like that of the early medieval period, was primarily household monarchy. Tasks and offices were not clearly and consistently defined. No firm line was drawn between the public and the private spheres and royal women moved between these two areas of action. They could not easily be excluded from an institution so loosely conceived.[76] Women such as Olympias or her mother-in-law, Eurydice, found benefit in the lack of definition of their role.

The Cassandreian inscription referring to Antigonus Gonatas' wife Phila implies (see above and PHILA 2) a more defined role for royal wives than that of earlier Argead women. Being a king's wife did not become an office with clearly defined duties, but it may have come closer to doing so than previously. The establishment of a title for royal women (see chap. 8) similarly seems to institutionalize the role of royal women to some degree. If some institutionalization of the role of royal women did occur, it may actually have circumscribed the power of such women by defining it. The institutionalization and definition of the roles of both kings and their wives acted to limit royal women and to elevate royal men, much as similar developments did in medieval monarchy.[77]

Greek affairs and attitudes affected the Antigonids more than they had Argead rulers. In the middle period of the Antigonid dynasty, there seem to have been no prestigious international marriage alliances, perhaps because the other rulers saw Macedonia as a backwater, perhaps because the Antigonids were reluctant to involve themselves outside the Greek peninsula.[78] Intensified Hellenization may have helped to limit the role of royal women as well as to cause discomfort with royal polygamy, particularly given the number of kings' wives who seem to have come from mainland Greece rather than one of the other Macedonian dynasties. Greeks were unused to polygamy and suspicious of political roles for women. This attitude was nothing new, but the need of the Macedonian royal house to cater to Greek opinion was now greater than it had previously been.

The other Hellenistic dynasties needed legitimization. The new dynasties had to create a monarchy out of whole cloth and therefore often used their women members as vehicles of legitimization. The Antigonids, once back in Macedonia, seemed comparatively unconcerned about legitimacy. Perhaps Macedonian fear of the reappearance of chaos if the Antigonids were rejected gave the dynasty a built-in security that the other dynasties lacked. Within Macedonia, there was apparently no need for the ruler cults or practices such as royal sibling marriage that shored up the other Hellenistic monarchies and often elevated the status of women in the dynasty.

A number of factors, as I have argued, made it much less necessary to give prominence to the women of the Antigonid dynasty and, that granted, Antigonid kings preferred to limit the importance of women in their families. Allotting a wider public role to royal women inevitably meant that some power and prestige was conferred on those other than the king, and it is not surprising that a ruler would prefer to avoid such seepage of royal power if it were possible to do so. This tendency, in turn, may have made Antigonid rulers less preferable grooms for royal fathers looking for husbands for their daughters. We know that Demetrius II's wife Stratonice grew restless under the limits imposed by the Macedonian situation, and it is possible that another Seleucid princess did as well (see Laodice). The narrow horizons of Antigonid Macedonia limited the role royal women played in its monarchy.

CHAPTER EIGHT

Changes in the Public Role
of Macedonian Royal Women
in the Hellenistic Period

The early Hellenistic period (the era of the Successors, (323–281) was one of tremendous change for royal women. Some of these changes proved merely ephemeral, but others endured.[1] Much of the evidence considered in this chapter comes from the early Hellenistic period because this comparatively brief span of time saw the establishment of most of the innovations in the role of Macedonian royal women for the entire Hellenistic period. It will sometimes be necessary to look back to the reign of Philip, less often to that of Alexander, and sometimes equally important to trace developments into the mid-third century.

My focus remains the Macedonian homeland. The other Hellenistic kingdoms are richer in information about women in general and particularly about royal women. Many changes in the role of royal women, although originating in Macedonia proper, were abandoned there or limited in their use but pursued and extended in the Successor kingdoms. Philip II, the Ptolemies, and the Seleucids emphasized dynasty and therefore included royal women in a prominent role, in a way and to a degree that Alexander and the Antigonids did not (see chap. 7).

WEDDING FESTIVALS and EXTRAVAGANZAS

Before the marriage of Philip's daughter Cleopatra to her uncle, the brother of Olympias, we know of no grand royal wedding celebrations. For much of its history Macedonia was too chaotic, the income of the kings too limited, and their prestige too low outside of Macedonia to make such an international festival possible or likely. Royal weddings may have been seen as private or at least Macedonian events. The celebration of 336 was an innovation, one that would create a precedent for kings of Macedonian blood after Philip.

Turning his daughter's wedding into an international festival was extremely clever because it satisfied various political, cultural, religious, and dynastic needs. First, it resolved a specific political problem by offering public proof of the reconciliation of the Argead dynasty of Philip and the Aeacid dynasty of Olympias, reconfirming the alliance originally established by Olympias' marriage but jeopardized by events arising from Philip's last marriage (see chap. 3; OLYMPIAS; CLEOPATRA 3). Quarrels between Philip and his son by Olympias, Alexander, had caused upset not only in Macedonia and Epirus but also in the Greek world (Plut. *Alex.* 9.6, *Mor.* 179c) in the critical period just before the departure of the Graeco-Macedonian expedition Philip planned to lead to Asia.[2] If Justin (9.6.3) correctly reports that Philip marched in the procession to the theater between his son and his new son-in-law, between his heir and Olympias' brother, then the ceremony made literal the reconciliation.

Second, the celebration was directly related to Philip's new role as *hegemon* (leader) of the Greeks and to imminent invasion of the Persian Empire. Philip wanted to generate greater unity in the league. Many of the cities of the league he had created, as well as prominent individuals, gave him golden crowns during the festival (Diod. 16.92.1). Diodorus' (16.91.4–93.1) account of the festivities emphasizes Philip's desire to cater to Greek opinion and to involve many Greeks in the festivities, partly to indicate his gratefulness for the honor of his new position. Ironically, Philip's wish to stress his role as leader of the league contributed to his murder: Diodorus (16.93.1) says that he kept his usual bodyguard at a distance to demonstrate that he was protected not by guards but by the goodwill of the Greeks.

Third, Philip's innovative festival displayed both his wealth and his Hellenism. Diodorus describes sacrifices to the gods, musical competitions, great banquets, dramatic recitations and presentations, and athletic competitions (the latter also noted by Justin [9.6.3]). Philip wanted as many as possible to see this display: he invited personal friends, encouraged courtiers to bring along their foreign friends, and also invited official delegations from city-states. He turned his daughter's marriage into a kind of ancient media event.

WOMEN AND MONARCHY IN MACEDONIA

Fourth, the wedding festivities served a religious purpose. Cleopatra's wedding was not simply a huge, splendid party. Philip transformed it into a Panhellenic festival. Such festivals traditionally had a religious foundation, and so did Philip's. Diodorus (16.92.1) called it a *paneguris*, a term often used for festivals in honor of a god. Philip ordered great sacrifices to be celebrated jointly with the wedding (Diod. 16.91.4), probably in connection with the annual Olympic festival in honor of Zeus.[3] But the most notorious part of Philip's program (Diod. 19.92.5) was the appearance of his own godlike statue, following impressive images of the twelve Olympians, making him enthroned with (*sunthronos*) them.

Fifth, Cleopatra's wedding served a dynastic purpose. Philip's wedding festival, the model for Hellenistic rulers, displayed an ideology of monarchy and dynasty similar to that of subsequent rulers. It emphasized the nearly divine specialness of the royal house and transformed the domestic into the Panhellenic, the familial into the Olympian. That the festival ended in the sudden murder of the man who had conceived it only served to guarantee that most of the Macedonian and Greek elite would recall it vividly.

The wedding festival served a number of different but hardly mutually exclusive purposes. W. R. Connor suggests that traditional scholarship on connections between political leaders and cults and festivals has too narrowly interpreted such occasions as propaganda. He argues that festivals organized by leaders ought to be understood as interactive events, not simply occasions for the imposition of the will of an individual on the masses. Participants could indicate their consent and approval. Such events built unity, not only by creating a communal experience, but also by involving participants and those who staged them in a common enterprise.[4] Seen in the light of Connor's understanding of festivals, Philip's wedding festival for his daughter played a role and served a purpose similar to that Simon Price has argued ruler cults served, a way to integrate the power of rulers into existing institutions, particularly polis institutions, and to express the relationship between rulers and cities and control or modify it.[5] In this context, the "convergence between festivals and political disturbance" that Connor notes makes sense and helps to explain why the assassin of Philip II chose the wedding festival as the occasion for his act.[6] If festivals were ordinarily vehicles for the population to offer consent or approval to rulers, they could also be events that enabled groups or individuals to indicate disapproval.[7]

Philip's son Alexander, a ruler more focused on his personal achievement than dynastic stability, as demonstrated by the fabulous wealth and ceremony surrounding the mass marriages at Susa, did not entirely forget his father's innovation. Alexander's purposes at Susa, however, were not so much dynastic as imperial.[8] In the early days after Alexander's death, the marriages of the Successors tended to be hurried affairs. By the end of the century, after the Successors began to call themselves kings, the wedding festival prototype of Philip's reasserted itself.

The first to imitate it was Demetrius Poliorcetes.[9] When he married Deidameia, sister of Pyrrhus, like Philip II he did so in association with a festival, that of Hera (Plut. *Demetr.* 25.2). Soon after the battle of Ipsus, when marriages between the developing dynasties proliferated,[10] Demetrius further developed Philip's precedent. He turned his trip to Asia to bring his daughter Stratonice to marry Seleucus (ca. 299) into an international event, complete with his fleet. The two kings feasted back and forth. The departure of bride and groom for Antioch grew into a ceremony (Plut. *Demetr.* 31.3–32.3).

The royal wedding now became so central an aspect of Hellenistic monarchy that it could stand for royal legitimacy. It was twice used to trick would-be wives into accepting marriage with royal men they rightly suspected. One of these trick weddings lured Arsinoe's sons into a death trap (see ARSINOE), and another fooled Nicaea into delivering the citadel of Corinth to Antigonus Gonatas (see NICAEA).

It is fitting that one of the last royal wedding extravaganzas—certainly the last Antigonid one—was at once the sign of the resurgence of Antigonid power and the source, in part, of enmity that helped to destroy the dynasty. Perseus' marriage to Laodice, daughter of Seleucus IV in 178/7 involved the conveyance of the bride by the Rhodian fleet (suitably rewarded with golden crowns and gifts of lumber; Polyb. 35.4.9–10). Livy (42.12.3–4) says that this marriage (as well as the one Perseus arranged for his sister with Prusias) impressed even the other kings with his authority and precipitated a flurry of diplomatic activity in his favor. Eumenes of Pergamum used these marriages and the elaborate ceremony surrounding them against Perseus (App. *Mac.* 9.11.1–2). For both Eumenes and the Roman senate, the weddings symbolized the dynastic power they disliked.

Philip II's innovation, the transformation of the initiation of a marriage alliance into a Panhellenic festival celebrating the wealth and power of royal dynasties, was a success. The Diadochi, ever in need of legitimizing devices, took it up with enthusiasm and, thanks to the physical distances separating their kingdoms, even improved on it by adding the bride's trip to the wedding to the event, thus reaching an even larger audience, the assorted peoples and shrines along the way as well as those assembled for the actual wedding.[11] The importance of the relationship between husbands and wives increased during the Hellenistic period.[12] Royal marriage festivals may have caused, contributed, or reinforced this more general phenomenon.

CITIES NAMED AFTER ROYAL WOMEN

When Philip II founded a city ca. 356 and named it after himself, his action was virtually unprecedented.[13] He and his contemporaries probably knew of no other *oikist* (city founder) who had given his own name to a city.[14] Alexander, while still merely a prince ca. 340, imitated his father and subsequently became an eponymous oikist many times over (Plut. *Alex.* 9.1; Steph. Byz. s.v. "Alexandreia, 3"). The Successors, before they had taken royal titles but when they were beginning to feel their way toward doing so, followed suit. In this same period the first city named after a royal woman, Thessaloniki, appeared.[15] By the beginning of the third century, the naming of cities after women in royal dynasties had become common.

Cassander, the first of Alexander's Successors to become an eponymous oikist,[16] founded both Cassandreia (Diod. 19.52.2) and Thessaloniki, a city he named after his Argead wife (Steph. Byz. s.v. "Thessaloniki"), ca. 316.[17] Cassander was the most vulnerable of the Successors to charges of usurpation (because of his murder of Olympias, his "arrest" of Alexander IV, and his control of the Macedonian homeland). His peculiar vulnerability probably led to his innovation. By naming his new city after his wife, he stressed his connection to the Argead dynasty and particularly to Philip, his bride's father. Her very name commemorated a victory of her father's and the Macedonian army.[18] The practice of naming of cities after women of royal dynasties began as a means of legitimization and was implemented by the Successor most in need of it.

Female eponymous foundations became commonplace among the Successors at the same time that dynastic marriages did, after Ipsus.[19] Kings who had initially claimed sovereignty on the basis of personal achievement then moved rapidly to advance claims of dynastic legitimacy as well. Naming a city after the mother, wife, or daughter of a king was an assertion of this new dynastic power; it is this context, rather than the mere fact that women's names were commemorated by city names (Greek cities were named after a great variety of things, some trivial, some quite important), that suggests the custom's importance.

Having a city named after herself did not necessarily convey any power to a woman, but it was an honor and one sometimes given because of her prominence. The Antigonids, not inclined in any event to stress the public role of royal women, founded few cities. In Macedonia there is only one other city named after a woman, Phila, founded by Demetrius II and named after his mother (Steph. Byz. s.v. "Phila").[20]

Oikists commonly had cults devoted to them (e.g., Cassander had a founder's cult at Cassandreia), but, of all the women after whom cities were named, only Amastris (niece of Darius III and wife, at various times, of Craterus, Dionysius of Heraclea Pontica, and Lysimachus) is known to have herself founded the city that was named after her (Memnon *FGrH* 434, F 4.4.9; Strab. 12.3.10; Steph. Byz. s.v. "Amastris"). No direct evidence demonstrates that eponymous royal women such as Thessalonice received cults in the cities named after them but not founded by them.

Nonetheless, Thessalonice and others like her may have received cult worship. Plutarch (*Mor.* 255a–e) tells a story—not historical but illustrative of a possible historical development—that suggests that an eponymous woman might receive cult honors although she did not found the city. According to Plutarch's tale, the conquerors of a city formerly called Pityoessa, out of gratitude to Lampsace for her help in bringing about the conquest, renamed the city after her, buried her within the city walls, and ultimately transmuted the original heroic honors she had been given to those of a god.[21] More historically, Messene, although not the *oikist* of the city named after her, received cult worship there.[22]

Not long after Thessaloniki's foundation, it began to be said that Thessalonice herself, not her husband, had founded it (Heidel. Epit. *FGrH* 155, F 2.4). Such a transposition, however literally untrue,[23] is not uncommon in the historical tradition of cities.[24] The unpopularity of Cassander and the Antipatrid dynasty, particularly after the murder of Thessalonice by one of her sons, probably inspired the transformation of Thessalonice into an *oikist* and could, in turn, have led to a cult for her.

Certainly Macedonian interest in the Argeads persisted as late as the third century A.D. A cult for Alexander existed in this period,[25] and cults for other prominent Argeads may have.[26] A statue base, apparently for a statue of Thessalonice and dating to the second or third century A.D. (in the inscription on the base, *IG* X 2.1 277, Thessalonice is called *basilissa* and her patronymic is given, but there is no reference to her husband), has been found in a house of Roman date in Thessaloniki, along with similar statue bases for Alexander the Great (referred to as *basileus* and the son of a god but not as a god himself) and his son Alexander (referred to as the son of Alexander, the son of a god, but *not* referred to as *basileus*; *IG* X 2.1 275 and 276).

These three statue bases could mean that all three Argeads received cults in Thessaloniki at this period, but the bases and inscriptions do not prove that they did. In any event, even if the statue base does mean that Thessalonice received a cult, its context would suggest that she did so as an Argead, not because the city was named after her or because she was later believed to have founded it.[27] Propaganda themes of the Severan dynasty might account for interest in Alexander, Philip II, and Olympias but could not explain reference to Thessalonice or Alexander IV. It is likely that interest in Argeads, including but not limited to cults, went back to Hellenistic times[28] and may have involved a city cult to Thessalonice.

The spread of these foundations speaks to a rapid return to a conceptualization of monarchy in familial rather than individual terms, to the need to legitimize not just the generation of the Successors but their descendants as well. The practice contributed to an understanding of monarchs as superhuman figures who could impose on the societies they controlled elements of their ordinary domestic lives but on a grand, perhaps Olympian, scale. Just as one recognized the statue of a god or a god king by its superhuman size, so one might recognize a clan as superhuman by the naming of that most basic unit of Hellenic culture, the polis, after a member of the dynasty.

CULT WORSHIP FOR ROYAL WOMEN AND THEIR IMAGES

Another innovation of the period was cultic honors for royal women. Although private, civic, and dynastic cults began to be directed at women associated with royal men by the late fourth century, virtually all the scanty scholarship on this topic deals with the Ptolemies and often goes no farther back than Arsinoe Philadelphus and the 270s. Cults for earlier Macedonian women are either ignored or mentioned in passing. Little analysis of the reasons for the initiation and existence of female cults has been attempted.[29]

I intend to trace the early development of cult worship of women at the end of the Argead dynasty and in the period of the Diadochi, link it to what we know about early Ptolemaic cults of royal women, and consider the reasons for the initiation of female cults. In pursuing this task, I have made certain assumptions about the general nature of ruler cults in the Hellenic world based on the work of earlier scholars.

Let me sketch briefly my views on this subject. The Greeks did not always draw a *firm* line between the human and the divine, although they usually understood them as distinct categories.[30] After all, a ruler cult is unlikely to develop in a culture that saw human and divine as entirely separate. It was a Homeric commonplace to call a warrior *isotheos* (equal to the gods, godlike). Similarly, women such as Briseis or Cassandra might be said to be *ikele* (like, resembling) golden Aphrodite (Hom. *Il.* 19.282, 24.699). The myth of Heracles, a mortal made immortal, demonstrated that a mortal might raise himself or herself to divinity by means of unusual achievement. Whereas Heracles was the exceptional human hero who became a god, female mortals, heroines, much more frequently achieved divine status.[31] Literature nagged Greeks to remember the distinction between human and divine (e.g., Pind. *Isthm.* 5.14; Alcm. frgs. 16–17); they needed reminding. The gods were like people, except that they had more power, much more.

Central to Greek cults was the recognition of the power of the gods. As Price has argued, ruler cults involved the recognition of the power of a human being over an individual or a city. They provided a way to integrate this power into existing institutions, a way to express the relationship between rulers and cities or individuals and to control or modulate it.[32] The first cult for a person established during that person's lifetime came during the career of Lysander.[33] Philip II flirted with divine cults and suggested his parity with the Olympians, but it is not certain that he received cult worship in his lifetime.[34] His son went further, first asserting divine sonship instead of mere divine ancestry and finally, in the last year of his life, having cults dedicated to him. After Alexander, cults instituted by Greek cities to the Successors appeared. Later dynastic cults administered by the kings themselves became commonplace.

Of course, the development of ruler cults is usually described in stages, as I have just done. The difficulty with such descriptions is that they imply the existence of clear distinctions in various steps along a linear path. Such distinctions are convenient but artificial. They are particularly unsuited to visual images, yet images are, I argue, critical to the development of cults. Assumptions about the motivation of image makers have little evidentiary basis. We have not come to terms with the essential ambiguity of physical images and recognized that their power derives from their ambiguity. Linear categorization should be used cautiously when considering the ways in which Greek peoples connected human and divine nature.

In contrast to the dearth of work that has been done on female cults, a great abundance of work has been done on male ruler cults. The quantity of scholarship on the deification of rulers in the Graeco-Roman world[35] derives from the recognition that ruler cult worship was a critical Greco-Roman institution. The existence of this large body of work also testifies to our near-inability to comprehend this institution. Our understanding of ruler cults will always be limited. The single god of the desert and the religions that worship him stand between us and those who put up altars and gave sacrifices and festivals in the name of Antigonus or dedicated votives to Arsinoe Aphrodite. It matters little whether an individual still believes in these religions. They continue to define even unbelief. Not one of us would think that a self-proclaimed atheist or agnostic was expressing disbelief in the gifts of golden Aphrodite or the truth of Apollo's oracles.

Our understanding of the nature of religious experience itself is so shaped by the nature of Christian experience that we have great difficulty recognizing as religious at all any belief or practice that departs from our Judaeo-Christian norm. Defining a religion in terms of personal belief is an idea we have imposed on a culture to which it is alien. Because of this imposition, the ruler cult has not been understood as religion at all but as politics, even though this distinction is ours and not that of antiquity.[36] Recent disdain for ritual tends to make us ignore its power.

The difficulties I have discussed are compounded when one looks at women's cults. Female cults developed in the same period that male ruler cults did and in similar, but not identical, fashion.[37] Indeed, the same monument, the Philippeum, is critical to understanding both.[38] Pausanias (5.20.9–10) recounts that at Olympia, within the Altis (which was apparently extended to include it),[39] was a round building called the Philippeum, constructed by Philip[40] after his defeat of the Greeks at Chaeroneia. Inside in Pausanias' day in the second century A.D. were three statues of ivory and gold of Philip II, Alexander, and Philip's father, Amyntas. Pausanias (5.17.4) notes that two other chryselephantine statues, of Olympias and Philip's mother, Eurydice,[41] once also stood there but were transferred to the nearby Heraeum by the time Pausanias visited the site. It would be interesting to know when and why the two female statues were moved. The action seems to suggest that their presence, unlike that of the male statues, was deemed somehow inappropriate by someone at a subsequent period.[42]

The statues stood on an elaborately carved, semicircular base that faced the door and was centered on it. Since the women's statues were no longer on the base, Pausanias is unlikely to have known what their placement had been. He described them last because they were no longer in the building. Philip's image may have been in the middle, opposite the door, images of his father and son on either side of him, and the female statues may have stood at each end.[43] All previous chryselephantine statues were cult images.

The purpose of the Philippeum, the nature of the building, and the intent of its presumed builder have been much disputed. This uncertainty is not accidental. The Philippeum is not only an ambiguous monument; it is a monument to ambiguity, a subtle piece of imagery from that master of public image, Philip. Philip decided to have it built after Chaeroneia. Any role Alexander had in its construction was nominal as the building is likely to have been completed no later than Alexander's departure for Asia in 334.[44] The monument's emphasis on dynastic rather than individual power suits Philip's priorities better than those of his son. The presence of the statue of Olympias is unremarkable and cannot be used to date the building and the choice of statuary.[45]

The Philippeum looked like a temple and was placed where one would expect a temple to be. It contained statues that looked like cult statues, yet there is no evidence for a divine cult. It was *not* a temple. It was *not* a treasury (the other treasuries contained no cult images and were not placed within the Altis). Its shape resembled that of *heroa* (heroes' shrines), but there is no evidence for heroic honors. It was *not* a *heroön*. We know what it was not but cannot be sure what it was, and that is the point.

What was it then? Philip offered those who visited the Panhellenic shrine a way to think about the power he had come to exercise. The Philippeum did not assert that this power was divine, but it implied that it might be and that this power was *like* the power of the gods. It parallels his decision to have his own statue appear with those of the twelve Olympians, but the Philippeum differs from that public image in an important way because it is also a dynastic monument. Five godlike statues, not one, once stood there. By implication, not only Philip but also the other four members of the dynasty were each *isotheos*. The picture of Philip as the thirteenth god presented at Cleopatra's wedding was a picture for the immediate future. At Olympia Philip chose to express his power in familial rather than individual terms because he intended Greek understanding of Macedonian power to be long-term and dynastic. The Philippeum stated or pictured things the way they were, in the terms Philip wanted them understood.[46]

It is important that the two women's statues were there. Philip included them in his public presentation of dynastic power. They were part of, not apart from, *basileia*.[47] Both Eurydice and Olympias played prominent and controversial roles in Greek affairs. Their inclusion is part of Philip's statement of the facts of power. They are part of the power the Greeks need to understand, and that is why they are there. It is critical that these too were chryselephantine statues. Philip's coy hints at divine status extended to the women of the clan.

These lavish images of two royal women were among the first public images of individual women in Greece. That statuary was long associated primarily with men is suggested by the word *andrias* (statue), derived from the word for a male human, although it was sometimes applied to the image of a woman (e.g., Phryne in Ath. 591b). No study of the development of female portraiture in Greek art exists, but general discussions of Greek portraiture suggest that portraiture of women paralleled the development of portraiture for men but on a much-reduced scale because of the much smaller public role of women.[48] Portraits of women, however, tended to be much more generalized than those of men and harder to distinguish from images of deities.[49] The development of portraiture parallels the development of cults for mortals.

The statues of Olympias and Eurydice were probably the very first in mainland Greece to commemorate women for what was, in effect, a political role. Of course, images of women had appeared on grave *stelai*, and earlier yet there were the *korai*, but none of these were genuine portraits.[50] An Athenian priestess named Lysimache had a portrait statue, dating to the very late fifth or early fourth century (Pliny *HN* 34.76),[51] and statuettes and statues of *kanephorai* (sacred basket bearers) once existed, although whether they were genuine portraits may be doubted.[52] A golden statue of the famous *hetaira* Phryne was dedicated at Delphi; it stood between the images of Philip II and Archidamus, king of Sparta (Ath. 591b–c; Paus. 10.14.4; Plut. *Mor.* 753 f.).[53] That the statue was gold, or at least looked golden, may suggest that Phryne, who tradition says was Praxiteles' model for Cnidian Aphrodite (Ath. 591a; Pliny *HN* 36.5.4), was alluding to a godlike status, perhaps even to the proverbially golden Aphrodite.[54] Also in the mid-fourth century, among the statues of initiates to the Eleusinian mysteries in the Athenian agora appeared those of a husband and wife.[55] And in Caria, on the coast of Asia Minor, a satrapy ruled by the Hecatomnid dynasty that practiced brother-sister marriage, public images of the women of the dynasty began to appear at about the same time.[56]

In Macedonia proper there is no good evidence for statues of royal women before those in the Philippeum at Olympia.[57] The statues Eurydice dedicated to Eucleia were probably statues of the goddess, not Eurydice, but another statue base found near Vergina may once have supported a statue of Eurydice.[58] Neither the heads, including some women, found on top of an archaic grave at Vergina[59] nor the small ivory heads from Tomb II at Vergina appear to be portraits.[60] Indeed, with the exception of the Roman statue base for an image of Thessalonice, there is no certain evidence in the following period.[61]

The inclusion of the women in the statue group was probably shocking at the time the Philippeum was built, both because public images of women were so rare and because their presence demonstrated how different from the world of the polis was the power of *dunasteia*. The triumph of the clan over the city-state was made concrete. Greeks often objected to monarchy because of the role royal women played, or were supposed to play, in it. Philip's household had been the source of much scandal (Plut. *Mor.* 179c). The Philippeum made no apologies; it flaunted the importance of royal women.

The relationship between image and cult is complex and critical.[62] Greek writers often referred to the statue as the person (e.g., Pausanias at both 5.17.4 and 5.20.10 speaks of Olympias or Amyntas, not of *statues* of Olympias or Amyntas, and uses the term *eikon* only when he must refer to the material of which the image is made), and Greek practice often shows a failure to make a firm distinction between the image and that of which it is an image, a phenomenon particularly observable in cult statues.[63] Statues and other images had some of the qualities of living beings.[64] Ancient writers often associated both the size of a statue and the material of its fabrication with divinity. Yet I do not believe, as some do,[65] that the multiplicity of images in our own culture blinds us to the impact of statues.

Such views exaggerate the differences between our perceptions and those of the people of the ancient world by arbitrarily attributing to us a degree of sophistication about physical images that many of us do not demonstrably possess. Although the erection of portrait statues is now comparatively rare, people today continue to transform monuments, even those without images of human figures, from mere representation to the thing itself.[66] The behavior of those who visit the Vietnam War Memorial in Washington, D.C., demonstrates a process not unlike that which made one refer not to a statue of Aphrodite but to Aphrodite. One writes letters of remembrance to people, not to inscribed walls.

Similarly, today we are not immune to the impact of statues. Indeed, much of the current power of the Vietnam Memorial derives from the personal engagement of those viewing it with the events and people it commemorates. The memorial groups of human figures, more recently added to the original wall of names commemorating those who died in the war and now generally considered less compelling, may become more so as the viewer's distance from these events increases. In fact, the figures were added because of popular pressure for their inclusion. Anyone who has ever excused herself or himself to a store mannequin, has come to feel uneasy in some undefinable way when viewing an exhibit of modern sculpture that includes groups of human figures riding a bus or eating in a restaurant, or has felt while sitting on a park bench somehow part of a group including the statue can begin to understand the role of statues in ancient culture.

Nor are we as indifferent to the size or material of statues as some seem to assume. The statue of Abraham Lincoln at his memorial in Washington, D.C., commands attention, yet it is hard to imagine a smaller version having the same effect. A walk through a museum displaying sizable gold images of human beings—I think, for instance, of the size and reaction of the crowds viewing the golden mask in the Tutankhamun exhibit at the Metropolitan Museum in the late 1970s—demonstrates that such images still inspire awe.

The links between visible wealth (of which gold remains the most universal example) and power, the sense of the viewer's diminished power in the presence of the potent and unchanging image, the awe generated by a larger-than-life human figure, and, above all, the oddly compelling impact of any human-sized replication of the human figure (thus the continuing appeal of Madame Tussaud's)—these are all things we may experience, if less intensely than did the Greeks. More difficult to replicate is the circumstances in which statues once appeared. For the Philippeum, one must imagine those five large statues, raised enough above ordinary eye level to force the viewer to look upward,[67] seen in a half-light from the two windows on either side of the door, gleaming with gold, pale with ivory, images (at least several of them) of living individuals and yet displayed like those of the gods.

Any life-size statue of a human figure, because of its size and the distinction that had caused it to be set up, may have alluded to the capacity of human beings to equal the gods through their achievements.[68] Pausanias (1.40.2) distinguished an *agalma*, an image that received cult worship, from an *eikon*, one that did not. The distinction, sometimes verbally blurred, was drawn on the basis of the treatment of the image, not the way it looked, and that treatment could change over time.[69] When images of individual women, royal and otherwise, began to be found among such statues in public places throughout the Greek world, Greeks must have had to make a considerable adjustment.[70]

Having attempted to recognize the critical role of statues in the early stages of cult worship, I now return to my task of establishing the early development of cults for women. The next evidence we have about women and cults relates to one of the women depicted in the Philppeum,

Olympias, mother of Alexander the Great. Plutarch (*Alex.* 3.2) cites Eratosthenes for the idea that Olympias herself first told Alexander of his divine sonship and other sources for the view that she rejected the notion. Despite this dubious anecdotal material, Alexander's belief in his divine sonship was clearly his own. Olympias was not with him at Siwah. Moreover, she risked more by implying that anyone other than Philip was Alexander's father than did Alexander, at least after his victories.

Alexander may have intended to deify Olympias after her death. Curtius (9.6.26) has Alexander state this intention as part of a speech made after his wound among the Malli. Curtius (10.5.30) also refers to this intention when summing up Alexander's character after his death. No other source mentions this possibility. Curtius' statements could easily be anachronistic, derived from Roman practice about Roman empresses, but there is nothing innately anachronistic about the two passages. Alexander had already claimed that Zeus Ammon was his father and was soon to receive divine honors himself. A divinized mother would seem an appropriate match for a divine father.[71]

Better, more contemporary evidence survives for cult worship for a mortal woman during the last years of Alexander's reign. The evidence has to do with Alexander's controversial treasurer Harpalus and involves his idiosyncratic and perhaps bizarre relationships with *hetairai*, not royal women. If elements similar to those in the stories about Harpalus and cult worship for women did not recur in other places, about other women, one would tend to attribute these stories to his erratic character (or perhaps to hostile tradition about him).[72]

Most of this information about Harpalus, cult worship, *hetairai*, and royal women comes from a long passage in Athenaeus that preserves fragments of several roughly contemporary writers and seems to refer to ca. 324 (Ath. 595a–596b).[73] Athenaeus (595a–c) cites Theopompus' *Letter to Alexander* for complaints about Harpalus' splendid funerary monuments at Athens and Babylon to a *hetaira* named Pythionice. She had died in Babylon, and Theompompus says that Harpalus had constructed for her a *hieron* (temple), a *temenos* (sacred precinct), and a *bomos* (altar) under the name of Pythionice Aphrodite.[74] Thus Harpalus' private cult to Pythionice apparently was, like that Alexander supposedly contemplated for Olympias, posthumous. Athenaeus (595c–d) then quotes a passage from Philemon's *Babylonians* that, in reference to Pythionice and

Harpalus, seems to term the courtesan *basilissa* of Babylon. He turns again to Theopompus for the information that Harpalus put up a bronze image of Glycera (a *hetaira* Harpalus brought out to Babylon after the death of Pythionice); had her live in the royal residence with him at Tarsus; and permitted her to receive *proskynesis* (the gesture that Persians performed to their social superiors, particularly to their kings, but that Greeks performed only to their gods) from the people, to be hailed as *basilissa*, and to receive other gifts that would be suitable for Alexander's mother or wife.[75] Athenaeus (595d–596b) then remarks that similar tales were preserved in another play produced after Harpalus had fled from Alexander.

Although the cult Harpalus established was clearly only his own doing,[76] he was the first of many to associate a mortal woman with Aphrodite in cult honors. As we shall see, some of these women were, like Glycera, *hetairai*, but some were royal women. The juxtaposition of the role of the *hetaira* with that of royal women seems shocking to us, and yet it too will reappear.

Both royal men and royal women began to receive cult worship before either men or women used a royal title. Phila, wife of Demetrius Poliorcetes, received cult worship at Athens ca. 307, about the time her husband and father-in-law did.[77] Once more the evidence is preserved in Athenaeus. Athenaeus (254a) reports that in a play of Alexis, a character drinks a toast with a libation to the *theoi soteres* (savior gods), Antigonus and Demetrius, and to Phila Aphrodite.[78] Athenaeus (255c) says his source was Dionysius, son of Tryphon, for the information that Adeimantus of Lampsacus set up a building with an *agalma* of Phila Aphrodite at Thria in Attica and that the place was called the Philaeum after Phila, wife of Demetrius. Adeimantus' cult may have been private, but the context of Athenaeus' description of the cult to Phila Aphrodite referred to in the toast, a long passage lamenting the decline of the Athenian populace into toadying subservience to powerful men, strongly implies that he is referring to a city cult to Phila.

The Athenians also put up temples to two of Demetrius Poliorcetes' *hetairai*, as Leaenea Aphrodite and Lamia Aphrodite, according to Demochares (Ath. 253a), and the Thebans also built a *naos* (temple) to Aphrodite Lamia, hoping, according to Polemon, to flatter Demetrius (253b). Since Athenaeus says that the Thebans and Athenians instituted these cults, one must conclude that all these cults to Demetrius' *hetairai* were civic. Dating the cults of these *hetairai* is more difficult than dating that of Phila because of the lack of apparent chronological context in the passage. The cults could date to the same period as Phila's, or they could have begun somewhat later, ca. 304–303, when Demetrius' activities with some of these same *hetairai* in the Parthenon were particularly notorious (Plut. *Demetr.* 23–24).

The Athenians instituted cults to Demetrius and sometimes to his father in gratitude for Demetrius' salvation of Athens. Cults for Demetrius and his father took various forms in various periods, sometimes associating the men with major gods, as with Phila and the *hetairai*, and sometimes not. The cult of Antigonus and Demetrius was (if we make use of Price's interpretation) a way for the Athenians to recognize and integrate the power of the Antigonids into the existing polis structure, a way of conceptualizing their power. This interpretation would explain the civic cult for Phila. Before the advent of the Macedonian kings, women had not had public power in Greek cities, but now they did and this power too had to be integrated.[79]

A certain Stratonice received a *temenos* at Delos ca. 300 (*OGIS* XI 4. 415). She was probably the daughter of Demetrius Poliorcetes, married at about this time to Seleucus Nicator. She was long a patron at Delos and the recipient of cult worship elsewhere (e.g., a civic cult at Smyrna, as Aphrodite Stratonice, *OGIS* 228, 229; *SIG* 575, 990; see STRATONICE 2). Her daughter Phila, wife of Antigonus Gonatas, also received a civic cult at Samos (see PHILA 2). In traditional Macedonia proper there were no dynastic cults for male or female Antigonids (possibly because, unlike the other Hellenistic dynasties that ruled conquered lands, the Antigonids were a nationally based dynasty), although city cults for kings did exist (e.g., Cassander's at Cassandreia: *SIG.* 332),[80] and a cult may have existed for Thessalonice as quasi-*oikist*.

In Egypt the Ptolemies, rather than simply receive cult worship from Greek cities, began to generate their own, ultimately a dynastic cult involving Alexander and all the Ptolemaic rulers. Berenice, wife of Ptolemy I, who received cult worship with her husband as one of the *theoi soteres*,[81] may also have received a cult in association with Aphrodite in her lifetime, and was associated with the goddess after her death.[82] Her daughter Arsinoe received a cult in her lifetime as one of the *theoi soteres*, and may have had an individual cult in her lifetime as well.[83] Arsinoe was associated with Aphrodite,[84] as were many later Ptolemaic queens. In Egypt, of course, connections between royal women and Aphrodite in cults often, although not always, involved connection to Isis as well.[85] In Ptolemaic Egypt we once more find cults for both a royal wife and a mistress and cults associated with Aphrodite. Bilistiche, a *hetaira* of Ptolemy Philadelphus, had a *naos* and *hiera* as Aphrodite Bilistiche (Plut. *Mor.* 753e–f).[86]

Thus my survey of the initial development of cultic honors for women in the Greek world suggests that it began at the end of the fourth century with the association of royal wives and royal *hetairai* with Aphrodite in both civic and private cults and then, as rulers themselves began to generate cults in the third century, became part of those as well. Although the Philippeum was not the site of a dynastic cult, its nature suggests the understanding of royal power as dynastic that would ultimately lead to dynastic cults. Although the first cult of a woman we know of was posthumous, living women began to receive civic cult before the end of the fourth century. The kings' *hetairai* in this early period were nearly as likely to receive cults as their wives. Being the wife of a man titled *basileus* cannot have been the only reason women received cults. Phila received a cult before her husband took the title *basileus,* and a king's *hetairai* got cult recognition although not married to a king.

Let us consider the implications and motivation of the early and persistent association of women with Aphrodite in civic and private cults. In the fragments preserved in Athenaeus and in inscriptions recording these cults, the name of the mortal woman and the name of the goddess are simply juxtaposed (indeed, Fraser terms this form of relationship between goddess and royal woman "identity by juxtaposition"),[87] more often, but not always, with the goddess's name coming first. It is a practice much more common for royal women than men.[88] This practice is commonly referred to as "assimilation" or "identification"—"symbiosis" is a better choice[89]—but what it means has not been much discussed.[90] Is there any significance in whether the goddess or the mortal is named first?[91] Are we talking about Phila as Aphrodite or Aphrodite as Phila? Alternatively, could it be Phila in Aphrodite or Aphrodite in Phila? The parallel usage would seem to be the various subcults of major deities, for example, Hera Basileia. The usage presupposes a manifestation of divine in mortal form, but the nature of the manifestation is vague. The power of royal women was equally undefined, however real.[92]

I am aware of no rigorous analysis of the reasons for associating royal women and Aphrodite in cult worship that directly addresses not only Ptolemaic examples but also the earlier, non-Egyptian examples from the fourth century.[93] Some earlier explanations of this phenomenon of cultic association with Aphrodite have dealt only with Ptolemaic Egypt.[94] They have found specifically Ptolemaic explanations: Ptolemaic control of Cyprus; Ptolemaic interest in sea power (in association with Aphrodite's role, as at Zephyrium, as a protector of seafarers); assimilation of Ptolemaic kings to Dionysus; emphasis on the personal, sexual relationship of the early Ptolemaic wives with their husbands.[95] One must also recall the long pharaonic tradition associating kings' wives with Hathor and, to some degree, Isis.

More general explanations of assimilation to Aphrodite have been offered. Some have seen assimilation of royal women to Aphrodite as flattery directed at the woman and her husband and primarily related to the woman's beauty; at best, such an explanation would apply only to cults initiated by cities or individuals, not those instigated by rulers themselves.[96] W. Neumer-Pfau theorized that Aphrodite was a model for all women in the Hellenistic period and thus the most appropriate choice for assimilation by royal women.[97] P. M. Fraser suggested that the identification of Ptolemaic queens with various deities (not just Aphrodite) was part of the general Hellenistic phenomenon of syncretism and that identification "created a more genuine feeling of the effective divinity of the queens, and of the ruling house as a whole, than the direct worship of individuals."[98] Let us see how well these suggestions may apply to earlier, non-Ptolemaic assimilations of women to Aphrodite, particularly women associated with kings.

The choice of Aphrodite as the deity to be assimilated has been treated as an inevitability.[99] Why are *both* royal wives and courtesans connected to Aphrodite? Why are not the wives, at least, associated with Hera instead? Both goddesses had responsibilities for marriage, yet Hera was queen of the gods, consort of the king Zeus, and in some places received cult worship with him in that role.[100] Assimilation of royal wives to Hera is not common, however.[101] The answer to the question I have posed relates to the traditional personality of Hera, particularly in

Homer. In the assimilation of human beings with already existing divinities, the "personality" of the god or goddess probably matters more than the cult because the association of the human and divine individual functions as a way to understand and explain the power of the human. Hera's personality was probably perceived as either too threatening or too unpleasant to make her a likely choice for divine association.

A passage about Pericles' famous mistress Aspasia hints at one reason why assimilation to Hera was rare. Plutarch (*Per.* 24.6), clearly incensed at Aspasia's political influence over Pericles despite what he considers her sexual disreputableness, notes that she was called the new Omphale, the new Deianeira, and (the new) Hera and quotes a line from Cratinus in which she is assimilated to Hera, clearly with negative intent. The references to Omphale and Deianeira are negative and threatening to male power. Omphale purchased Heracles as a slave and is said to have made him wear female dress and perform female tasks such as spinning (Apollod. 2.6.3; Diod. 4.31.5–8), and Deianeira, albeit unwittingly, caused the painful death of her husband, Heracles.

The reference associates her with two women who interfered in male activities. It suggests that the primary frame of reference for Hera was similar, most likely epitomized by Hera's treacherous seduction of Zeus so as to get her own political way, as shown in the *Iliad* (14.153–353). In myth and cult Hera is portrayed as having royal authority. She sits on a golden throne and wields a scepter. She offers to Paris as bribe her particular gift, royal power. Aspasia is linked to Hera because of her political influence and the perception of that influence as sinister interference, doubtless the consequence of her sexual power over Pericles.

The male Successors tended to prefer Dionysus, an Eastern conqueror, to Zeus, a hereditary ruler as they, after all, were not. Demetrius Poliorcetes was closely connected to him, as many of the Ptolemaic rulers would be. Although not linked in myth, Dionysus and Aphrodite may have seemed a more appropriate pairing.[102] It may be that, as the fourth century went on, Hera was losing out to Aphrodite as the goddess most typically associated with marriage. Aside from the fact that cults of Aphrodite were more widespread than those of Hera, other factors make it likely that this suggestion was increasingly true as the fourth century ended and the Hellenistic period began. The patronage of the Ptolemies, particularly Arsinoe II's role, had this effect: for example, dedications

WOMEN AND MONARCHY IN MACEDONIA

made at the time of marriage. Social changes, beginning in the fourth century, made private life more important than previously. The development of romantic comedy and romantic love is suggestive, as is the sense that Hera's "personality" made her an inappropriate goddess of marriage.[103]

None of this is a sufficient explanation for the association of royal women with Aphrodite in city and dynastic cults. If Hera was not acceptable, why was the choice for assimilation Aphrodite instead of, say, Demeter? We should look for explanations having to do not with typicality but with royal power. With Aphrodite too we should pay attention to the "personality" of the goddess in Homer and later literature, although there is less discrepancy in her case between her literary and cultic character than is true for Hera. From the point of view of political power, Aphrodite is much less threatening than Hera. When she dares to interfere in battle, she is humiliated by a mortal and very clearly told that warfare is not her sphere of action (Hom. *Il.* 5.311–430). In Homer (*Od.* 8.226–366) she can be comic, or at least amusing. The sea-born goddess had long been associated with the sea and the preservation of seafarers; clearly Arsinoe's cult as Aphrodite at Zephyrium fits this tradition and conforms to Ptolemaic naval ambitions, but the marine connection will hardly work for all the examples of assimilation I have noted.[104] In relation to the power for which Aphrodite is best known, her control of sexual desire, she can be very scary indeed; one thinks of the old men of Troy looking at Aphrodite's pawn, Helen (*Hom. Il.* 3.156–60), or the scene in which Aphrodite compels an unwilling Helen to go to bed with Paris (373–420).[105] When she is associated with marriage, it is most often with its sexual aspect. Through marriage Aphrodite tamed the supposed sexual voracity of women and became a stabilizing force, promoting, among other things, the creation of children.[106]

Her association with *hetairai* is obvious. In Corinth and Cyprus her cult involved temple prostitution (e.g., Ath. 573c–d). She was elsewhere seen as the special protector of courtesans as Aphrodite Hetairia (571c–e). Her very name was the way Greeks referred to the sexual act. Aphrodite *was* sex.

More interesting is why *both* royal wives and prostitutes are assimilated to her. There is one obvious thing that both kinds of women have in common: both Lamia and Phila, for instance, had a sexual relationship with the same man, a man who was receiving cult worship in Athens and elsewhere. In literature assimilation to Aphrodite may indeed be linked in part to a cult of beauty, but in cults sexuality is the relevant point of reference. In Greek myth people (particularly women) who have sexual relationships with gods are somehow transformed by the experience; in a number of cases they are deified.[107] Both groups of women had power, recognized by cults, because of their sexual influence over godlike royal men. Associating their sexual partners with deities made men feel—or think they looked—more powerful. Greek cities clearly thought they would be pleased. If, as has been surmised, Arsinoe II herself helped to shape her association with Aphrodite in cult worship,[108] then this identification was one that appealed to royal women as well as royal men.

Both royal courtesans and royal wives were public figures in a way that ordinary Greek women could never be, even in the somewhat more relaxed fourth century and Hellenistic periods.[109] The images of both royal wives and *hetairai* appeared in the public places of Greek cities and the Panhellenic shrines. Both kinds of women commanded considerable wealth and might themselves fund statues, buildings, or charities. Both kinds of women were able to act independently, if only occasionally. Royal wives and royal courtesans, therefore, had public power, and that power derived, ultimately, from their relationship—fundamentally sexual for both—to the kings, to the new powers Greek cities had to cope with and develop working relationships with. Understanding the women associated with the kings as Aphrodites was a way of recognizing their power (not their typicality) that was less unsettling and probably more meaningful than understanding them as Heras.

The sources often criticize these cults of *hetairai*.[110] Athenaeus (595a–e) and his source, Theompompus, condemn Harpalus's cults of *hetairai* as showing contempt for the vengeance of the gods and for Alexander's powers. Plutarch (*Mor.* 753 f.) contrasts with seeming disapproval the cult to Bilistiche with her origins as a barbarian and a slave. Similarly, Athenaeus puts the Athenian cults to Demetrius's courtesans in the context of extreme flattery (252 f.) and treats the Theban cult of Lamia in the same fashion (253b; he also puts the toast to Antigonus, the *theoi soteres*, and Phila Aphrodite in the same context (254a–b). This disapproval does not mean that these cults were generally disapproved of or even that those initiated by the kings themselves indicated their trivialization of either the *hetaira* or the royal woman who received similar honors.[111] The statements reflect an intellectual tradition officially critical of apotheosis but also the curiously ambivalent attitude toward *hetairai* demonstrated by the many stories about them preserved in Athenaeus and often originating in comedy.[112] The tone of these references is difficult to capture. It combines self-satisfied moral disapproval, interest in explicit sexuality, and tacit approval of the public notoriety of these women. *Hetairai* were celebrities, not entirely subject to ordinary rules of conduct.

Cults to royal wives and royal *hetairai*, especially those instituted by people other than their husbands or lovers, had to do with power and accessibility to power. In the new Hellenistic world of rulers powerful as gods, cults for royal men helped to make them and their power accessible to the general populace, but they were not enough. The cult of the women connected to these divinely powerful men made them and their power somehow more accessible yet, perhaps by highlighting their sexuality and domesticity, as the Aphrodite equation implies. They suggest a need to imagine power as *both* male and female, as is implied not only by female cults but also by the creation of a female royal title and by other changes in the role of royal women in the Hellenistic period (see below).

DEVELOPMENT OF A FEMALE TITLE: *BASILISSA*

Few inscriptions referring to Macedonian royal women survive from the period before the death of Alexander.[113] In none of the extant inscriptions from this period do royal women use a title. They appear with a personal name and sometimes a patronymic.[114] Similarly, no inscription before the reign of Alexander uses *basileus* as a title for Macedonian kings. Alexander began to use the title during his reign, although not on all occasions.[115] Antigonus and his son Demetrius Poliorcetes took the royal title in 306/5, after their great military victory at Salamis, and their rivals soon followed suit (Diod. 20.53.2–4; Plut. *Demetr.* 18.1–2).[116] It is therefore not surprising to learn that the first extant inscription in which a woman is given the title *basilissa* refers to Phila, wife of Demetrius Poliorcetes, and dates to a period shortly after 306 (*SIG* 333.6–7).[117] Since other evidence dating to ca. 300 indicates that both Apamea, wife of Seleucus, and Berenice, wife of Ptolemy, had taken the title *basilissa*,[118] it is reasonable to conclude that, like their husbands, the wives of the Successors rapidly followed the pattern established by the Antigonid clan.[119]

The application of the title *basilissa* to a woman did not signify that she had any well-defined office. Title and office had been separate issues for men. Argead males ruled Macedonia long before they bothered to call themselves *basileus*. Kingship itself was probably not conceived of as an office until after the end of the Argead dynasty and even then, in the Macedonian homeland as opposed to the new kingdoms, perhaps in limited fashion (see chap. 7). The position of the wife of the king or of the daughter of the king varied too widely to suggest that it was ever defined.

The development of a female title was linked to the pressing need of the Successors to legitimize power they had essentially usurped. They moved rapidly to transform their claim to individual legitimacy into a claim to dynastic legitimacy, as is demonstrated by the speed at which the various incipient dynasties appropriated the female title.[120] Like grand weddings, public statuary, and cults for royal women, the female title helped to institutionalize royal women as public figures. Some of these women were able to use their high public profile to their personal advantage, but most were not. As Philip II's policies demonstrated, emphasis on dynasty almost necessarily involved some emphasis on the women of the dynasty. Whether this emphasis ever became anything more than a designation of status—membership in a royal family—depended on circumstance and personality.

Basilissa was not an exclusive title. Phila and Berenice I could both be called *basilissa* in the same period. Similarly, after the end of the Argead dynasty, *basileus* was not an exclusive title and was used in correspondence between kings. As with the male title, *basilissa* was not connected to any geographic area. But here meaningful parallelism between the male and female titles ends.

Whereas the use of the male title within one kingdom was limited to the sovereign and did not apply to his heir unless the heir had been made a co-ruler, among the Ptolemies kings' daughters, even if they never married, used the title *basilissa*.[121] Inscriptional evidence strongly suggests that the practice of referring to a king's daughter as well as the wife of king as *basilissa* was widespread, not limited to the Ptolemies. Trying to link this use to some dynasties and not others, given both our spotty evidence, often of uncertain date, and the international nature of

WOMEN AND MONARCHY IN MACEDONIA

the evidence (e.g., is it reasonable to think that Delos treated Ptolemaic and Antigonid women differently?), does not make sense. *Not* referring to a king's daughter as *basilissa* would surely have reflected negatively on the status of her dynasty.[122]

There are inscriptions that refer to a woman as *basilissa* X and give only a patronymic.[123] Whether such inscriptions date from a period before to the woman's marriage or after it, the implication of this usage seems to be that the status of *basilissa* derived from the father and not necessarily from the husband, if he existed.[124] A body of inscriptions that refer to *basilissa* X, daughter of *basileus* Y, and wife *(gune)* of *basileus* Z,[125] as well as the tendency of Greeks to refer to women we would call queens as wives of kings,[126] suggest that *basilissa* was a general category and royal wife or daughter was a kind of subset within this category.

The meaning of *basilissa* is not so straightforward as has often been assumed. The word was created by adding a feminine suffix to the root of *basileus*, "king" (a construct roughly equivalent to the English word *princess*), and does not appear before the early fourth century; in the course of the century it gradually replaced earlier formations like *anassa*, *basileia*, and *basilis*.[127] Adding a feminine ending to *basileus* certainly did not mean that the person so titled had the power of a *basileus*, nor, as we have seen, did it always refer to the wife of a king. *Basilissa* cannot, therefore, automatically be translated either "female king" or "queen," although its usage encompassed such women in a broader category that also included kings' daughters. No one English word conveys the meaning of *basilissa*, when used as a title. The terms "royal woman" or perhaps "female royalty" are the best one can do.[128]

As a title, *basilissa* appears to refer to a status that one might acquire by birth or by marriage, rather than to a position. If so, discussions that refer to the desire of someone to be queen need to be rethought (e.g., Just. 24.3.3). In my view, Arsinoe, for instance, could always be styled *basilissa* because she was Ptolemy's daughter. If she believed that her position would be improved by marriage to Ptolemy Ceraunus or Ptolemy Philadelphus (see ARSINOE), then we must conclude that she needed to be married to a king, that being a royal daughter (or royal widow) either meant little or constituted too insecure a situation. She needed not the status conferred by her father or her first marriage but the position of being a living ruler's wife.

My view on the usage of *basilissa* as a title specifically contradicts Justin's (24.3.3) statement that Arsinoe was happy to accept Ptolemy Ceraunus's offer of marriage because she would regain the name *regina* (royal woman) that she had lost with Lysimachus's death. Contemporary documentary evidence should be valued more than the possibly anachronistic Justin. Justin's understanding of *regina* may not have been identical to the early-third-century B.C. understanding of *basilissa*. Even if Justin's usage is not anachronistic, his report may simply mean that Arsinoe wanted to emphasize her role as wife of the new king.

ROYAL POLYGAMY: A STATUS REPORT

While the Successors continued the Argead habit of polygamy (Plut. *Comp. Demetr. et Ant.* 4.1), it is sometimes asserted and more often and more insidiously assumed (though rarely argued), that after this first generation, Hellenistic kings were officially monogamous, however many mistresses they might maintain.[129] There has been a tendency to assume that the presumed disappearance of polygamy was linked to the evolution of a formal position as chief wife.

An examination of the evidence suggests that the practice of polygamy by kings of Macedonian origin certainly declined as the fourth century ended and the third century began but did not entirely disappear. I shall not attempt to demonstrate its continuance outside of Macedonia, or even past the reign of Demetrius II within Macedonia (see chap. 7), but rather suggest that each instance in which a Hellenistic king marries again when he is known to have had an earlier wife should be examined on its merits.

One cannot simply assume that a king divorced one wife when he married another. The departure of an early wife, especially when she remained within the kingdom of the man she had married, should not automatically be taken as evidence of divorce but rather as decline in status in comparison to other royal women. Kings could make their own rules, and little could stop them; imitating the practices of Philip or Alexander, even if there had been no polygamous marriages in some time, must always have remained an option, particularly in Macedonia proper.[130]

The precipitate decline of a practice of some antiquity, one followed by the two monarchs whose policies most often served as models for

Hellenistic rulers, Philip II and Demetrius Poliorcetes, is undeniably important, and the reasons require analysis. A variety of factors led to similar developments for somewhat different reasons in the various monarchies.

According to a dubious tale in Plutarch (*Mor.* 178 f.), Alexander complained because his father had children by more women (than Olympias presumably) and Philip responded by telling him that competition is good because Alexander would obtain rule through his own action, not through his father. The anecdote is not exactly a complaint about polygamy but rather about the problem that Argead polygamy had often produced: too many and thus competing heirs. Factors other than the qualms referred to in the anecdote may have made Alexander delay marriage (see chap. 4), but they did not prevent him from practicing polygamy. The first indication that royal polygamy was beginning to be problematic is subtle.[131] It involves that enthusiastic polygamist Demetrius. In 300-299, after the wedding of his daughter Stratonice to Seleucus (another polygamous marriage), Demetrius sent his wife Phila to her brother Cassander, hoping that she would represent his interests to Cassander against another of Antipater's sons, Pleistarchus. Plutarch (*Demetr.* 32.3) reports that, at this point, Demetrius was joined by another wife, Deidameia, sister of Pyrrhus. Plutarch's narrative clearly suggests that it was no coincidence that one royal wife left and another arrived. The implication is obvious that Demetrius (and perhaps the wives) chose not to have both wives present at the same time. Indeed, though it is often hard to tie down the whereabouts of these various wives, it may well be that those of comparable status did not live with the king at the same time.

This sort of delicacy about making the reality of polygamy obvious is new. At the time of Alexander's death in Babylon, Roxane and his Achaemenid wife were both present and not all potential brides or father of brides were squeamish. For instance, Cratesipolis, perhaps after having failed to marry Ptolemy (not a man short of wives), turned to Demetrius in about 307 (Plut. *Demetr.* 9.3–4), only to fail there too. Cratesipolis lacked the distinguished lineage of Deidameia or Phila and was likely to be less choosy.[132]

In about 290 Demetrius again figures in an incident that suggests that the practice of royal polygamy has become more difficult and complex (see chap. 7). Lanassa left her current husband, Pyrrhus, and invited

Pyrrhus's enemy Demetrius to marry her. Lanassa certainly did not object to polygamy: she asked Demetrius exactly because she knew that, of all the kings, he was the one most disposed to take wives. Her objection to Pyrrhus had not been that he had many wives but that he paid more attention to his barbarian wives than to her. This incident confirms that royal women, at least, were concerned about their status and its recognition within a polygamous marriage and sensitive to indications of it.

Arsinoe's dealings with Ptolemy Ceraunus, ca. 281/0, indicate the further problematizing of polygamy. Arsinoe had grown up in the midst of a court torn by the struggle between her mother and an earlier wife of her father and had already demonstrated her personal dislike of situations in which there was potential rivalry between the sons of kings by two different wives (see ARSINOE). Husbandless after the death of the aged Lysimachus, she next married Ceraunus, her half brother and another veteran of the war between her father's wives. Ceraunus merely used the marriage to gain control of Cassandreia and murder two of Arsinoe's sons by Lysimachus. Arsinoe herself barely escaped.

What is interesting is the bait Justin (24.2.9) says Ceraunus used to lure Arsinoe: he would take no other wife and have no other sons than hers. That Ceraunus did not mean it does not detract from the significance of his offer. He knew, given the circumstances in which both had grown up, that she would see polygamy as a disadvantage and that she would be concerned for the fate of her sons. But the passage clearly indicates that Ceraunus' offer was made exactly because without it Arsinoe could not assume that she would be his only *uxor* (wife). On her return to Egypt, she would once more demonstrate her determination to be the only wife of a reigning king.

Events relating to the marriages of Demetrius II demonstrate, on the one hand, how unpopular polygamy had become with royal brides and, on the other, that it continued to be practiced, at least through the reign of this king. Stratonice, the Seleucid wife of Demetrius, chose to leave him toward the end of the 240s. Justin (28.1.4) says that she left because of his new marriage, to one of the last of the Aeacids, Phthia. Even this late, the problem may have been the taking of a second wife, as Phthia's status threatened that of Stratonice, particularly because Stratonice had produced no male heir (see STRATONICE 2). Demetrius had a child, the future Philip V, by another wife while he was married to Phthia (see PHTHIA; CHRYSEIS; chap. 4).

Why did polygamy decline and, toward the end of the Hellenistic period, possibly disappear? It was unpopular with Greeks, whose good opinion Hellenistic kings were eager to acquire. Concern for Greek opinion would have been particularly potent for the Antigonids. Some potential royal brides were not Macedonian, and may have been less comfortable with royal polygamy. If Macedonian aristocrats had not been polygamous, given that the Hellenistic dynasties sprang from various aristocratic Macedonian clans, it is quite possible that this particular habit of Argead monarchy proved unacceptable once the initial transition to the new dynasties had been accomplished. The advent of Roman power also had the effect of making any international marriage, let alone multiple ones, difficult.

Royal women, and quite possibly their fathers, saw polygamy as a threat, an unnecessary complication, particularly if it involved wives of similar status. As the prestige of royal women grew, thanks to their use in so many aspects of the struggle for legitimization, they or those who acted for them increasingly saw polygamous situations as risky and problematic. A significant increase in the number of royal women who brokered their own marriages (or whose mothers rather than their fathers did so) happened after the death of Alexander.[133] Most of these women were widows; those who were not tended to have been married before. Many are also known to have had military power (e.g., control of a citadel or a fleet); those who did not are likely to have had control of wealth. As a consequence of their independence, more women were able to avoid polygamy or, as with Arsinoe, act to eliminate it.

Some factors peculiar to particular Hellenistic kingdoms contributed to the decline of polygamy. In Egypt, as the third century went on, the increasing predominance of brother-sister marriage all but destroyed it.[134] To some degree the same applies to the Seleucids. In Macedonia there is a noticeable narrowing of the public presentation of *basileia*. If multiple wives existed, they were not flaunted. There appears to have been a reluctance to have more than one son (see chap. 7).

I have already argued that *basilissa* was not an exclusive title in the sense that a king's daughter and a king's wife might both use it, even within the same kingdom. But, if a king did indeed have more than one wife, did both retain the title? (It is difficult to answer this question with any certainty; we need clearly contemporary inscriptions referring to wives of the same king.) My sense is that in the days of Successors, the answer would probably be yes,[135] but it is less clear how long this continued to be the case. Later, during the reign of Demetrius II, Athenian decrees apparently referred to Phthia, and only to Phthia, as *basilissa*, at a period when her husband had another wife.[136] This usage could imply that a working exclusivity of the title did develop, most probably as monogamy gradually came to seem the norm and polygamy the exception.[137] However, the wording of the inscription may only signify that, as had long been the case, one wife tended to predominate (as, for instance, in the case of Phila or Olympias) without necessarily being the only *basilissa*. The Athenians may have chosen to refer only to Demetrius' most important *basilissa*.

ROYAL ROBES and DIADEMS

Evidence on characteristic dress for royal women is poor. It is obvious that royal women were luxuriously dressed, as befitted the wealth of their fathers and husbands as well as their own. As the fabric and jewelry found in the antechamber of Tomb II at Vergina hint, purple and gold were a part of their dress, although neither was an exclusive privilege of either male or female royals.[138] Two passages could suggest that wives of Macedonian kings were recognizable as such by more than the mere luxury of their equipage: Plutarch (*Arat.* 17.2–5) refers to the royal trappings of Nicaea's litter, and Polyaenus (8.57) refers both to a royal litter and to a royal robe of Arsinoe.[139] There seems to be a close link between royal trappings and royal status.

Diadems have been the subject of much controversy and puzzlement.[140] Whatever their earlier history, we know that when Antigonus and Demetrius took the royal title, they also put on the diadem, as the other Successors apparently did (Plut. *Demetr.* 18.1–2; Diod. 20.53.2–4). From this point on the diadem is clearly associated with monarchy and, in both Plutarch and Diodorus, specifically with the taking of a royal title. Seleucid women took the female title either at the same time the men did or very soon thereafter. Did they put on the diadem too? Did the women of other dynasties? The comparative paucity of images of royal women, the tendency for other items of headdress (e.g., the *stephane*, or veil) to prevent one from being able to tell if the diadem is worn, and the difficulty of distinguishing a diadem from other items of headdress make this question hard to resolve. Whereas there is evidence of the diadem for Ptolemaic women,[141] there is no physical evidence of diadems for Antigonid women as they did not appear on coins and no generally accepted portrait of one survives. However, when Justin (24.3.3) reports that the duplicitous Ptolemy Ceraunus proclaimed Arsinoe *basilissa* outside the walls of Cassandreia, he also says that Ceraunus placed a diadem on her head. Despite the uncertain dependability of Justin, the passage seems to suggest that one woman who was wife, however briefly, to one Macedonian king did wear the diadem.[142]

Because much of the debate about diadems for men has centered on the *meaning* of wearing them, it is difficult to assess what significance we should attach to the wearing of a diadem by the wife or daughter of a king,[143] other than to conclude that it had something to do with the fact that she was the daughter or wife of a king. Wearing the diadem was probably associated with the title *basilissa*.[144] Athenaeus (593a) preserves a report that Demetrius Poliorcetes shared his *basileia* with his *hetaira* Myrrhine, except for the diadem. This is an interesting distinction. The *hetaira* was not excluded from *basileia*, just as we have seen royal *hetairai* were not excluded from royal and city cults, but she was excluded from the diadem. The passage confirms a close association of the title *basilissa* and the wearing of the diadem at the same time that it implies that there were aspects of monarchy of which women associated with kings might partake that were not defined by any formal status.[145]

Even if more consensus grows about the implications of diadems for men, it is dangerous to take parallelism between the sexes very far. *Basilissa* may have been formed by putting a feminine ending on the Greek name for king, but, as we have seen, this hardly means that a *basilissa* was a female king (although a few were).

Whatever diadems worn by women may have signified at the time (willful ambiguity, as in the case of the Philippeum, may be the true significance of diadems), it is now impossible to conclude much more than that they are part of the bag of tricks that enabled the Successors to transform their upstart lines into royal dynasties. Many of these tricks involved a public role, sometimes active, more often passive, for the women of the clan, a role that often paralleled that of royal males. In the dynasties other than the Ptolemies, this parallelism was usually superficial, but it did signify that the women of these dynasties were an integral part of *basileia* as the rulers chose to display it.

CHAPTER NINE

Royal Female Burials

No burials in Macedonia can be ascribed with absolute certainty to any member, female or male, of one of the ruling dynasties of Macedonia. Since 1977, however, most of the scholarly world have identified Vergina with ancient Aegae, burial place of Macedonian kings, and agreed that the three tombs found under the Great Tumulus at Vergina belonged to fourth-century B.C. members of the royal family.[1] P. B. Faklaris's recent challenge[2] to the identification of Vergina as Aegae has failed to change the generally held view.[3]

Although several factors have led to general agreement that the three tombs are royal, the most important is the Great Tumulus itself. Only kings are likely to have been commemorated in this grand fashion[4] and probably only by other kings (the excavator Manolis Andronicos's original suggestion that the great mound was the work of Antigonus Gonatas remains persuasive).[5]

No consensus on the individual identities of those buried under the Great Tumulus has developed, although most scholars would now identify the occupant of Tomb III as Alexander IV. Enduring controversy, however, surrounds the identity of the man and woman buried in Tomb II. Within a few weeks of the discovery of the tomb, Andronicos asserted that the male was Philip II. Many scholars have accepted his assertion, but many others have rejected it, convinced that the man in Tomb II was his obscure and mentally limited son, Philip Arrhidaeus.[6]

Philip Arrhidaeus had only one wife, Adea Eurydice, and if he did indeed lie in the main chamber of Tomb II, then she must have been buried in the antechamber (see ADEA EURYDICE). As his famous father had seven wives, it is less clear which one might have been buried with Philip, if it is indeed he. While most scholars who believe that Philip II lay in the main chamber of Tomb II think it likely that the woman in the antechamber is Philip's last wife, Cleopatra, known to have been killed

Diagram of Tomb II at Vergina. Photo from National Geographic Society, reprinted by permission.

soon after her husband (see CLEOPATRA 3), Hammond continues to reject this conclusion in favor of either Meda (a Getic princess married to Philip; see MEDA) or an unattested Scythian wife.[7]

Meda may have been more likely to have possessed some of the warlike objects found in the antechamber than Cleopatra (if all the objects in the antechamber do indeed belong to its occupant rather than to the man in the main chamber),[8] but it is difficult to accept Hammond's suggestion that any non-Hellenic royal wife committed suttee. None of our sources mentioned so spectacular an event, despite the fascination of Alexander historians with similar Indian practices (Plut. *Alex.* 69.3; Arr. 6.29.4–8). Hammond also doubted that Cleopatra died soon enough after Philip for her burial to be planned by the builder of the tomb (as the structure suggests), but she may well have.[9]

Much less attention has been paid to Tomb I, perhaps because it is the only one of the three to be looted. There has been a tendency to identify its occupants in terms of who one believes was buried in Tomb II. Those who believe that Philip was buried in Tomb II tend either to ignore Tomb I or to suggest that Amyntas, Philip's father, was once buried there, whereas those who believe that Philip Arrhidaeus was placed in Tomb II tend to conclude that his father, Philip II, lay in Tomb I. There were, in fact, three burials in Tomb I (these were inhumation burials, whereas the burials in Tombs II and III were cremations): a small-boned male "in the prime of his life," a woman in her midtwenties, and a newborn infant.[10]

Problems surround all the suggested identifications for the occupants of Tombs I and II. Given the current state of our knowledge, certainty is not possible. Common sense, however, strongly suggests that the builder of the Great Tumulus believed that the most respected of Macedonian rulers, Philip II, lay under the red earth mound he covered with the much larger tumulus. A structure apparently unprecedented in size, created long after the deaths of those buried there, over tombs dating to the midfourth century, built by a ruler not part of the same dynasty can signify little else. The Great Tumulus must have been constructed as a memorial to the last of the Argeads, and it is unbelievable that the most famous of them would have been omitted. Philip II must have been placed in Tomb I or Tomb II.

Although many of the original factors that led Andronicos to his early identification of the man in Tomb II as Philip II have proved ephemeral, others continue to make this identification compelling but by no means

WOMEN AND MONARCHY IN MACEDONIA

a certainty. The strongest evidence for an identification of Philip II is that which Jonathan Musgrave has derived from the male bones: he concludes that they show evidence of an eye injury of a sort appropriate to Philip's known wounds. This conclusion was not shared by others who have examined the bones,[11] but another finding by Musgrave makes the alternative identification difficult.[12] Musgrave determined that the bones of both the man and the woman in Tomb II were cremated soon after death.[13] It is hard to fit this and other aspects of these burials with what is known about the deaths of Adea Eurydice and Philip Arrhidaeus. So splendid a cremation as that arranged for the occupants of Tomb II (gold acorn remnants from the golden oak wreath and from a chryselephantine couch were found with the funeral pyre),[14] even if Olympias had wanted an impressive burial, would have been nearly impossible to accomplish in the remote region where the royal pair had been captured and killed. If these are indeed the bones of Philip Arrhidaeus and Adea Eurydice, one must conclude that Olympias had them transported back to Aegae soon after their deaths and cremated and buried there.

However, the contents and nature of the antechamber in Tomb II raise serious, although not insuperable, problems for Andronicos's identification. If Philip II was in the main chamber, then the woman in the antechamber must have been one of his wives. As we have seen, the evidence from the antechamber does not easily suit either one of Philip's barbarian wives. Nor is it a good match for Cleopatra; even if one assumes that all the military apparatus in the antechamber belonged to the male,[15] one must still account for the absence of her baby, supposedly killed at the same time. The bones seem to have belonged to a woman a little older than either Cleopatra or Adea Eurydice were likely to have been at the time of their deaths (see ADEA EURYDICE; CLEOPATRA 3). The unusual size of the antechamber, planned from the start, would better fit the burial of a royal wife who was an Argead.[16]

Although we might expect that the most splendid burial found under the Great Tumulus, that of Tomb II, would belong to the most splendid king buried there, the even more splendid burial of King Tutankhamun demonstrates that this need not be the case. Tomb II could have contained the burial of a Macedonian Tutankhamun, Philip Arrhidaeus.[17] But the difficulties already discussed make it impossible to insist, as some have done, on the certainty of his presence in Tomb II.

The near-total looting of Tomb I tends to distort any comparative judgment of the two burials. The remarkable paintings on the walls of Tomb I have no real parallel even in the heavily damaged frieze on the facade of Tomb II. It is the size and the large collection of beautifully made objects that make Tomb II so impressive, yet we have little sense of the nature of the contents of Tomb I, other than to surmise that their thorough looting suggests their high quality and value. Moreover, the difference in the structures of the two tombs (small cist vs. a large "Macedonian" type) tends to make Tomb II seem more impressive, but, in the light of our as yet uncertain knowledge of the development of tombs in Macedonia, such an impression may be anachronistic, particularly if the Tomb of the Throne dates after the death of Philip II but before the building of Tomb II (i.e., if Philip Arrhidaeus is in Tomb II). (See below on the date of the Tomb of the Throne and problems with our understanding of the development of tombs in Macedonia.) The evidence remains too poor to permit a secure identification of the occupants of Tomb II.

The identity of those in Tomb I requires more attention. Piecemeal identification of occupants of the various tombs ignores the fact that, twice over, they were made part of the same unit, one tomb complex. If, as I have suggested, Philip II must have been in either Tomb I or II, no identification is complete unless both tombs are discussed. If Andronicos's dating of Tomb I is roughly correct, then its male occupant cannot have been Amyntas, who died an old man. Hammond recently suggested that Amyntas was indeed buried in Tomb I, his cremated remains placed in a valuable *larnax* (box or cinerary chest), which the tomb robbers removed, and that the human remains found in the tomb are part of a secondary burial, probably that of his son Alexander II and a wife and child.[18] This ingenious suggestion explains the physical remains, but no evidence supports it. Tomb I was the tomb of one of one of the three sons of Amyntas, most likely Philip or Perdiccas.[19]

Let me turn to the two female burials under the Great Tumulus. Tomb I tells us little about the royal woman buried there. The splendid frescoes covering three of the walls of this cist tomb, including the Rape of Persephone, testify to the wealth of those who had the tomb constructed and imply that its contents would have been similarly impressive, as does the thoroughness of the looting. In addition to the bits of human bone on the floor of the tomb, there were fragments of stamped black-glazed pots and a marble shell and an ivory comb.[20] There is no way of telling for which of its occupants the tomb was first built. Hammond was right to argue that the Persephone theme need not have any particular reference to age or gender.[21] Although it seems likely that the three occupants of the tomb were a husband, his wife, and their baby, even that is not certain. The dating of this tomb, both absolute and relative to the other two tombs, remains problematic. If it is royal and Andronicos's identification of the occupant of Tomb II is correct, then it must have been built before Andronicos's earliest date of 350.[22]

Thus it is likely that Tomb I once contained the bones of either Philip II and his last wife, Cleopatra, as well as their baby, or those of one of his brothers, a wife, and a baby. There are problems with both identifications. Whichever choice is the correct one, Tomb I suggests no significant difference between the burials of royal women and those of the rest of the elite. Women were often buried with other family members and tended to have rich objects, indicators of their family status, buried with them. The magnificent frescoes are not typical but, again, may have been created for a man, not for a woman.

The female burial in Tomb II is more revealing and yet more ambiguous. The woman's burial was placed in the tomb's antechamber. Her burial and the antechamber were completed somewhat later than the main chamber and the male burial there, although the structure of the tomb implies that a second burial was planned from the start.[23] The woman's burial is unusual because of both what is there and what is not. Other than the bones themselves,[24] very little associated with the burial is characteristically female. The golden myrtle wreath, the "Illyrian" pin, the *alabastra* (perfume jars), and the small golden disks with the starburst pattern are all things found in both male and female burials. However, jewelry, the most standard feature of female burials, is absent, except for the lovely "diadem" found in the golden *larnax*; many graves of other Macedonian women contain more jewelry.[25]

The graves of Macedonian women do not contain weapons, and yet there are a number of military items, quite unusual ones at that, in the antechamber. Propped in the doorway between the chamber and the antechamber (or lying on the doorstep) were a gold-covered gorytus, arrowheads, gilded greaves, and at least one spear. Nearby, probably once displayed on a table of sorts, was a gilded Thracian pectoral and five more spears.[26] The antechamber also held a cuirass, of which only the metal parts, made of gold, survive.[27] This odd assortment of rather grand armor and weaponry cannot be said to constitute a full panoply, separate from that in the main chamber, but cannot easily be categorized as supplemental to the military items found in the main chamber.[28] Moreover, it is now believed that the gold and ivory couch in the antechamber (see below) was decorated with battle scenes,[29] a curious choice for the conventional Macedonian woman.

The burial in the antechamber is unusual for another reason: its limited parallelism to the burial in the main chamber. Both sets of bones were wrapped in purple cloth. The solid gold *larnakes* with sunburst designs and the marble sarcophagi in which they were enclosed are common to both and very similar. Elaborately decorated chryselephantine couches stood in front of or perhaps over each sarcophagus.[30] Although the designs of the two *larnakes* are certainly similar and clearly products of the same workshop and period, and the male's *larnax* only somewhat larger than the female's, looking at the two together[31] makes one aware of an apparently conscious attempt to distinguish one from the other, to make the *larnax* for the woman plainer and less impressive. This conscious distinction may be as important as the equally conscious similarity. The main chamber contains many more items than does the antechamber, and a number of things point to the higher status of the male in the main chamber, but the parallelism is nonetheless significant. The presence of the female burial in the antechamber—in itself extremely rare[32]—is another important element in this parallelism.

How one analyzes this burial is linked to the two common identifications of the person buried; each possibility permits a plausible interpretation. If it is Cleopatra in Tomb II, then one concludes that the military items in the antechamber belonged to Philip and that only the items in the immediate area of the *larnax* and sarcophagus are hers. The puzzling absence of more jewelry can be explained by concluding that Alexander placed her in the antechamber to avoid scandal associated with her death but that he did no more than was absolutely necessary and may even have slighted her where he could. Andronicos's suggestion that her other jewelry was consumed on the pyre is unsatisfactory.[33] Fire would not destroy semiprecious stones or precious metals.[34] Moreover, many aristocratic burials contained considerable quantities of jewelry and one wonders whether a quantity surely at least equal to that could have vanished. Andronicos's explanation implausibly assumes that the only jewelry the woman owned was worn on her body on the pyre and would not have been replaced. One wonders why the Illyrian pin, other than the diadem itself, is the only survivor.[35]

If the woman in the antechamber was Adea Eurydice, then the weapons were meant to relate to her burial, although they may not have belonged to her personally. She had been captured on a battlefield and later murdered by her enemy. Her possessions may have been pillaged, and others may have been found to suit the burial. The absence of jewelry can be attributed either to the same circumstance or to her own lack of interest.[36] The parallelism of the burials and perhaps her inclusion in the antechamber make sense when one recalls that she was an Argead by blood as well as by marriage and that she was apparently responsible for Cassander's initial legitimization of rule in Macedonia and that he was the one who buried her at Aegae (see ADEA EURYDICE).

There are a number of difficulties with reconciling the contents of the antechamber with either woman. Anthropologists believe the bones were those of a woman no younger than twenty and probably older.[37] Our evidence on the ages of both Adea Eurydice and Cleopatra at the time of their deaths is quite poor (see ADEA EURYDICE; CLEOPATRA 2), but it is distinctly possible that both women were younger than twenty at the time of their deaths. Not only is it impossible to rule either out of consideration for Tomb II, but the apparent age of the bones raises some doubts about whether these are the bones of either woman.[38]

One would expect not only their husbands but a third person to be buried with each of our candidates. Our evidence for the death of Cynnane (Diod. 19.52.5; Diyllus *FGrH* 73, F 1) has been taken to signify that Cassander buried Philip Arrhidaeus, Adea Eurydice, and her mother, Cynnane, together,[39] but the Greek need not be so translated.[40] One does wonder why Cassander would have buried Cynnane separately, however. There is no trace of the bones of a baby in the remains of the woman in the antechamber.[41] Babies were often but not always buried with their mothers. Nonetheless, the absence of Cleopatra's baby, murdered at the same time she was, seems odd.

The evidence so far available permits two interpretations of the same burial. It could have been the public facade of a political sham to cover up the powerlessness of one young royal wife, or it could have been the enshrinement of another with royal blood and power nearly equal to her husband's, whose murder was the excuse for the usurpation that the man who buried her managed to accomplish.

No general recognition of other female burials at Vergina as royal exists, but Andronicos's excavations in the years after his discovery of the three tombs under the Great Tumulus produced a number of other burials, one of which he believed to be that of Philip's mother and others of which may have been those of royal women. A brief discussion of these discoveries is therefore relevant.

In 1987 Andronicos discovered an extremely large, vaulted tomb, about four meters east of the Rhomaios tomb. Because the excavator concluded that it was the tomb of Philip's mother, he and some others have referred to it as the "Tomb of Eurydice"; I shall refer to the tomb in more noncommittal fashion as the "Tomb of the Throne."[42] Looters entered through the plain front facade of the tomb, leaving the front doors of the tomb untouched but the door from the antechamber to the main chamber ajar. The antechamber, covered with high-quality plaster, although looted, contained much fine-quality Attic pottery, including a vase with Eleusinian scenes attributed to the "Eleusinian Painter."[43] The back wall of the main chamber has a false Ionic facade, richly painted and well preserved, with a false door and two false windows. Within the main chamber, to the right of the false door in the facade, is a large (2 meters wide at the front and 2 meters high), magnificent marble throne, painted and gilded, decorated with sphinxes, griffins, lions, deer, caryatids, and a sunburst design similar to that found on objects in many Macedonian tombs, including those of Tomb II under the Great Tumulus. On the panel of the throne back is a painting of Hades and Persephone in a chariot.[44] In front of the throne is a footstool, decorated in a fashion similar to that of the throne. A marble *larnax* was found lying on its side in front of the footstool, whereas the robbers left the lid of the *larnax* on the throne itself. The interior of the *larnax* and its lid preserves traces of purple, apparently from the purple fabric in which the bones were originally wrapped. The western wall shows the marks of chests that must once have preserved many now-vanished valuables. Just outside the tomb, in the remains of what appears to have been a pyre, was a Panathenaic amphora handle fragment with a partial archon name datable to 344/3 B.C.[45]

Andronicos believed that this was the tomb of a woman,[46] yet the pub-

WOMEN AND MONARCHY IN MACEDONIA

lished evidence on the tomb offers little support for his conclusion. No weapons were found in the tomb, but, as Tomb I demonstrates, their absence does not necessitate a female burial.[47] Alabastra like those found with the tomb, while common in female burials, are found in male burials as well.[48] Some nearby burials are female, but they are of a much earlier date, and the gender of the person buried in the Rhomaios tomb, probably much closer in date to the Tomb of the Throne, is uncertain.[49] The presence of a throne could signify a female burial, but Andronicos did not think so.[50]

Andronicos suggested that it could have been the tomb of Philip II's mother, Eurydice.[51] Connecting Eurydice to the tomb is problematic,[52] given that the burial must have occurred after 343, perhaps long after. Borza doubted the tomb could be Eurydice's. He argued that the Panathenaic fragment provides only a *terminus post quem* and that such items were often long preserved as heirlooms. He wondered whether Eurydice lived so long into her son's reign and pointed to the discrepancy between Andronicos's insistence on Eurydice as the occupant of the tomb he dated prior to 340 and his belief that Eurydice dedicated statues to Eucleia after 338.[53]

The Tomb of the Throne certainly seems to be royal, and the burial resembles that of Tomb II. If one accepts the ca. 340 date Andronicos and Hammond prefer and similarly agrees to their arguments in favor of Philip II for Tomb II, one is faced with a quandary. Andronicos, Hammond, and many others have long believed that Tomb II and Tomb III were constructed very close to each other in time,[54] yet Tomb III is universally dated to ca. 309. One cannot have it both ways.

Problems in dating the Tomb of the Throne reflect general difficulties in dating all tombs of the Macedonian type. Efforts to write a history of the development of Macedonian tombs have so far been preliminary.[55] They have suffered from the assumption of linearity in development and from the belief that once a new feature appeared, all subsequent tombs used it and did not retain the older feature. Such a tidy pattern of development would seem surprising in a matter so likely to be steeped in tradition as royal burial and in structures that were largely concealed once completed. Stella Miller rejects the idea of morphological development among the tombs.[56]

During his last active season at Vergina in 1990, Andronicos directed the excavation of a tomb (K3) found very near the Tomb of the Throne. It was made of porous stone and contained three burials. The skeletal remains of a woman of twenty to twenty-five were found on a stone *kline* (couch). Most of the remains of a fourteen-year-old had been swept into a corner of the tomb. The fragmentary remains of a young child of five or so were also found. The tomb had been looted of valuable objects but contained numerous clay images, female busts, and a number of other objects. The burials seem to have been made at different periods from the early to the late fourth century. Granted that the burial of the adolescent girl clearly predated that of the young woman, it would appear that we have a rather grand and once-rich tomb originally constructed for a very young, perhaps unmarried, and probably royal woman.[57]

In the same year as the discovery of the Tomb of the Throne Andronicos uncovered another female burial, also in the area of the Rhomaios tomb (about 13 meters from the facade of the Tomb of the Throne). This was an earlier, ca. 500–490 cist tomb.[58] At the bottom of a deep, rubble-filled pit were the remains of a wooden coffin and a large number of high-quality grave goods: an elaborately decorated diadem (whose decorative scheme was repeated on gold attachments apparently once sewed to the himation); fine earrings, snake's head bracelets; a double-strand gold bead necklace with pendants; gold pins and "Illyrian" fibulae; a silver chain with serpent head endings; a gold sheet covering the breast area; silver-covered sandals, gilded on the underside; a bronze *hydria;* a silver *phiale;* bronze *phialai;* six terra-cotta female protomes; a decorated bone object; an iron tripod with bronze *lebes;* and several other items. The quality and quantity of these goods (comparable to those found at Sindos), granted their early date, suggests a woman of high rank, quite possibly a royal woman.

Andronicos subsequently found eight more rich female graves from ca. 530–420. He suggested that these finds indicated the existence of a cemetery for women of high social status.[59] Obviously, these rich earlier burials could easily be those of royal women. One would like to know why there are so many single female burials in one area.

The rapid advance of Macedonian archaeology, coupled with Andronicos's recent discoveries of so many rich and possibly royal female burials, makes it difficult to reach conclusions about female royal burials in Macedonia and what they may tell us about the role of royal women. If Vergina is the site of ancient Aegae and Tomb II a royal burial, then the female burial in the antechamber would offer some confirmation that some Argead women played prominent roles in Macedonian society.

Conclusion

In a number of respects the nonbiographical sections of this book chronicle royal women's rise to a position of power and influence within the institution of monarchy in Macedonia and their subsequent fall. The comparative lack of evidence on royal women in very early Macedonian history and again in later Antigonid times may have exaggerated this pattern of growth and decline to some degree, but the pattern is real and clear enough.

I have argued that changes in the nature of monarchy in Macedonia have a great deal to do with the fluctuations in the position of royal women. The original understanding of monarchy as the rule of a clan generated a circumstance in which women were sometimes placed in situations where they exercised real power. More often, royal women functioned as an important part of the public image of the monarchy as its power increased because they were so clearly part of the dynasty.

With the collapse of the Argead dynasty, monarchy changed. In the transitional period individual women continued to play important political roles, and in the kingdoms established by two of the Successors of Alexander the prominence and to some degree the power of royal women was institutionalized and even increased in a number of respects. In Egypt, for instance, royal women began to reign with their brother-husbands. But in Macedonia proper, at least once the Antigonids were firmly entrenched, this prominence did not endure and another change in the nature of Macedonian monarchy, an understanding of it as an office held by an individual rather than as the domination of a dynasty, led to the comparative exclusion of royal women from many, although certainly not all, aspects of monarchy in Macedonia.

Indeed, despite this change in the nature of Macedonian monarchy and the consequent decline in the role of its women, I maintain that historians should always consider the role of women in any monarchy they examine. Because monarchy is a hereditary institution and women are therefore inescapable participants in the determination of succession, they should never be excluded from consideration or regarded as idiosyncratic light relief from the serious business of political history.

Moreover, the histories of monarchies are by definition the histories of families, although how family is defined may vary considerably (e.g., nuclear, cross-generational, clan) from one period or reign to another. The royal family, however constituted, often corresponded to more general societal patterns, whether it simply replicated on a grander scale broader social patterns (e.g., the importance of cults for both royal and ordinary women) and thus validated and reinforced them or whether it changed social roles, as some have believed Ptolemaic royal women did by their example.

The biographical sections of this book, although providing much support for the general pattern of growth and decline I have noted, also tell a more complicated story. The lives of individuals, even lives whose details and motivations are so imperfectly known as even the most famous of these women most certainly are, do not entirely conform to any pattern. The lives of many of these women were, quite simply, very sad, examples (e.g., Barsine) of the way in which the rivalries and battles of the great distorted and often destroyed the lives of those who possessed much less power but did have dangerous proximity to the powerful. The careers of a few of these women, for example, Olympias and Cynnane, were strikingly different. These women certainly suffered (both, after all, died violently, as did their daughters), but they also caused suffering. Like the careers and personalities of Philip II and Alexander the Great, those of these women have a larger-than-life quality, a considerable element of physical bravery, and a willingness to embrace risk and adventure that continue to fascinate us at the same time as their ruthlessness and violence may repel us.

To a much greater degree than those of their male kin, the lives of royal women are irrecoverable, partly because so much less is known about them than about royal males, but partly because we know so very little about what it was like to be a woman, to lead a woman's life anywhere at any period in the ancient Hellenic world. I can imagine Olympias, old by her world's standards but game, probably being carried in a litter, traveling over the mountain paths from the remote kingdom where she had grown up, back into Macedonia for one last battle, this time an attempt to ensure that her grandson, a half-Asian boy she had just met for the first time, lived long enough to be a real king, not just a tool with a title. But I can only guess, as I have done, at her motivation, because many ancient sources had no interest in what drove her and others explained her actions only in terms of their stereotypical expectations of women.

It is at least as hard, perhaps even harder, to understand the motivation of one of the overtly conventional and less threatening royal women, one of the "good girls" like Phila, daughter of Antipater and wife of Demetrius Poliorcetes. Whereas the sources distort the life of Olympias into a caricature of the power-hungry woman, the sources, by turning Phila into a kind of royal female saint, an icon of respectability by royal Macedonian standards, provide even less information about the forces that motivated her. I can try to imagine her contemplating suicide after an eventful life full of *peripeteia* (reversal). I picture her choice of self-inflicted death as one made out of strength of character, out of the kind of commitment to *arete* (excellence) and *time* that characterized so many male leaders. I suspect that her choice of death over what she apparently believed was a life of dishonor showed her strength of character, just as I believe that her husband's decision to go on living, however dishonorable or humiliating that life was, was a sign of his weaker character. I suppose these things, but I am much less confident in my supposition than I am in my conclusions about the forces that drove Olympias or Cynnane. Curiously enough, a positive rather than a hostile source tradition actually makes it more difficult to recover any genuine understanding of the actions of a royal woman, or, for that matter, any woman.

Most difficult to understand are the many women (really the typical royal women) who appear in our sources as mere dynastic tokens, often because that is what they really were, although sometimes simply because our sources are too uninterested in them to provide something like a full report of their actions. Did a woman like the second Phila, wife of Antigonus Gonatas, understand herself as an actor in events, as her more famous namesake seems to have done, or did she understand her life as only the fulfillment of duty to the dynasties of her birth and of her marriage?

Despite the many limitations our evidence and the prejudice of our sources as well as our own prejudices impose, the lives of these women are a precious possession. So little remains of the lives actually lived by individual women in the ancient world that we must prize what we know about the careers of these royal rarities. Atypical their lives may have been, but we know at least something about them, though not nearly enough.

Genealogical Charts

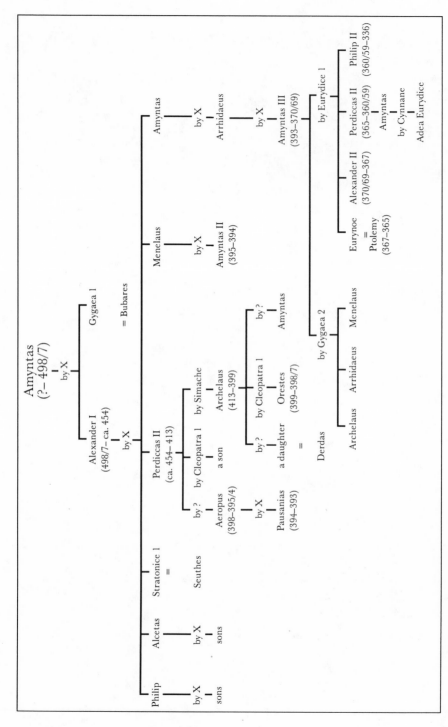

The Argead House until Philip II

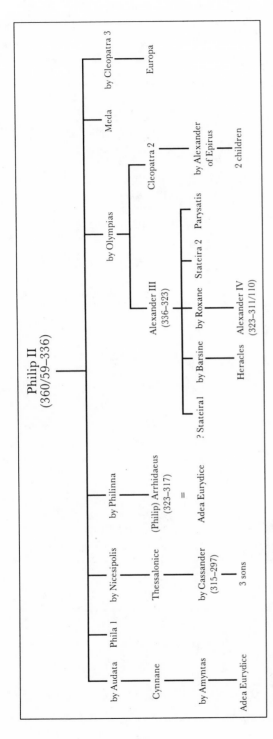

The Argead House from Philip II to the End

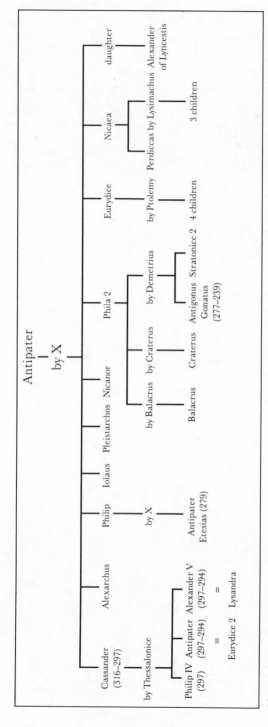

House of Antipater

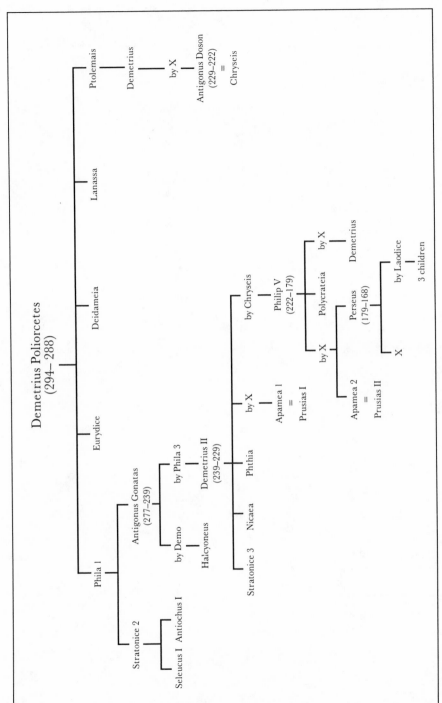

Demetrius Poliorcetes
(294– 288)

Phila 1 — Eurydice — Deidameia — Lanassa — Ptolemais

Stratonice 2

Seleucus I — Antiochus I

Antigonus Gonatas
(277–239)

by Demo — Halcyoneus

by Phila 3 — Demetrius II
(239–229)

Stratonice 3 — Nicaea — Phthia

by X — Apamea 1 = Prusias I

by Chryseis — Philip V
(222–179)

by X — Apamea 2 = Prusias II

Polycrateia — Perseus
(179–168)

by X — Demetrius

X

by Laodice — 3 children

Demetrius

by X — Antigonus Doson
(229–222) = Chryseis

Antigonid House

Notes

CHAPTER 1

1. See Fantham et al. 1994 and Blundell 1995 for recent discussions of the role of women in the Hellenic world.

2. On the general history of ancient Macedonia, see Hammond and Griffith 1979; Hammond and Walbank 1988; Borza 1990; Errington 1990.

3. For the reign of Philip, see Ellis 1976; Cawkwell 1978. On Alexander's reign, see Bosworth 1988, 1996.

4. See Green 1990 for a recent survey of Hellenistic history and the Roman conquest of the Hellenistic kingdoms.

5. See Borza 1990: 1–179; Errington 1990: 1–28.

6. See general discussions in Edson 1970: 17–44; Borza 1990: 236–41.

7. The argument presented in the following section is based on that given in Carney 1995: 367–91. See Borza 1990: 231–48 for discussion of both interpretations of the nature of the monarchy, references, and an argument in favor of the anti-constitutionalist view. Hatzopoulos (1996) takes the opposing view.

8. E.g., the death of Parmenio. Alexander ordered it without a trial or public hearing; see Hamilton 1969: 137–38.

9. Carney 1983: 260–72; Greenwalt 1989: 19–43; Borza 1990: 240.

10. Borza (1990: 240) contrasts the stability of the rule of the Argead clan with the instability of the rule of individual Argeads. Greenwalt (1989: 35) speaks of the "corporate aura surrounding the royal family which distinguished it from all others in the realm." See further Goody 1966: 24.

11. Ptolemy of Alorus is ordinarily assumed to have been an Argead; see Hammond 1979: 181–83; Borza 1990: 190–95.

12. The nature of modern governmental structures and cultures has led scholars to an unconscious and inappropriate assumption that power was synonymous with office. See further Carney 1995a.

13. Hammond (1988a: 382–84, 390) has argued that inscriptional evidence demonstrates that Alexander used the title *basileus* (king) early in his reign, before his departure for Asia.

14. See, for instance, *IG* I 3.89, in which Perdiccas appears as the first signatory of a treaty, followed by other Argeads in what may be status order.

15. Carney 1995: 370 n. 10.

16. See Carney 1995: 371–74 for examples.

17. See Carney 1995: 375–76; and below, chap. 4.

18. Heckel (1986: 295 n. 10) notes the comparative poverty of references, especially named references, to women in the reign of Alexander, as compared to men.

19. For instance, Adams (1977: 22 n. 23) suggests that Olympias may not have had a right to speak in the Macedonian assembly because women could not speak in the Athenian assembly. Cynnane, Adea Eurydice, and Cleopatra, Philip's daughter, all spoke in public circumstances (see references in their respective lives), as did Homeric women, the more appropriate parallel. Hatzopoulos (1996: 1:275) assumes that Olympias had a right to speak but that Cassander, hoping to avoid her possibly compelling appearance, tried to avoid it by arranging her murder. See further chap. 5 and OLYMPIAS: PART 3.

20. See Badian 1982b and Borza 1990: 90–97 for discussion and references on the issue of Macedonian ethnicity.

21. Pomeroy 1984: 18–19.

22. See further Carney 1995: 382.

23. See Saller 1980 for an excellent discussion of the dangers of uncritical use of anecdotal material.

24. See Carney 1984: 167–70 for a medieval example of this phenomenon.

25. For instance, the story of an elite Macedonian who laughs when seeing the ceremony of *proskynesis* for the first time is told about Cassander (Plut. *Alex.* 74.1–2), Polyperchon (Curt. 8.5.21–24), and Leonnatus (Arr. 4.12.2). Heckel (1978b: 459–61) offers a plausible scholarly explanation for the three versions of the story but ignores the attractiveness of the narrative of the anecdote as a factor in its duplication.

26. An egregious example is the story that Philip stopped sleeping with Olympias because he once saw a snake sleeping by her side, a snake who turns out to be Zeus (Plut. *Alex.* 2.4, 3.1). Quite apart from other less than historical aspects of this tale (see Carney 1992a: 171), it assumes that Philip felt compelled to explain to some one why he was not sleeping with one of his many wives.

27. Diodorus' (17.16.2) report that Parmenio and Antipater advised Alexander to marry before he left for Asia and delay his departure until he had an heir is a good example of this kind of anecdote. The story conforms to conventional understanding of the two generals' characters but assumes either that such a conversation took place in some public place or that one of the two generals repeated the tale. Neither assumption is plausible, and other details make it likely that the story is spurious (see further chap. 4).

28. For instance, the story preserved in Diodorus (19.11.9) first singles Olympias out for special opprobrium in terms of political enemies she had slaughtered (her action was typical of leaders in the period of the Successors, and yet no author singles out any of the male Successors for similar blame; see OLYMPIAS) and then reminds the reader that Antipater had supposedly uttered

a deathbed warning against primary rule by a woman. Similarly Plutarch (*Alex.* 68.3) recounts that when Alexander heard that Olympias and her daughter Cleopatra had divided Epirus and Macedonia between them, with Olympias taking Epirus (on the uncertain historicity of this episode, see OLYMPIAS and CLEOPATRA 2), he said that Olympias had made the better choice because the Macedonians would not tolerate being ruled by a woman. In both cases, whatever the veracity of the anecdote, the narrative is also interested in establishing a norm—women should not rule in Macedonia—at least as much as reporting events.

29. For instance, while we may doubt that Philip married Olympias because he fell in love with her as Plutarch (*Alex.* 2.1) claims, Plutarch's allusion to the meeting of these two at Samothrace and their participation in the mysteries deserves more belief (see OLYMPIAS), exactly because the information about Samothrace is merely incidental and not the "point" of the story.

30. E.g., Plutarch's (*Alex.* 9.3) description of Olympias as *chalepotes* (difficult, harsh, ill-tempered), *duszelos* (very jealous), and *baruthmos* (sullen). See Carney 1993b: 29–36; OLYMPIAS. Plutarch's diction doubtless suits Antipater's view of Olympias but probably does not fit the view of her friend Eumenes or her daughter Cleopatra.

31. The expectation of "niceness" for women is insidious but helps to explain why scholars have overreacted to Olympias' violence and underreacted to that of male Successors; see Carney 1993b: 38–41.

32. See Carney 1993b: 39–41.

33. See Carney (1993b: 37–55), who argues that Justin's (9.7.12) version of this murder is the more plausible. An early medieval example invites a similar irrational reaction. Fredegund, a Merovingian royal woman, is said to have killed her husband in order to become regent, led the army to victory carrying her infant son into battle, killed troublemakers with an ax, but, surprisingly squeamishly, left the murder of ecclesiastics to minions (see Wemple 1981: 64–65). This story, which at once so appealingly inverts traditional expectations about female behavior and yet somehow confirms them at the same time, tempts one to tell the tale with comparative indifference to its truth.

34. See Stafford 1983: 1–30 for a discussion of a similar circumstance in terms of Merovingian sources.

35. On accusations of witchcraft, particularly common in polygamous circumstances, see Harris 1973: 145–59; Stafford 1983: 29–30; Gluckman 1963: 116. The story of Olympias and the snake (see n. 26) is a good example of the sexual undertone often involved in stories of witchcraft or magic.

36. On the enduring appeal of these stereotypes, see the essays in Garlick, Dixon, and Allen 1992.

37. See, e.g., Carney 1993b: 29–55 for an attempt to sort out truth from stereotypes in terms of the violent actions of Olympias.

38. See Carney 1993b: 30–32 for examples of imputation to Olympias of one motivation, madness, unmentioned by any ancient source.

39. See Carney 1993a.

40. For discussions of women in Homer, see Foley 1978: 7–19; Mossé 1981: 149–57; Pedrick 1988: 85–101; Marquandt 1985: 32–48; Vernant 1981: 49–66. None focuses specifically on royal women.

41. See Carney 1993a: 315–16. As my discussion indicates, I am not persuaded by Mortensen's (1997: 50–52) argument that the freedom of action of Olympias and other royal women dated to the period after the death of her husband and that my Homeric examples are in various ways exceptions (e.g., Penelope's husband's absence and the pressure of the Suitors led to a unique situation). Although I would agree that royal women (both historical Macedonian and mythic) were generally more likely to appear in public in the absence of royal men, this hardly means that they "lived largely secluded lives" (Mortensen 1997: 50). Royal women, at least from the time of Eurydice on (possibly earlier, but in the absence of evidence, we cannot tell), had various kinds of public roles in Macedonian society (see below), roles that can hardly have been played out in seclusion. It is likely, however, that there were separate women's quarters and considerable separation between the lives of royal men and royal women. But separation and seclusion are different circumstances.

42. Prestianni-Giallombardo 1976–77: 96; Hammond 1956: 3 n. 12.

43. See Lacey 1968: 66–69; Vernant 1973: 51–74; Pomeroy 1975: 34–57; Starr 1977: 129–33; Fantham et al. 1994: 11, 34–45.

44. See further Gernet 1968: 290–301; Carney 1993a: 316–18.

45. Sancisi-Weerdenberg 1987: 37–44; Hall 1989: 201–2, 1995: 110; Brosius 1996: 188.

46. See discussions in Sancisi-Weerdenberg 1983, 1987; Hall 1989: 95, 209; Briant 1989; Carney 1993a: 320–22.

47. Borza 1990: 102–5.

48. See below for possibility that Macedonian practices about women's names may have been related to Persian.

49. See Borza 1992: 102 for discussion and reference.

50. Borza 1992: 103.

51. Macurdy 1932a: 14.

52. Samuel 1988: 1270–86. His suggestion that Macedonian kings should be understood, like Merovingian kings, to be leaders of war bands who were compelled to reward the members of the band with frequent booty-generating conquests seems most applicable to the period before the reign of Philip II but increasingly an oversimplification when applied to the reigns of Philip and his son.

53. Carney (1987b: 37–38), discussing the career of Olympias, first suggested that the role of women in the early Frankish monarchy could be a useful model for that of women in the Macedonian monarchy; Greenwalt (1989: 32–34) made similar use of Frankish material in his discussion of polygamy and succession in the Macedonian monarchy; Samuel (1988: 1270–86) argued that the

nature of Merovingian monarchy helps to explain the general nature of Macedonian monarchy (he does not discuss women or succession patterns).

54. See discussions on Merovingian royal women in Stafford 1978: 79–100, 1983; Nelson 1978: 31–78; Wemple 1981: 63–70, 97–98.

55. The inscription cited records a treaty between Macedonia and Athens signed—clearly in rank order— first by Perdiccas himself, then his brother Alcetas, and next Archelaus. The date of the treaty is disputed: Hammond (1979: 154–56) argues for a late date of ca. 425; Borza (1990: 153, 295) prefers ca. 423; and Errington (1990: 25) opts for the very early date of ca. 440.

56. Hammond 1979: 154; Greenwalt 1989: 25.

57. Greenwalt (1989: 25) suggests that the slur, while incorrect, indicates lower prestige.

58. Greenwalt 1989: 25.

59. The great uncertainty about the date of the treaty (see above, n. 55) makes Archelaus' age unknown, other than that he was old enough to succeed by ca. 413. Perdiccas could have married Simache as early as the 450s, although a somewhat later date for the marriage and the birth of Archelaus seems preferable.

60. If so, then it came soon after Alexander I's death in the late 450s, in the period in which Perdiccas faced rival claims by several brothers: see Hammond 1979; 115; Borza 1990: 134–35; Errington 1990: 15.

61. Greenwalt 1989: 34.

62. Nelson 1978: 59; Stafford 1983: 11, 25, 124–27, 178–82.

63. Certainly female regents were common among the Franks (Stafford 1983: 141–58), whereas they were unknown in Macedonia. (Olympias' role after her son's death is a possible partial exception; see OLYMPIAS. Thessalonice, although often termed a regent, was not; see THESSALONICE.)

64. This important point is made not only by Stafford (1983: 178–82). Goody (1966: 20) also stresses the cross-cultural importance of mothers as succession advocates for their sons in polygamous situations with indeterminate successions.

65. The earliest examples of the marriages of royal women seem to demonstrate this: Gygaea, daughter of Amyntas I and sister of Alexander I, married a high-ranking Persian (Herod. 5.21; see GYGAEA 1), and the two daughters of Archelaus also made political marriages, one to a ruler of Elimeia and the other to another Argead (Arist. *Pol.* 1311b11).

66. Greenwalt 1988a: 93–97.

67. See Seibert 1967: 122–27 for a useful discussion of Hellenistic marriage alliances. Although Seibert deals with a later period, many of his conclusions seem relevant to Argead times as well. See MEDA, one of the wives of Philip II, for an example of a wife probably acquired for very short term reasons. Greenwalt (1989: 36–37) suggests that Philip's marriages to Audata and Phila had similar short-term goals.

68. Heckel 1986: 294–95.

69. See Seibert 1967: 122–23; Carney 1992b: 169–71; chaps. 3 and 4 below.

70. The marriage of Olympias to Philip was probably arranged for long-term benefit: Philip's role in putting her brother on the throne; the marriage he arranged between his daughter by Olympias and her brother; the role of Cleopatra as apparent regent in Molossia during her brother's reign; and the engagement of Deidameia, daughter of Aeacides, to Alexander IV (Plut. *Pyrrh.* 4.2) all tend to confirm this understanding of the marriage. Amyntas III's marriage to Eurydice would appear to fall in this category (see EURYDICE 1). Greenwalt (1989: 37) implies that such distinctions between long and short term only emerged over time, based on "developing circumstance," but the case of Olympias seems to imply the opposite. See also Seibert 1967: 125–26.

71. Clearly the first possibility is more likely in marriages for long-term purposes; it may well be that Olympias did in fact act as her family's ambassador to the Argeads, but it is impossible to demonstrate (see OLYMPIAS). Phila, sister of Cassander and wife of Demetrius Poliorcetes, certainly did enter into peace negotiations between her husband and brothers (Plut. *Demetr.* 2.3), and there are probably many other examples we have no evidence for. Meda, in contrast, would appear to have been something close to a party favor. Not only do we know nothing more about her, but the alliance presumably commemorated by her marriage does not seem to have continuing importance: see Seibert 1967: 123–24, 126–27; and MEDA and STRATONICE 1.

72. Borza 1990: 146–48; Hammond 1979: 129.

73. Some fairly certain examples in the Argead dynasty: Cynnane, daughter of Philip II, married her first cousin, Amyntas, the son of Philip's brother Perdiccas; Cynnane's daughter, Adea Eurydice, married her uncle, Philip Arrhidaeus; Archelaus probably married his father's widow, Cleopatra (see CLEOPATRA 1); Gygaea, one of the wives of Amyntas III, may herself have been an Argead (see GYGAEA 2); and Eurydice, widow of Amyntas III, may have married one of his successors, Ptolemy Alorites (see EURYDICE 1). For some early medieval parallels for the marriages of royal widows, see Nelson 1978: 36; Stafford 1983: 49.

74. Macurdy 1932a: 15–16; Whitehorne 1994: 17–29 contra Hammond 1979: 169 n. 2.

75. The son's name was probably Orestes, the boy king who succeeded Archelaus and, according to Diodorus (14.37.6), was killed by Aeropus. See Errington 1990: 28; Borza 1990: 178.

76. Hammond 1979: 169 n.2.

77. Tataki (1988: 321), examining the evidence from Veria, but only in the Roman period, produces figures that suggest that the name became fairly common there (though not so common as a number of other names). Whitehorne (1994: 22) denies that there is any evidence for Hammond's assertion.

78. Best known in Macedonia proper are the daughter of Philip II (CLEOPA-

TRA 2) and his last wife (CLEOPATRA 3), but the name also appears as the mother of Argaeus on a list of early Argead kings of dubious historicity (Satyr. *FGrH* 630, F 1; *POxy.* 27 (1962 2465, 121 f.) Hammond (1979: 13) suggests that this Hellenistic list simply projected names from the fifth and fourth centuries back in time. Whitehorne (1994: 9–13) takes the list very seriously, but see Greenwalt (1996: 47–50). The name was common in royal dynasties in the Hellenistic period.

79. The identity of this Amyntas is disputed; Hammond (1979: 169) argues that the Greek refers to a son of Amyntas and that it was Amyntas "the little," but Macurdy (1932a: 14–15) understands it, emended, to refer to Amyntas, son of Arrhibaeus.

80. Whitehorne (1994: 26–29).

81. Greenwalt made this suggestion in private conversation.

82. Hammond 1979: 169 n. 2.

83. Clignet (1970: 13) discusses great variations in polygamous systems.

84. Ellis 1976: 211–17; Griffith 1979: 214–15; Tronson 1984: 116–26; Bosworth 1988: 6–7; Borza 1990: 206–8 contra Green 1982: 138–46. On Philip's marriages and the status of his wives, see chap. 3.

85. My discussion of the likelihood of royal polygamy pre-Philip II largely follows the arguments of Greenwalt (1989: 22–28).

86. See Greenwalt 1989: 25–28; chap. 2.

87. See Greenwalt 1989: 22–25; this part of his argument is somewhat less persuasive than his discussion of the marriage of Amyntas III.

88. Greenwalt 1989: 22–23.

89. Greenwalt 1989: 19–43, esp. 42–43. See Stafford 1983: 71–78 for a discussion of the similarly destabilizing effect of polygamy in Frankish monarchy.

90. Greenwalt (1989: 32) rightly points to Goody (1966: 25), who cautions that tidy and well-defined methods of choosing heirs to thrones are quite uncommon around the world. Stafford (1983: 173) makes the same points and links it to the important role of women in succession politics; struggles for the throne, she notes, tend to enhance the importance of a mother to a son.

91. Here I follow the arguments of Greenwalt 1989: 19–43 contra a number of earlier scholars (see Greenwalt 1989: 19 n. 1 for references) and, more recently, Hatzopoulos 1986: 279–92.

92. See discussion in Greenwalt 1989: 34–43. Greenwalt, however, believes that the nationality of the potential heir's mother was a factor in successful succession, particularly in the troubles Alexander experienced at the end of Philip II's reign (39–42); I am less certain that it was very important (see below).

93. Borza (1990: 240) estimates that about half the Argead kings of the fifth and fourth centuries fell to assassination plots. Perdiccas III (see chap. 2) died in battle in his twenties; we know that he had a son, but we do not know the name of his wife.

94. See Muhsam 1956–57: 6–16; Clignet 1970: 29, esp. n. 17; McClintock 1971: 244–45. I owe these references to Kate Mortensen.

95. See Mortensen 1997: 168 for a chart of Philip's probable absences from the Macedonian court. His frequent absences on campaigns must have significantly reduced sexual contact with his various wives.

96. Herodotus (1.61) reports that the polygamous Athenian tyrant Peisistratus, partly because he wanted to protect the interests of his sons by an earlier and less prestigious wife, chose not to have sexual intercourse with the daughter of Megacles in a way that could produce children. Philip might have chosen to do the same.

97. Of Philip's wives, only the mother of Thessalonice, Nicesipolis, is known to have died in childbirth (see NICESIPOLIS), but others, like Phila and Meda of whom nothing is known except for their marriages, might have died in childbirth. They may equally well have lived on in obscurity.

98. Clignet (1970: 35, 51) notes that in the African systems he studied the senior wife tended to be dominant but that the degree of dominance varied, particularly if the status of senior wife was inferior to that of subsequent wives. There is no evidence that in Macedonian polygamy the first wife had any particular status; see chap. 3 for discussions of Philip's marriages.

99. See Carney 1992a: 171–89; OLYMPIAS.

100. Greenwalt 1989: 34–43.

101. Greenwalt 1989: 39–40 contra Ellis 1976: 42, 215, and Badian 1982a: 103–4. This issue is most often raised in terms of Philip II's mother, Eurydice, but her ethnicity is mixed and disputed, and in terms of Attalus's implication that Alexander III, whose mother was Molossian, was not *gnesios* (legitimate, lawful; Plut. *Alex.* 9.4; see OLYMPIAS).

102. On the competitive nature of the Macedonian court, see Carney 1992a; Fredricksmeyer 1990.

103. So Clignet 1970: 34, 41, 51, in discussing societies with similar features.

104. Clignet 1970: 30–31, 45, 52–53.

105. Heckel (1992: 213) suggested that Phila, a childless wife of Philip II, was able to exercise influence on behalf of her birth family during her husband's reign. See PHILA 1.

106. Andronicos (1964: 6; 1984: 39) did not designate any area in the Vergina palace as women's quarters, but both the missing upper story, which covered at least the east wing, or the mysterious building west of the main palace might have fulfilled such a purpose. Since royal polygamy was in decline (see chaps. 6, 8) by the reign of Cassander (the apparent occupant of the main palace at Vergina), who had, as far as we know, only one wife, this structure may not reflect the usage of the Argeads in more polygamous times or under more polygamous kings.

107. Three Macedonian palaces have been discovered so far. The chronology of the palace at Pella is a problem (Petsas 1978: 30; Lauter 1987: 347; Siganidou 1987: 124; Ginouvès 1994: 89), but some of the structure dated to Argead times. The palace at Demetrias was only of Hellenistic date (Lauter

1987: 347). The palace at Vergina is now dated to the period of Cassander (Andronicos 1984: 39; Ginouvès 1994: 87). Petsas (1978: 29–30) notes the presence of several rooms identifiable as an *andron* in ordinary houses at Pella from the late fourth century. Andronicos (1984: 42,44) and Ginouvès (1994: 87) find evidence for at least five different areas of the palace at Vergina being used as an *andron*. Faklaris (1994: 609–16) rejects Vergina's identification as Aegae and thus brings into question the assumption that the structure was a royal palace (see chap. 9). See also Nielsen 1994: 81–99, 260–68. Nielsen (1994: 23, 136) finds no specific evidence for women's quarters, but her general discussion of life at Hellenistic courts (largely based on evidence from the reign of Ptolemy IV) does assume that there were separate women's quarters with both bedrooms and dining areas.

108. Herodotus (5.17–21) tells a story about the women of the family of Amyntas I and Alexander I that stresses the fact that Argead women would not ordinarily have been present when male guests were in attendance, but the story is of dubious historicity (see references in Carney 1993a: 314 n. 4), intended to demonstrate, among other things, the Hellenic ways of the Argeads. It is worth noting, however, that the female burial in the antechamber of Tomb II at Vergina, a probable royal burial, contains no banqueting vessels at all, whereas such vessels were a prominent part of the male burial in the main chamber: see Drogou et al. 1996: 57.

109. Royal women seem to have had some sort of household entourage, some of which was male: Alexander's sister Cleopatra funded a tomb for a court musician (Paus. 1.44.6); Cynnane had some sort of military escort (see CYNNANE); and Adea Eurydice had a secretary (*FGrH* 156, F 9.30–33) and someone named Polycles who was an adviser of sorts (Diod. 19.11.3).

110. One thinks, for instance, of the confrontation of Cleopatra, sister of Alexander, with Antipater (see CLEOPATRA 2), or Olympias' apparent management of the siege of Pydna and of the events surrounding her death (see OLYMPIAS).

111. Olympias and her daughter knew Eumenes and corresponded with him and with Perdiccas and Leonnatus, which implies previous acquaintance. Dionysius of Heracleia applied to Cleopatra to use her influence with Alexander to protect him from the king's wrath (Memnon *FGrH* 434, F 4. 37). Olympias' long-running quarrel with Antipater also implies acquaintanceship, at the very least.

112. For example, Philip's mother Eurydice's attempt to persuade Iphicrates to protect her sons (see EURYDICE 1), Olympias' attempt to intervene in the Harpalus affair (Diod. 17.108.7), or Cynnane's abrupt departure for Asia when she heard of Alexander's death there (see CYNNANE).

113. The sources preserve a tradition of voluminous correspondence for Olympias, the authenticity of which is uncertain (see Carney 1987b: 49, 54–55). Whatever the dependability of individual letters, our sources assume that

Olympias was literate. Diogenes Laertius (5.27) refers to a collection of letters Aristotle supposedly addressed to Olympias. For her daughter, we have evidence of a correspondence between her and her brother and others (Memnon *FGrH* 434, F 4.37), including Leonnatus (Plut. *Eum.* 3.3–6). Events imply a correspondence between Adea Eurydice and Cassander (Just. 14.5.1–4). Barsine is said to have had a Greek education, apparently in imitation of Macedonian women (Plut. *Alex.* 21.4), but this may refer to her upbringing, not her literacy. Both Pomeroy (1977: 61) and Cole (1981: 230) conclude that Macedonian royal women could read.

114. Cole (1981: 230) makes this point about Olympias, but it applies to many other royal women.

115. Thanks to Euripides' stay in Macedonia, his works seem to have been particularly well known among the Macedonian elite: see Borza 1990: 172–73; Instinsky 1960: 253; Aymard 1949: 48–49.

116. Contra Hammond (1979: 154 and 1989: 31, followed by Pomeroy 1984: 4 nn. 4, 5), who believes that Macedonian royal women regularly wove the clothing and made the meals for their menfolk and asserts that there was no staff of slaves; he also assumes that this situation endured into the fourth century, as I do not; see below.

117. Hammond (1979: 154; 1989: 31) cites Curt. 5.2.20; Aristid. 45.55; and Herod. 8.137.2. Curtius has the women of Alexander's family weaving him a garment, in contrast to the Asian luxury of the women of Darius's family. The tale is obviously suspect for any number of reasons (see Carney 1996; Briant 1994: 286 n. 9). It is likely enough that Argead women did fine work in fabric, but they are unlikely to have made all garments or even most of them, at least by the later period. The second century A.D. work of Aristides refers to the supposed use of a hand grain mill by a royal woman in the late fifth century. The Herodotus passage, in recounting the legendary beginnings of the Argead dynasty, refers to a king's wife (not an Argead) baking for the household and includes Herodotus' observation that in past times even kings' wives cooked. None of these passages deserves belief. Hammond offers no evidence for his assertion about the lack of slaves, although it seems likely that there would not have been many in early Argead times. Only with the great military success of Philip would war captives and thus slaves have become plentiful and have come to supplement the service of groups like the Royal Youths (Pages). Mirón Pérez (1999) argues that these stories are Argead propaganda, meant to demonstrate their Hellenism.

118. Ginouvès 1994: 85.

119. Berve (1926: 1: 41–42) and Scholl (1987: 108–21) discuss the role of slaves in the court of Alexander, but this may have been much changed from the days before the Persian campaign.

120. See above. One thinks of Penelope, who spent her time at genteel and even political weaving but who left many household tasks to Eurycleia. See chap. 9 for the possibility that the fabric found in the *larnax* of the antechamber of Tomb II at Vergina may have been the work of a royal woman.

121. Lanice: see Berve 1926: 2:231.

122. Leonidas, the early chief tutor of Alexander, was a relative of Olympias (Plut. *Alex.* 5.4). Whether or not he was chosen by Olympias, his choice certainly flattered her and her family. Plutarch (*Alex.* 2.5) later represents Leonidas as being at odds with Olympias in terms of the degree of austerity he wanted in the boy's education, with Olympias resisting. Alexander's later education with Aristotle at Mieza was not a sign of Philip's desire to remove Alexander from his mother's influence—no ancient source says so—but probably typical of the more professional and less familial education of older boys in Hellenic elites.

123. See CLEOPATRA 2, OLYMPIAS, CYNNANE, and ADEA EURYDICE for examples of mothers and daughters who remained close in adulthood. The mothers attempted to arrange marriages for their daughters.

124. Olympias and her daughter, for instance, seem to be able to travel distances, sometimes with considerable entourages, with no male relative in any obvious role. Cynnane was somehow able to raise a military force and take it to Asia; her daughter helped to lead an army. See details and references in their lives.

125. Cabanes (1980: 324–51) points out that Epirote women could, among other things, function as heads of family, if their fathers or husbands were dead. That would appear to be the circumstance not only with Epirote Olympias and her daughter but also with Cynnane, who had Illyrian roots.

126. Consider the situation in Macedonia that developed after the departure of Alexander. Plutarch (*Alex.* 68.3) says Olympias and Cleopatra shared Alexander's *arche* (rule) in a faction against Antipater. In Plutarch, Alexander does not seem to act as *kurios* (guardian) for either his mother or his sister; he simply allows events to take their course.

127. See OLYMPIAS; CLEOPATRA 2; ADEA EURYDICE. See above for precedents from the archaic period.

128. For instance, Alexander's full sister, Cleopatra, certainly benefited in many ways from the fact that her full brother became king; apparently, it enhanced her status more than it did that of her half sisters; see CLEOPATRA 2.

129. See Stafford 1978: 79–100 and Carney 1987b: 37–38 for the analogous situation of mothers and sons in Merovingian and Carolingian times. On the tensions between aging royal father and adult or near-adult sons, consider the examples of Philip II and Alexander (see Fredricksmeyer 1990: 300–15; Carney 1992a: 169–77) and Lysimachus and Agathocles (see ARSINOE). Antipater's curious preference for Polyperchon over his own son Cassander may be another example (see chap. 6).

130. Dixon 1988: 63.

131. E.g., Eurydice, mother of Philip II: see Oikonomedes 1983: 62–4 and Plut. *Mor.* 14c; Olympias, mother of Alexander: see *SIG* 252N. 5–7; *SEG* IX 2.

132. See OLYMPIAS; Heckel 1981b: 80–86.

133. Both involve apparently identical women who are given different names

by different sources. In each case, one of these names is Eurydice; see AUDATA and CLEOPATRA 3. In neither case is there any indication that any source was aware that either woman was known by more than one name, and each could easily be a mistake in one of the surviving texts. There is no evidence that Philip II's mother, also known as Eurydice, was ever called anything else (Heckel [1978a: 156] seems to suggest that she might have been). A possible model for Macedonian name changing: the tyrant Periander changed his wife's name (Diog. Laert. 1.94).

134. See EUROPA and THESSALONICE. There is an Athenian precedent. Themistocles named his daughters to commemorate his ambitions and achievements (Plut. *Them.* 32.2). See Carney 1991a: 168 n. 38 for the possibility that these public names for girls are part of an older, archaic and aristocratic attitude toward women that was preserved into the fourth century in Macedonia. See above for the archaic period and aristocratic custom, especially that of tyrants, as possible models or influences on the role of women in Argead monarchy.

135. Brosius (1996: 184–86) points to the recurrence of certain women's names throughout the Achaemenid dynasty and concludes that Achaemenid women, like men, may have changed their names either when married to a king or at the time of their father's accession. She also discusses significant naming of royal women in memory of earlier holders of the name, perhaps for political purposes. These similarities between Achaemenid and Argead practice—whose extent is difficult to determine—may suggest Achaemenid influence on Argead practice or may be coincidental. They do suggest a similar, quasi-public aspect to the position of royal women.

136. See Greenwalt (forthcoming) on the idea that Argead names were often chosen or changed to allude to past figures in the clan and their political legacies. The most obvious example would be shown in the only attested name change for a male, Arrhidaeus, who took the name of his famous father. Argeads named Alexander must surely have been meant to reflect the glory of the first Alexander of their dynasty, and so on.

137. Heckel (1978a: 155–58), following up an idea of Macurdy (1932a: 24–25), suggested that "Eurydice" was becoming a throne or dynastic name. See contra Badian 1982a; Carney 1991b: 159–60 esp. n. 30.

138. See Carney 1991b: 160. Cratesipolis, wife of Alexander son of Polyperchon, is sometimes said to have changed her name after the conquest of Sicyon (Heckel 1981b: 85 n. 34; Pomeroy 1984: 10), but Macurdy (1929: 273–78) argues persuasively against this possibility. If Heckel and Pomeroy are correct, however, then Cratesipolis, like Olympias, seems to have changed names of her own accord, to commemorate her accomplishments. See PHTHIA and CHRYSEIS for arguments against a possible name change by a wife of Demetrius II in Antigonid times.

139. For references see EURYDICE 1; Mortensen 1992: 163–65.

140. Ath. 659 f. refers to a letter sent to Alexander by Olympias in which she urges him to buy a cook knowledgeable about sacrificial rites, both Bacchic and

Argead, as well as those she offers for him. See Fredricksmeyer 1966: 179–81 and above, on slaves at court.

141. For the role of royal women in religion in the post-Argead period, see Le Bohec 1993b: 229–45.

142. Pomeroy (1984: 3), on the basis of grave goods demonstrating a sexual division similar to that of Athens, and Tataki (1988: 433), on the basis of inscriptional evidence, largely of post–fourth-century material, believe that women's roles in Macedonia were similar to those of women in southern Greece; Hammond (1989: 5), on the basis of his theory about the importance of pastoral transhumance to Macedonia, concludes that women played a less circumscribed role in Macedonia than in southern Greece. What little evidence survives seems to support the former view, but too little survives to reach any firm conclusion.

143. See Carney 1995: 384–85. The evidence is minimal but suggests a pattern similar to that of Macedonian royal women rather than Hellenic women in general. Aristocratic women, like royal women, occasionally played a political role.

144. See further Carney 1983: 264. On the importance of hunting in Macedonia, see Briant 1993: 267–77.

145. Riginos (1994: 103–19) examines the evidence for the many wounds of Philip. Alexander had many as well; he nearly lost his life as consequence of the wounds he received at a citadel of the Malli; see Hamilton 1969: 176–78 for discussion.

146. Borza 1983: 55; 1990: 241–42.

147. Mortensen 1997: 119–29. On the sexual element in assassination plots, see Carney 1983: 260–72. One wonders if sexual tension was an element in the resentment of Hephaestion by the other men close to Alexander (e.g., Plut. *Eum.* 3).

148. The obvious example is the sources' treatment of Olympias; see OLYMPIAS and Carney 1993b: 41–42, 48–50. See also EURYDICE 1 and ARSINOE. Note, however, that Adea Eurydice is not condemned for her actions against Antipater, even though they nearly ended in his death (see ADEA EURYDICE).

149. CYNNANE, AUDATA, and ADEA EURYDICE offer examples of women who went into battle; OLYMPIAS appeared in battle but did not actually fight. CLEOPATRA 2 risked and lost her life in an attempt to escape the control of Antigonus. OLYMPIAS, despite her age, returned to Macedonia in a dangerous attempt to safeguard the throne for her grandson and was ultimately killed. BARSINE accompanied her son Heracles when he went to his father's homeland in what proved to be a fatal attempt to gain the throne.

150. Walcot (1987a: 20–22) blames the timocratic quality of much of Hellenic society on vicariously ambitious mothers (he pictures them working out their own frustrations by goading their sons), citing Olympias and Alexander as a good example. This reverses the truth: the competitive warrior values of the male world were embraced by women as well; part of being a good mother in-

volved reinforcing those values. See Fredricksmeyer (1990: 304 n. 18) who notes that this is an area where Philip and Olympias would have agreed.

151. See examples in the careers of Olympias, Arsinoe, Eurydice.

152. See OLYMPIAS for her role in the attempt to substitute Alexander for Arrhidaeus in the Pixodarus marriage alliance; see also her attempts to arrange a marriage for her daughter Cleopatra with Perdiccas, in competition with the candidacies of the daughter of Antipater; see also CYNNANE, who also introduced her daughter, at about the same time, to competition in the post-Alexander Asian marriage market.

153. Cynnane was killed in the attempt; Cleopatra (see CLEOPATRA 2), although she escaped death at the hands of Antipater, was held more or less captive by Antigonus and died, as we have seen, attempting to arrange a marriage with Ptolemy. Arsinoe managed to survive her marriage to Ptolemy Ceraunus, but it cost her the life of two of her sons.

154. The *basileia* mentioned may refer to Epirus rather than Macedonia, but the context seems to suggest the latter. The story of Cleopatra's supposed affair may well be apocryphal; if not, it almost certainly relates to the period of her widowhood as her husband died early in Alexander's reign. The literal truth of the tale is less significant than the conceptualization of Cleopatra's role.

155. Naturally a Greek, used to the extreme separation of the worlds of men and women, found the permeability of Macedonian court life to women upsetting. See further Carney 1993b: 33.

156. For example, Thessalonice spent most of her life in the shadows but apparently played an important role in the critical period after the deaths of her husband and oldest son (see THESSALONICE). Cynnane, similarly obscure for years, took sudden and decisive action on her daughter's behalf after Alexander's death (see CYNNANE).

CHAPTER 2
1. See Hammond 1979: 182–85; Borza 1990: 191–93.

2. On these events, see Hammond 1979: 172–88; Errington 1990: 28–37; Borza 1990: 180–97.

3. See Mortensen 1992: 157 n. 2 on the possibility that *adelphos* can mean brother-in-law. *LSJ* suggests that the term can refer to a kinsman, not just a brother.

4. Hammond 1979: 182–83; Greenwalt 1988b: 42; Greenwalt 1989: 28; Mortensen 1992: 156–71. See EURYDICE 1.

5. Macurdy (1927: 209; 1932a: 18, 20) suggests (followed by Mortensen 1992: 157), on the basis of Diod. 16.71.1 (which says he was a son of Amyntas and brother of Alexander II), that Ptolemy was a bastard son of Amyntas III. Hammond (1979: 182), on the basis of the Diodorus passage, suggests that Ptolemy was a son of Amyntas "the little." See contra Errington 1990: 36 n. 2. Green (1991: 14) considers the reference to Amyntas mere propaganda.

6. Mortensen (1992: 167 n. 43) suggests death in childbirth. If her mother did marry Ptolemy and he was Eurynoe's husband, she was almost certainly dead. Polygamy was common enough in Macedonia, but marriages to a mother and daughter at the same time are unlikely.

7. See Hammond 1979: 183 for references.

8. Mortensen (1992: 167 n. 43) concludes that Philoxenus was probably too old to be Eurynoe's son. See Berve 1926: 2.389–91 for discussion of four possible descendants of this Philoxenus.

9. Macurdy (1927: 207–8, 212) first pointed to Eurydice's pivotal role as the first royal woman to act politically but denied that Eurydice had any "political power"; her judgment derives from her failure to distinguish between authority—something Eurydice, not being king or regent, did not have—and influence—something she demonstrably did possess (see below). Power and office were not synonymous in Macedonia, as she assumed; see chap. 1. Greenwalt (1989: 41–42) notes the development with Eurydice of a "public persona, status and role." Mortensen (1992: 163) seems to agree.

10. The name of Eurydice's father is now certain because of three inscriptions found at Vergina that read, in part, *Eurydika Sirra*. See Oikonomedes 1983: 62–64; Andronicos 1984: 49–51; Saatsoglou-Paliadeli 1987: 733–44, 1993: 1339–71.

11. For references, see above, n. 10.

12. See Greenwalt (1989: 37–44) who believes that Eurydice's father, Sirras, was Lyncestian (as do Hammond [1979: 15] and Oikonomedes [1983: 63]) and Mortensen (1991: 51–55) who believes he was Illyrian (as do Papazoglou [1965: 150]; Bosworth [1971: 93–105]; Ellis [1967: 42, 249–50] and Badian [1982: 103]).

13. The passage (from an essay that may not be a genuine work of Plutarch; see Mortensen 1992: 159 n. 16) includes an inscription that refers to a woman named Eurydice who is termed "Illyrian and three times barbarian." Like Mortensen (1991: 52), I doubt Oikonomedes' (1983: 63 n. 4) suggestion that "Illyrian" was used by Attic orators to describe anyone they believed to be barbarian; it is not clear why Plutarch or anyone else would have described Eurydice as, in effect, "barbarian and three times barbarian," particularly as the context of the passage is anything but hostile to Eurydice. A literal understanding of the term better suits the context.

14. As Mortensen (1992: 159 n. 16) notes, the identification of the Eurydice in the Plutarch passage and the preserved inscription with the mother of Philip II has been generally accepted. The first line of the text of the inscription embedded in the Plutarch passage has now been considerably emended to read *Eurudike Sirra polietisi tond' anetheken* (see Robert and Robert 1984: 450–51; Wilhelm 1949: 625–33). The discovery of the three other Eurydice descriptions with the patronymic "Sirra" makes that portion of the emendation especially plausible (see also Oikonomedes 1983: 62–64) and thus the identification of Eurydice as the mother of Philip.

15. Greenwalt (1988a: 37, 42–43) ties her supposed Lyncestian ethnicity not

only to a political alliance with that house but also to changes in the monarchy. Mortensen (1991: 52–55) connects her supposed Illyrian ethnicity to an Illyrian/Lyncestian alliance.

16. So Hammond 1979: 178; Greenwalt 1988a: 37; Errington 1990: 29, all of whom think she was Lyncestian. Mortensen (1991: 53) and Bosworth (1971b: 100), who think she was Illyrian, date it a little later, to 391–390, and connect the marriage to the Illyrian invasion.

17. Papazoglou (1965: 153) and Hammond (1979: 178) suggest a birthdate of ca. 410. See Greenwalt 1988: 93–97 on the ages of Argeads at marriage. Mortensen (1991: 53) suggests the period 410 to 406. It seems unlikely that she would have married earlier than fourteen or much later than eighteen.

18. See Ellis 1973: 350–54; Griffith 1979: 699–701.

19. Greenwalt 1989: 27.

20. Greenwalt (1988a: 41–44; 1989: 26–28) argues that Eurydice's status, which he ties to her supposed ethnic origins, was the determinant and that Amyntas consciously promoted her status to strengthen his own security and stability. Certainly inscriptional and archaeological evidence seems to confirm the latter theory. While the identification of Eurydice as the daughter of a Lyncestian seems unconvincing to me, Greenwalt's suggestion that Eurydice's status mattered in her ultimate victory makes sense, so long as one recognizes that other factors were present as well (see chap. 1).

21. See Borza 1990: 90–95 on the identity of Ptolemy.

22. Macurdy 1932a: 21–22.

23. Mortensen 1992: 165–66.

24. Mortensen 1992: 158.

25. See further Mortensen 1992: 158.

26. See Mortensen 1992: 156–71. Only Errington (1990: 35–36) and Green (1991: 14) continue to accept Justin's account.

27. Greenwalt 1989: 28. Mortensen (1992: 162–63) agrees, noting that Philip, Eurydice's youngest son, would have been particularly vulnerable to slurs on his legitimacy based on his mother's supposed adultery (Suda s.v. "Karanos" seems to confirm this suggestion) but also considers the possibility that Eurydice's marriage to Ptolemy generated scandal.

28. See n. 10 for references, as well as Saatsoglou-Paliadeli 1987: 733–44; *AR* 1983–84: 47, *AR* 1990–91: 56; *Ergon* 1990: 83–85, 1991: 65–68. A headless statue of Eucleia (contra Hammond 1994: 184) was discovered near the second inscription.

29. Greenwalt 1988a: 42; Borza 1990: 192–93, 308–9; Mortensen 1992: 165. Oikonomedes (1983: 62), apparently unaware of Andronicos's dating, tied the first inscription to "the early fourth century," on the basis of letter shape.

30. If that were the case, Eurydice would have been celebrating her son's victory against those who had killed her elder son and at the same time would have been suggesting that, whatever her ethnic heritage, the Illyrians were her and her family's enemies.

31. Borza 1992: 192–93. The Vergina temple does indeed seem to have been on the edge of the marketplace.

32. Greenwalt (1988a: 42) argued for the reign of Amyntas and suggested that Amyntas encouraged the public development of her role for purposes of dynastic security. Mortensen (1992: 164–65) doubts his early date, primarily because she seems to doubt Amyntas had a need to emphasize Eurydice's role. In light of the various Argead pretenders active in the reigns of her husband and those of her sons, emphasizing Eurydice and her dynastic role might have been important on many occasions. Still, Greenwalt's apparent date in the 380s or 370s seems to stretch the date of the lettering of the inscriptions very far. If there is any connection between these inscriptions and the inscription preserved in Plutarch (*Mor*.14c), which refers to grown sons, then a date for the Eucleia inscriptions after 370 does seem plausible. See further Mortensen 1992: 165.

33. So Greenwalt 1988a: 42 contra the doubts of Mortensen 1992: 164. That we now have two statue bases dedicated by her seems very persuasive, and the evidence for the role of royal women in religion in later Argead and Hellenistic times (see chaps. 1, 8) also seems suggestive.

34. The dedication, as emended (Hammond [1994: 17] seems unaware of the suggested emendations), suggests that she functioned as a patron, perhaps of female education, to the women of the city (Wilhelm [1949] and Robert and Robert [1984] argue that this is a dedication not to the muses but to women citizens), and the reference to grown sons would appear to date the inscription after the death of Amyntas; see further Wilhelm 1949: 625–33 and Robert and Robert 1984: 450–51; note Wilhelm's (632) warning that Plutarch's gloss on the inscription indicates that he somewhat misread it.

35. Borza 1992: 308–9 points out the obvious difficulty inherent in Andronicos's belief that Eurydice's Eucleia dedications were post-338 and that the Tomb of Throne, which he dated to 343–340, was also Eurydice's.

36. Ellis 1973: 351; Mortensen 1992: 168.

37. The existence of a wife is to be presumed from the existence of his son, Amyntas (Just. 7.5.8).

38. Beloch (1927: 3:266) suggests that she was a descendant of Menelaus; Macurdy (1927: 204–5; 1932a: 14–15) more plausibly—granted the name of her eldest son—suggests that Gygaea's father was Archelaus. Ellis (1973: 351), Hatzopoulos (1986: 281), Greenwalt (1988: 43), and Mortensen (1992: 169) endorse the idea that Gygaea was an Argead.

39. Heckel 1986: 295 n. 10. By the Hellenistic period, epigraphic information significantly increases, but we cannot assume that usage of a name did not change over time.

40. Macurdy 1932: 17; Ellis 1973: 351; Badian 1982a: 104; Hatzopoulos 1986: 282; Greenwalt 1988b: 37. Only Greenwalt (1989: 26–28) challenges this assumption.

41. Incorrectly cited in Greenwalt 1988b: 26 as Diod. 15.60.3.

42. Aeschines could, of course, be thinking only of full brothers. These three sources come out of different traditions.

43. Greenwalt 1989: 26–28.

44. Greenwalt 1989: 27.

45. So Hatzopoulos 1986: 281. Hatzopoulos' theory that only sons born to a king while he was king were eligible seems particularly implausible in this situation.

46. See Greenwalt 1989: 25–28.

47. Although Greenwalt (1989: 22–25) makes a good argument for the view that Perdiccas II was probably polygamous, it is certainly possible, if unlikely, that Amyntas was the first Argead polygamist. See chap. 1.

48. For instance, Pausanias, the Argead claimant who challenged Philip at the beginning of his reign and had support prior to the reign of Philip (Aeschin. 2.27; Diod. 16.2.6).

49. Greenwalt (1988b: 439–40; 1989: 27) argues that Eurydice's status was critical to the succession of her sons, a status he connects to her parentage, which he believed to have been primarily Lyncestian. See EURYDICE 1.

50. Greenwalt (1988b: 42–43) suggests that Amyntas consciously promoted Eurydice and thus her line of descent.

CHAPTER 3

1. On the reign of Philip, see Ellis 1976; Cawkwell 1978; Griffith 1979: 203–646, 675–98.

2. This is a late-second-century A.D. work that uses the literary frame of a symposium to collect excerpts from a large number of ancient authors on a vast variety of topics. Many of the excerpts come from works and authors otherwise lost to us. See further Baldwin 1976: 21–42; Hawley 1993: 73–91.

3. Satyrus the Peripatetic was probably active in the third century B.C. Among other things, he wrote a series of lives of famous men now known to us primarily from citations in Athenaeus and a few other writers from later antiquity. The surviving fragments suggest that Satyrus was somewhat prone to gossip, sensationalism, and moralizing. See further Tronson 1984: 117–18; Hawley 1993: 73–91.

4. My discussion of the significance of the Athenaeus/Satyrus passage follows the fundamental discussion of Tronson (1984: 116–26) in most respects (the conclusions that the list is chronologically organized, that the *kata polemon* observation is Athenaeus', not Satyrus', that this is a list of wives rather than a list of wives and concubines) but differs in suggesting that Satyrus may not have known the order of Philip's first five marriages (I therefore stress the fact that only the last three marriages are described in words that clearly indicate chronological order) and in taking a broader perspective on the information contained in the passage.

5. Tronson (1984: 119) translates this phrase, on the basis of Satyrus' use of *oikeiousthai*, as "he wanted to appropriate the Thessalian people as well, on grounds of kinship."

6. See Tronson 1984: 116–26 and Ellis 1981: 11–23 for general discussion and references.

7. See arguments in Tronson 1984: 120.

8. Although Tronson (1984: 119) concedes that there is little or no "formal structure" in Athenaeus' discourse, he nonetheless takes it more seriously than the evidence warrants, particularly in terms of his discussion of the "theme" of Asian versus Greek attitudes toward polygamy. (I am not persuaded by the arguments of Hawley [1993: 81–87] that Athenaeus' order and pursuit of themes is organized and coherent.) He considers the passage about Philip to be the concluding part of Athenaeus' exposition of the theme. Athenaeus (13. 556b–c) does indeed say that although Asian queens tolerate polygamy, among Greeks the practice is not tolerated. Once he proceeds to offer Greek examples, however, he moves rapidly from a discussion of Greek women's resentment of the practice to examples of Greeks who had many wives, from that to Greek men who acquired wives on their travels (the views of their wives about the practice not being mentioned), and from that to the fact that Philip did not take women with him. It is therefore no surprise that the Philip passage does not refer to his wives' resentment of polygamy but rather (if anything), to his son's. (See below.)

9. Tronson (1984: 119) reasonably translates *kata polemon* as "to do with, according to," but Ellis (1981: 111) says "for military purposes," and Errington (1975b: 41 n. 1) seems to translate it as "in wartime." These "translations" appear to try to make sense of Athenaeus's dim thinking rather than to read the Greek. In any event, the many attempts to connect these marriages to the completion of various of Philip's campaigns, or at least of phases of them, imply that the authors assume that they happened after the campaign.

10. As Tronson (1984: 121) observes, even when military circumstances are noted, specific wars are not, and the examples seem to demonstrate, to the degree they demonstrate anything, political, not military, motivation.

11. See Tronson 1984: 120 on this possibility in terms of this particular passage; see Tronson 1984: 125 n. 54 and 55 and Brunt 1980: 480–81 for varying views on the general dependability of Athenaeus' quotations. Tronson suggests that, in this instance, Athenaeus may have combined information from two different Satyrus passages: one a list of wives and children and another the account of the Attalus quarrel. Brunt, however, makes a good case for the general accuracy of Athenaeus' reports and argues that the structure of the list, as I have noted, suggests that it is Satyrus' organization, not Athenaeus'.

12. Contra Tronson (1984: 123), who hypothesizes that Satyrus only listed and Athenaeus added the explanations. Had that been the case, the explanations would probably have been more consistently offered and more overtly connected to war.

13. Contra Gryzbek (1986: 228–29), who suggests that Philip married Perdiccas' widow, the mother of Amyntas. No ancient evidence supports this suggestion, which depends on the much-disputed question of Philip's regency.

14. Tronson 1984: 122 makes this important point.

15. See discussion in chap. 1 and Prestianni-Giallombardo 1976–77: 109; Tronson 1984: 121–22.

16. See Tronson 1984: 116–17 for the history of this argument.

17. Tronson (1984: 122 n. 39) suggests that Athenaeus' choice (or Satyrus') of an earlier verb in the passage (*paidopoeisthai*) may simply have reflected his desire to avoid using the same verb again and again. The same could apply to *epeisagein*, but its repetition in terms of Cleopatra as well as Meda might speak to emphasis.

18. Martin 1982: 67 makes this important point, one that Tronson's (1984: 119–20) translation obscures. Tronson repeatedly employs a word in reference to the earlier marriage that implies chronological sequence in English (*then*), despite the fact that the Greek *de* (consistently applied to the first marriages) does not.

19. Ellis (1981: 113) asserts that the lack of chronology is conscious choice, not the consequence of either Satyrus' or Athenaeus' ignorance, although he offers no support for his view. Tronson (1984: 122) simply assumes that Satyrus would have been as familiar with Philip's life in 359/8 as with the later period.

20. I do not mean to suggest that all seven women were present at court. We know that Nicesipolis died in childbirth (see NICESIPOLIS) and several other wives may have done so as well. Nonetheless, Philip's court always must have included several wives and his three daughters. His mother, as we have seen, may also have been at court in the early years of his reign. Judging by the quality of grave goods in female burials of the elite in Macedonia (see chap. 1, 9), this cluster of royal women would have provided a conspicuous display of family wealth.

21. Macurdy 1932a: 48; Ellis 1976: 47; Hammond 1994: 27. Dell (1980: 94) and Mortensen (1991: 56–57), without entirely rejecting this possibility, think that Audata could have been a relative of a successor of Bardylis, perhaps someone chosen by Philip.

22. Ellis 1976: 47–48; see EURYDICE 1. Such a relationship would help to explain the marriage alliance.

23. Ellis (1976: 47–48) suggests this possibility.

24. As Hammond (1994: 27 n. 23), observes, before his defeat, Bardylis had no motivation for such a marriage, especially since he was planning an invasion of Macedonia (Diod. 16.2.6). Griffith (1979: 211) suggests that the delay in Bardylis' invasion plan might be attributed to purposely protracted negotiations by Philip, intended to delay the projected invasion and thus give him time to prepare. Mortensen (1991: 56) suggests that the delay may have come either from internal problems in Bardylis' state or from his concern about Philip's rapid series of successes.

25. On the broader role of women in Illyrian society, see Wilkes 1992: 110, 187, 238; Stipçevic 1977: 168.

26. See Mortensen 1997: 227 for the suggestion that Audata may have been

the advocate of her daughter's marriage to Amyntas. Assuming that she did indeed live so long, the suggestion is plausible because it parallels the known actions of her daughter and of Olympias.

27. So Pomeroy 1984: 6. Athenaeus (560 f.) actually refers to the half-Macedonian Cynnane as "the Illyrian," a choice of words that speaks to her apparent cultural identity, if not exactly to her ethnicity. Audata's daughter's name, Cynnane, is probably Illyrian (so Wilkes 1992: 86; Heckel [1985: 196] is less certain) and may indicate her mother's resolve to maintain an Illyrian identity for her daughter.

28. Badian (1982a: 104) implies that the evidence for a change to "Eurydice" by Audata is even poorer than that for Philip's wife Cleopatra (see CLEOPATRA 3) because there is more chance that the names derives not from Arrian but from Photius.

29. Ellis (1976: 47–48) makes the curious assumption that Philip II would have changed his new wife's name to that of his mother only under compulsion. His assumption appears to derive from his acceptance of only the hostile tradition about her (see EURYDICE 1 for refutation). The name change, if genuine, is more likely the act of a son remembering his recently dead mother.

30. Contra Berve (1926: 2:229) and Macurdy (1932a: 25) who simply assume it to be true.

31. See discussion and references in Bosworth 1971b: 96; Ellis 1976: 46, 60 n. 84; Heckel 1992: 213–14; Hammond 1994: 28.

32. There were marriages between the two houses in the reigns of Alexander I and Archelaus. For references and discussion, see Bosworth 1971b: 100; Ellis 1976: 38; Griffith 1979: 214.

33. Whether Phila is seen as Philip's first or second wife, virtually everyone connects his marriage to Phila to his annexation of Elimeia. The marriage is generally assumed to have been early. Ellis (1976: 38, 46) makes the unlikely suggestion that it could have happened before the death of Perdiccas III. Griffith (1970: 70 n. 1; 1979: 214) and Hammond (1994: 28) prefer a later date, probably after Philip's victory against the Illyrians and Philip's marriage to Audata. Griffith (1979: 215) and Ellis (1976: 38) put this marriage before the marriage to Audata.

34. See discussion of Harpalus and his kin in Heckel (1992: 213–14), who notes the importance of the clan and attributes its decline to Harpalus's disgrace and Alexander's death. See also Berve 1926: 2:75–80, 384–85, 371–72; Ellis 1976: 60. Andronicos (1984: 124) suggests that a silver wine strainer from the antechamber of Tomb II at Vergina, inscribed with the name MACHATA, may have belonged to Phila's brother.

35. Ellis (1976: 46) suggests that she must have died soon after marriage, been divorced at the time of the Audata marriage, or been ignored because she was childless.

36. Heckel 1992: 213.

37. Tronson 1984: 122.

38. Ellis (1976: 83 n. 108), although he considers Nicesipolis a wife of Philip, doubts that she was a member of the tyrant's family and suggests instead that she belong to a clan in the elite that had supported the tyrants. Griffith (1979: 278) and Hammond (1994: 48) accept the relationship to Jason and put it in the context of Philip's general policy of reconciliation in Thessaly. If the anecdote preserved in Plutarch (*Mor.* 141b–c) refers to Nicesipolis (the woman is simply described as a Thessalian whom Philip loved), the description of her would be consistent with this status.

39. On Philip's choice of this significant name for his daughter, see THES-SALONICE and chap. 1 on significant names for royal women.

40. Ehrhardt 1967: 296–97; Griffith 1979: 677; Ellis 1981: 112 n. 16; Green 1982: 143.

41. Tronson 1984: 122; Sawada 1993: 38 n. 98. Martin (1982: 68–69), while not certain, considers it possible that the Nicesipolis marriage came early.

42. See Martin 1982: 68–69; Tronson 1984: 122.

43. Tronson 1984: 122. Not all would agree that this passage implies that Philip married the two Thessalian women: see Westlake 1935: 168; Green 1982: 143; and general discussion above.

44. Ellis 1976: 61; Greenwalt 1985b: 70–71; Griffith 1970: 70–71; Griffith 1979: 225; Hammond 1994: 29.

45. Arrian, in his narrative of events after Alexander's death (*FGrH* 156, F 1.35), refers to a certain Amphimachus as the brother of the king (Philip Arrhidaeus). Amphimachus was old enough to be awarded a satrapy at Triparadeisus in 321 (Berve 1926: 2:32; Greenwalt 1985b: 71), so he cannot have been a son of Philinna's by a marriage contracted after the death of Philip in 336, and he cannot have been a son of Philinna's by Philip, of course. Philinna must therefore have been a widow when Philip married her.

46. Greenwalt 1985b: 71; Hammond 1994: 29.

47. Ehrhardt (1967: 296–97) claimed that Arrhidaeus could have planned to marry at the age of fifteen and that Philip did not involve himself in Thessaly before 353 or 352, but Griffith (1970: 67–71) argued against this, and his views have won general acceptance (Ellis 1976: 61 n. 90; Greenwalt 1985b: 70; Hammond 1994: 29).

48. See Greenwalt 1985: 72–74.

49. See Hammond 1967: 412–14 on possible Chaonian connections for Olympias, based on her claim of descent from Helenus (*FGrH* 115, F 355).

50. On her brother, see Berve 1926: 2:19–21.

51. See Carney 1987b: 51 n. 47. An account in Plutarch (*Pyrrh.* 5.5–6) reveals that male and female royal Molossians (Olympias' granddaughter and grandson) drank together, contrary to both Greek and Macedonian custom.

52. See Heckel 1981b: 79–86; Mortensen 1997: 25–31. Both generally prefer the testimony of Plutarch to that of Justin.

53. Carney 1987b: 45 n. 31.

54. Both Mortensen (1997: 17–23) and Greenwalt (pers. com.) believe that though the romantic aspect of Plutarch's story is implausible, the reference to Samothrace is significant.

55. Carney 1993b: 29–56.

56. See Greenwalt 1985b: 69–77.

57. Carney 1992a: 171–73.

58. Carney 1987b: 42 n. 22. Justin (8.6.6) says that Philip and his brother-in-law became lovers. If true, this relationship would also have contributed to Philip's support for Alexander. See Mortensen 1997: 118–29.

59. On the relationship between father and son, see Carney 1992a: 169–71; Fredricksmeyer 1990: 300–15.

60. Perhaps not. If the anecdote recounted in Plut. *Alex.* 22.4 is to be trusted, Leonidas believed that Olympias would try to circumvent his austere regime for her son.

61. Plutarch (*Alex.* 2.4) says that Philip stopped sleeping with Olympias on a regular basis when he saw a snake sleeping by her side, either because he feared she might practice magic on him or because he feared that she was sleeping with a god in the form of a snake. Olympias may well have kept snakes, but the claim that a divine snake fathered her son is probably a subsequent invention, not something Philip or Olympias believed at the time. See discussion in Hamilton 1969: 5.

62. See Mortensen 1997: 73–84 for a discussion of Olympias, Dionysiac religion, and snakes. See also OLYMPIAS: PART 3 for her appearance as a Bacchant in front of the army at a time of military and political crisis.

63. Carney 1992a: 170–71.

64. Carney 1987b: 44 n. 28; Mortensen 1997: 185, 207.

65. Carney 1987b: 44 n. 29. Mortensen (1997: 205–6) suggests that Olympias may actually have suggested the marriage alliance herself.

66. Contra Errington (1981: 76–77), who is reluctant to date such interest far back in Philip's reign.

67. See Carney 1992a: 172 on this point.

68. See Ellis 1976: 166; Griffith 1979: 560; Hammond 1994: 124; *FGrH* 115, F 217.

69. Ellis (1976: 167) and (Green 1982: 140) suggest late 342. Hammond (1994: 124) seems to date it to spring 341, apparently following Griffith (1979: 560), but Hammond (1989: 36) says that the marriage probably happened in 339 (apparently associating the marriage with Philip's Scythian campaign against Atheas; curiously Griffith [1979: 677] also dates the marriage to 339).

70. Contra Green (1982: 145), who not only considers the possibility that she died in childbirth or of disease but also that she was repudiated, perhaps by ca. 340.

71. Hammond 1991: 76–77; 1994: 182.

72. See Heckel 1985: 195–200 for a discussion of the variant forms of her name. He is not certain of its ethnicity, but Wilkes (1992: 86) believes that it was Illyrian.

73. As Pomeroy (1984: 6) observes, this clearly constitutes evidence for the preservation of tradition in the female line.

74. Stipçevic 1977: 168.

75. On Amyntas, see Berve 1926: 2:30–31; Kaerst 1894a: 2007. On Amyntas' activities prior to his murder, see Ellis 1970: 68–75; Ellis 1971: 15–24; Griffith 1979: 702–4; Badian 1963: 244; Bosworth 1971: 103.

76. Adams 1980: 72 n. 60.

77. Greenwalt 1988: 93–97.

78. Contra Berve (1926: 2:229), Adams (1980: 72 n. 60), and Heckel (1983–84: 193), who think that she was born in 358 or 357. Their estimates depend on assumptions about the date of her parents' marriage and ignore the implications of her own apparent marriage date.

79. Berve (1926: 2:30) estimates that Amyntas was born about 365, but the only real evidence is that Amyntas was alive and quite young at the time of his father's death in 359. If Amyntas had been born in 365, it would require that his father married young for a male Argead (he was probably about twenty-four or a bit older at the time of his death; see Errington 1990: 37; Hammond 1979: 181–88) and that Philip put off a marriage for Amyntas until later than usual for male Argeads (see Greenwalt 1988: 93–97).

80. Carney 1988b: 393.

81. Carney 1992a: 180.

82. So Heckel 1983–84: 194.

83. How passive one imagines Amyntas to have been depends in good part on whether one believes that he had, as a young child or an infant, briefly been king and Philip only regent and that Philip subsequently displaced him and became king in his own right. The evidence is unclear: see discussion and references in Carney 1987a: 497 n. 5. Even if Amyntas had once been king and therefore hated his uncle for depriving him of his position, one need not assume that he failed to rebel because he lacked the desire to do so, but only that he had not yet found the opportunity.

84. As do Schachermeyr 1973: 97; Heckel 1992: 4.

85. See Carney 1992a: 174–77. Athenaeus (557e) says simply that Philip countenanced Attalus' insults, while Plutarch (*Alex.* 9.5) and Justin (9.7.4) actually say that Philip, rather than defend his heir, sided with Attalus and attacked his own son.

86. According to Diodorus (16.93.8–9), Philip, although angry at Attalus, found it inconvenient to punish him. He unsuccessfully attempted to calm Pausanias by gifts and a promotion. Justin (9.6.8) says that Philip not only postponed action on his complaints but made fun of Pausanias.

87. Arist. *Pol.* 1311b; Diod. 16.93–94; Just. 9.6.4–7.14; *POxy.* 1798; Plut. *Alex.* 10.4. On Pausanias and the rape that led to the assassination, see Carney 1992a: 180–82. It is possible that factors in addition to the rape may have contributed to Pausanias' crime.

88. Diodorus (16.93.9) mentions only Attalus as *strategos* (general) for the advance force but later (17.2.4) says that he shared this command with Parmenio. Justin (9.5.8–9) says that Attalus, Parmenio, and Amyntas were all sent to Asia as duces.

89. See discussion in Heckel 1992: 5. The chronology of events immediately after Philip's murder is notoriously uncertain. While the sources seem to assume that both Cleopatra and Attalus were killed soon after Philip's death, Ellis (1981: 122–23; 1982: 70–72) and Burstein (1982b: 159–61) have argued that both events occurred somewhat later.

90. Justin (11.5.1) says that Alexander killed all of his stepmother's relatives to whom Philip had given important civil or military commands, but Heckel (1992: 5–12) has argued that Cleopatra's nephew survived and that only Attalus was killed. Heckel is right to doubt that all members of the family were eliminated when one member was executed, but this need not mean that only Attalus was killed.

91. Heckel 1981a: 57.

92. The context for this description is the beginning of the Pausanias episode. Heckel (1992: 4 n. 3) claims that Diodorus' description refers only to the period after Philip's marriage. He may be right, but the passage does not put any chronological limits on the description.

93. The term Diodorus employs probably refers to the fact that Philip was Attalus' in-law but can signify friendship rather than kinship. Diodorus (17.5.2) uses the term in just that way to refer to Parmenio's friendship with Alexander.

94. Diodorus (16.93.9) says that he had proved his bravery in battle.

95. See PHILA 1. Estimates of the power accrued to the family of a royal wife are often inflated. Hammond (1994: 172) makes the dubious claim that it was the policy of Macedonian kings to marry foreign women because choosing a Macedonian bride would "place the honoured family on a level with the royal house." Whitehorne (1994: 36) even less plausibly asserts that "any son born" to Cleopatra had the "inside track" and that Alexander was hardly in consideration for the succession.

96. Hamilton (1969: 24) implausibly suggests that Philip was essentially forced to marry Cleopatra because Attalus and his father-in-law, Parmenio, were "not prepared to accept the son of the barbarian Olympias as Philip's successor." Bosworth's (1971b) arguments for a regional political context for the marriage have not won general acceptance: see Heckel 1981a: 52 n. 7 for refutation. Heckel (1986: 298) rightly points out that, whatever Attalus' clout before Philip's death, Alexander was able to eliminate him fairly quickly and Parmenio, his in-law, found it opportune to cooperate in his elimination.

97. Sources often mistake the nature of her relationship to Attalus: see Berve 1926: 2:213 n. 4.

98. Heckel 1979: 389–92; 1981a: 54.

99. See EUROPA and Heckel 1979: 285–303 for the widely accepted argument

that Cleopatra had only one child, a daughter; contra Unz 1985: 171–74. On the date, see Hatzopoulos 1982a: 38–42.

100. See discussion and references in Carney 1992a.

101. Berve (1926: 2:213) estimates that she was born ca. 353, but Heckel (1992: 8) unconvincingly suggests that she may have been born as early as 355 (his suggestion that Plutarch's description of her age somehow compares her to Olympias does not make sense in the context of the passage).

102. See Carney 1992a: 174 n. 15 for references.

103. Greenwalt 1989: 29–43; Borza 1990: 208.

104. Athenaeus (557d) refers to Cleopatra as the sister of Hippostratus and niece of Attalus. Had Hippostratus still been alive, he rather than his uncle would probably have been guardian. Heckel (1992: 4, 8) suggests that he was the Hippostratus who died in Philip's Illyrian campaign of 344/3 and that Cleopatra's father's name was therefore Amyntas (Didymus ap. Marsyas of Pella *FGrH* 135–36, F 17). On a possible nephew of Cleopatra's, see below.

105. See CLEOPATRA 1 on the comparative rarity of this name and on its possible royal associations.

106. I do not mean to suggest that, even if this hypothesis is correct, it was the only reason that Alexander and Olympias were alarmed. See Carney 1992a: 169–89.

107. Ellis (1976: 302 n. 3) argues that Diod. 16.93.6 dates the death of the first Pausanias after the wedding of Cleopatra and dates both the wedding and the campaign in which Pausanias died to summer 337. The Diodorus passage, however, merely implies that by the time the second Pausanias was complaining to Philip about the rape, Attalus was powerful, Cleopatra probably married, and Attalus appointed to command. Heckel (1992: 4) dates the campaign after the wedding, to early 336, and assumes the rape came soon after, and thus that Pausanias' complaints came in late winter or early spring 336, when Attalus had his military appointment but before he departed. The campaign could have come in the fall, perhaps after the wedding.

108. Curtius (6.9.17) is the only source to mention this marriage. Although Curtius does not say when the marriage was arranged, the implication of the passage (Philotas is described as marrying his sister to Alexander's enemy) is that this marriage happened after Cleopatra's marriage, because only then did Attalus become Alexander's enemy. Heckel (1992: 14 n. 34) suggests that the marriage to Parmenio's daughter probably dates to fall 337, shortly after Cleopatra's marriage to Philip. Fears (1975: 133) believed that Curtius invented the marriage of Attalus, but few have followed him.

109. See Heckel 1992: 15.

110. Carney 1991a: 18 n. 7, 8.

111. Carney 1993b: 50–54.

112. See Badian 1982a: 99–110 for discussion of this view.

113. So Heckel 1978: 155–58. His idea, developed from a statement of Macurdy's (1932a: 25) that the name "Eurydice" had a tendency to become dynas-

tic, and his assumption that the name somehow marked her as foremost among the wives are not persuasive. Bosworth (1980b: 282) claims implausibly that Eurydice was "the established name for a Macedonian queen." See contra Badian 1982a.

114. Prestianni-Giallombardo 1981: 295–306. If Cleopatra was of Argead descent, it is likely to have been her original name, whether or not it was ever subsequently changed.

115. Whitehorne (1994: 44) terms Plutarch's inclusion of Cleopatra "ridiculous" because, apparently, he believes that Cleopatra's pregnancy would prevent her from being involved. Being a few months pregnant would not prevent her from being part of what Plutarch seems to suggest is a clan vendetta. However, she may not have been pregnant at this time (see above).

116. Whitehorne (1994: 44) believes that the reference derives from later propaganda "invented . . . to excuse Olympias' later mistreatment" of Cleopatra and her daughter. Tradition, in fact, tends to favor Cleopatra and dislike Olympias; see Carney 1993b passim). In any event, Plutarch's reference is made so much in passing and without any embroidery or moralizing that it is difficult to place it in the context of hostile propaganda. The tone is completely matter-of-fact, and nothing more is made of her involvement.

117. See further Carney 1992a: 178–79.

118. Berve (1926: 2:212), suggests a birthdate of 355. Macurdy (1932a: 26), suggests 354. Neither offers an explanation for these dates, but, as Cleopatra married in 336 and is unlikely to have been older than her brother or younger than fourteen at the time, it seems safe to conclude that she must have been born between 355 and 350 and that her apparent role as regent in her husband's absence, beginning in 334, tends to suggest a date closer to 355 than to 350. On the ages of the Argeads at the time of marriage, see Greenwalt 1988: 93–97.

119. See OLYMPIAS; Carney 1992a: 169–89.

120. See Carney 1992a: 181–89 on the assassination.

121. On the Pixodarus incident, see discussion and references in Carney 1992a: 179–80, as well as below.

122. On name changing in general, see chap. 1.

123. See further Heckel 1979: 285–303, pointing to contradictions in the testimony of Justin and Pausanias and arguing that there was not enough time between Cleopatra's marriage and her husband's death for two pregnancies and births; for contra, see Green 1991: 103, 112, 115, 141–42.

124. The details of the murders provided by both Pausanias and Justin are dubious; see Carney 1993b: 29–56 and chap. 4.

125. See Carney 1991b: 159–60 nn. 38, 39.

126. See further discussion and references in Carney 1992a: 172–3, esp. nn. 9–12.

127. Whether Attalus' ability to get what he wanted from Philip derived solely from his niece's royal marriage or from other factors as well is not certain (see CLEOPATRA 3), but it was an important reason.

128. See Carney 1992a: 169–89 for a more detailed discussion of the possible role of Olympias in the Philip's murder. See Carney 1993b: 29–56 on the prejudices relating to the career of Olympias that make determination of her possible culpability in Philip's murder so difficult.

129. See Carney 1992a: 169–80.

130. See Carney 1987b: 44 n. 28.

131. An anecdote preserved by Plutarch (*Mor.* 141b–c) about a Thessalian woman Philip was enamored of shows Olympias to be watchful of the influence of other women on Philip but hardly jealous. Tronson (1984: 123–24) suffers from the presumption of sexual jealousy, although he notes that, despite his expectation (based on Athenaeus' earlier statements about Greek women's problems with polygamy) that Olympias should demonstrate jealousy and outrage, it is in fact Alexander who does so. (See above.) Trouble began with the men at the banquet and not with Olympias, who was not present.

132. See further Carney 1992a: 181–85.

CHAPTER 4

1. Of the innumerable accounts of Alexander's reign, Bosworth 1988 and Green 1991 remain the best.

2. On Amyntas, see Berve 1926: 2:30–31; Kaerst 1894a: 2007. See also CYNNANE: PART 1.

3. Soon after Alexander had her husband, Amyntas, executed, he planned to have Cynnane marry Langarus, leader of the Agriani, but Langarus died before the marriage could take place (Arr. 1.5.4–5). See further CYNNANE: PART 2.

4. See Carney 1993b: 37–41. The conflicting accounts and scanty evidence for the murder of Cleopatra suggest that it was done in private and perhaps concealed for a time, as was Cassander's murder of Alexander IV (see chap. 5). The careers of Cynnane and her daughter Adea Eurydice demonstrate what kind of damage Cleopatra and her daughter could have done to Olympias' branch of the family (see CYNNANE: PART 2; ADEA EURYDICE).

5. Kingsley (1986: 171–77) makes a persuasive argument for this date for the Cyrene inscription. Blackwell (1999: 96–98) argues for an even earlier date, possibly 334/3. See their discussions for rejection of later dates.

6. On the significance of the appearance of both Olympias and Cleopatra (see below) on the lists with only personal names, see Charneux 1966: 178; Hammond 1980: 74.

7. Some have doubted that either Olympias or Antipater requested Harpalus; see convincing arguments against these doubts, as well as references, in Blackwell 1999: 20–27.

8. Blackwell (1999: 95–96) suggests that the passage can be read somewhat more generally, to refer to a longer period of time than that just before Alexander's death.

9. Hammond (1967: 559) suggested that the Plutarch passage means that Antipater fomented the Epirote alliance to check Olympias and Cleopatra and that Alexander supported this policy. The date of the formation of the Epirote alliance is disputed, as is its significance: see contra Carney 1987b: 51 n. 47.

10. Carney 1987b: 53 n. 53.

11. The authenticity of all of Alexander's supposed correspondence is at best dubious. Some of the reported exchanges between Alexander and Olympias are particularly likely to relate to the later propaganda wars of Olympias and Cassander. See further Carney 1987b: 49, 54–55, especially nn. 43, 54.

12. Carney 1987b: 54–56. The "bad advice" theme associated with Olympias is very similar to that connected to Parmenio. This similarity should make us suspicious of both themes.

13. See Blackwell 1999: 104 for the suggestion that the young men Olympias is said to have harbored were part of a bodyguard she had created.

14. See Hamilton 1969: 104 for a discussion of the authenticity of the letter about Alexander's gifts to his friends. Diodorus' account of the reasons for the arrest of Lyncestian Alexander has often been rejected in favor of Arrian's (1.25.1–10), and Diodorus (17.32.2) says that Olympias' charge was not the only reason. See further Bosworth 1980: 164 (who thinks Olympias' position was part of her opposition to Antipater, the Lyncestian's father-in-law) and Carney 1980: 30–32. Amyntas, son of Andromenes, was acquitted, but more likely because of Alexander's desire to conciliate some of the surviving supporters of Parmenio and Philotas.

15. Pausanias' (1.11.3) assertion that Olympias returned to Epirus out of fear is surely an overstatement. As long as her son lived, Olympias cannot really have feared Antipater. Apparently Olympias willingly left Macedonia, probably because she thought she could do better for herself in her homeland, away from Antipater's power (so Cross 1932: 48). There is no evidence for any public scolding of Olympias by Alexander (contra Berve 1926: 2:285–86; Macurdy 1932a: 33; Hamilton 1969: 105).

16. Contra Bosworth 1971a: 126 and Hamilton 1969: 105.

17. For Cleopatra's children, see Berve 1926: 2:186, 273; for her husband, see Berve 1926: 2:19–21.

18. Kingsley 1986: 169–70 contra Oliverio 1933: 34–35. See also Blackwell 1999: 96–98.

19. Hammond (1967: 559) suggested that the Plutarch passage (*Alex.* 68.3) means that Antipater fomented the Epirote alliance to check Olympias and Cleopatra and that Alexander supported this policy. The date of the formation of this alliance is disputed, as is its significance: see Hammond 1980: 472 n. 46 but c.f. Cabanes 1976: 177–81; Carney 1987b: 51 n. 47; Blackwell 1999: 101, esp. n. 73.

20. On the absence of evidence for quarrels between mother and daughter, see Carney 1988b: 397 n. 34. Just as Cynnane and Adea Eurydice acted as a political unit, so did Olympias and Cleopatra.

21. Kingsley (1986: 167), suggests that she may have been involved in her brother's policy. See Carney 1988b: 396 n. 31 for references to earlier and opposing views. The two countries, already linked by Olympias' marriage, grew closer when Philip II removed Olympias' uncle Arybbas from the throne and replaced him with her brother. On these events, see Griffith 1979: 306–8.

22. Einhard (*Vita Caroli* 19) describes how Charlemagne kept his daughters at court instead of allowing them to marry. He attributes Charlemagne's policy to their beauty and his affection for them but admits, in a genteel manner, that his policy did cause them to act scandalously in sexual matters, although the king shut his eyes to it. For the more political and less sentimental interpretation of the king's motivation, see Stafford 1983: 28, 35, 109; Munz 1969: 47.

23. Plutarch's story suggests an astonishing degree of sexual license for a royal woman. It would be surprising if Alexander or any other male Argead dared, publicly or not, to take the risk inherent in allowing a royal daughter of childbearing age to take a lover. Even if one accepts the truth of Plutarch's passage, it may relate to Alexander's views and not to those of Argeads in general. On Plutarch's apparent understanding of Cleopatra's role, that she is somehow part of *basileia*, see Carney 1995 and chap. 1 above.

24. Hammond's belief in Olympias' very late departure for Epirus seems untenable. See OLYMPIAS: PART 2 and CLEOPATRA 2: PART 2 for discussion of evidence that Olympias was present in Epirus much earlier.

25. Hammond 1980: 471–76; 1985: 158–59; 1988b: 90–91; 1989: 33–34. See contra Carney 1987b: 50–53, 58 n. 61; 1988b: 397 n. 33; and 1995.

26. See Carney 1987b: 53, esp. n. 52, for a discussion of the possible reasons for Olympias' move from Macedonia to Epirus; Blackwell (1999: 100–101) suggests that Olympias left because Antipater's victory against Agis limited her chances for increasing her power in Macedonia itself.

27. Badian (1961: 36–40) makes a strong case for a dramatic deterioration in relations between Alexander and Antipater; he is largely followed by Bosworth (1988: 161–62); Baynham (1994: 343–46) is more noncommittal.

28. Mendels (1984: 138–39) argues that as early as the Cyrene grain shipments Alexander consciously supported the development of a "zone of influence" for his mother against Antipater; Blackwell (1999: 91) rightly rejects this suggestion as implausible so early in the reign, when Alexander still needed help in the form of reinforcements from Antipater and still had Greek allies. However, Alexander did have a lifelong tendency to play favorites off against each other, but that hardly supports something so defined as a "zone of influence."

29. On Ada and the Carian dynasty, see Judeich 1893: 339; Berve 1926: 2:11–12. And see discussion and references in Bosworth 1980b: 152–54; Ruzicka 1992.

30. See Hamilton 1969: 54; Bosworth 1980b: 220–22; Bosworth 1988: 63–64; Carney 1996.

31. On Sisygambis, see Berve 1926: 2:356–57. See also Bosworth 1988: 63–64 for the obvious comparison to Ada. Alexander addressed both women as mother.

32. For Darius' elder daughter, Stateira, see STATEIRA 2. Darius' younger daughter was Drypetis: see Staehelin 1918: 415; Berve 1926: 2:148. Justin (11.9.16) has Alexander promise them worthy marriages, as does Diodorus (17.38.1). See also Carney 1996.

33. Curtius (3.11.24) gives him a name, Ochus. See Berve 1926: 2:409–10. Diodorus (17.38.3) and Curtius (3.12.26) say Alexander kissed and cuddled the boy as well.

34. Plutarch (*Alex.* 21.4) claims that Alexander's sexual relationship with Barsine (See BARSINE: PART 1) was the sole exception to Alexander's sexual self-restraint. Darius's wife Stateira may have become pregnant while under Alexander's power, possibly by Alexander; see STATEIRA 1.

35. According to Curtius (4.10.31–34), Alexander's elaborate funeral arrangements for Stateira as well as his apparently extravagant public grief (shades of Hephaestion) aroused Darius' suspicions. Justin (11.12.6–7) feels compelled to state that Alexander's reaction to Stateira's death was "non amoris, sed humanitatis causa." Curtius (4.10.18) attributes her death to travel fatigue, and Diodorus (17.54.7) offers no explanation.

36. Bosworth 1980b: 221; Berve 1926: 2:363; Hamilton 1969: 78; Schachermeyr 1973: 227 n. 249; Atkinson 1980: 392. Welles (1963: 275 n. 3) and Green (1991: 287) suggest that the late dating of Stateira's death in the sources may reflect a tradition that rejected the idea that Alexander did not have relations with Stateira.

37. For the possible political implications of his relationship with Barsine, see BARSINE. On the complexities and ambiguities of Alexander's Persianizing, see Bosworth 1980a: 1–21.

38. Alexander may simply have been waiting for the death of Darius. Green (1991: 300) may imply that her death and Darius' second escape caused the long delay before Alexander's marriage to her daughter.

39. See chap. 1; Carney 1996 for discussion and references. Green (1991: 234) and Bosworth (1980b: 221) emphasize the importance of the women in any claim to legitimate rule.

40. Green (1991: 153) says, "His interest in women was (to put it mildly) tepid, and could not begin to compare with his burning sense of destiny."

41. See BARSINE: PART 1. On his relationship with Bagoas, see Badian 1958b: 144–57. That Alexander's sexual appetites seemed modest in ancient eyes, perhaps especially in contrast to his father's, is suggested by a story preserved in Athenaeus (10.435a) that has Alexander suffering from some sort of physical problem that prompted his anxious parents to send in a *hetaira*. But tradition preserves reference to a mistress of Alexander's (Luc. *Imag.* 7; Pliny *NH* 35.86; Ael. *VH* 12.34: see Berve 1926: 2:297), a possible reference to a sexual relationship with Thais (Ath. 13.576e), and one to Alexander's erotic interest in a female harp player (Plut. *Mor.* 180 f.). The historicity of all these references is uncertain, but they imply that Alexander was not assumed to be completely uninterested in sexual relationships with women.

42. Plutarch's attitude is typical: in the course of his discussion of Alexander's self-mastery, he moves from Alexander's sexual restraint toward women to his sexual restraint toward boys and then back again to sexual restraint toward women (*Alex.* 21.4–22.3). Plutarch follows this with mention of self-restraint in diet (22.4). (See a similar association in stories about Alexander in *Mor.* 1099c–d). See Dover 1973: 64–65 on the importance of self-control, sexual and otherwise, in Hellenic culture.

43. Demosthenes' famous remark (59.122) that a man had a wife for the production of legitimate children, a concubine for regular sexual relations, and a courtesan for pleasure should be recalled. See Walcot 1987b: 6. This pragmatic attitude toward marriage would only be truer of a monarch who needed to produce heirs; see chap. 1.

44. I owe to Peter Green the point that, in Plutarch (*Alex.* 22.3; *Mor.* 65F; 717F), Alexander associated mortality and sexuality.

45. So Burn 1962: 65–66, who refers to Alexander's "irresponsibility" and "recklessness" and indifference to what would go on after his death; Errington 1990: 114–15. So also Green 1991: 153, although he notes that other factors also influenced Alexander.

46. See Carney 1988b: 88; CYNNANE: PART 2; CLEOPATRA 2: PART 2; THESSALONICE.

47. Ellis (1981:135–36) and Hatzopoulos (1982b: 59–66), argue unconvincingly for its rejection. See contra Develin 1981: 95; Bosworth 1988: 22; Carney 1992a; above, chap. 3.

48. Bosworth (1971b: 104) argues that Alexander's fear of dividing Macedonia along regional lines kept him from marrying.

49. On Elizabeth's manipulation of the public image of her virginity, see Levin 1989: 95–110.

50. Tarn (1921: 18–28; 1949: 2: 330) denied that Barsine was Alexander's mistress and that Heracles was his son, but Brunt's (1975: 23–34) arguments against Tarn's views are now nearly universally accepted and followed here, with modifications. Some portions of what follows appeared in Carney 1996.

51. On Artabazus' career, see Judeich 1895: 1299; Berve 1926: 2:82–84. On his royal lineage, asserted specifically only by Plutarch, see Brunt 1975: 24–25; Weiskopf 1989: 2–28, 55–56 (who believes he was of Achaemenid descent on both sides) contra Burn 1985: 381–82.

52. See Berve 1926: 2:82; Brunt 1975: 25.

53. Contra Burn 1985: 381–82.

54. Curtius (6.5.4) says that he had nine grown sons in 330. Diodorus may have incorrectly assumed that all these children were by the sister of the Rhodian mercenaries (so Brunt 1975: 25).

55. Berve (1926: 2:102) suggests a date of 360; Brunt (1975: 25) says that she was born after 362 and could not have been born later than 357/6. Lane Fox (1973: 177) implies a birthdate of 360. But if she married Mentor, she can hardly

have done so before her family's return from exile and, granted that Mentor is assumed to have died soon after their return in 342, she is likely to have been at least fourteen by that year. Unlike Brunt (1975: 25), I would be unwilling to base estimates of her age on whether Alexander found older women attractive, but it is certainly relevant to recall the young age of Greek girls at marriage.

56. See Cook 1983: 220–24; Olmstead 1948: 421–28; Parke 1933: 121–24.

57. On the education of Greek women in the fourth century, see Pomeroy 1977: 51–68.

58. Lane Fox 1973: 177.

59. Frye 1963: 119.

60. For the career of Mentor, see Kahrstedt (1931b: 964–65), who supposes that he died soon after the affair of Hermias (Diod. 16.52.5–8). See Brunt 1975: 27 for arguments on the likelihood of this marriage.

61. On Memnon, see Berve 1926: 2:250–54; Kahrstedt 1931a: 652–53.

62. Arr. 2.1.3. See Berve 1926: 2:379–80; Lenschau 1938: 1848.

63. See Brunt 1975: 27 for the probability of an earlier marriage for both brothers.

64. On Heracles, see Berve 1926: 2:168; Schoch 1924: 731.

65. Justin (15.2.3) says that Heracles was fourteen when he died and thus was born in 324. The testimony of Diodorus is usually preferred: see Brunt 1975: 2:28.

66. Brosius (1996: 78) states that Alexander married Barsine but cites only the Plutarch passage, which does not mention marriage.

67. Berve (1926: 2.103) bases this estimate on the assumption that Barsine and Alexander began their relationship about the time of his return from Egypt.

68. See Bosworth 1980a: 1–21.

69. Schachermeyr (1973: 133) suggests that Alexander's pragmatic attempts to mix Macedonians and Persians in the rule of his empire may have had their origin in his early acquaintance with the family of Artabazus. Lane Fox (1980: 64) makes similar remarks but also suggests that Barsine and her "bilingual and high ranking" family were central to his attempts to understand and rule the old Persian empire (65, 262).

70. On Heracles' name as related to Alexander's hero emulation, see Schachermeyr 1973: 409. On coins and Heracles as an ancestor, see Borza 1990: 173.

71. So Schachermeyr 1973: 212; Brunt 1975: 29–30, tentatively; Berve 1926 2:103. This assumption may derive from difficulties with accepting the reality of polygamy.

72. Tarn (1921: 24) doubted that Alexander ever took Parmenio's advice; Brunt (1975: 28–29) argued for acceptance of the story.

73. Neither Tarn (1921: 24) nor Brunt (1975: 28 f.) takes into account the problem of the series of anecdotes. Many have suggested that the advice motif is official, apologetic history: Badian 1960: 328; Berve 1926: 2:300–303; Hamilton 1969: 89; Heckel 1977: 11–12 n. 13; Pearson 1960: 47.

74. See Berve 1926: 2:84.

75. So Brunt (1975: 29–30), who hypothesizes as an increasing coldness between the king and Barsine as Artabazus's motivation.

76. Brunt 1975: 29–30.

77. See Brosius 1996: 31, 190–91.

78. Green 1991: 370.

79. See Bosworth 1980a: 10–11; Holt 1988: 65–70.

80. Bosworth 1980a: 7–9.

81. See Carney 1996 on Alexander and Persian women.

82. Berve 1926: 2:292.

83. Staehelin 1914: 1155–56; Berve 1926: 2:346–47; Holt 1988: 66–68, 92, 98.

84. Holt 1988: 66, esp. n. 64. See also Bosworth 1980a: 10–11. Arrian (4.19.4–6) says the family of Oxyartes, including Roxane, was captured on the rock of Sogdiana, apparently in spring 327, and reports (4.20.4) that their capture and good treatment precipitated Oxyartes' surrender. Curtius does not connect the family of Oxyartes to the Sogdian rock and dates their capture to spring 328 (7.11.1) and has Roxane first appear at a banquet in spring 327 (8.4.21–30).

85. So Holt 1988: 66; Berve 1926: 292; Bosworth 1988: 117. If this view is correct, then Oxyartes, like Artabazus, the father of Barsine, converted to Alexander's side only after Alexander's capture of his daughter and distinctive treatment of her.

86. See Renard and Servais 1955: 29–50; Bosworth 1988: 117. Berve (1926: 2.347) and Lane Fox (1973: 317), believe the marriage followed Iranian custom in whole or in part.

87. Lane Fox (1973: 317) rejects the otherwise nearly universal skepticism about the marriage to Roxane as a love match.

88. See Bosworth 1980a: 10–11; Holt 1988: 65–70.

89. Berve (1926: 2:347) and Hammond (1988b: 100) accept the birth as genuine.

90. Contra Green (1991: 369), who considers the testimony of the Metz Epitome "dubious" and implies that Roxane had no sexual relations with Alexander until after the death of Hephaestion. Concluding that the absence of children speaks to lack of sexual relations between Alexander and Roxane is most unwise. Whatever the nature of Alexander's relationship with Hephaestion, it did not prevent him from having sexual relations with Barsine or Bagoas. There is no reason to think his treatment of Roxane would be any different. Moreover, whether or not the Metz Epitome is accurate, we cannot assume that ancient sources would mention failed pregnancies, stillbirths, or infant deaths. The fertility of either Alexander or Roxane could affect the frequency of pregnancy.

91. See Bosworth 1988: 156–57.

92. Darius III's eldest daughter is everywhere referred to as "Stateira" except in Arrian (7.4.4), where she is called Barsine. Berve (1926: 2:363) suggests

that he had probably confused her with Artabazus' daughter and rejects the possibility that she changed her name at the time of her marriage (see discussion and references in Berve 1926: 2:363). Brosius (1996: 77–78) believes that her name was probably changed.

93. On Darius' wife, see STATEIRA 1. She is called "Stateira" only in Plutarch *Alex.* 30.3–4.

94. On Sisygambis, see Berve 1926: 2:356–57.

95. On her sister Drypetis, later married to Hephaestion, see Berve 1926: 2:148; on her brother, Ochus, see Berve 1926: 2:409–10.

96. Plut. *Alex.*; Just. 11.9.15; Curt. 3.12.12, 24; Diod. 17.38.1–4. Arrian, Curtius, and Justin specifically mention their retention of the title of "queen." Justin (11.9.16) and Diodorus (17.38.1) have Alexander play the role of father or brother for the daughters of Darius in promising to arrange marriages, and Curtius (3.12.21) says Alexander treated the daughters of Darius as though they had the same mother. Curtius (3.12.17, 25) and Diodorus (17.37.6) have Alexander address Sisygambis as "mother." On Alexander's treatment of the royal women in general, see Carney 1996.

97. On the problems surrounding the correspondence (the number of letters and offers Alexander received; the nature of Darius' offers; the nature of Alexander's response; the date and/or occasion of such offers) see Hamilton 1969: 76–77; Bosworth 1980b: 227–29, 256–57; Atkinson 1980: 320. Despite the source problems, it is clear that Stateira functioned as the token of choice for the Achaemenids in whatever settlement was offered.

98. Tarn (1949: 2:336) argues that the decision to have the daughters of Darius taught Greek signified that he intended to marry one, presumably the eldest, from the start. Arrian (3.22.6) refers to Alexander's arrangements for the education of the royal children, probably meaning the same thing (so Bosworth 1988: 348).

99. See Bosworth 1980a: 2–4, 10–12, 20; Bosworth 1988: 156–57; Plut. *Alex.* 70.2; Plut. *Mor.* 329e, 338d–e; Arr. 7.4.4–6; Just. 12.10.9–10; Curt. 10. 3.12; Diod. 17.107.6.

100. Hammond (1988b: 119) suggests that Roxane may have murdered the daughters of Darius because they were pregnant. One might expect that had they been pregnant, their murders would have been more widely reported and their pregnancies mentioned. Perdiccas may have seen an heir by Roxane as less troublesome to his interests than any possible son of Stateira.

101. Berve 1926: 2:306.

102. Bosworth (1988: 156), Green (1991: 448), Hammond (1988b: 119), and Lane Fox (1973: 418) accept Aristobulus's statement. Hamilton (1969: 195) is less certain.

103. Plutarch refers to the second murder victim only as the sister of Stateira—she is not named (on Drypetis, see Berve 1926: 2:148; Staehelin 1918: 415).

104. See Brosius 1996: 77–78, 184–86, on the possibility that Persian women of the royal family and the elite changed their names on marriage.

105. Had Hephaestion still been alive at the time of Alexander's death, there would have been every reason to murder him and his Achaemenid wife, but there seems to be little incentive for her murder after Hephaestion's death.

106. E.g., the marriage of Henry V and Katherine. See further Carney 1996; Tarn 1949: 2:336.

107. Bosworth (1988: 63–64), sees the marriage to Stateira in 324 as the final stage in process of the integration of the Persian royal women into Alexander's rule and notes that in the early years of Alexander's reign, when the "war of revenge" still had meaning, the marriage was not yet possible. See also Green 1991: 300. Of course, if Alexander did impregnate the elder Stateira (see above), he may have tried and temporarily abandoned the policy early in his reign.

108. According to Diod. 17.118.8; Curt. 10.5.21; Just. 13.1.5, she killed herself by starving to death; the murder of her two granddaughters, as reported by Plutarch (*Alex.* 77.4), whether happening before or after, speaks to the same reality.

CHAPTER 5

1. Much of the material in this chapter appeared in somewhat different form in Carney 1994b.

2. On the Hellenistic period, see Will 1979–82; Green 1990. On Macedonia during the period of the collapse of the Argead house, see Errington 1990: 114–129; Hammond 1988: 95–179.

3. So Errington 1990: 129; Green 1990: 19–20; Hammond 1988b: 141.

4. Hammond (1989: 34), refers to Olympias' "insane revenge." Errington (1990: 127) also assumes that Olympias' return to Macedonia was revenge driven. The sources rarely offer information on the motivation of the Successors and, in any event, can only speculate. On the determination of revenge as a motive, see below. Green (1990: 18) terms Olympias' return to Macedonia as "intervention" and describes her rival Adea Eurydice as "too ambitious," suggesting that she too involved herself in matters not considered her affair. Similar judgments of the male Successors are not common. On the treatment of Olympias and other royal women in scholarship, see chap. 2; and Carney 1993b: 29–56.

5. Macedonian troops, rebellious because of the murder of Philip II's daughter Cynnane, forced the generals to marry her daughter Adea Eurydice to one of the co-kings, Arrhidaeus (*FGrH* 156, F 9.22–23). Adea Eurydice moved other Macedonian troops to more rebellion (Diod. 18.39.1–4; *FGrH* 156, F 9.30–33). The mere sight of Olympias inspired the Macedonian army to go over to her (Diod. 19.11.1–3). Despite having been persuaded by Cassander, son of Antipater, to condemn Olympias, the Macedonians refused to execute her (Just. 14.6.6–12; Diod. 19.51.4–6). Despite many years of Cassander's efficient and stable rule, Cassander was pressed to allow first Alexander IV and later Heracles

to take the throne (Diod. 19.105.2; .20.2–4, 28.1). See further discussion of these incidents below.

6. Westlake (1969: 326) points out that Greeks like Eumenes in Macedonian service tended to remain loyal.

7. Westlake (1969: 326) insists that the cause of the Argead house "was not inevitably doomed from the outset" but seems to confuse the desire some people retained for the perpetuation of the royal house with its likelihood.

8. See Carney 1993b: 41–42 for a comparison of acts of violence by royal women and Macedonian generals in the period.

9. Carney 1983: 260–72; Borza 1990: 240.

10. His Asian wives played no active role in the events after his death, unless one believes that Roxane could have dared to have Darius' daughters killed if Perdiccas had not willed it (Plut. *Alex.* 77.4; see ROXANE and BARSINE). The racism of their treatment is exemplified by Polyperchon's offer of the *epimeleia* of Alexander IV to his European grandmother rather than his mother, Roxane.

11. Heracles was geographically closer to them, and his mother, Barsine, was almost certainly well known to them (see BARSINE: PART 1). Since Barsine was herself half-Greek, Heracles was also the less Asian of Alexander's sons.

12. Some of them created an *agema* (e.g., Diod. 19.28.3) and accepted kinglike honors or gave kinglike gifts (Plut. *Eum.* 8.7; Diod. 19.48.1), and Cassander and perhaps some of the others began eponymous foundations in imitation of the city founding of Philip and Alexander (Diod. 19.52.2).

13. Diodorus (19.1.2–3) notes that it is difficult for those who have gotten hope of rule to abstain from monarchy. See 18.23.3, 25.3, 58.3, 4; 19.52.1, 5, 56.2).

14. See discussion and references in Gruen 1985: 253–71.

15. Even Antipater, for instance, had joined in a military alliance against Perdiccas, the man to whom Alexander had supposedly given his ring. In fact, Antipater and most of the others simply had their real power legitimized after they had come to possess it.

16. The most famous example is that of Eumenes: see Carney 1994: 361 n. 7.

17. See Carney 1987b: 57 n. 59 for discussion.

18. See also Carney 1987b: 58 n. 61; and 1995: 368–76.

19. Nepos (*Eum.* 6.1–2)also mentions a letter, but the passage does not inspire confidence: Eumenes advises that she wait until Alexander IV gained *regnum* (suggesting that the entire situation and its danger is misunderstood) and adds advice clearly meant to demonstrate that she ignored it when she did go to Macedonia.

20. Macurdy 1932b: 256–61.

21. Aeacides' daughter Deidameia was betrothed to young Alexander IV and accompanied Olympias to Pydna (Plut. *Pyrrh.* 4.2); this renewal of the Molossian-Macedonian alliance may explain Aeacides' support.

22. It is hard to know whether to believe Duris' testimony. Adea Eurydice, with her military training, may actually have planned to fight (see ADEA EURY-

DICE), but Olympias would surely have simply appeared to inspire the army, as she did. The *tumpanon* drum (small, hand held, like a castanet without the jingles) was used in Dionysiac cult (see OLYMPIAS: PART 1 on her involvement in such cults), but the drum could have a military rather than a religious significance. If Olympias appeared as a Dionysiac, she must have believed that the Macedonians would see this as an appropriate and impressive role for her, as they seem to have done.

23. But see Westlake 1969: 329 for the possibility that Polyperchon was the victim of a hostile source tradition.

24. She may have attempted to escape. Polyaenus (4.11.3) reports that Polyperchon attempted to arrange her escape but that Cassander thwarted the plan and thereby so convinced Olympias that she could not trust Polyperchon that she surrendered. Diodorus (19.51.2–3), however, reports a somewhat similar episode after Olympias had already been condemned, in which the "escape" was actually a ruse to enable Cassander to murder her without as much criticism as a public murder would cause. Neither story inspires much faith.

25. Justin's description of her death is particularly florid and suspect; female bravery in the face of death, often with the theme, as in this case, that the woman in question died a death worthy of her male relatives, is a recognizable topos (literary theme) in classical literature. Of course, florid or not, it may be true. See further Carney 1993b: 1.

26. Hatzopoulos (1996: 275) argues that Cassander ended the trial and arranged the murder because he feared Olympias might persuade her audience to spare her.

27. Errington 1975a: 148.

28. Berve 1926: 2:232–35; Heckel 1992: 91–106. Seibert (1967: 20) attributes the projected marriage to Leonnatus' blood relationship to the royal house.

29. Errington 1975a: 148.

30. See Berve 1926: 2:313–16; Heckel 1992: 134–63.

31. On these events, see Errington 1970: 49–65. Diodorus and Justin claim that from the beginning Perdiccas planned to marry Cleopatra and get rid of Nicaea, as Antigonus later successfully persuaded Antipater and Craterus (Diod. 18.25.3; Arr. *FGrH* 156, F 9.26). Errington (1975a: 149; 1970: 64) and Briant (1973: 175), both reject the truth of Antigonus' claims, but Will (1979–82: 35) and Hornblower (1981: 162) accept their veracity. The latter arguments are more convincing. Staehelin (1921: 737) implausibly claims that she actually married him.

32. Hammond (1988b: 124) observes that Cleopatra was "an uncommitted notability" in a period when such a position was risky. Errington (1990: 119) suggests that she was not comfortable with intrigue. Her departure for Sardis argues against this.

33. Hornblower 1981: 161.

34. On Eumenes' dealings with Olympias and Cleopatra, see Carney 1988b: 400 n. 41. On Eumenes and Cleopatra at Sardis, see Carney 1988b: 401 n. 43.

35. Public confrontation or not, no evidence supports Droysen (1953: 92), who thought that this confrontation somehow constituted a formal trial.

36. Diodorus (20.37.4) mentions Cassander as one of Cleopatra's suitors. Seibert (1967: 21), concludes that this information is correct and suggests that Cassander's interest probably dated to the period before his marriage to Thessalonice. Antipater might have hoped that a marriage to Cleopatra would end the feud between the two families and thus stabilize affairs.

37. So Errington 1970: 150.

38. Contra Hornblower 1981: 161–62.

39. See Carney 1988b: 388 for the possibility that Olympias did not introduce Thessalonice to the marriage market, in part, to protect Cleopatra. Had Thessalonice been available as a bride, Cleopatra might not have lived as long as she did.

40. Amundsen and Diers (1970: 79–86) conclude that the usual age range for menopause in antiquity lay between 40 and 50. Fertility, however, tends to decline rapidly for women in their thirties. It is likely that this decline was observable in antiquity too. In 320 b.c. Cleopatra was between 30 and 35 years old; by 309/8, the year of her death, she was between 42 and 47.

41. So Carney 1988b: 403. Hammond (1988b: 169) suggests that she feared for the fate of Alexander IV. He bases this view on his rejection of both the conventional dating of the death of Alexander IV and Heracles and the conventional order (165–66). Even if one accepts his views, it is dubious that Cleopatra's motivation would have been concern for Alexander IV rather than for her own physical safety. As I have argued, whereas Olympias's ambitions by the last stage of her life were necessarily tied to those of her grandson's (OLYMPIAS), Cleopatra's were not necessarily identical with those of her nephew.

42. Carney 1988b: 385–404.

43. Palagia (1999) has suggested that Amyntas and Cynnane has another daughter, younger than Adea Eurydice, who subsequently married Cassander and had a short-lived daughter by him. See further chap. 6. Alexander was able to thwart whatever designs Amyntas had on the throne and had him executed, late in 336 or more likely early in 335 (Plut. *Mor.* 327c; Curt. 6.9.17; Just. 12.6.14; Arr. 1.5.4–5 and *FGrH* 156, F 9.22).

44. He was a leader of the Agriani who had provided critical aid to Alexander in the chaotic period immediately after Philip's death. See Staehelin 1924b: 677; Berve 1926: 2:230.

45. Langarus had been acceptable primarily because a marriage between him and Cynnane offered no serious threat to Alexander and would have removed Cynnane from both court and country. The difference in the status of Amyntas and of Langarus suggests the difference between Alexander and his father on dynastic matters. Whatever the ethnicity of the Agriani, to Greeks and Macedonians they were barbarians. This second marriage not only would have denoted a lower status than Cynnane's first but also implies that Alexander considered her a barbarian.

46. He was Philip's mentally deficient son. See Greenwalt 1985b: 74–76; Carney 1987a: 499 n. 9.

47. Heckel (1983–84: 195), rightly calls it "a stroke of brilliance."

48. Polyaenus (8.60) makes it sound as though Cynnane died in battle against Alcetas, rather than simply being murdered by him.

49. See discussion and references in Carney 1988b: 393–94, nn. 21, 22, on what the troops' reaction to the murder of Cynnane signifies about the reputation of Philip and Alexander and about the reputation of the Argeads generally.

50. So Carney 1988b: 404; I have rethought this point.

51. See Seibert 1967: 11–19 on these marriages.

52. See Kaerst 1894a: 2007; Berve 1926: 2:30–31.

53. Polyaenus (8.60.4) says that the murder of Amyntas (difficult to date exactly but likely to have happened in 335) followed his marriage "swiftly," obviously a relative term. See CYNNANE: PART 1; Carney 1991b: 18 n. 4.

54. Ellis (1970: 68–75; 1971: 15–24) argues that Philip ruled as king from the beginning, but see contra Tronson 1984: 34; Hammond 1979: 208 n. 4, 651 n. 1. See also Hatzopoulos 1982b: 21–42. On Amyntas' activities after Alexander's accession, see Ellis 1970: 68–75; Ellis 1971: 15–24; Griffith 1979: 687 f., 702–4; Badian 1963: 244; Bosworth 1971: 103.

55. See Greenwalt 1985b: 74–76 for a review of the evidence on the nature of Arrhidaeus's ills. See also Carney 1987a: 499 n. 9.

56. Arr. *FGrH* 156, F 9.23. On name changing by royal women, see chap. 1; Carney 1987a: 498 n. 6. Greenwalt (forthcoming) argues that Adea Eurydice herself chose her new name, for political reasons, to honor the tradition of Philip II's mother.

57. As Billows (1990: 67 n. 30), observes, Diodorus (18.36.6–7) does not seem to understand the position as temporary, but Arrian (*FGrH* 156, F 9.30) says that it was.

58. As Billows (1990: 67–69) does by creating an account that simply combines all three sources.

59. Diodorus (18.39.2) says that they resigned, but Arrian (*FGrH* 156, F 9.30–31) claims that when she asserted herself, they resisted until the arrival of Antigonus and Antipater. Billows (1990: 67 n. 30) prefers Arrian's version because he thinks that Diodorus is too abbreviated.

60. For Asclepiodorus, see Berve 1926: 2:88–89; Kaerst 1896: 1636. For Attalus, see Berve 1926: 2:95; Kaerst 1984b: 2158. Little is known of either man. Billows (1990: 68 n. 31) believes that this particular Attalus was Perdiccas' brother-in-law.

61. Orosius (3.23.29–30) claims that Cassander allied himself with Adea Eurydice (see below) out of lust for her. Macurdy (1932a: 51) rightly rejects the truth of this story, but it may indicate Cassander's political plans, if not his lust. Shortly after the death of Adea Eurydice he married her half aunt, Thessalonice. For a man who wanted to rule Macedonia, marriage to Adea Eurydice, with Philip Arrhidaeus eliminated, would have been attractive.

62. Hammond (1988ba: 139) assumes that the separation of the two kings was a decision of Polyperchon's made because of fear of either Cassander's supporters or Adea Eurydice.

63. Referred to only in Diod. 18.75.1 and 19.35.7. Diodorus (18.75.2) says that he seized many of Polyperchon's elephants, and he found many Macedonians and Greeks turning to him, thanks to Polyperchon's failings and Cassander's skills. It is unlikely that he came without an invitation from Adea Eurydice.

64. See Hammond 1988b: 138 n. 1 for the possibility that Justin (14.5.3) means that the transfer in power was accomplished by letter, contra Dusanic (1965: 140–41), who believes that it was arranged in person, primarily because of his dating of Cassander's expedition, and that her invitation and his acceptance of regency were contemporary. Adams (1977: 20) also believes that it happened while he was in Macedonia.

65. Hammond (1985: 160 n. 36) rightly notes that Diodorus does not reveal how Adea Eurydice came to power but simply says that she had it, whereas Justin says she usurped it.

66. Hammond (1988b: 141) says that Cassander left her in the lurch, preferring to stay at Tegea, perhaps because he wanted her to fail or perhaps because he knew she would and did not want to get involved.

67. See Carney 1993b: 43–44 for the undependability of the details of Adea Eurydice's death.

68. Adea Eurydice and her husband may or may not have been buried in Tomb II at Vergina. See chap. 9.

69. Hornblower (1981: 161) sees a conflict between the two as inevitable; Westlake (1969: 326 n. 52) argues that Philip Arrhidaeus would inevitably have been eliminated or ignored.

70. See further Carney 1994b: 361–62 on Polyperchon's choice and policies.

71. Errington 1990: 122–25.

72. Hammond 1988b: 130–31.

73. E.g., his dealings with Heracles, Barsine's son; see below. Westlake (1969: 329, esp. n. 61) terms Polyperchon's reversal of Macedonian policy in Greece "shrewd." Had Polyperchon been able to defeat his opponents at Megalopolis, his policy would have been vindicated. His failure was military, not political.

74. All three passages make Olympias' possession of the *epimeleia* contingent on her return to Macedonia, yet Hammond (1988b: 131) assumes that she accepted his offer but that it was not necessary for her to return to Macedonia to do so.

75. My earlier views (discussed in Carney 1994b: 363–64) on the meaning of these terms have been somewhat modified; now see Carney 1995: 373–74; and chaps. 1 and 3 and OLYMPIAS and CLEOPATRA 2 below contra Hammond 1980: 473–76; 1985: 156–60; 1988b: 90, 138; 1989: 173, 240–41, 261. See also Errington 1970: 55–56; Badian 1964: 264–67.

76. Macurdy (1932b: 256–61) suggested that Roxane and Alexander IV never passed out of Polyperchon's control until the invasion of Macedonia and that Olympias and her cousin Aeacides and their forces met Polyperchon and his forces at the Macedonian border and then confronted Adea Eurydice's army.

77. This lack of clarity in the two rival alliances may result from the unprecedented involvement of royal women in political alliances.

78. See chap. 1 and Carney 1993b: 50–54 for a discussion of this passage and its dependability.

79. Adams (1977: 22 n. 23) suggests that women may not have been allowed to speak in assembly, as they were not in Athens. Women in Macedonia, at least royal women, appeared in public frequently. It is more likely that the situation was unprecedented. Hatzopoulos (1996: 273) argues that she would have spoken had Cassander not feared that by speaking she would escape conviction. See chap. 1.

80. In the incident mentioned, Cassander's general Apollonides had five hundred Argive supporters of Polyperchon trapped in the prytaneion and burned alive and then had yet more killed later. The assembly outlawed and condemned to death more than fifty followers of Perdiccas; among those killed was his sister (Diod. 18.37.2; Arr. *FGrH* 156, F 1.30, 39). See Billows 1990: 11 n. 27 for references to other atrocities carried out by various Successors. When Diodorus (19.35.1) describes Cassander's reactions to events in Macedonia, he mentions the murders of Philip Arrhidaeus and Adea Eurydice and Olympias maltreatment of his brother's tomb but not the deaths of one hundred supporters.

81. Virtually everyone agrees that Adea Eurydice and her husband, Philip Arrhidaeus, were killed in the fall, but there is no consensus about subsequent events. Errington (1977a: 478–504) and Billows (1990: 60, 86–105) reject the view that the siege of Pydna happened over the winter of 317–316 and argue that it happened a year later and that Cassander did not even move north until spring 316. The argument does not convince: see Bosworth 1992: 55–81. Diodorus' (19.35.1) narrative makes it clear that Cassander ended the siege of Tegea as soon as he heard of events in Macedonia, and nothing else about the narrative suggests delay but rather great speed. The confusing situation of the forces arrayed against him in Macedonia may be explained in part by the fact that Cassander did arrive in late fall, before they had expected him, and thus managed to find them less than fully prepared.

82. Blackwell (1999: 103), on the basis of Diod. 19.11.2, says that Olympias took "command of the Macedonian army itself." As I have tried to indicate, the evidence is less straightforward than that description implies. Clearly Olympias took various kinds of indirect or administrative military actions. It is not clear that she personally and literally led the army, especially in combat.

83. Although the absolute date of the siege of Pydna and of Eumenes' final battle is disputed (see above), Errington (1977a: 487) agrees with the conventional view that these two events transpired over the same winter.

84. Eumenes' faithfulness to Olympias and the royal family, however informed by enlightened self-interest, was well known. (See discussion and references in Westlake 1969: 323 n. 41.) Moreover, because his ethnicity prevented him from hoping for personal *basileia*, he was the ideal *epimeletes*.

85. A number of factors suggest this possibility: had Aristonous not been hoping for some sort of assistance form Eumenes, Diodorus' reference to his ignorance of Eumenes' death makes no sense; Aristonous' station at Amphipolis, hardly the direction from which Cassander's forces were approaching, also suggests interest in connection with forces in the east. Once Aristonous and Olympias were under siege, it is difficult to know how good their information would have been about Eumenes' whereabouts and success. The story of Eumenes' famous false letter (Diod. 19.23.1–4) shows how much the Macedonians in the east could be affected by "news" they may have wanted to hear; the same may apply to Olympias' forces in the homeland.

86. Contra Adams 1977: 22. Monimus simply drops from sight, but Diodorus tells us that Cassander had the relatives of the man Aristonous had just defeated and killed in battle kill Aristonous. Nothing in the description implies judicial procedure.

87. The ordinary procedure would have been for those voting for her condemnation to carry out her execution immediately. Hatzopoulos (1996: 275) argues that Diodorus should be read to mean not that they had already condemned her but that they were going to condemn her, that she had yet to speak, and that Cassander broke off the trial before a possibly favorable verdict might be reached. If a verdict was reached, whether because people admired Olympias or because they feared taking responsibility for her death, or both, they would not carry it out.

88. As already noted, Hatzopoulos (1996: 273–76), who takes the trial seriously, believes that Cassander ended the trial before a verdict was reached and arranged to eliminate Olympias by private means because he feared that she would persuade her audience to acquit her. He suggests that, like other controversial crimes (e.g., the murders of Cleopatra, sister of Alexander, and Alexander IV), it was disguised, this time as a vendetta by the kin of those she had killed.

89. Justin's (14.6.1–13) narrative of these events does not inspire confidence. His account is so abbreviated that Polyperchon does not appear. The description of the trial is quite unclear, and the death of Olympias is rendered with lurid drama.

90. See a detailed review of the evidence provided by Diodorus' narrative in Carney 1994a: 374–76.

91. Adams (1977: 23) rightly points out that Cassander not only showed skill as a commander himself but also built up a collection of very competent and loyal subordinates whose efforts did much to bring him success against Polyperchon.

92. So Hammond 1988b: 145.

93. See discussion and references in Adams 1991: 30.

94. Gruen (1985: 254) faults Diodorus' analysis here, terming it "anticipatory and conjectural," yet the fact that more time passed before any of them took the title of king need not mean that they had not, just as Cassander had, been acting to produce that ultimate goal for some time.

95. On the complex events at Babylon, see discussions in Errington 1970: 49–59; Schachermeyr 1970: 134–98. Arrian (7.27.3) reports that he has heard a tale he does not believe in which Roxane prevented her dying husband from killing himself in order to make belief in his divinity more likely.

96. So Green 1990: 6.

97. See Sancisi-Weerdenberg 1983: 20–33. Sancisi-Weerdenberg notes that the image of Asian women, particularly royal ones, is not only that they were murderous and cruel products of the evil harem system but also that they manipulated men by using womanly wiles. Perdiccas himself may have used this stereotype to escape primary blame for the murders.

98. The only exception to her general obscurity in the Greek world is a splendid dedication she made to the goddess Athena, probably in 319 or 318 (see discussion and references in Harris 1995: 140, 179, 234–35). Macurdy (1932b: 256–61) argues that Roxane and her son never went to Epirus but remained with Polyperchon until Olympias' return to Macedonia and notes (258) that Polyperchon had continued Antipater's policy of retaining personal control of the kings. Having lost control of Philip Arrhidaeus, he would be even less likely to lose control of his remaining source of power, Alexander IV (259).

99. Contra Hammond (1988b: 145, 167), who says that Alexander IV was too young to have pages yet, but see Heckel (1980: 249–50) and Burstein (1977: 223–25) for epigraphic evidence for the existence of "pages" of Alexander IV.

100. Adams 1991: 29 n. 15. Tarn, *CAH* 6.49; Errington 1990: 142, contra Hammond 1988b: 167, see the treaty as incentive for the subsequent murder of Alexander IV. The reference to a term of office that ended when Alexander IV reached adulthood, once read to apply only to Cassander, is now commonly held to apply to all four (Errington 1990: 141; Hammond 1988b: 161 n. 3; Billows 1990: 132). Although many have attributed the murder to the terms of the treaty (see discussion and references: Errington 1990: 142), Adams (1977: 29) seems to ascribe it to Cassander's growing confidence in his support. Hammond (1988b: 161) associates the murder with the need for heirs to the throne to have pages after age fourteen. See below.

101. Contra Hammond 1988b: 165–68. For a convincing argument against Hammond's view, see Adams 1991: 29 n. 16 and BARSINE. Justin and Diodorus vaguely refer to secrecy and concealment, whereas Pausanias claims that both sons of Alexander and their mothers were killed by poison.

102. The murders must have become known sometime between their occurrence and the assumption of royal titles by various of the Successors in 306/5. The variation and vagueness in accounts of the murders (see above) speak both

to their secrecy and to the likelihood of the passage of time before they were publicly discussed.

103. So Holt 1988: 92,98.

104. Contra Adams 1977: 29. Errington (1990: 142); and Hammond (1988b: 164) both take the risk seriously.

105. Brunt (1975: 30) suggests this possibility; it was in Artabazus's old satrapy.

106. Hammond (1988b: 129) suggests, on the basis of Strabo's reference (794) to the children of Alexander, that when Antipater returned to Macedonia, he brought with him not only Roxane and Alexander IV but also Heracles and Barsine. A little later, however, Hammond has them back in Pergamum for Polyperchon's summons (169). It seems likely that they did not leave Pergamum before the message from Polyperchon.

107. See Errington 1970: 49–77.

108. Carney 1988b: 385, 403–4.

109. Carney 1988b: 385.

110. Contra Hammond (1988b: 165–68), who recently argued that Alexander IV outlived his older half brother. See Adams 1991: 30 for arguments against Hammond. Diodorus' narrative of the events leading to the murder of Heracles (20.20.1–4, 28.1–4) clearly presupposes that Alexander IV was dead; there is no mention of Alexander IV and frequent reference to the appeal of restoring Heracles to his ancestral kingdom, and, most tellingly, he refers (20.20.4, 28.1,2) to Heracles as *basileus*, a term he had previously reserved for Alexander IV.

111. As Errington (1970: 74) notes, Heracles' rejection at Babylon was not a consequence of doubts about his parentage but rather arose from a preference for other candidates perceived to be more viable.

CHAPTER 6

1. On the events of this period, see Walbank 1988: 199–258; Errington 1990: 130–61.

2. Contra Macurdy (1932a: 69), who dates the decline of the importance of royal women to the period after the death of Olympias; however, Macurdy (1932a: 75–76) more appropriately put the change after the departure of Phila, wife of Demetrius Poliorcetes. If we consider Arsinoe (see below), then it seems best to date the change to the end of chaos and the beginning of Antigonus Gonatas' rule. Hatzopoulos (1990: 144–47), followed by Le Bohec (1993b: 229–45), would not agree that the power of royal women declined: see discussion in chap. 7 below.

3. Errington (1990: 133) suggests that Cassander took the title between 306 and 297; Hammond (1988b: 174) thinks that Cassander was acclaimed king after the burial of Alexander IV; Adams (1977: 25) believes that he took the title in 301.

4. Contra Hammond (1988b: 145), who implausibly argues that Cassander initially had no sinister intent toward Alexander IV and secluded him for his own good. Cassander (see below) named his eldest son Philip rather than Antipater, as would have been customary. Cassander's preference for the maternal but royal grandfather's name over his own father's speaks to his ambitions. See further chap. 5.

5. Adams 1977: 23. Palagia (1999) has made the intriguing suggestion that a funerary inscription commemorating a young girl named Adea, whose mother was Cynnane (or Cynna) and whose father was Cassander (see Tataki 1988: 85 n. 26 for references) refers to a daughter of the famous Cassander by a daughter of Cynnane (daughter of Philip II and Amyntas), to a younger sister of Adea Eurydice. Palagia has suggested that Cassander married his first wife ca. 319. Dr. Palagia was kind enough to provide me with a copy of her paper.

6. So Green 1982: 143; Ellis 1976: 84; Griffith 1979: 524.

7. Berve (1926: 2:179) and Macurdy (1932a: 52) argue convincingly that ca. 346/5 is the earliest plausible date for her birth, and Greenwalt (1988a: 94) rightly concludes that a birthdate in the late 340s would be more appropriate, granted the date of her marriage.

8. So Berve 1926: 2:179, followed by Macurdy 1932a: 52–53.

9. Macurdy (1932a: 53) suggested that Olympias wanted to prevent the possibility of "pretenders"; in reality, it was the fact that children of Thessalonice's need not have been so labeled that made her marriage dangerous to Olympias' heirs.

10. Polyaenus (8.60) reports that, once widowed, Cynnane did not wish to remarry and we know of no interest in remarriage on Cleopatra's part until her brother's death, when she may have feared for her safety. Her long stay in Sardis without seeking a replacement groom for her intended husband Perdiccas may signify that she had now returned to her earlier reluctance to remarry, and only the reemergence of physical danger may have caused her to return to the marriage market.

11. Diodorus (19.52.1) asserts that Cassander married Thessalonice because he wanted the *basileia* of Macedonia and therefore wished to establish a relationship with the royal family. Diodorus places the marriage first in a list of kinglike acts Cassander performed immediately after the death of Olympias (19.52.1–5). Adams (1977:27), mentions the possible advantages of being the uncle by marriage of the child king Alexander IV, granted that his role as regent was otherwise dubious.

12. Beloch 1927: 4:2. 127 n. 2.

13. Hammond (1989: 277) suggests that members of the Macedonian aristocracy imitated the polygamy of the kings. The remarkable number of children attributed to Antipater (see Berve 1926: 2:46; Heckel 1992: 39) could be explained by polygamy. Cassander's monogamy is even more striking if it reversed his father's practice. See chap. 8 on the decline of royal polygamy in Macedonia in subsequent years.

14. Cassander's nephew, Antipater "Etesias," the son of his brother Philip, reigned for forty-five days during the most chaotic period after the death of Ceraunus but was then rejected in favor of Sosthenes, a man who refused to take the royal title. "Etesias," who had preserved some sort of regional following in Macedonia, was ultimately driven from the country by Antigonus Gonatas at the time he assumed rule (Polyaen. 4.6.17). See Walbank 1988: 353–54, 257.

15. See Carney forthcoming.

16. Pausanias (9.7.2–3) says that young Philip died of consumption, but attributes Cassander's death to phthiriasis (his body was consumed by worms) and implies that this terrible death was due to his elimination of the house of Alexander. Eusebius (1.231 f.) and Syncellus (265 A 504 Bonn), however, attribute Cassander's death to a wasting disease—consumption. Africa (1982: 6, 15) plausibly suggests that the phthiriasis story derived from a "propaganda smear" by Hieronymus. Antigonus Doson also probably died of tuberculosis: see Walbank 1988: 362.

17. Ancient medicine was unable to diagnose the early and nearly asymptomatic stages of the disease, but Greek medical descriptions of advanced pulmonary tuberculosis are quite accurate (Dubos and Dubos 1952: 70–72; Morse 1967: 260), and the house of Antipater, with its close ties to Aristotle and Greek intellectual leaders, doubtless had access to the best advice available. I assume, therefore, that Cassander and those around him knew he had tuberculosis.

18. What used to be called "galloping" consumption can kill in a few months, but it was rare. More typically the disease was contracted in early childhood, remained virtually invisible until puberty, and then waxed and waned, only gradually becoming symptomatic and finally life-threatening. See Dubos and Dubos 1952: 4.

19. Greenwalt (1988a: 93–94) concluded that most Argead males married in their early twenties. See THESSALONICE for a discussion of their probable date of birth, but both must have been teenagers.

20. Macurdy (1932a: 55), followed by Heckel (1989: 34), suggested that Cassander was the likely arranger of the marriages because of the identity of the brides. Seibert (1967: 75–76, 96–97) seems unaware of Macurdy's suggestion and simply assumes both marriages happened after Cassander's death.

21. See Seibert 1967: 96–97.

22. Errington (1990: 134) notes with apparent approval Diodorus' (20.106.3) observation that Cassander tended to turn to Lysimachus in times of anxiety because of his proximity and his character.

23. Seibert (1967: 97 n. 20) suggests that Lysimachus' treatment of his daughter and elimination of Antipater may have had to do with the marriage of Lysimachus's son Agathocles to the widow of Antipater's brother and his ability to use this marriage as a possible basis for claim to Macedonian rule. In contrast, Macurdy (1932a: 56) suggests that Arsinoe, Lysimachus' young wife, may have influenced his decision. See ARSINOE.

24. Seibert (1967: 97) points to the inherent problem of dynastic alliances, as demonstrated in this case: the groom and the father of the bride had different motivations, which often conflicted.

25. One could of course conclude that the passage in Eusebius is a fiction, but it is difficult to see why such an alliance would have been invented.

26. Seibert (1967: 75) considers this a possibility.

27. Macurdy (1932a: 58) suggests that Ptolemy may have offered Lysandra to Alexander V to prevent him from marrying one of Phila's daughters by Demetrius.

28. See Seibert 1967: 76.

29. See Macurdy 1932a: 56–57; Seibert 1967: 75 n. 16.

30. Macurdy 1932a: 58.

31. On the sources, see Walbank 1988: 200 n. 1.

32. Errington (1978: 126 n. 124) and Walbank (1988: 210 n. 3) note the fact that she is nowhere described as regent and cite several scholars who nonetheless assume she was. I was once among them (see Carney 1988b: 391 n. 14).

33. Neither Olympias nor Adea Eurydice, although each exercised some control over a noncompetent king, functioned as regent in the way that Antipater or Polyperchon did; see OLYMPIAS and ADEA EURYDICE.

34. Lévêque (1957: 126) assumes that this division was geographic, but Walbank (1988: 211 n. 1) argues that the Macedonians would never have agreed to such a geographic division. Granted that they had in the past (see n. 35), Walbank's view is unconvincing.

35. After the death of Alexander I ca. 454, three of his sons had some sort of *arche* over different parts of the kingdom (Thuc. 2.99.2). Borza (1990: 134–35), following Cole 1974: 55–57 contra Hammond 1979: 115, argues that this shared rule was probably the consequence of a decision of Alexander I's rather than of a struggle for power after Alexander's death. More recently, Philip Arrhidaeus and Alexander IV had been co-kings, although, of course, they themselves had not ruled. Neither precedent could be considered encouraging. The first led to a prolonged struggle for the throne, and the second hastened the end of the Argead dynasty.

36. Beloch 1927: 4:22; Walbank 1988: 209; Errington 1990: 148.

37. Carney 1988b: 393 n. 15.

38. See Greenwalt 1988a: 93–97.

39. On this possibility, see further Carney forthcoming.

40. Obviously, other factors contributed to the demise of the Antipatrid dynasty, most prominent among them the lack of competence both of the younger sons of Antipater so consistently displayed. They acted more like the sons of Polyperchon than of Cassander. See further Carney forthcoming.

41. For discussion of these events and the evidence for them, see Walbank 1988: 210–18; Errington 1990: 147–50.

42. This work will deal at length only with Phila and Lanassa, the two

women Demetrius is known to have been married to at the time he was king of Macedonia. His marriage to Eurydice, an Athenian, preceded his period as Macedonian monarch; it is not clear that she was alive at the time he was king (see Macurdy 1932a: 63; Seibert 1967: 27). His marriage to Deidameia, sister of Pyrrhus, also happened before his stint as Macedonian monarch, but Deidameia died before he became king (Macurdy 1932a: 63–64; Seibert 1967: 28–30). He married Ptolemaïs, daughter of Ptolemy, after he had given up the kingship of Macedonia (see below and Seibert 1967: 30–32).

43. Another, unnamed daughter of Antipater was married to Lyncestian Alexander by 336 (Curt. 7.1.7; Just. 11.7.1, 13.14.1), but this does not disprove Diodorus' assertion. Contra Beloch 1927: 3:2.84.

44. This estimate is based on the marriage date of her younger sister, and the knowledge that she was considerably older than Demetrius at the time of her marriage to him (Plut. *Demetr.* 27.4). See Berve 1926: 2:382; Wehrli 1964: 140–41.

45. The marriage to Balacrus (see Berve 1926: 2:100–101) was once doubted (e.g., Wehrli 1964: 141) because the only evidence was a dubious passage attributed to Antonius Diogenes (ap. Phot. 111b), but Heckel (1987: 161–62; and 1989: 33) has argued convincingly that a Delian inscription naming a certain Antipater, son of Balacrus (*IG* XI 2 287b.57) demonstrates that Phila did indeed marry Balacrus and that the marriage probably took place before 334. Badian (1988: 116–18) accepts Heckel's evidence for the existence of the marriage but rejects the authenticity of the passage from Antonius Diogenes.

46. Berve (1926: 2:282) states that she stayed at her father's court; Heckel (1989: 33) believes that she may have joined Balacrus in Cilicia and that Craterus found her still there in 324, a recent widow. Badian (1988: 177) prefers Berve's view.

47. See Seibert 1967: 11–19.

48. Seibert (1967: 13 n. 9) believed that this son must have been posthumous, but Badian (1988: 118) argues that this need not have been the case.

49. See Seibert 1967: 27–33.

50. We do not know whether this practice was a usage limited to one wife when Phila and other royal wives began to use and be given a title (see chap. 8). Cults created for Phila, Lanassa, or various of Demetrius' *hetairai* were not unique. Phila's situation, like that of Demetrius' other wives, was fluid, and similar to the situation of Philip II's wives.

51. Macurdy 1932a: 61; Wehrli 1964: 141. Diodorus' (20.93.4) reference to the presents she dispatched to Demetrius during the siege of Rhodes implies that Phila was then living in Cilicia.

52. *SIG* 333.6–7: a Samian decree honoring a certain Demarchus, said to be a guard in *basilissa* Phila's entourage. Its original editor dated it to shortly after 306), most probably to the siege of Rhodes (305–4) and Robert (1946: 17 nn. 1–2) agrees and suggests that an Ephesian decree honoring a certain Melisippus, part of *basilissa* Phila's entourage, should be dated to the same period. Wehrli (1964: 140–43) accepts this dating for both documents. See chap. 8.

53. Tarn 1913: 19.

54. Macurdy (1932a: 63) seems to approve Tarn's suggestion, whereas Wehrli (1964: 143) is less willing to commit himself. Since Tarn (1913: 19) actually believed that Phila and Demetrius separated for a time because of this new marriage, it becomes obvious that his suggestion derives from his—not Macedonian—discomfort with polygamy.

55. Macurdy (1932a: 64–66) suggests that she returned to Macedonia.

56. See the encomium-like treatment of both Tarn 1913: 17–18 and Macurdy 1932a: 59–61. Green (1990: 121) portrays Phila as loving and long-suffering.

57. See Hornblower 1981: 226–28.

58. Hornblower (1981: 228) suggests that the portraits of Phila and Demetrius in his more likable youth may have been intended to contrast with the rather ruthless patriarch, Antigonus. Tarn (1913: 18) likens Phila to Octavia, and there are similarities in their public images. One wonders if—just as some have suggested—the image of Octavia was in some degree manipulated to make her the "good wife" in opposition to either Fulvia or Cleopatra or both (see Delia 1991: 197–217 esp. n. 82)—Phila's image was "airbrushed," perhaps for dynastic purposes (e.g., good Phila vs. bad Olympias or Adea Eurydice).

59. See Carney 1992a: 170–71.

60. See Carney 1993b: 51–55 on suicide by women, especially royal women, including Phila.

61. See Pomeroy 1984: 12–40 for a discussion of the role and public image of the queen in the Hellenistic period, particularly in Egypt.

62. The date of Lanassa's marriage to Pyrrhus is uncertain. Staehelin (1924: 617) and Seibert (1967: 101) suggest 295.

63. After the death of Agathocles, Pyrrhus tried to claim a role in Sicilian politics (App. *Sam.* 11.1). The Syracusans, because of Pyrrhus' son by Lanassa, hoped for his help (Diod. 22.8.2), and Pyrrhus did indeed try to use this connection for political gain in Sicily (Just. 23.3.3). See discussion in Staehelin 1924: 618.

64. So Staehelin 1924: 617–18; Lévêque 1957: 139; Walbank 1988: 223.

65. Seibert 1967: 107–8; Lévêque 1957: 140.

66. Contra Seibert 1967: 107–8. Seibert's argument that Agathocles' alliance with Demetrius was not begun by Lanassa's marriage but came after depends on the dubious assumption that this was not a political marriage. Similarly, his assertion that Lanassa must have acted alone because her motivation was solely personal is equally unconvincing. Agathocles would always have been concerned about the honor of his dynasty and desirous of his daughter making a marriage appropriate to the status of his dynasty.

67. It is not clear that the stories preserved in Athenaeus about the Athenians' treatment of Demetrius refer to Lanassa, and involve Demetrius and Lanassa being greeted as Dionysus and Demeter, as Scott (1928: 228–29) and Tarn (1913: 49 n. 25) believed. See contra Cerfaux and Tondriau 1957: 181–84.

68. See Seibert 1967: 107 n. 16.

69. Macurdy 1932a: 66–67.

70. See Kuhrt and Sherwin-White 1991: 84–85 for the unusual role that Stratonice played in Seleucid kingship. They suggest that, as a "stakeholder", an instrument in the transition from father to son, she was a "powerful political figure." While the cuneiform text they discuss does suggest the importance of her role in the continuity of power, it demonstrates no independent action of her own and thus cannot be said to indicate that she was a "powerful political figure"—though she may have been—but rather that she was a potent political symbol.

71. A Delian inscription, *IG* XI 4. 415, ca. 300, refers to a cult statue of Stratonice and is usually assumed to refer to the daughter of Demetrius Poliorcetes; see Habicht 1970: 61. Billows (1990: 235 n. 118) suggests that the inscription might instead refer to Antigonus' mother. She received cult worship at Smyrna (*OGIS* 228, 229; *SIG* 575, 990). See chap. 8.

72. Tarn 1913: 349–51; Macurdy 1932a: 80. Ferrario (1962: 78–82), however, has raised compelling questions about the authenticity of the inscription.

73. Her death is usually linked to the establishment of a vase foundation at Delos in her honor: Macurdy 1932a: 80; Hammond 1988a: 598.

74. See Tarn 1913: 348–53; Macurdy 1932a: 81, esp. n. 23. She never describes herself as wife of either Seleucid but rather as daughter of both parents or simply as Demetrius' daughter. See chap. 8.

75. So Tarn 1913: 352–53. Among her many Delian offerings are dedications made on the occasion of each of her daughters' marriages. Each of those marriages was to an Antigonid, perhaps not a coincidence (see Tarn 1913: 350).

76. Tarn 1913: 350–51.

77. Macurdy 1932a: 81.

78. On the conflicting and ambiguous testimony of Appian, Nepos, and Memnon on the chronological relationship between Ceraunus' visit to Seleucus and his stay at Lysimachus' court, see Heinen 1972: 4, arguing that he went to Seleucus only after his residence in Lysimachus' court, contra Errington 1990: 157.

79. See Carney 1994a: 123–31 for a lengthier discussion of Arsinoe's earlier career and its impact.

80. Heckel 1989: 34–35 dates her predominance to this period, on the basis on dynastic marriages arranged for her children but not Eurydice's.

81. The second marriage involved Lysandra, Ptolemy's daughter by Eurydice, and Agathocles, Lysimachus' son by Nicaea, and probably occurred somewhat later, although it may have been planned at the same time. See Seibert 1967: 75–76.

82. Justin (24.3.5) says that Lysimachus was 16 and Philip 13 at the time Ptolemy Ceraunus murdered them ca. 280. Heinen (1972: 10) therefore suggests that her eldest son was born sometime between her marriage ca. 300 and 297/6, the date of the birth of the second brother.

83. Macurdy (1932a: 57) suggests they may have perpetuated girlhood rivalries; this is too superficial an interpretation. The two young women had come

to maturity in the midst of a very real power struggle between their mothers, primarily over which of their brothers would succeed to their father's position. Each would show continued allegiance to their respective full brother's future. On the power struggle between the children of Eurydice and Berenice, see also Heckel 1989: 34–36.

84. As Burstein (1982: 199 n. 7) cautions, the date of Nicaea's death is not certain. Burstein's reference to the *basilissa* title in this context is not helpful because we do not have an inscription from the 290s attesting either woman as a *basilissa* (Ferrario [1962: 78–82] has shown that *OGIS* 14, which appears to refer to Arsinoe as *basilissa* ca. 299, is probably a fake or altered) and we cannot be sure *basilissa* was an exclusive title (see chap. 8). We do know, however, that Lysimachus ended his recent marriage to Amastris for the sake of Arsinoe: Memnon *FGrH* 434, F 4.9).

85. Burstein (1982a: 198) alone suggests that the name referred to Lysimachus' similarly named daughter, despite the fact that Strabo specifically refers to his wife. On eponymous foundations for women, see chap. 8. See Lund 1994: 175 on another Arsinoea in Aetolia.

86. She is often said to have controlled and ruled Heracleia, Cassandreia, and Ephesus (Arsinoea). Lund (1994: 194) points out that it is certain only that Lysimachus gave her Heracleia ca. 284 (Memnon *FGrH* 434, F 5.4–5) and that even this may have entailed only revenues and not direct rule. Many cities named after women were never ruled by them, and Arsinoe's role in Cassandreia soon after Lysimachus' death may speak only to her ability to pay mercenaries.

87. Fraser (1960: 51) favors the period of her marriage to Lysimachus and is followed by Cole (1984: 22) and Lund (1994: 168). Roux (1981: 231–39) argues unconvincingly for a date during her marriage to Philadelphus.

88. Roux 1992: 236 n. 15. See Burstein 1982a: 200 n. 10 and Lund 1994: 197–98 n. 41 for discussion of an inscription commemorating a statue of Arsinoe put up at Thebes by Arsinoe's son Ptolemy on behalf of his father, Lysimachus. The inscription may date before or after the death of Agathocles and therefore cannot be used to prove that Arsinoe's status, along with that of her son, had risen prior to the elimination of Agathocles, although it may indeed signify exactly that.

89. The sources for these events are notoriously poor and contradictory and the chronological relationship of many events in the period uncertain. Heinen 1972: 4–19 and Lund 1994: 184–206 provide the best discussions of the period and the sources.

90. Pausanius (1.10.4) reports that Philetarus, who controlled Pergamum and its wealth, went over to Seleucus out of anger at the death of Agathocles and hostility to Arsinoe. It has often been assumed that a considerable portion of Lysimachus' realm revolted before Corupedion, but Lund (1994: 199–200) argues convincingly that there is little evidence for extensive revolt before Lysimachus's defeat.

91. Ritter (1965: 116 n. 3) doubted the historicity of the episode, apparently because he believed it to be too similar to one both Phylarchus (ap. Ath. 13.593e) and Polyaenus (8.61) tell about Mysta, a *hetaira* of Seleucus II. Ritter (1965: 172–73) notes a kind of *topos* of disguised flight. Doubtless there are literary elements involved in these tales, but this need not mean they are untrue.

92. Lund (1994: 91, 184, 187–89) argues convincingly against the validity of choosing one source to the exclusion of others and warns of the dangers of sources demonstrably colored by literary *topoi* and sexual stereotypes.

93. Burstein 1982a: 200.

94. Macurdy 1932a: 113; Walbank 1988: 299.

95. Heinen (1972: 10–16) first suggested (contra Tarn 1913: 125) that Memnon's reference to Ptolemy Ceraunus as the murderer of Agathocles was a mistake for Ptolemy, son of Lysimachus (probably created by subsequent *epitomators* of Memnon), and has been widely followed: Walbank 1988: 297; Lund 1994: 88.

96. Pausanius (1.10.3) says that Arsinoe feared that her children might fall into Agathocles' hands after Lysimachus' death. Lund (1994: 198) suggests that Agathocles really did, as is implied by Strabo (13.4.1), plot against his father and his father was therefore compelled to eliminate him.

97. So Lund (1994: 196–98), who points to the notorious tensions that develop between an aging ruler and his apparent heir. There is an obvious parallel here to the situation of Philip II and Alexander in the last years of Philip's reign; see Fredricksmeyer 1990: 300–15; Carney 1992a: 169–89.

98. Lund (1994: 193–95) doubts the extent of Arsinoe's influence over Lysimachus and questions the evidence.

99. Heinen (1972: 76–77) points out the variation in Justin's explanations. Justin at 17.2.7–8 suggests nothing sinister about the marriage proposal (Ceraunus wants to increase his popularity) but in 24.2.1 clearly says that Ceraunus had determined to use the marriage as a means to murder her sons and seize control of Cassandreia. Neither Justin nor his sources can have known for a certainty, but Justin's narrative suggests so short a time from the marriage to the murder as to allow no time or reason for a change of motivation, and Ceraunus' murder of Seleucus suggests that Ceraunus generally found murder a useful solution to conflicting claims to succession.

100. Walbank 1988: 248 n. 3.

101. Justin does not say that he left, but he did not appear at the ceremony with his brothers (see below) and was therefore not available to be murdered. The prologue to 24 reports a subsequent war between Ceraunus and the combined forces of Lysimachus' son and an Illyrian named Monimus. Heinen (1962: 83) suggests that he may have fled between the marriage ceremony and Ceraunus' entry into Cassandreia, but there is no certainty.

102. The date of her return is usually assumed to have been relatively soon after ca. 280 or 279. See Burstein 1982a: 200.

103. He became the ruler of Telmessus in Lycia, and his dynasty seems to

have lasted into the second century. See Volkmann 1959: 1596 f.; Heinen 1972: 82 n. 314; Burstein 1982a: 206 n. 45.

104. So Errington 1990: 159 and Heinen 1972: 81–83, which suggests that the murder of the younger sons may have been precipitated by the departure of the elder.

105. See Carney 1987a: 420–39.

106. So Burstein 1982a: 210; Carney 1987b: 426–27.

107. Burstein 1982a: 207 implausibly sees as proof of Arsinoe's lack of influence with her brother the "exclusion of her son by Lysimachus from succession to the throne by forcing her to adopt his children by his first wife as her own." No matter how influential Arsinoe was, it would have been extremely unlikely that she could have convinced her brother to prefer her son by another man to his own son. We do not know that she tried. Her son's position in Telmessus may owe something to his mother's influence, but that too is unknown. As suggested above, each may have been too embittered for further contact.

108. While Burstein 1982a: 197–212 stands as a healthy corrective to the excessive claims made for Arsinoe by earlier scholars such as Longega, Pomeroy (1984: 19) rightly argues that the evidence of the Egyptian sources tends to support the idea that Arsinoe exercised unprecedented power in her years as her brother's wife.

109. See chap. 8; Gryzbek 1990: 103–12; Gutzwiller 1992: 365.

110. Lund (1994: 189) refers to the "'cherchez la femme' school of history" and notes how common stereotypes about powerful women were in ancient historiography. See also Carney 1993b passim; Garlick, Dixon, and Allen 1992, esp. 209–25.

CHAPTER 7

1. On the reign of Antigonus Gonatas, see Walbank 1988: 259–316; Errington 1990: 162–73; Gabbert 1997. On the Antigonid period, see Walbank 1988: 259–579; Errington 1990: 162–217.

2. Macurdy 1932a: 69 puts it after the death of Olympias, but Macurdy 1932a: 75–76 more plausibly places it after the death of Phila, wife of Poliorcetes (see PHILA 2).

3. So Hatzopoulos 1990: 144–47, followed by Le Bohec 1993b: 229–45. They argue, primarily on the basis of a new inscription from Cassandreia (see below for discussion), that we have underestimated the role of the royal wife in the Antigonid period.

4. In the subsequent passage, however, Athenaeus notes that Heracleides of Lembus claims that Demo was Demetrius' (apparently Poliorcetes) and that his father Antigonus fell in love with her (Ath. 13.578b). Tarn (1913: 248 n. 92) plausibly argues that this passage, like Plut. *Demetr.* 27.4, confuses and conflates stories about Demitrius Poliorcetes' mistress Mania with his son's mistress Demo.

5. For a discussion of Halcyoneus' activities, see Kroll 1912: 2273; Walbank 1988: 267.

6. So Kirchner 1901: 2863; Tarn 1913: 248 n. 92.

7. Gabbert (1997: 15) suggests ca. 290.

8. Tarn 1913: 248, esp. n. 92. Macurdy (1932a: 70) is more modest; she simply says that Gonatas "brought Halcyoneus up as a prince."

9. Antigonus first scolded and then praised the youth for various actions in the Pyrrhus campaign (see Gabbert 1997: 31) and gave him a remarkably extravagant birthday party (Diog. Laert. 4.41).

10. So Tarn 1913: 248. If Tarn's view is correct, then Gonatas' reaction resembles that of Alexander in the early years of his reign; see chap. 4.

11. Walbank 1988: 251.

12. Hoffman (1938b: 2088) notes that she must have been born between 300 and 294/3 B.C. because the latter date marks the end of her mother's marriage to her father. Thus she would have been in her late teens or early twenties at the time of her marriage. Gabbert (1997: 78) suggests that she was eighteen.

13. *IG* II 1367. So Tarn 1913: 174; see also Hammond 1989: 315; Green 1990: 142; Gabbert 1997: 76 n. 27. On the uses of royal weddings, see chap. 8.

14. Errington 1990: 165–66; Edson 1934: 213–35.

15. This conclusion was initially based on an inscription that, if correctly restored, has *basilissa* Phila dedicating jointly with Patron, son of Antiochus, and is dated to this year (*SIG* 2635). See Tarn 1913: 389 n. 60. Tarn's surmise has now been confirmed by the 1980 discovery of another inscription, an Athenian decree dated 247/6 or 246/5, which very clearly refers to sacrifices for *basileus* Antigonus and *basilissa* Phila and their descendants. See Dontas 1983: 48–63, esp. 52, ll. 24–25.

16. A statue base in the Propylaea at Delos, erected by a private person. *OGIS* 216. See Tarn 1913: 289 n. 60.

17. The original editor of the Samian inscription found at Cos referring to a *temenos* of Phila (Laurenzi 1941: 27, l. 22–24) concluded that it referred to the wife of Poliorcetes and dated it ca. 306. Robert (1949: 177 n. 4) concluded, however, that the orthography and formulaic language of the inscription require dating to a later period and connecting to Phila, wife of Gonatas. His view has now won general acceptance. See Le Bohec 1993b: 237 n. 64.

18. See Le Bohec 1993b: 237–38 for references to these inscriptions, as well as discussion. They include a Delian dedication to Phila by a private person; a Samian inscription, perhaps related to a cult for Phila; an Athenian decree; and the new inscription from Cassandreia. See Hatzopoulos 1990: 135–47; 1996: 1:144, and 2:64; and below for discussion of the latter inscription.

19. See Hatzopoulos 1990: 147–48; Le Bohec 1993b: 244–45. The inscription implies that the courtier referred to is a kind of liaison between Phila and citizens of Cassandreia who visit her on public and private business.

20. On the reign of Demetrius II as well as the possibility that he co-ruled with his father for some time, see Walbank 1988: 317–36; Errington 1990: 173–75.

21. See Walbank 1988: 316 n. 1.

22. So Le Bohec 1993b: 232.

23. Beloch (1927: 3:2, 93); and Geyer (1931b: 320) suggest 255–53; Tarn (1913: 348), narrows the date to 253; Seibert (1967: 34–36) and Errington (1990: 171) merely suggest the 250s.

24. So Walbank 1988: 322.

25. Tarn (1913: 369) and Walbank (1988: 323) judge the motivation of Stratonice's departure and its date as a problem incapable of solution.

26. Errington (1977b: 115–22) attempted to refute the view that Demetrius ever co-ruled with his father, but Walbank (1988: 317–18), continues to hold the idea of a co-kingship. One wonders, though, if Justin would refer to Demetrius as *rex* (king), without reference to his father, if his father still lived.

27. Macurdy 1932a: 71.

28. Geyer 1931b: 321; Macurdy (1932a: 71 n. 179) considers it possible.

29. Wilhelm 1908: 79–81.

30. Walbank (1967: 475–76) points out that the Piraeus inscription is irrelevant to the problem of the "first" Apamea, that there is no reason to prefer Stephanus to Strabo and Hermippus, and that since not only Strabo but also Stephanus himself (s.v. "Prousa") attribute the refoundation of Cius to Prusias, it is reasonable to conclude that he refounded and renamed Myrleia too (Strabo pairs the refoundations and connects them to the activities of Philip V). See Walbank 1967: 476 for references to opposing views, most notably those in Habicht 1957: 1086–87, 1095–96.

31. On Alexander's revolt, see discussion and references in Walbank 1988: 301 n. 1 and Errington 1990: 172 n. 36.

32. Tarn (1913: 370 n. 4), argues for 247 B.C. and is followed by Fine (1934: 100); Seibert (1967: 36); and Errington (1990: 172) prefer 244 B.C.; Walbank (1988: 305) seems to imply a date of early 245.

33. Tarn (1913: 370 n. 4) and Fine (1934: 100) reject the actuality of marriage. See contra Seibert 1967: 36 n. 40.

34. See Errington 1990: 288 n. 36; Walbank 1988: 301 n. 2.

35. So Tarn 1913: 372.

36. Tarn (1913: 370 n. 4) and Fine (1934: 100) argue that Nicaea would only agree to the marriage if it conveyed "legitimate queenship," yet neither really demonstrates that such an entity, if it existed, was limited to one woman. Walbank (1988: 305) rejects these views and believes that Stratonice remained Demetrius's wife until some subsequent period. See chap. 8.

37. Macurdy (1932a: 71 n. 181) suggests that it was the marriage to Nicaea that precipitated Stratonice's departure. This view not only contradicts Justin but also ignores the lower status of Nicaea. Both women were older, and Nicaea was apparently childless, so she offered even less chance of producing an heir. Her supposed father-in-law's treatment of her suggests the contempt with which he regarded her. She had no dynastic standing and mattered only because of the fortress and troops she so briefly controlled.

38. See Hammond 1967: 591–94 on the dynasty's end.

39. *IG* II 1299 (*SIG* 485) and *IG* II 790, 11, 16–17.

40. *ID* 407.20; 443B.137; 444B.57; 461B.46. Since these are later inventories, it is not possible to determine the date of Phthia's offering.

41. Rather than assume, as Dow and Edson (1937: 148–49) do, that the reference to multiple children by Demetrius and Phthia is conventional and implies nothing about their literal existence, I am inclined to take the reference seriously but note that royal daughters, even as adults, are often unknown and unnamed and that even male children who died very young are unlikely to be known to us. Phthia may have had several children by this date, none of them Philip V and none of them known to us.

42. Justin (28.1.1–2) associates the death of Phthia's father, Alexander of Epirus, and Phthia's marriage, but the date of his death is unknown: see Walbank 1988: 322–23.

43. Le Bohec (1981: 36–39) questions the reliability of these sources. All the sources are very late and the Syncellus passage may be derived from the Eusebius passage. Eusebius does conflate Demetrius II and Demetrius the Fair and has some other difficulties. Nonetheless, we have three ancient sources naming Chryseis as the mother of Philip V and none that name Phthia.

44. Tarn (1940: 492) rightly dismisses the arguments of Dow and Edson (1937: 155) that she was merely a mistress and not a wife. Although I believe that her son might still have taken the throne, in the absence of any other living son of Demetrius II, even if she were only a mistress (contra Le Bohec 1981: 43), there would have been no reason for Doson to marry her had she not been both Philip's mother and Demetrius' wife. Plutarch (*Aem.* 8.2) attributes to leading Macedonians the decision to call in Doson, marry him to Philip V's mother, and make him regent and then king. See chap. 1 for other marriages of kings to royal widows and reference to medieval examples. Dow and Edson (1937: 153–55) do bring forward evidence suggesting that those with the given name of Chryseis were often of humble social status (hardly enough to be decisive), but since they also suggest that Demetrius gave her the name because she was a captive, her name cannot be said to indicate her status at birth except—if they are right—to recall the fact that she had been a captive.

45. Le Bohec (1981: 42–46; 1993: 143–49) argues for a third possibility, one I do not consider very likely. She believes that Phthia was the mother of Philip V and that Doson married her on the death of Demetrius II but that she died or was repudiated soon thereafter and that he then married Chryseis. While her doubts about the late sources that name Chryseis as Philip's mother are not without basis (see above), her arguments ignore all the positive ancient evidence and seem to depend on her presumption that Demetrius II had to be monogamous and that if his mother were not married to his father he could not inherit. See below.

46. Tarn 1940: 483–501, followed by Walbank 1940: 94; 1988: 238. Errington (1990: 174) rejects the idea. For others who have followed Tarn and for a lucid

exposition of the problem and the history of the argument, See Le Bohec 1981: 34–46.

47. One could use the argument of Dow and Edson (1937: 155 n. 1), to conclude that Eusebius' diction (he says that Demetrius married one of the captives and called her [*proseipon*] Chryseis) signifies that he had changed her name.

48. Le Bohec 1981: 37.

49. Philip V may have had a daughter other than one probably called Apamea (see below APAMEA 2). Polyb. 15.25.13 and Livy 32.38.1–3 imply the existence of daughters, not all of whom could be Apamea. See Seibert 1967: 40–42.

50. On the struggle between the two sons of Philip V and the king's role in it, see discussion and references in Gruen 1974: 221–46 and Edson 1935: 191–202.

51. Beloch 1927: 4:2, 139–40. His suggestions have been accepted by Macurdy 1932a: 72; Seibert 1967: 39; Hammond 1988b: 490; Errington 1990: 72–73; Le Bohec 1993b: 232.

52. See Gruen 1974: 221–46 for discussion and references on the problem of source hostility to Philip V and Perseus, much of it shaped by the struggle between Perseus and his half brother, Demetrius, for the succession.

53. Hammond 1988b: 474.

54. So Ziegler 1952: 1726.

55. Beloch 1927: 4:140 points to Perseus as an Argive hero and therefore to the name as appropriate for the son of an Argive woman. It seems peculiar that the older son (Livy 40.6.4) was not given the name of the paternal grandfather and the younger one was, but this could be explained by the existence of an earlier son named Demetrius dead in childhood, or perhaps by the higher status, because she was Macedonian, attached to the mother of Demetrius.

56. The mothers of Macedonian kings tended to be either foreign royalty or Macedonian nobility. Perseus' mother, it would seem, was neither. Seibert (1967: 39) remarks on Philip V's lack of interest in using marriage alliances for political purposes. The relatively modest yet foreign status of Perseus' mother apparently made his claim to the succession harder to argue.

57. Beloch (1927: 4:140) notes that whoever Philip's second wife was, she could not have been a member of any royal dynasty or we would have mention of it. He suggests that she was probably of a noble Macedonian family, or perhaps Thessalian as Chryseis is sometimes supposed to have been, and that to the Macedonians, her son Demetrius would have seemed better born than Perseus, the son of an Argive woman. Seibert (1967: 39–40) comments on Philip's failure to make political use of dynastic marriage and argues that Philip even failed to make use of two alliances offered him by foreign rulers.

58. Livy (40.5.11) reports the offer of the sister of a member of a Bastarnian embassy for marriage to a son of Philip. Walbank (1940: 246) believes that the son was Perseus and that marriage took place (partly because Livy [52.5.3] says that Perseus was married when he took the throne) but that his wife soon

after died or was put away. Seibert (1967: 42) is less certain that it happened. If she existed, she could have been the wife whom anecdote (Livy 42.5.4) says he murdered. Hammond (1988b: 493) accepts the historicity of the Bastarnian wife but discounts the murder story as propaganda. More implausibly, Hammond (1988b: 493 n. 2) takes App. *Mac.* 11.2 to refer to yet another wife of Perseus, but the Appian passage seems to refer to the marriage of Perseus's sister as well as his own marriage, not to a second marriage of Perseus. Perseus may have been polygamous, but this is not good evidence. However, nothing suggests that the Bastarnian wife died.

59. Seibert 1967: 44.

60. See Hammond 1988b: 558 n. 1 for references to other versions of the capture of Perseus and for discussion.

61. On the basis of Livy 40.5.10, Walbank (1940: 246) suggests that Perseus married a Bastarnian princess. Hammond (1988b: 493) accepts this view and dates the wedding to 182.

62. The second marriage alliance seems to be that arranged between Perseus' sister (possibly called Apamea—see APAMEA 2) and Prusias, king of Bithynia. Hammond (1988b: 493 n. 2), however, takes this to be a reference to yet another marriage of Perseus.

63. Adams 1982: 246, 251.

64. Green 1990: 426.

65. Seibert 1967: 44.

66. Dittenberger, the original editor of the inscription, suggested that the occasion that inspired it was the arrival of Laodice on Delos on her way to her wedding, but Durrbach, a later editor, doubts this. See discussion in Le Bohec 1993b: 241.

67. See Hammond 1988b: 558 n. 1 for references to other, lengthier versions of Perseus' capture.

68. Macurdy 1932a: 75; Staehelin 1924a: 708.

69. See Wilhelm 1908: 79–81.

70. While the new epigraphic material on Antigonus Gonatas' wife Phila is significant (see n. 3 and below), it is insufficient to contradict this obvious conclusion.

71. Macurdy 1932a: 75–76.

72. Macurdy 1932a: 76.

73. Macurdy (1932a: 7) also attributes the unimportance of Antigonid royal women to the fact that they lacked, "eponymous priestesses and all the pomp and paraphernalia that went with deification and state worship." Yet Argead women also lacked such things but did not suffer from the universal political obscurity of Antigonid women. It is more likely the situation of royal women in particular and the dynasty in general that led to the absence of royal cults for either men or women in Macedonia, rather than that the absence of cults made either unimportant.

74. See Carney 1995: 375–76, espec. nn. 21–23.

75. Stafford (1983: 134, 194) points to medieval connections between succes-

sion patterns and the role of royal women; she argues that uncertain succession patterns, like that of the Argeads, tended to empower women, however accidentally, whereas more certain ones tended to exclude women from succession politics.

76. See chap. 1 on the appropriateness of medieval parallels between Macedonian and early medieval monarchy in general and particularly between the roles of women in each monarchy. Facinger (1968: 4), followed by Bornstein (1983: 76), suggests that the lack of distinction between public and private in medieval monarchy empowered royal women.

77. Facinger (1968: 39) argues that as power and definition of medieval monarchy grew, it focused more on the person of the king and that the power of queens declined. So also Bornstein 1983: 76. Stafford (1983: 195) suggests that Facinger's view oversimplifies by neglecting the continuing importance of personal politics.

78. Seibert (1967: 45) notes the absence of dynastic politics from Antigonid policy and particularly the absence of connection to the Ptolemies.

CHAPTER 8

1. The best general discussion of royal women in this period is Pomeroy 1984: 3–40, but it focuses on Ptolemaic women. Le Bohec 1993b: 229–45 is limited by the lack of interest in change over time. Macurdy 1932a does not deal with institutional change.

2. On the general political situation in this period, see discussion and references in Carney 1992a: 169–89.

3. So Hatzopoulos (1982a: 38–42), who suggests that some of Philip's earlier weddings were in conjunction with this same festival. Mortensen (1997: 31–35) argues that Philip's marriage to Olympias was celebrated on this same occasion and that her name was changed to commemorate the festival that coincided with her wedding (see chap. 1 on name changes for royal women). Whether or not these surmises are correct, no evidence suggests that any of these wedding celebrations became the spectacle Cleopatra's did.

4. Connor (1987: 40–50) deals primarily with the Archaic period, but he does refer to Demetrius Poliorcetes' ceremonial entry into Athens (44 n. 22). Connor's views are based on scholarship on the role of ritual and ceremony in civic life in medieval and Renaissance times (see 40 n. 2 for references).

5. Price 1984b: 27–30; see below for discussion of the development of cults for royal women.

6. Connor 1987: 41. Among other examples of this phenomenon, he refers to the tyrannicides Harmodius and Aristogeiton, who did their deed during the Panathenaic festival.

7. Clearly wedding festivals were not the only festivals used by Hellenistic rulers to connect themselves to the citizen bodies. Philip's festival for Cleopatra's marriage seems to be the first such festival, however.

8. Arr. 7.4.1–8; Diod. 17.107.6; Just. 12.10.9–10; Plut. *Alex.* 70.3; Chares ap. Ath. 538a. Alexander himself made an Achaemenid marriage, and many prominent members of his court married Persian women. See Bosworth 1988: 156–58.

9. He played a formative role in the creation of Hellenistic monarchy; Scott 1928: 137; PHILA 2; STRATONICE 2.

10. Cohen (1974: 177–79) suggested that the defeat of Antigonus at Ipsus in 301 signaled genuine recognition of mutual sovereignty by the Successors, not the assumption of royal titles ca. 306.

11. Even the Ptolemies put on wedding displays, despite the domestic nature of their sibling marriages; Vatin 1970: 78–80.

12. Vatin 1970: 58.

13. See Carney 1988a: 13–42 for a lengthier discussion of cities named after royal women, but new material and arguments are included in what follows.

14. Malkin 1985: 114–30; contra Griffith (1979: 360), who argued that earlier prototypes existed but conceded that Philip may have been unaware of them. See also Fredricksmeyer (1990: 306–7) and Badian (1996: 13 n. 11), who believes that Philippi was not named after him until long after 356 and thus concludes that Philippopolis ca. 340 is the earliest certain precedent.

15. Lyons (1997: 30–32) discusses a number of eponymous heroines, most clearly mythical. Messene, founded in 369 by Epaminondas, had an eponymous heroine, with a cult. She was not royal but was probably historical. Messene, however, was commemorated because of an act of her own (the foundation of a cult), whereas Thessalonice was commemorated because of who she was, not because of what she had done.

16. Leschhorn 1984: 252–53. It is difficult, however, to tie down the dates of many city foundings; see Carney 1988a: 134 n. 3.

17. Carney 1988a: 136–68; contra Mikrogiannakes 1973: 228.

18. See Carney 1988a: 138 n. 22.

19. Carney 1988a: 134–35. The 290s saw its rapid spread.

20. Le Bohec 1993b: 239; Papazoglou 1988: 115–16; PHILA 3. See Cohen 1995: 100–101 for the possibility that Stratonicea in the Chalcidice was founded by Antigonus Gonatas, commemorating his sister Stratonice.

21. See Malkin 1985: 119 for further discussion.

22. Lyons (1997: 32), although noting that Messene was a cult founder, not a city founder, argues that she was given "at least a symbolic role in the refoundation of Messenian polity."

23. See Carney 1988a: 136–67.

24. Cohen 1978: 11.

25. A dedication dated to the mid-third century calls Alexander *theos* (a god; Rizakes and Touratsoglou 1985: 137–38, no. 148); an inscription from Thessaloniki from the second or third century refers to a priest of Alexander (*IG* X 2, 1 278); and an inscription from Thessaloniki may also refer to Alexander as *theos* (*IG* X 2, 1 933), but see editor's comments).

26. Stewart (1993: 278, 420) states that, in addition to the Alexander cult, Thessaloniki also had cults to Philip II and Thessalonice. In support of these as-

sertions he cites but does not discuss *IG* X 2, 1 275, 276, 277 (see discussion below) as well as the inscriptions already referred to (n. 25). None of his evidence confirms the existence of cults in Roman Thessaloniki for anyone other than Alexander. Rizakes and Touratsoglou (1985: 137–38) argued that the images on *stele* no. 148 (a young man with *thorax*, spear, and sword; a bearded man with a scepter and *phiale*; a woman with a scepter and *phiale*; and a smaller female figure) correspond to Alexander, Philip, and Olympias (they offer no explanation for the fourth, small female figure) and spoke of a cult of Alexander and Olympias. Even if their identifications are correct, they do not confirm cults for other Argeads. Gagé (1975: 8–10) cites some possible evidence for Olympias' popularity in Roman Macedonia, but none of it confirms a cult for her.

27. On the other hand, the inclusion of a statue of the otherwise obscure Thessalonice in a set of royal statues in a late Roman house in Thessaloniki could signify that her eponymous role made her more important in the city named after her than she might otherwise have been. Vickers (1972: 166 n. 71) mentions a female statue that he believes could represent either Thessalonice or merely Tyche.

28. Gagé (1975: 1) denies that Macedonian interest in Argeads in Roman times had anything other than a Roman origin, but Stewart 1993: 278 rightly questions such a presumption.

29. Cerfaux and Tondriau 1957: 194–201; Tondriau 1948: 12–33; 1948b: 1–15; 1948c: 1–15; 1956 15–22. Pomeroy 1984: 28–40 is the most useful discussion, but her focus is on the Ptolemies and so earlier precedents are not generally discussed. See now Míron Pérez 1998a: 23–46 and 1998b: 215–35. These publications, kindly sent me by their author, arrived too late to make full discussion of their arguments possible.

30. Contra Price 1984a: 79–95; 1984b: xi, 7–38, whose views are currently more dominant. See also Burkert 1981:205 ("The wall which separates them is impermeable . . ." Among scholars of Macedonian historian, Badian has most adamantly insisted that a strong line was drawn between people and gods (see, most recently, Badian 1996: 14–15). Many scholars continue, however, to understand Greek religious views, even early on, to distinguish between divine and human, but not to see the boundary between them as impenetrable. Lane Fox 1974: 439 describes it as an "open frontier"; Vermeule 1979: 126–27, following Nock 1944: 141–73, points out that the supposedly impassable barrier was, during the archaic period, frequently crossed by those achieving or losing divine status. See also Lyons 1997: 5–6. Among Macedonian historians, Fredricksmeyer (see below) takes a similar view. It seems clear that many Greeks, over centuries, saw distinctions in status and recognized them in cult practice, but much less clear that these status distinctions were immutable.

31. See discussion and references in Lyons 1997: 5–6.

32. Price 1984b: 27–30.

33. Contra Badian 1981: 27–71; see Flower 1988: 124–34.

34. See Borza 1990: 249–50 for a succinct discussion of the problem. In recent years, Fredricksmeyer (1979) has been the main proponent of the idea that Philip planned for divine honors and even dynastic cult, and Badian (1981)

has argued that no good evidence demonstrates lifetime cult for Philip and that even cults for Alexander were established only late in his reign (see references in Borza, as well as Badian 1996). As Borza (1990: 250) observes, whatever the date of certain cults, Philip and Alexander were clearly changing the nature of Macedonian monarchy in a manner that involved association with divinity.

35. The major general works: Habicht 1970; Cerfaux and Tondriau 1957; Taeger 1957.

36. Price 1984a: 79–95; 1984b: xi, 7–38.

37. Hammond 1994: 184 suggested that Eurydice, mother of Philip, received posthumous cult. His evidence is not convincing: a splendid tomb that may or may not be hers (see chapter 9) and his own theory that the female statue found near two of the statue bases at Vergina she dedicated to Eucleia was actually one of Eurydice herself.

38. For recent discussion and references, see Miller 1973: 189–218; Fredricksmeyer 1979: 52–56; Badian 1981: 71; Carney 1995: 380–81; Míron Pérez 1999b:216–24. See also Gardner 1925: 128–36; Wiesner 1939: 105–107; Schleif 1944: 3–23; Schleif 1944: 3–24; Zschietzschmann 1944: 24–52; Drees 1968: 121–23; Mallwitz 1972: 128–33.

39. Gardner 1925: 136.

40. Pausanias 5.20.10 has usually been understood to mean that the building was constructed by Philip, but Badian 1981: 71 is not certain. If the building had been built for rather than by Philip, one would expect Pausanias to name the donor.

41. Paus. 5.17.4 refers to her as the daughter or wife of Arrhidaeus, whereas Philip's mother was the daughter of Sirras and the wife of Amyntas. (Paus. 5.20.10 simply calls her Eurydice.) It is usually assumed that this was simply a textual error.

42. See Drees 1968: 113; Gardner 1925: 213.

43. Zschietzschmann (1944: 52) suggests that Alexander may have been in the middle. He notes (51 n. 1) that the remaining stones of the statue base suggest that the central figure held either a scepter or a lance and, convinced that the women would have been placed next to their respective husbands, concludes that Alexander rather than Philip must have been in the middle. I consider his argument unpersuasive: it would be odd to call the building the Philippeum and place Alexander in the focal point.

44. Miller 1973: 191.

45. Fredricksmeyer (1979: 53–55) rightly rejects the view that the presence of the image of Olympias signifies that the structure cannot have been completed in the last years of Philip's reign. Such a view depends on false assumptions about the nature of Macedonian royal marriage in general and the incorrect belief that Philip divorced Olympias when he married Olympias; see further Ellis 1976: 211–12; Carney 1992a; chap. 3.

46. See Borza 1990: 250 for a similar analysis of the function of the

Philippeum but one that emphasizes its implications about the nature of Macedonian monarchy in general rather than the importance of the inclusion of women or its dynastic implications.

47. See chap. 1; Carney 1995: 367–91.

48. Richter 1965: 1: 3–5; Breckenridge 1968: 81–142; Havelock 1971: 19–20; Pollitt 1986: 59–65. See also Ridgway's study (1987: 399–409) of women and Greek art.

49. Smith 1988: 48. Lyons (1997: 5–6), noting that some deny that Greeks distinguished between heroines and goddesses (a denial she rejects), does point out that more heroines than heroes were deified. I wonder if the difficulty in distinguishing female human and female divine in terms of image does not mirror this situation, perhaps reflecting a sense that this was a more permeable barrier. Similarly, as we shall see, more women than men seem to have been assimilated to divinities, mainly Aphrodite.

50. Pollitt (1986: 59) defines a portrait as the "intentional representation of a person containing a sufficient number of specific features to make the representation recognizable to others."

51. Breckenridge 1968: 100; Ridgway 1987: 405.

52. See discussion and references in Roccos 1995: 645, esp. n. 37.

53. On Phryne, see Raubitschek 1941: 893–207; Havelock 1995: 42–47. On her statue, see Ridgway 1987: 91, esp. n. 43.

54. On Aphrodite's goldenness and its association with beauty, see Friedrich 1978: 77–78. See Scott 1931: 101–23 and Gordon 1979: 13 on the connection between the use of gold and silver in statuary and the Greek conception of divinity that was so often associated with brightness or gleamingness. Gordon suggests that the use of costly material for divine statues was a way around the somewhat limiting nature of the anthropomorphic images of the gods. See below on the association of the cult of *hetairai* with Aphrodite. See Havelock 1995: 3, 42, 133, on the difficulty ancients had distinguishing between Phryne, her statue, and Aphrodite. Elsewhere Phryne is considered a ministrant of Aphrodite (Ath. 590e–f).

55. Ridgway 1987: 405 n. 35. Earlier statues of women had appeared in tombs and sanctuaries, but, as Pollitt (1986: 59) remarks, the agora was a quasi-sacred area. Nonetheless, statues of women continued to be more common in sanctuaries than in agoras.

56. Ridgway 1987: 91–92 nn. 45, 46. See Van Bremen 1996: 180–86 on the gradual development, after the rise of the Hellenistic kings, of civic statues for female benefactors and for a discussion (12–13) of whether this development was modeled on the benefactions of royal women.

57. Le Bohec's (1993b: 238) conclusion that the female statues in the Philippeum represented "tradition . . . chez les Macédoniens" remains unsubstantiated, although possible.

58. Contra Hammond (1994:184), who thinks the statue found nearby might

be that of Eurydice. See Borza 1990: 192–93. See Saatsoglou-Paliadeli 1993: 1339–71 for the probability that a third Eurydice inscription (found near Vergina) that gives her name and patronymic but no dedication was inscribed on the base of a portrait statue. Saatsoglou-Paliadeli also suggests that the statue may have formed part of a dynastic group, indentical to that in the Philippeum, and that this group was once placed in the "heroön" associated with the Great Tumulus.

59. Ginouvès (1994: 38) thinks both male and female heads were chthonic deities. While the two male heads show some individual traits, the two female heads are very general and nearly identical.

60. Although Andronicos (1984: 129–31) considered at least some of the small heads portraits, including perhaps Olympias, even he stepped back from a certain identification of Alexander's mother, and Smith's (1988: 62–63) doubts that any of the heads are female, let alone portraits, are persuasive.

61. Le Bohec (1993b: 239) suggested that Antigonus Gonatas would have included statues of his ancestresses among those of his ancestors in his dynastic monument at Delos. The narrow public presentation of monarchy in Antigonid times (see chap. 7) would not necessitate their inclusion.

62. The discussion in this section has been influenced by the fundamental work of Gordon (1979: 5–34).

63. Clerc 1915; Gordon 1979: 7–10; Kassel 1983: 1–12; Freedberg 1989: 28–48; Flory 1994.

64. Gordon 1979: 8–10.

65. So Pollitt 1986: 19; Smith 1988: 15.

66. I can offer a personal example of the continuation of this phenomenon. My university recently erected a piece of statuary intended to commemorate those of its graduates who had died during World War II. For months after the monument was unveiled, small noncommercial bouquets of wildflowers were regularly placed at its base.

67. Cult statues were often, although not always, larger than life size. As Gordon (1979: 14) observes, size is not a trivial issue; larger-than-life-size statues indicated the "otherness," the nonhumanness of the gods. It is impossible to tell exactly how large the images in the Philippeum were. Zschietzschmann (1944: 51 n. 1) supposes that the statues in the Philippeion were not larger than life size, apparently because of the comparatively modest size of the statue base (each of the separate supporting bases is roughly 0.8 m across), substantial parts of which survive. Whereas Gardner (1925: 133) lists the height of the base as 1.92 meters, a height that would certainly have forced the viewer to look upward at a sharp angle and hardly implies that the statues it supported were small, Schleif (1944: 21, esp. pl. 17) seems to suggest a height of about 0.914 meter. Even this lower height, granted the comparatively small size of the building, would force the viewer to look sharply upward and could surely have supported life-size or nearly life-size figures.

68. Gordon 1979: 14.

69. Nock 1930: 53–54. Nock cites an example from Egypt of an *eikon* receiving cult. Smith (1988: 15 f.) notes that our understanding of this distinction depends on inscription. *Agalma* continued to apply only to cult statues, but *eikon* could be used to refer to either cult or honorific statues.

70. Because of the absence of evidence for Macedonia proper and because of the scarcity of identified images of royal women from anywhere in the Hellenistic world (Smith 1988: 43–48), I shall not attempt to trace the development of this custom further. Images of royal males on Macedonian coins were a rarity, and none survive of royal women, but in Ptolemaic Egypt royal women appeared on coins as early as 309: Kahrstedt 1910: 261–314; Koch 1923: 67–106.

71. Macurdy 1932a: 34; Hammond (1980: 473–76) accepted the truth of Curtius statements but not on plausible grounds. Curtius' assertion could, nonetheless, be correct.

72. Jaschinski (1981: 23) argues that Harpalus' treatment of the courtesans, including cults, would have been read as treason, particularly because he had these women treated like queens. The implication seems to be that he was using these notorious hetairai as part of his public image as counterking at Babylon.

73. The dating depends on Athenaeus' reference to a satyr play called the *Agen*, performed at Alexander's court sometime between 326 and summer 324. On the dating, see discussion and references in Flower 1997: 260 n. 19.

74. Pausanius (1.37.5) also speaks of an especially large and beautiful tomb of Pythionice in Attica. Flower (1997: 269) suggests that the tomb was also the temple. Lane Fox (1973: 439, 545; 1986: 118), followed by Flower (1997: 258–62), believes that this passage offers proof that Alexander received lifetime divine honors since they translate Ath. 595c as referring to insults directed at honors Alexander has received (see Flower 1997: 259 n. 16). Since Pythionice had cult honors, they conclude that these are the honors referred to.

75. Flower (1997: 261) argues that this passage means that Olympias and Roxane could appropriately receive both *proskynesis* and the title *basilissa*, Roxane as wife of the king of Asia and Olympias as the mother of a god. I am not convinced by this argument, particularly because of Alexander's previous failed attempt to impose the performance of *proskynesis* on his Greek and Macedonian courtiers and evidence that Olympias did not use a title (see Carney 1991b: 158). I have no doubt that the anecdote dates to the period of Harpalus, but that does not make it true. He was a controversial figure: see Carney 1991b: 167 n. 27.

76. The suggestion of Flower (1997: 260) that the Athenians may have had a civic cult for her and that this cult may have been a model for those Athenian cults to Demetrius Poliorcetes' courtesans as Lamia or Leaenea Aphrodite is implausible. The change in mind-set and cult practice in Greek cities after the death of Alexander was dramatic. Moreover, Harpalus's role was hardly parallel to that of Demetrius in Athens.

77. Cerfaux and Tondriau 1957: 173–84; Habicht 1970: 44–48; Scott 1928:

137–66, 217–39; Ferguson 1911: 107–43. The first attested cult directed to any of Alexander's Successors, the city cult for Antigonus and Demetrius at Scepsis, dates to 311 (*OGIS* 6).

78. The date of Phila's cult is somewhat less certain than that of her husband and father-in-law, but the information cited in Athenaeus implies a period between 307 and 305: the toast associates her identification with the cult of the *theoi soteres* and thus to the period between Demetrius' salvation of Athens and his departure for his victorious campaign against Ptolemy. The Alexis quotation also suggests a date no later than 305. It is usually assumed that the temple and *agalma* date to the same period. Scott 1928: 152–53; Ferguson 1911: 114 n. 7; Cerfaux and Tondriau 1957: 176; Green 1990: 49.

79. Fraser (1972: 1:246) says that it is likely that the Ptolemaic assimilations created a more genuine feeling of the effective divinity of queens and ruling houses than direct worship of individuals did. See below on why *hetairai* as well as royal wives were included in cult worship and why both kinds of women were associated with Aphrodite.

80. There were cults for Lysimachus at Priene, Samothrace, and Cassandreia, all set up in the 280s: see Walbank, *CAH* VII.i.92, n. 105. See Míron Pérez 1998b: 229–30 for a discussion of a festival in honor of Ptolemy Ceraunus' mother, Eurydice, briefly celebrated in Cassandreia because she had somehow restored the freedom of the city (Polyaen. 6.7.2). This Eurydice was the sister of Cassander, the city's founder, and she controlled the city for a short time. The festival, if historical, does not demonstrate the existence of a cult, but Míron Pérez rightly points out that later city cults were often motivated by appreciation for similar benefactions.

81. See Fraser 1972: 2:367–68, 373.

82. See Gutzwiller 1992: 363–65, esp. n. 20, on the evidence for Berenice I's lifetime identification with Aphrodite. The evidence includes an epigram stressing the resemblance between Berenice (it is not clear that the Berenice referred to is Berenice I, but likely: see Cameron 1990: 294–95) and Aphrodite (*Anth. Pal.* 12.77), as well as Theoc. *Id.* 17.51–52, which says that Aphrodite saved Berenice from the afterworld and placed her in the same temple with the goddess. Gutzwiller (1992: 365 n. 20) concedes that Arsinoe II may have "projected" her own connection to Aphrodite back to her mother. See discussions in Tondriau 1948a: 2–3; Tondrian 1948b: 14; Fraser 1972: 1:197.

83. Gryzbek (1990: 103–12) now dates the death of Arsinoe Philadelphus to 268 instead of the date previously generally accepted, 270. If his date is accepted (Gutzwiller 1992: 365), then her individual cult as Arsinoe Philadelphus would also have been established in her lifetime. Arsinoe's cult in association with Aphrodite at Zephyrium (see below) may also have begun in her lifetime; so Neumer-Pfau 1982: 57; Gutzwiller 1992: 365.

84. Callicrates erected a shrine to her as Arsinoe–Aphrodite Zephyritis. Arsinoe patronized the Adonia (Theoc. *Id.* 15.22–24; Fraser 1972: 197, 239–40; Pomeroy 1984: 30). Fraser suggests that Arsinoe herself was responsible for the

popularity of Aphrodite. Later Ptolemaic royal women were associated with Aphrodite.

85. Whereas Aphrodite and Isis were closely identified in the Hellenistic world (Fraser 1972: 198), in Ptolemaic times Aphrodite was sometimes identified with Hathor (Fraser 1972: 197), and, as early as Herodotus, Isis was sometimes associated with Demeter (Fraser 1972: 259). Moreover, in later periods Isis and Hathor were often merged (Heyob 1975: 43). Granted that from early in the pharaonic period Egyptian queens were often shown with the attributes of various female deities (Robins 1993: 23–25) and that the goddesses Hathor and Isis were closely associated (see further Quirke 1992; Shafer 1991), the Ptolemaic association of Isis and Aphrodite with cults for various royal women may have developed not so much from the identification of the two goddesses as from the Ptolemaic need to serve two monarchic traditions: the pharaonic, which associated royal women with Isis (as well as many other Egyptian deities), and the much more recent Macedonian tradition, which connected royal women and Aphrodite.

86. Fraser 1972: 1:240 and n. 401.

87. Fraser 1972: 1:245. He can find no instance after the third century.

88. Fraser (1972: 1:236) makes this point about the Ptolemies, but it would appear to be more generally true.

89. Préaux 1978: 252.

90. Havelock (1995: 128) suggests that those who identified themselves with deities claimed kinship with them and thus claimed their power but did not claim to be reincarnations of deities as occurred in late Hellenistic times. She points out that Arsinoe, for instance, was not represented as Aphrodite, so far as we know. Fraser (1972: 1:245) remarks that it is difficult to speak with certainty as we know about assimilation only from documents that refer to but do not explain it. He adds that such identifications must have carried with them absorption of attributes and concludes that it is a form of syncretism.

91. The passages cited all refer to the goddess's name and the individual's in the same case, whereas the inscription from Eresus (*GHI* 191.5–6) uses a phrase that one might translate as either "altars of Zeus to Philip" or "altars to Philip of Zeus." Badian (1996: 13) insists that this is a cult of "Philip's Zeus"— Zeus as Philip's protector—not Philip as Zeus, and castigates Bosworth (1988: 281) for his views, but Bosworth seems closer to the messy ambiguity of the phrasing of the inscription when he says, "The precise meaning of this act cannot be recovered, but it seems certain that Philip was deeply associated in the cult of Zeus, and the sacrifices made to Zeus were also in a sense offered to Philip."

92. Nock (1928: 21–42) recognizes the ambiguity of this aspect of the ruler cult. Smith (1988: 44) warns against limiting the meaning and therefore the ambiguity of constructs like "Phila Aphrodite."

93. Tondriau (1948b: 40, 44) mentions both non-Ptolemaic and Ptolemaic

examples, but his analysis can scarcely be termed "rigorous" as he simply assumes that the natural choice of the goddess for royal women to be assimilated to was Aphrodite. Fraser (1972: 236–59) refers only to the Ptolemies, although some of his suggestions have implications for non-Ptolemaic cults. Pomeroy (1984: 30) states that "no binding precedents" existed for royal women as did (the cult of Alexander) for royal men. While I would agree that the cults to Phila and Demetrius' *hetairai* in association with Aphrodite can hardly be considered as precedent setting as Alexander's was for the male Ptolemies, Pomeroy's subsequent discussion of the development of various kinds of female cults under Arsinoe II leaves the impression, possibly unintentionally, that were no earlier precedents at all. Míron Pérez (1998b: 230–35) argues that Aphrodite was chosen as the goddess for assimilation because she epitomized the erotic power of women over men; Míron Pérez also stresses the role of beauty in female deification.

94. Pomeroy (1984: 30–38) provides a useful general discussion of the choice of Aphrodite; she refers to the Cypriote connection (as does Fraser 1972: 197) to Aphrodite as patroness of the sea and her past role in cults as a marriage goddess. The last explanation will prove the one most relevant to non-Ptolemaic assimilations to Aphrodite.

95. Gutzwiller (1992: 363–68), while following Pomeroy (see above), emphasizes the sexual aspect of the equation, the "power of erotic persuasion over the king" also shown by deification of the king's *hetairai*. She suggests that the emphasis on shared affection in marriage and its promotion through assimilation to Aphrodite may have been politically helpful for Berenice I and her daughter because the marriage of each was in some degree controversial. Griffiths (1981: 247–73) argues that Arsinoe II used her sponsorship of Aphrodite to create acceptance of her own power as well as to maintain the social status quo. See also Havelock 1995: 127.

96. Tondriau (1948b: 12–13) speaks of flattery, particularly of a woman's real or supposed beauty, taken as a token of her divinization. But as Tondriau (1956: 20–21) concedes, beauty is more prominent in literary references to deification than in cults. See, however, a passage in Athenaeus (13.566a–e) that generally associates female and male beauty with power, divinity, and monarchy. Athenaeus (566c) actually says, "beauty is related to royalty."

97. Neumer-Pfau 1982: 55–60. The thesis lacks a strong evidentiary basis, partly because it is so broad as to be unprovable. The idea that the model for queens derived from a general societal model (the reverse, in a sense, of Pomeroy's [1984: 40] view that queens provided the societal model) is problematized by the difficulty of relating the role of royal women to that of ordinary women.

98. Fraser 1972: 245–46.

99. Tondriau (1948a: 40) observes that Aphrodite was "naturally" chosen as a model for assimilation and that this "goddess of womanly beauty and power" (44) was naturally the best choice. See also Taeger 1957–60 1:260.

100. There is no general study of either the cult of Aphrodite or that of Hera. For Hera, see Farnell 1971: 1:179–223; Pomeroy 1975: 7–8; Burkert 1985: 131–35; O'Brien 1993. For Aphrodite, see Farnell 1971: 2:618–677; Pomeroy 1975: 6–7; Friedrich 1978; Burkert 1985: 152–56; Pirenne-Delforgé 1994. Friedrich and O'Brien concentrate on the archaic period and myth, not cult. Pirenne-Delforge deals only with the classical and Hellenistic periods.

101. Their number is modest by comparison to the many assimilations to Aphrodite. Theocritus (*Id.* 17.126–34) compares the marriage of Zeus and Hera to the marriage of Ptolemy Philadelphus and his sister, thereby justifying it. Arsinoe took Hera's cult names of *basileia* and *teleia* (Fraser 1972: 237–38). Apollonis, wife of Attalus I, was sunnaos with Hera Basileia at Pergamum (Préaux 1978: 254). Cults to Hera were generally less widespread than those to Aphrodite; (Farnell 1971: 179, 618; Fraser 1972:194–95; Parke 1977; Simon 1983).

102. On the tendency to associate Demetrius with Dionysus, see Cerfaux and Tondriau (1957: 180), who suggest that the same tendency may be true of his father. Scott (1928: 222–35) suggests that the Dionysus/Aphrodite equation relating to Demetrius and various of the women associated with him may have been the prototype for the Ptolemies. On associating male rulers with Dionysus and royal women with Aphrodite, see Tondriau 1948c: 35; Smith 1988: 37–38.

103. See Neumer-Pfau 1982; 56 n. 289.

104. On Aphrodite as a marine goddess, see Farnell 1971: 636–41; Pirenne-Delforgé 1994: 433–39. Pirenne-Delforgé contrasts her power to soothe or quiet the seas with Poseidon's, which often disturbed them. She had numerous cults on the seashore and in harbors. On the Arsinoe cult at Zephyrium, see Fraser 1972: 1:245. It is more difficult to connect *hetairai* to naval power. Granted Demetrius' role as a naval leader, it is possible that Phila's identification with Aphrodite relates to that aspect of the goddess's cult; Ath. 253c says that the Athenians hymned that Demetrius was born of Poseidon and the Aphrodite. Again, it is more difficult to associate this aspect of the Aphrodite cult with royal *hetairai*.

105. A story told about Phryne's trial at Athens (Ath. 590e–f) suggests that this sense of the powers of Aphrodite continued to be understood as frightening in some ways (the story may well be a fiction, but it is the fact that it was told that signifies): when it looked as though she might lose, her defender Hypereides laid bare her bosom as he finished his emotional speech. According to the story, this made the jurors experience fear of the gods for this servant and interpreter of Aphrodite and so they spared her.

106. Vatin 1970: 42–43, 54.

107. For instance, the sisters Ino and Semele. See Lyons 1997: 6.

108. Pomeroy (1984: 30), pointing to Arsinoe's known sponsorship of the festival of Aphrodite and Adonis (Theoc. *Id.* 15.22–24), says, "She herself influenced the direction of her own dynastic cult"; see also Tondriau 1948a: 28 n. 31. Fraser (1972: 197) suggests that Arsinoe's mother may have preceded her as a patron

of Aphrodite; Gutzwiller (1992: 363–65) agrees and believes that if Berenice herself did not initiate the identification with Aphrodite, then her daughter did (see above).

109. Hawley (1993: 76) points to the great difference between the conventionally silent respectable women of Athens whose names were not even mentioned in public (see Schaps 1977: 323–30) and *hetairai* so notorious as to be the subject of many anecdotes in which their names are clearly assumed to be well known. The irony is that royal women also were named (often, like courtesans, without reference to the names of husbands or fathers) and were recognizable in public (see chap. 1 and OLYMPIAS PART 1) and might even be the subject of anecdotes very similar to those told about courtesans (e.g., Olympias; see Ath. 609c).

110. Pomeroy 1984: 54.

111. A possibility suggested by Pomeroy (1984: 54), although not necessarily endorsed by her.

112. See Henry 1992: 250–68; Hawley 1993: 73–91, who warns that the image of the *hetaira* is a "constructed fiction" (75). Davidson (1997: 134) notes that scholars have had a hard time determining where *hetairai* fit in Greek society, partly because of the kind of ambiguous treatment they receive in many sources.

113. See Carney 1991b: 154–72 for more information on the development of a female title. Some material in this section is not developed in Carney's article.

114. For Eurydice, mother of Philip II, see Oikonomedes 1983: 62–64; Robert and Robert 1984: 450–51. For Olympias: *SIG* 252N. 5–7; *SEG* IX 2; a tomb inscription, originally dated later (Edson 1949: 84) but now plausibly argued to date to the period immediately after Olympias' death (Oikonomedes 1982: 9–16). She is referred to in the same manner in contemporary speeches (Hyp. *Eux.* 19, 20, 24, 25). In a dedication to Athena almost certainly made in 319 or 318 (see Harris 1995: 140, 179, 234–35 for discussion and references) Roxane, the widow of Alexander, uses no title and still refers to herself only as the wife of King Alexander.

115. On the general absence of the male title, see Errington 1974: 20; Aymard 1948: 232–63; and Aymard 1950: 61–97. Hammond (1988a: 382–84, 390) has argued that two inscriptions (see his references, 382) show Alexander using the title *basileus* before his departure for Asia. Badian (1996: 12) continues to maintain that there is no good evidence that Alexander used a title before early 331.

116. Gruen 1985: 253–71.

117. Dated by the editor to shortly after 306, probably to the period of the siege of Rhodes (305/4). The document is a Samian decree honoring a certain Demarchus, said to be a guard in *basilissa* Phila's entourage. Robert (1946: 17 nn. 1–2) confirms the date and suggests that an Ephesian decree (*Ephesus* 2003) honoring a certain Melesippus, also said to be part of the entourage of *basilissa* Phila

and originally dated to 300/299, may in fact date to the same period as the Samian decree. Wehrli (1964: 140–43) accepts both dates.

118. For Apamea: *Didyma* 480. See Holleaux 1923: 5 n. 4. For Berenice (perhaps Berenice II), coins from Cyrene: see Koch 1923: 74–79; Kahrstedt 1910: 262. See Ritter 1965: 116 nn. 1–2 for other early uses of *basilissa*.

119. The earliest inscription from Macedonia referring to a royal woman as *basilissa* is one from Cassandreia, dating to late in the reign of Antigonus Gonatas and referring to his wife Phila: see Hatzopoulos 1990: 135–55.

120. Practices involving the changing of royal women's names on marriage and the naming of daughters after the accomplishments of fathers die out about this time; Carney 1991b: 160.

121. *OGIS* 35 refers to *basilissa* Philotera, an unmarried daughter of Ptolemy I. Vatin 1970: 74 f.; Ritter 1965: 116. See also *OGIS* 56.l.47 ff.

122. Ritter (1965: 116) argues that both the Ptolemies and the Seleucids used *basilissa* for king's daughters. Tarn (1913: 351 n. 27) argues that *OGIS* 745 probably shows that Seleucid kings' daughters used it too (contra Bikerman 1938: 27) and probably the Epirote house as well. Tarn suggests that Stratonice's offerings may have set a fashion. See also Brosius (1996: 19), who seems to believe the practice was common to all the dynasties.

123. Phthia, daughter of the last Epirote king, appears as *basilissa* Phthia on Delphic inventories (*ID* 407, 20; 443b137; 44B57; 461Bv46) with only a patronymic, although she was the wife of Demetrius II. The inventories might or might not derive from the period before her marriage. Stratonice, daughter of Demetrius Poliorcetes, often appears in inscriptions with only a patronymic (sometimes with a matronymic as well). It is difficult to believe that all these inscriptions involving Stratonice date only from the brief periods of her maidenhood or widowhood (if one assumes widows did not employ *basilissa*; see below), and there is no reason to believe that shrines were reluctant to name either of her royal husbands (contra Macurdy 1932a: 81; Roux and Lehmann 1992: 233).

124. One of the inscriptions that name the woman and her father but not her husband (*OGIS* 14) had been dated to a period in which Stratonice was married (see references and discussion in Tarn 1913: 350–51, esp. n. 27), but the authenticity of *OGIS* 14 has since been seriously questioned: see Ferrario 1962: 78–82.

125. *OGIS* 15 refers to *basilissa* Arsinoe, *thugater* (daughter) of *basileus* Ptolemy, *gune* of *basileus* X. In *OGIS* 216, we have *basilissa* Phila, *thugater* of Seleucus (Nicator), and *gune* of Antigonus (Gonatas). *SIG* 639 speaks of *basilissa* Laodice, daughter of Seleucus, and *gune* of *basileus* Demetrius. Roux and Lehmann 1992: 233 claims that no *basilissa* referred to her filiation in a dedication once married unless she was a Lagid married to a Lagid and thus dates *OGIS* 15 to the period of Arsinoe's marriage to Ptolemy II. There are simply too few surviving inscriptions involving dedications by royal women to determine whether the point of Roux and Lehmann is significant; one does wonder, however, whether international shrines would have chosen a usage (*SIG* 639 or

OGIS 216) that was consistently different from the preference of the women themselves or somehow perceived to honor royal fathers at the expense of royal husbands, as Roux and Lehmann claimed such usage did.

126. Macurdy 1928: 276–82.

127. Carney 1991b: 156 nn. 11–13. Pomeroy (1994: 276–77, 303) suggests that Xenophon may have coined the word. Occasional use of earlier formations like *basileia* continued, although not as titles (see Brosius 1996: 20).

128. See below as to whether the title was limited to only one wife of a given *basileus*. The usage of *basilissa* as a title may also have changed over time. *Basilissa* began as a title of status or honor but came to be applied to women who had power as well, like later Ptolemaic women who co-ruled. Brosius (1996: 20) suggests that *basileia* be translated in the same way, since it can apply either to a king's wife or mother.

129. Le Bohec 1993: 232. See contra chap. 7 above. Frequently scholars simply assume that if a king takes another wife, his first must be dead or repudiated, even if there is little or no evidence for such an assumption. Vatin (1970: 74) specifically associates this assumption with Greek practice and ignores the polygamous Macedonian precedent.

130. Macurdy 1932a: 106; Pomeroy 1984: 13 (who notes that serial and simultaneous liaisons continued to occur, as did a blurring of the wife/concubine distinction [as we have seen with Aphrodite assimilations]); Green 1990: 119 n. 4.

131. Carney (1994a: 130–31) offers a brief version of the following section.

132. See Macurdy 1929: 273–78.

133. See Cleopatra 2; Lanassa; Arsinoe; Stratonice 2; Nicaea. Cratesipolis and Berenice II are also known to have arranged or attempted to arrange marriages for themselves. Cynnane and Olympias brokered marriages for their daughters.

134. On the factors leading to the reappearance of royal brother-sister marriage in Egypt, see Carney 1987c: 420–39.

135. Apamea apparently kept her title after her husband's marriage to Stratonice (Macurdy 1932a: 78), and Arsinoe I certainly retained her Egyptian titles (Macurdy 1932a: 110–11), which may well mean that she remained *basilissa*.

136. *IG* II 1299 = *SIG* 485; *IG* II 790.16–17. See Phthia.

137. The Athenians, for instance, must have felt comfortable with a reference to only one wife, even if one assumes, as is sometimes done, that the reference to children might include all Demetrius' children or descendants, not just those through Phthia.

138. Le Bohec 1993b: 238. The bones in two presumably royal female burials at Vergina were wrapped in purple fabric, as were the male royal burials in Tomb II's main chamber and Tomb III at Vergina (see chap. 9).

139. Ritter (1965: 117 n. 3) questioned the historicity of the Polyaenus story, but see contra in Arsinoe.

140. See discussion and references in Smith 1988: 34–38.

141. Smith (1988: 43) says that female royal portraits wore either a *stephane* or a diadem, but also remarks that even for the more plentiful portraits of Ptolemaic women, diadems are rare and that some of these women may have worn neither a *stephane* nor a diadem (89). Pomeroy (1984: 24) suggests that the *stephane* was associated with Aphrodite, although Smith (1988: 43) insists that it was an attribute common to several goddesses.

142. See above on the accuracy of Justin's testimony. Ritter (1965: 114) argues that this is the first evidence for the wife of a Hellenistic ruler wearing the diadem, but if Kahrstedt's (1910: 261–62) dating and identification of Berenice I on a coin showing her wearing a diadem is correct, that would be an earlier example. Some Seleucid women had a ceremony separate from their wedding in which they were proclaimed *basilissa* (see Bikerman 1938: 26), and Justin's account describes an analogous situation; whether the similarity ought to inspire confidence or distrust is difficult to say.

143. Ritter's (1965: 114–24) discussion tends to assume that practice was universal in the Hellenistic world. It may have been, but differences in royal cults among the various monarchies should make us careful to assume commonality. Pomeroy's (1984: 29) view that the appearance of Arsinoe II with a diadem on Egyptian coins is evidence of deification goes too far.

144. Ritter 1965: 114–24.

145. Diog. Laert. 6.63 preserves an anecdote about Diogenes in which the famous philosopher supposedly called the *hetairai* of kings *basilissai* because they made kings do what they wanted. The anecdote's historicity is dubious, but it does evidence the same tendency demonstrated in the other passage, on the one hand, to suggest that very little distinguished a royal woman from a royal courtesan, and, on the other, to recognize a distinction (in this case, by means of the joke about *basilissai*).

CHAPTER 9

1. See Carney 1991a: 17 n. 1 for a general bibliography of the royal tombs at Vergina, to which should be added Hammond 1991: 69–82.

2. Faklaris 1994: 609–16.

3. Hatzopoulos 1996: 264–69; Hammond 1997: 177–79; Greenwalt 1997a; Carney forthcoming in *Arch News* all reject Faklaris's arguments.

4. Andronicos (1984: 224–26) offers his reasons for considering the burials under the Great Tumulus royal; see also Carney forthcoming in *Arch News*.

5. Andronicos 1984: 82 contra Hammond 1991: 78. See Carney 1992b: 9 n. 49 for further discussion.

6. See Carney 1991a: 17 n. 1 for a general bibliography of the dispute about the identity of those buried in Tomb II.

7. Hammond 1991: 77.

8. See Carney 1991a: 21–23; Greenwalt 1997: 131–33; and below.

9. See Carney 1991a: 18 nn.7, 8.

10. Musgrave 1991: 7 n. 21; 1985: 8.

11. Musgrave 1991: 3–4 contra Xirotiris and Langenscheidt 1981: 158.

12. Musgrave (1990: 277, 281) argues that the great care shown in preservation of these bones as opposed to those of the royal youth in Tomb III or those of the woman in the antechamber might suggest Philip. This point does not seem very convincing: Cassander had every reason to bury Philip Arrhidaeus carefully; it indicated that he was a legitimate successor who had avenged his death. Adea Eurydice was a woman, so it is hardly surprising that her bones got less attention. Assuming that the youth buried in Tomb III was Alexander IV (see above), Cassander, the murderer of the youth, would have wanted an appropriate-looking burial but would hardly have cared about such details (on the murder, see ROXANE).

13. Musgrave 1990: 25; 1991: 5.

14. Andronicos 1984: 227; Drogou et al. 1996: 103.

15. Hammond (1991: 77) rightly concludes that such an assumption is difficult to sustain; see also Greenwalt 1997: 131–31. See below for a discussion of other, more recently discovered military elements in the antechamber burial (cuirass; battle theme of the couch) that make it increasingly difficult to argue that these elements had nothing to do with the woman buried in the antechamber. Originally, the military aspects of the burial seemed to be limited to the objects on the threshold to the main chamber, but we now know that was not the case.

16. Adams 1991: 31. Borza (1987: 121) points to the unusual size of the antechamber. Andronicos (1980: 170) reveals that the large antechamber was part of the original plan.

17. The parallel is fairly close: Tutankhamun, like Philip Arrhidaeus, reigned briefly at the end of a dynasty. For much of Tutankhamun's reign, others ruled for him.

18. Hammond 1991: 74, 77–78.

19. See Carney 1992b: 2–3 for further arguments.

20. See Andronicos 1984: 86–95 for a detailed description of the tomb and its contents. The comb is mentioned in Andronicos 1978: 70.

21. Hammond 1978: 338.

22. See Carney 1992b: 6 n. 7.

23. See above n. 14 and Carney 1991a: 18 n. 5.

24. Borza (1991: 35–36) points out that Musgrave's identification of the bones as female, though confirmed by the diadem, is based on the comparatively subjective consideration of gracility.

25. See Carney 1991a: 21 for a discussion of these points and references to comparanda.

26. Greenwalt (1997: 131–33) argues convincingly that the pectoral was once placed on one of the two offering tables that Andronicos believed had once

been in the tomb. Greenwalt also points to the iconographic similarity between the figure, four times reproduced, on the central band of the pectoral and the obverse of Amyntas III's Rider *stater* and suggests that the pectoral was not simply booty crafted for someone else but had symbols central to the Argead family.

27. Drogou et al. 1996: 107.

28. So Carney 1991a: 22. See also Hammond 1991: 77 n. 45 for the observation that the dramatically uneven greaves in the antechamber must belong to the woman because they are quite different from the three "matching" pairs in the main chamber.

29. Drogou et al. 1996: 103.

30. Drogou et al. 1996: 97–105. They believe (103) that the couch in the antechamber was even more "richly decorated" than that in the main chamber.

31. Most easily done in *TAM*, pls. 18 and 19, figs. 86 and 120, seen on facing pages.

32. A tomb at Amphipolis had a *kline* in the antechamber, probably because the main chamber was too small to permit a second burial: see Andronicos 1986: 28 n. 24.

33. Andronicos 1984: 179–80.

34. Borza 1991: 38 n. 8.

35. See Carney 1991a: 22.

36. Prestianni-Giallombardo and Tripodi (1980: 994) suggest that the arms in the antechamber are not personal possessions but rather serve to stress the warrior character of the dead woman and also argue (998) that many of the items in the tomb were not made for the grave but were selected from family treasure. Borza (1987: 110–18) hypothesized that a number of the military items found in the main chamber of Tomb II once belonged to Alexander the Great. Both suggestions share the assumption that the grave goods were in some sense reconstituted.

37. Xirotiris and Langenscheidt (1981: 156) suggest an age of 25 for the bones, but add that their owner was not younger than 20 or older than 30. Musgrave (1991: 4) concurs, although urging caution in the light of the comparatively small number of bones preserved. He finds the evidence firmer for the lower age estimate. See also Musgrave 1993: 1133 n. 9. Musgrave informs me in conversation that a possible later menarche, due perhaps to nutritional considerations, would only push his estimate upward, not downward (see discussion on ancient age for menarche in Musgrave 1991: 5 n.12).

38. The discrepancy between the age estimates reached by the anthropologists (see n. 34) and the likely ages at death of Adea Eurydice and Cleopatra is small in terms of the number of years, but significant. The anthropologists found that the pelvic bones of the woman in Tomb II were completely mature. Those of Eurydice and Cleopatra would not have been if our age estimates are correct.

39. Musgrave 1991: 5 n. 14.

40. Adams 1991: 31.

41. Musgrave (1985: 9) once thought that the *larnax* might contain fragments of an infant's cranium, but further investigation has led him to reject this possibility.

42. For descriptions of the tomb, see Andronicos 1987a: 45–49; 1987c: 81–84 (figs. 7–11); 1987d: 375 ff.; 1994: 154–61 (figs. 1,135–37); Hammond 1991: 70–71; *AR* 1987–88: 52 and 1988–89: 78–79 (figs. 108–110, cover photo). It is somewhat larger than Tomb II, previously the largest known. Andronicos (1994: 161 n. 44) rightly points out that designating this tomb "Tomb of the Throne" could be confusing because two other tombs at Vergina also contain thrones, but as each of these has already acquired other conventional designations that do not refer to the throne ("Rhomaios Tomb" and "Bella Tumulus, tomb 2") I shall continue to call it Tomb of the Throne.

43. Andronicos (1987c: 83), dates it to ca. 340.

44. Andronicos (1994: 160) observes that reddish stains on the back and arms of the throne may have been left by purple cloth draped across the throne.

45. Andronicos 1987c: 83. Hammond (1991: 71) points to similarities between the Tomb of the Throne and both burials in Tomb II. In all three cases the bones of the deceased were wrapped in purple cloth and placed in a *larnax*. Outside both tombs were objects apparently from a pyre.

46. Andronicos 1987c: 84; 1994: 161.

47. *AR* 1987: 52 says that Andronicos believed it belonged to a woman because of the absence of weapons. He held the same belief about Tomb I (Andronicos 1984: 87), until analysis of the bone fragments demonstrated that the burial included an adult male as well as a female.

48. Kurtz and Boardman 1971: 208. Andronicos (1987c: 83) mentions the presence of fragments of alabastra.

49. Hammond (1991: 71) refers to the presence of female burials.

50. Andronicos 1994: 150. He cites the presence of a semithrone in the second tomb under the Bella Tumulus. He believed it to be a male burial because the facade includes three large painted figures, two of whom are males and warriors. The presence of thrones could be seen as suggestive of a female burial, if not certain proof, granted representations of funerary banquets with seated women and reclining men.

51. Andronicos 1987c: 84, followed by Hammond 1991: 71.

52. Even if one accepts the tomb as Eurydice's, such a conclusion hardly supports Hammond's (1994: 184) suggestion that the splendor of the tomb was proof Eurydice received a cult.

53. Borza 1992: 308. See EURYDICE 1.

54. See Carney 1992b: 9 n. 43 for references.

55. Andronicos (1987b: 1–16; 1994; 147–50) and Hammond (1991: 69–82) have tried.

56. Miller 1993: 2–3. Biers (1992: 79–82) doubts that the identity of the oc-

cupants of Tomb II can be resolved because he doubts that changes in material culture were significant enough to make it possible. This observation applies to the dating of many of the tombs.

57. See *Ergon* 1990: 80–82; Musgrave 1994: 309. The very young and possibly female child could have been the first occupant.

58. See descriptions in *AR* 1987–88: 52 and 1988–89: 80; *Ergon* 1988: 72–80 (figs. 62–66); and Andronicos 1994: 35–36 (figs. 27–30). The dating is particularly dependent on some Ionic-style protomes (*Ergon* 1988: 79).

59. *AR* 1990–91: 56; Andronicos 1994: 35–38.

Abbreviations

AAA	*Athens Annals of Archaeology*
AC	*L'Antiquité classique*
AE	*Archaiologika Ephemeris*
AEMTH	*To archaiologiko ergo ste Makedonia kai Thrake*
AHB	*Ancient History Bulletin*
AHR	*American Historical Review*
AJA	*American Journal of Archaeology*
AJAH	*American Journal of Ancient History*
AJP	*American Journal of Philology*
AM	*Archaia Makedonia/Ancient Macedonia,* Proceedings of the International Symposia on Ancient Macedonia
AncW	*Ancient World*
AnnPisa	*Annali della Scuola Normale Superiore di Pisa*
AncSoc	*Ancient Society*
AR	*Archaeological Reports*
ArchNews	*Archaeological News*
BCH	*Bulletin de correspondance hellénique*
BSA	*Annual of the British School at Athens*
BSRAA	*Bulletin de la Société royal d'archéologie d'Alexandrie*
CA	*Classical Antiquity*
CAH	*Cambridge Ancient History*
Choix	F. Dürrbach, *Choix d'inscriptions de Délos.* Paris 1921.
CJ	*Classical Journal*
CP	*Classical Philology*
CQ	*Classical Quarterly*
CW	*Classical World*
EchCl	*Echos du monde classique. Classical Views*
Ergon	*Ergon tes archaiologikes Etaireias*
EtPap	*Études de papyrologie*

FGrH	F. Jacoby, *Die Fragmente der griechischen Historiker*
FHG	C. Müller, *Fragmenta Historicorum Graecorum*
GHI	M. N. Tod, *A Selection of Greek Historical Inscriptions*
G&R	*Greece and Rome*
GRBS	*Greek, Roman and Byzantine Studies*
HSCP	*Harvard Studies in Classical Philology*
HThR	*Harvard Theological Review*
ID	F. Dürrbach, Inscriptions de Délos. Paris, 1929.
IG	*Inscriptiones Graecae*
JHS	*Journal of Hellenic Studies*
LSJ	H. G. Liddell, R. Scott, and H. Stuart Jones, *Greek-English Lexicon*, 9th ed. Oxford, 1940.
MDAI(A)	*Mitteilungen des Deutschen Archäologischen Instituts Abteilung Athens*
NC	*Numismatic Chronicle*
OGIS	W. Dittenberger, *Orientis Graecae Inscriptions Selectae*. Leipzig, 1903–5.
PF	*Philosophical Forum*
PP	*La Parola del Passato*
P&P	*Past and Present*
RE	Pauly-Wissowa, *Realencyclopädie des classischen Altertumswissenschaft*
REA	*Revue des études anciennes*
REG	*Revue des études grecques*
RendIstLomb	*Rendiconti. Istituto lombardo, Accademia di scienze e lettere*
RFIC	*Rivista di filologia e d'istruzione classica*
RIDA	*Revue internationale des droits de l'antiquité*
RSA	*Rivista storica dell'antichita*
SEG	*Supplementum Epigraphicum* Graecum
SIG	W. Dittenberger, *Sylloge Inscriptionum Graecarum*, 3d ed. Leipzig, 1915–24.
TAM	K. Ninou, *Treasures of Ancient Macedonia*
TAPA	*Transactions and Proceedings of the American Philological Association*
ZfN	*Zeitschrift für Numismatik*
ZPE	*Zeitschrift für Papyrologie und Epigraphik*

Bibliography

Adams, W. L. 1977. "The Dynamics of Internal Macedonian Politics in the Time of Cassander." *AM* 3: 17–30.

—————. 1980. "The Royal Macedonian Tomb at Vergina: An Historical Interpretation." *AncW* 3: 67–72.

—————. 1982. "Perseus and the Third Macedonian War." In Adams and Borza 1982: 237–56.

—————. 1991. "Cassander, Alexander IV, and the Tombs at Vergina." *AncW* 22: 27–33.

Adams, W. L., and E. N. Borza, eds. 1982. *Philip II, Alexander the Great, and the Macedonian Heritage*. Washington, D.C.

Africa, T. 1982. "Worms and the Death of Kings: A Cautionary Note on Disease and History." *CA* 1: 1–17.

Amundsen, D. W., and C. J. Diers. 1970. "The Age of Menopause in Classical Greece and Rome." *Human Biology* 42: 79–86.

Andronicos, M. 1964. *Vergina, the Prehistoric Necropolis and the Hellenistic Palace*. Studies in Mediterranean Archaeology 13.Lund.

—————. 1978. "Regal Treasure from a Macedonian Tomb." *National Geographic* 154: 54–77.

—————. 1980. "The Royal Tomb at Vergina and the Problem of the Dead." *AAA* 13: 168–78.

—————. 1984. *Vergina*. Athens.

—————. 1986. "Vergina. Archaiologia kai historia." In *Philia Epe. Festschrift George E. Mylonas*, 1: 19–37. Athens.

—————. 1987a. "Archaikos taphos. O neo "Basilikos" taphos." *Ergon* 1: 45–49.

—————. 1987b. "Some Reflections on the Macedonian Tombs." *BSA* 82: 1–16.

—————. 1987c. "Vergina. Anaskaphe 1987." *AEMTH* 1: 81–88.

—————. 1987d. "E zoographike sten archaia Makedonia." *AE* 126: 363–93.

—————. 1994. "The Tombs of Vergina" and "The Macedonian Tombs." In Ginouvès 1994: 35–38, 147–90.

Atkinson, J. R. 1980. *A Commentary on Quintus Curtius Rufus's Historiae Alexandri Magni Books 3 and 4*. London Studies in Classical Philology 4. Amsterdam.

Austin, M. M. 1981. *The Hellenistic World from Alexander to the Roman Conquest*. Cambridge.

Aymard, A. 1948. "Le protocole royal grec et son évolution." *REA* 50: 232–63.

——. 1949. "Sur quelques vers d'Euripide qui poussèrent Alexandre au meurtre." In *Mélanges Henri Grégoire* 1: 43–74. Paris.

——. 1950. "Basileus Makedon." *RIDA* 4: 61–97.

Badian, E. 1958a. "Alexander the Great and the Unity of Mankind." *Historia* 7: 425–44.

——. 1958b. "The Eunuch Bagoas." *CQ* 8: 144–57.

——. 1960. "The Death of Parmenio." *TAPA* 91:324–38.

——. 1961. "Harpalus." *JHS* 81: 16–43.

——. 1963. "The Death of Philip II." *Phoenix* 17: 244–50.

——. 1964. "The Struggle for the Succession to Alexander the Great." In *Studies in Greek and Roman History*, 262–70. Oxford.

——. 1981. "The Deification of Alexander the Great." In *Ancient Macedonian Studies in Honor of Charles F. Edson*, 27–71. Thessaloniki.

——. 1982b. "Greeks and Macedonians." In Barr-Sharrar and Borza 1982: 33–51.

——. 1982a. "Eurydice." In Adams and Borza 1982: 99–110.

——. 1988. "Two Postscripts on the Marriage of Phila and Balacrus." *ZPE* 73: 116–18.

——. 1996. "Alexander the Great between Two Thrones and Heaven: Variations on an Old Theme." In *Subject and Ruler: The Cult of the Ruling Power in Classical Antiquity. Journal of Roman Archaeology* supplement no. 17, edited by D. Fishwick and A. Small, 11–26.

Baker, D. 1978. *Medieval Women*. Oxford.

Baldwin, B. 1976. "Athenaeus and His Work." *Acta Classica* 19: 21–42.

Barr-Sharrar, B., and E. N. Borza, eds. 1982. *Macedonia and Greece in Late Classical and Early Hellenistic Times*. Studies in the History of Art, vol. 10. National Gallery of Art, Washington, D.C.

Baynham, E. J. 1994. "Antipater: Manager of Kings." In Worthington 1994: 331–56.

Beloch, K. J. 1927. *Griechische Geschichte*, 2d ed. Vols. 3 and 4. Leipzig-Berlin.

Berve, H. 1926. *Das Alexanderreich*. Vol. 2. Munich.

Biers, W. R. 1992. *Art, Artefacts, and Chronology in Classical Archaeology*. London and New York.

Bi(c)kerman, E. 1938. *Institutions des Séleucides*. Paris.

Billows, R. A. 1990. *Antigonos the One-Eyed and the Creation of the Hellenistic State*. Berkeley.

Blackwell, C. W. 1999. *In the Absence of Alexander: Harpalus and the Failure of Macedonian Authority*. New York.

Blundell, Sue. 1995. *Women in Ancient Greece*. Cambridge, Mass.

Bornstein, D. 1983. *The Lady in the Tower, Medieval Courtesy Literature for Women*. Archon.

Borza, E. N. 1983. "The Symposium at Alexander's Court." *AM* 3: 45–55.

——. 1987. "The Royal Macedonian Tombs and the Paraphernalia of Alexander the Great." *Phoenix* 41: 105–21.

———. 1990. *In the Shadow of Olympus: The Emergence of Macedon.* Princeton.

———. 1991. "Commentary." *AncW* 22: 35–40.

———. 1992. (Paperback ed.) *In the Shadow of Olympus: The Emergence of Macedon.* Princeton.

Bosworth, A. B. 1971a. "The Death of Alexander the Great: Rumour and Propaganda." *CQ* 21: 112–36.

———. 1971b. "Philip II and Upper Macedonia." *CQ* 21: 93–105.

———. 1980a. "Alexander and the Iranians." *JHS* 100: 1–21.

———. 1980b. *A Historical Commentary on Arrian's History of Alexander.* Vol. 1. Oxford.

———. 1988. *Conquest and Empire.* Cambridge.

———. 1992. "Philip III Arrhidaeus and the Chronology of the Successors." *Chiron* 22: 55–81.

———. 1996. *Alexander and the East: The Tragedy of Triumph.* Oxford.

Breckenridge, J. D. 1968. *Likeness, a Conceptual History of Ancient Portraiture.* Evanston.

Briant, P. 1973. *Antigone le Borgne: Les débuts de sa carrière et les problèmes de l'assemblée macédonienne.* Les Annales Litteraires de l'universite de Besançon, 152. Paris.

———. 1982. *Rois, tributs et paysans. Études sur les formations tributaires du Moyen-Orient ancien.* Besançon.

———. 1989. "Histoire et idéologie. Les Grecs et la 'décadence perse.'" In *Mélanges P. Lévêque* 2: 33–47.

———. 1993. "Les Chasses d'Alexandre." *AM* 5 (1): 267–77.

———. 1994. "Sources gréco-hellénistiques, institutions perses et institutions macédoniens: Continuités, changements et bricolages." *Achaemenid History* 8: 283–310.

Brosius, Maria. 1996. *Women in Ancient Persia (559–331 B.C.).* Oxford.

Brunt, P. A. 1963. "Alexander's Macedonian Cavalry." *JHS* 83: 27–46.

———. 1975. "Alexander, Barsine, and Heracles." *RFIC* 103: 22–34.

———. 1976. "Anaximenes and King Alexander I of Macedon." *JHS* 96: 151–3.

———. 1980. "On Historical Fragments and Epitomes." *CQ* 31: 477–94.

Buck, D. D. 1914. "Is the Suffix of *Basilissa,* etc., of Macedonian Origin?" *CP* 9: 370–73.

Burkert, W. 1985. *Greek Religion.* Translated by J. Raffan. Cambridge, Mass.

Burn, A. R. 1962. *Alexander the Great and the Hellenistic World.* New York.

———. 1985. *Cambridge History of Iran.* Vol. 2. Cambridge.

Burstein, S. M. 1974. *Outpost of Hellenism: The Emergence of Heraclea on the Black Sea.* University of California Classical Studies 14. Berkeley.

———. 1977. "*IG* II 56 1 and the Court of Alexander IV." *ZPE* 24: 223–25.

———. 1982a. "Arsinoe Philadelphos: A Revisionist View." In Adams and Borza 1982: 197–212.

———. 1982b. "The Tomb of Philip II and the Succession of Alexander the Great." *EchCl* 26: 141–64.

Cabanes, P. 1976. *L'Épire de la mort de Pyrrhos à la conquête romaine.* Paris.

————. 1980. "Société et institutions dans les monarchies de grèce septentri-onale au IV siècle." *REG* 113: 324–51.

Cameron, A. 1990. "Two Mistresses of Ptolemy Philadelphus." *GRBS* 31: 287–311.

Carney, E. D. 1980. "Alexander the Lyncestian: The Disloyal Opposition." *GRBS* 20: 23–33.

————. 1983. "Regicide in Macedonia." *PP* 211: 260–72.

————. 1984. "Fact and Fiction in 'Queen Eleanor's Confession' (Childe No. 156)." *Folklore* 95: 167–70.

————. 1987a. "The Career of Adea Eurydice." *Historia* 36: 496–502.

————. 1987b. "Olympias." *AncSoc* 18: 35–62.

————. 1987c. "The Reappearance of Royal Sibling Marriage in Ptolemaic Egypt." *PP* 237: 420–39.

————. 1988a. "Eponymous women: Royal Women and City Names." *AHB* 2: 134–42.

————. 1988b. "The Sisters of Alexander the Great: Royal Relicts." *Historia* 37: 385–404.

————. 1991a. "The Female Burial in the Antechamber of Tomb II at Vergina." *AncW* 22: 17–26.

————. 1991b. "'What's in a Name?': The Emergence of a Title for Royal Women in the Hellenistic Period." In *Women's History and Ancient History*, edited by S. B. Pomeroy, 154–72. Chapel Hill.

————. 1992a. "The Politics of Polygamy: Olympias, Alexander, and the Death of Philip II." *Historia* 41: 169–89.

————. 1992b. "Tomb I at Vergina." *ArchNews* 17: 1–10.

————. 1993a. "Foreign Influence and the Changing Role of Royal Macedonian Women." *AM* 5,1: 313–23.

————. 1993b. "Olympias and the Image of the Royal Virago." *Phoenix* 47: 29–56.

————. 1994a. "Arsinoe before She Was Philadelphus." *AHB* 8: 123–31.

————. 1994b. "Olympias, Adea Eurydice, and the End of the Argead Dynasty." In Worthington 1994: 357–80.

————. 1995. "Women and Basileia: Legitimacy and Female Political Action in Macedonia." *CJ* 90: 367–91.

————. 1996. "Alexander and Persian Women." *AJP* 117:563–83.

————. n.d.a. "The Curious Death of the Antipatrid Dynasty." Forthcoming in *AM* 6.

————. n.d.b. "Were the Tombs under the Great Tumulus at Vergina Royal? Forthcoming in *ArchNews*.

Cawkwell, G. 1978. *Philip of Macedon.* London.

Cerfaux, L., and J. Tondriau. 1957. *Le Culte des souverains dans la civlisation gréco-romain.* Tournai.

Charneaux, P. 1966. "List Argienne de Thearodoques." BCH 90: 156–239.

Clerc, D. 1915. *Les theories relatives au culte des images chez es auteurs grécs du IIme siè-cle apres J.-C.* Paris.

Clignet, R. 1970. *Many Wives, Many Powers: Authority and Power in Polygamous Fam-ilies.* Evanston.

Cohen, G. M. 1974. "The Diadochoi and the New Monarchies." *Athenaeum* 52: 177–79.

———. 1978. *The Seleucid Colonies.* Historia Eizelschriften 30. Wiesbaden.

———. 1995. *The Hellenistic Settlements in Europe, the Islands, and Asia Minor.* Berke-ley.

Cole, J. W. 1974. "Perdiccas and Athens." *Phoenix* 28: 55–72.

Cole, S. G. 1981. "Could Greek Women Read and Write?" In Foley 1981: 219–46.

———. 1984. *Theoi Megaloi: The Cult of the Great Gods at Samothrace.* Leiden.

Connor, W. R. 1987. "Tribes, Festivals and Processions: Civic Ceremonial and Po-litical Manipulation in Archaic Greece." *JHS* 107: 40–50.

Cook, J. M. 1983. *The Persian Empire.* New York.

Cooper, C. 1995. "Hyperides and the Trial of Phryne." *Phoenix* 40: 303–18.

Cross, G. N. 1932. *Epirus, a Study in Greek Constitutional Development.* Cambridge.

Davidson, J. N. 1997. *Courtesans and Fishcakes, the Consuming Passions of Classical Athens.* London.

Delia, D. 1991. "Fulvia Reconsidered." In *Women's History and Ancient History*, edited by S. B. Pomeroy, 197–217. Chapel Hill.

Develin, R. 1981. "The Murder of Philip II." *Antichthon* 15: 86–99.

Dixon, Suzanne. 1988. *The Roman Mother.* Norman.

Dover, K. 1973. "Classical Greek Attitudes to Sexual Behaviour." *Arethusa* 6: 59–73.

Dontas, G. S. 1983. "The True Aglaurion." *Hesperia* 52: 48–63.

Dow, S., and C. F. Edson. 1937. "A Study of the Evidence in Regard to the Mother of Philip V." *HSCP* 48: 127–80.

Drees, L. 1968. *Olympia, Gods, Artists, Athletes.* New York.

Drogou, S. 1987. "To uphasma tes Verginas. Protes Paratereseis." *Ametos* 1: 303–16, Pls. 63–69.

Drogou, S., C. Saatsoglou-Paliadeli, P. Faklaris, A. Kottaridou, and E-B. Tsi-garida. 1996. Vergina. The Great Tumulus. Archaeological Guide. Thessa-loniki.

Droysen, G. G. 1953. *Geschichte des Hellenismus.* Vol. 2. Basel.

Dubos, R., and J. Dubos. 1952. *The White Plague: Tuberculosis, Man and Society.* Boston.

Dürrbach, F. 1921. *Choix d'inscriptions de Délos.* Paris

Dusanic, S. 1965. "The Year of the Athenian Archon Archippus II (318/17)." *BCH* 89: 128–41.

Edson, C. F. 1934. "The Antigonids, Heracles, and Beroea." *HSCP* 45:213–35.

———. 1935. "Perseus and Demetrius." *HSCP* 46: 191–202.

———. 1937. "Chryseis, a Study of the Evidence in Regard to the Mother of Philip V." *HSCP* 48: 127–80.

————. 1949. "The Tomb of Olympias." *Hesperia* 18: 84–95.

————. 1970. "Early Macedonia." *AM* 1: 17–44.

Ehrenberg, V. 1938. *Alexander and the Greeks.* Oxford.

Ehrhardt, C. 1967. "Two Notes on Philip òf Macedon's First Interventions in Thessaly." *CQ* 17: 296–301.

————. 1975. "Studies in the Reigns of Demetrius II and Antigonus Doson." Ph.D. diss., State University of New York, Buffalo.

Ellis, J. R. 1970. "The Security of the Macedonian Throne under Philip II." *AM* 1: 68–75.

————. 1971. "Amyntas Perdikka, Philip II and Alexander the Great." *JHS* 91: 15–24.

————. 1973. "The Step-Brothers of Philip II." *Historia* 22: 350–54.

————. 1976. *Philip II and Macedonian Imperialism.* London.

————. 1981. "The Assassination of Philip II." In *Ancient Macedonian Studies in Honor of Charles F. Edson*, 99–137. Thessaloniki.

————. 1982. "The First Months of Alexander's Reign." In Adams and Borza 1982: 69–73.

Ellis, W. M. 1994. *Ptolemy of Egypt.* London.

Errington, R. M. 1970. "From Babylon to Triparadeisos: 323–320 B.C." *JHS* 89: 49–77.

————. 1974. "Macedonian 'Royal Style' and Its Historical Significance." *JHS* 94: 20–37.

————. 1975a. "Alexander in the Hellenistic World." In *Alexandre le Grand: Image et réalité,* edited by E. Badian, 145–52. Foundation Hardt, Entretiens sur l'Antiquitè Classique 22. Geneva.

————. 1975b. "Arybbas the Molossian." *GRBS* 16: 41–50.

————. 1977a. "Diodorus and the Chronology of the Early Diadochoi, 320–311 B.C." *Hermes* 4: 478–504.

————. 1977b. "An Inscription from Beroea and the Alleged Co-Rule of Demetrius II." *AM* 2: 115–22.

————. 1978. "The Nature of the Macedonian State under the Monarchy." *Chiron* 8: 77–133.

————. 1981. "Review-Discussion: Four Interpretations of Philip II." *AJAH* 6: 69–88.

————. 1990. *A History of Macedonia.* Berkeley.

Facinger, M. F. 1968. "A Study of Medieval Queens: Capetian France, 987–1237." *Studies in Medieval and Renaissance History* 5: 3–48.

Faklaris, P. B. 1994. "Aegae: Determining the Site of the First Capital of the Macedonians." *AJA* 98: 609–16.

Fantham, E., H. P. Foley, N. B. Kampen, S. B. Pomeroy, and H. A. Shapiro. 1994. *Women in the Classical World.* Oxford.

Farnell, L. R. 1971. *The Cults of the Greek States.* Vol. 2. Chicago.

Fears, J. R. 1975. "Pausanias, the Assassin of Philip II." *Athenaeum* 53: 111–35.

Ferguson, W. S. 1911. *Hellenistic Athens: An Historical Essay*. New York.

Ferrario, F. 1962. "Arsinoe-Stratonice: A proposito di una iscrizione ellenistica." *RendIstLomb* 96: 78–82.

Fiehn, K. 1929a. "Stateira 2." *RE* 3A (2): 2170–71.

———. K. 1929b. "Stateira 3." *RE* 3A (2): 2171–72.

Fine, J. V. A. 1934. "The Mother of Philip V of Macedon." *CQ* 28: 99–104.

Flower, M. A. 1988. "Agesilaus of Sparta and the Origins of the Ruler Cult." *CQ* 38: 123–34.

———. 1997. *Theopompus of Chios*. Oxford.

Flory, M. 1994. "The Social Role of Ancient Statues." Paper presented at the Annual Meeting of CAMWS, April.

Foley, H. P. 1978. "Reverse Similes and Sex Roles in the Odyssey." *Arethusa* 11: 7–19.

Foley, H. P., ed. 1981. *Reflections of Women in Antiquity*. Philadelphia.

Fraser, P .M. 1960. *Samothrace, the Inscriptions on Stone*. Vol. 2, pt. 1. New York.

———. 1972. *Ptolemaic Alexandria*. 2 vols. Oxford.

Fredricksmeyer, E. A. 1966. "The Ancestral Rites of Alexander the Great." *CP* 61: 179–81.

———. 1979. "Divine Honors for Philip II." *TAPA* 109: 39–61.

———. 1990. "Alexander and Philip: Emulation and Resentment." *CQ* 85: 300–15.

Freedberg, D. 1989. *The Power of Images in History and Theory of Response*. Chicago.

Friedrich, P. 1978. *The Meaning of Aphrodite*. Chicago.

Frye, R. N. 1963. *The Heritage of Persia*. Cleveland.

Gabbert, J. J. 1997. *Antigonus II Gonatas: A Political Biography*. London.

Gagé, J. 1975. "Alexandre le Grand en Macédoine dans la 1ère moitié du IIIe Siècle après J.-C." *Historia* 24: 1–16.

Gardner, A. P. 1880. "Ares as a Sun-God and Solar Symbols on the Coins of Macedon and Thrace." *NC* 20:49–61.

Gardner, E. N. 1925. *Olympia, Its History and Remains*. Oxford.

Garlick, B., S. Dixon, and P. Allen, eds. 1992. *Stereotypes of Women in Power: Historical Perspectives and Revisionist Views*. New York.

Gernet, L. 1968. *The Anthropology of Greece*. Translated by J. Hamilton and B. Naby. Baltimore.

Geyer, F. 1931a. "Stratonike 8." *RE* 4 (A1): 319–20.

———. 1931b. "Stratonike 9." *RE* 4 (A1): 320–21.

Ginouvès, R., ed. 1994. *Macedonia, From Philip II to the Roman Conquest*. Princeton.

Given-Wilson, C. 1986. *The Royal Household and the King's Affinity: Service, Politics and Finance in England, 1360–1413*. New Haven.

Gluckman, Max. 1963. *Order and Rebellion in Tribal Africa*. London.

Goody, Jack. 1966. *Succession to High Office*. Cambridge.

Gordon, R. L. 1979. "The Real and the Imaginary: Production and Religion in the Graeco-Roman World." *Art History* 2(1): 5–34.

Green, P. 1982. "The Royal Tombs of Vergina: A Historical Analysis." In Adams and Borza 1982: 129–51.

———. 1990. *Alexander to Actium: The Historical Evolution of the Hellenistic Age.* Berkeley.

———. 1991. *Alexander of Macedon.* Berkeley.

Greenwalt, W. S. 1985a. "The Introduction of Caranus into the Argead King List." *GRBS* 26: 43–49.

———. 1985b. "The Search for Arrhidaeus." *AncW* 10: 69–77.

———. 1986. "Herodotus and the Foundation of Argead Macedonia." *AncW* 13: 117–22.

———. 1988a. "The Age of Marriageability at the Argead Court." *CW* 82: 93–97.

———. 1988b. "Amyntas III and the Political Stability of Argead Macedonia." *AncW* 18: 35–44.

———. 1989. "Polygamy and Succession in Argead Macedonia." *Arethusa* 22: 19–45.

———. 1992. "The Iconographical Significance of Amyntas III's Mounted Hunter Stater." *AM* 5(1): 509–19.

———. 1994a. "The Production of Coinage from Archelaus to Perdiccas III and the Evolution of the Argead State." In Worthington 1994: 105–34.

———. 1994b. "A Solar Dionysus and Argead Legitimacy." *AncW* 25: 3–8.

———. 1996. "'Proto-historical' Argead Women: Lan(ice?), Cleonice, Cleopatra, Prothoe, Niconoe." *AHB* 10: 47–50.

———. 1997. "Thracian Influence on the Ideology of Argead Kingship." In *Thrace Ancienne*, 1: 121–33. Actes 2e Symposium International des Études Thraciennes. Komotini.

———. Forthcoming. "Argead Name Changes." *AM* 6.

Griffith, G. T. 1970. "Philip of Macedon's Early Intervention in Thessaly (358–352 B.C.)" *CQ* 20: 67–80.

———. 1979. "Part Two." In Hammond and Griffith 1979: 203–646, 675–721.

Griffiths, F. T. 1981. "Home before Lunch: The Emancipated Woman in Theocritus." In Foley 1981: 247–73.

Gruen, Erich. 1974. "The Last Years of Philip V." *GRBS* 15: 221–46.

———. 1985. "The Coronation of the Diadochoi." In *The Craft of the Ancient Historian: Essays in Honor of Chester G. Starr*, edited by J. W. Eadie and J. Ober, 553–71. Lanham, MD.

Gryzbek, E. 1986. "Zu Philipp II und Alexander dem Grossen." *AM* 4: 223–29.

———. 1990. *Du Calendrier macédonien au calendrier ptolémaïque.* Basel.

Gutzwiller, Katherine. 1992. "Callimachus' Lock of Berenice: Fantasy, Romance, and Propaganda." *AJP* 113: 359–85.

Habicht, C. 1957. "Prusias 1." *RE* 23(1): 1086–87, 1095–96.

———. 1970. *Gottmenschentum und griechische Städte.* Ztemata 14. Munich.

Hall, E. 1989. *Inventing the Barbarian: Greek Self-Definition through Tragedy.* Oxford.

_____. 1995. "Asia Unmanned: Images of Victory in Classical Athens." In *War and Society in the Greek World*, edited by J. Rich and G. Shipley, 108–33. London.

Hamilton, J. R. 1969. *Plutarch: Alexander: A Commentary*. Oxford.

Hammond, N. G. L. 1956. "The Philaids and the Chersonese." *CQ* 6: 113–29.

_____. 1966. "The Kingdoms in Illyria circa 400–167 B.C." *BSA* 61: 239–53.

_____. 1967. *Epirus*. Oxford.

_____. 1972. *A History of Macedonia*. Vol. 1. Oxford.

_____. 1978. "Philip's Tomb in Historical Context." *GRBS* 19: 331–50.

_____. 1979. "Part One and Chapter 20." In Hammond and Griffith 1979: 3–200, 647–76.

_____. 1980. "Some Passages in Arrian concerning Alexander." *CQ* 30: 47–76.

_____. 1985. "Some Macedonian Offices c. 336–309 B.C." *JHS* 105: 156–60.

_____. 1988a. "The King and the Land in Macedonia." *CQ* 38: 382–91.

_____. 1988b. "Part One and Part Three." In Hammond and Walbank 1988: 3–196.

_____. 1989. *The Macedonian State: Origins, Institutions and History*. Oxford.

_____. 1991. "The Royal Tombs at Vergina: Evolution and Identities." *BSA* 86: 69–82.

_____. 1994. *Philip of Macedon*. Baltimore.

_____. 1997. "The Location of Aegae." *JHS* 117: 177–79.

Hammond, N. G. L., and G. T. Griffith. 1979. *A History of Macedonia*. Vol. 2. Oxford.

Hammond, N. G. L., and F. W. Walbank. 1988. *A History of Macedonia*. Vol. 3. Oxford.

Harris, Diane. 1995. *The Treasures of the Parthenon and Erechtheion*. Oxford.

Harris, Grace. 1973. "Furies, Witches, and Mothers." In *The Character of Kinship*, edited by Jack Goody, 145–59. Cambridge.

Hatzopoulos, M. B. 1982a. "The Oleveni Inscription and the Dates of Philip's Reign." In Adams and Borza 1982: 21–42.

_____. 1982b. "A Reconsideration of the Pixodarus Affair." In Barr-Sharrar and Borza 1982: 59–66.

_____. 1986. "Succession and Regency in Classical Macedonia." *AM* 4: 279–92.

_____. 1990. "Un nouveau document du règne d'Antigone Gonatas." *Mélétèmata* 10: 133–47.

_____. 1996. *Macedonian Institutions under the Kings*. Vols. 1 and 2. *Mélétèmata* 22. Athens.

Havelock, C. M. 1971. *Hellenistic Art*. Greenwich, Conn.

_____. 1995. *The Aphrodite of Knidos and Her Successors: A Historical Review of the Female Nude in Greek Art*. Ann Arbor.

Hawley, R. 1993. "'Pretty, Witty and Wise': Courtesans in Athenaeus' *Deipnosophistai* Book 13." *International Journal of Moral and Social Studies* 8: 73–91.

Heckel, W. 1977. "The Conspiracy against Philotas." *Phoenix* 31: 9–21.

_____. 1978a. "Cleopatra or Eurydice?" *Phoenix* 32: 155–58.

_____. 1978b. "Leonnatos, Polyperchon and the Introduction of *Proskynesis*." *AJP* 99: 459–61.

————. 1980. "*IG* II 561 and the Status of Alexander IV." *ZPE* 40: 249–50.

————. 1981a. "Philip and Olympias (337/6 B.C.)." In *Classical Contributions: Studies in Honour of M. F. McGregor*, edited by G. S. Shrimpton and D. J. McCargar, 51–57. Locust Valley, N.Y.

————. 1981b. "Polyxena, the Mother of Alexander the Great." *Chiron* 11: 79–96.

————. 1983–84. "Kynnane the Illyrian." *RSA* 13–14: 193–200.

————. 1986. "Factions and Macedonian Politics in the Reign of Alexander the Great." *AM* 4: 293–305.

————. 1987. "A Grandson of Antipatros at Delos." *ZPE* 70: 161–62.

————. 1989. "The Granddaughters of Iolaus." *Classicum* 15 (2): 32–39.

————. 1992. *The Marshals of Alexander's Empire*. London.

Heinen, H. 1972. *Untersuchungen zur hellenistischen Geschichte des 3. Jahrhunderts v. Chr. zur Geschichte der Zeit des Ptolemaios Keraunos und zum Chremonideischen Kriege.* Historia, Einzelschriften 20. Wiesbaden.

Henry, Madeleine. 1992. "The Edible Woman: Athenaeus' Concept of the Pornographic." In *Pornography and Representation in Greece and Rome*, edited by A. Richlin, 250–68. New York.

Heyob, S. K. 1975. *The Cult of Isis among Women in the Greco-Roman World.* Leiden.

Hoffman, W. 1938a. "Phila 3." *RE* 19 (2): 2087–88.

————. 1938b. "Phila 4." *RE* 19 (2): 2088.

————. 1941. "Phthia 8." *RE* 20 (1): 959–60.

Holleaux, M. 1923. "Le décret des milésiens en honneur d'Apame." *REG* 36: 1–13.

————. 1942. "Ptolemée de Telemessos." *Études d'épigraphie et d'histoire grecques* 3: 365–404.

Holt, F. L. 1988. *Alexander the Great and Bactria.* Supplements to Mnemosyne, 104. Leiden.

Hornblower, J. 1981. *Hieronymus of Cardia.* Oxford.

How, W. W., and J. Wells. 1912. *A Commentary on Herodotus.* Vol. 2. Oxford.

Hruza, E. 1894. Polygamie und Pellikat nach Griechischem Rechte. Erlangen.

Instinsky, H. U. 1960. "Alexander, Pindar, Euripides." *Historia* 10:248–55.

Jacoby, F. 1923–30. *Die Fragmente der Griechische Historiker.* 3 vols. Berlin.

Jaschinski, S. 1981. "Alexander und Griechenland unter dem Eindruck der Flucht des Harpalos." Ph.D. diss., Bonn.

Judeich, W. 1893. "Ada." *RE* 1:339.

————. 1895. "Artabazus 3." *RE* 2 (1): 1299.

Kaerst, J. 1893. "Alexandros 5." *RE* 1 (1): 1434–35.

————. 1894a. "Amyntas 15." *RE* 1: 2007.

————. 1894b. "Attalus 7." *RE* 1: 2158.

————. 1896. "Asklepiodorus 8." *RE* 2 (2): 1636.

————. 1897. "Barsine (Stateira)." *RE* 3 (1): 29.

————. 1907. "Eurydike 13." *RE* 6 (1) : 1326.

Kahrstedt, U. 1910. "Frauen auf antiken Münzen." *Klio* 10: 261–314.

———. 1931a. "Memnon 3." *RE* 15 (1): 652–52.

———. 1931b. "Mentor 6." *RE* 15 (1): 964–65.

Kapetanopoulos, E. 1994. "Sirras." *AncW* 25: 9–14.

Kassel, R. 1983. "Dialoge mit Statuen." *ZPE* 51: 1–12.

Kingsley, B. M. 1986. "Harpalos in the Megarid (333–331 B.C.) and the Grain Shipments from Cyrene." *ZPE* 66: 165–77.

Kirchner, J. 1901. "Demo 5." *RE* 4 (2): 2863.

Koch, W. 1923. "Ptolemäerinnen nach ihren Münzen." *ZfN* 34: 67–106.

Kroll, W. 1912. "Halkyoneus 1." *RE* 7 (2): 2273.

Kuhrt, A., and S. Sherwin-White. 1991. "Aspects of Seleucid Royal Ideology: The Cylinder of Antiochus I from Borsippa." *JHS* 111: 71–86.

Kurtz, D., and J. Boardman. 1971. *Greek Burial Customs.* Ithaca.

Lacey, W. K. 1968. *The Family in Classical Greece.* London.

Lane Fox, R. 1973. *Alexander the Great.* New York.

———. 1980. *The Search for Alexander.* Boston.

———. 1986. "Theopompus of Chios and the Greek World, 411–322." In *Chios: A Conference at the Homereion in Chios*, edited by J. Boardman and C. E. Vaphopoulou-Richardson, 105–120. Oxford.

Laurenzi, L. 1941. *Clara Rhodos* 10.

Lauter, H. 1987. "Les éléments de la *regia* hellénistique." In *Le système palatial en Orient, en Grèce et à Rome*, edited by E. Lévy, 345–55. Strasbourg.

Le Bohec, S. 1981. "Phthia, mère de Philippe V: Examen critique des sources." *REG* 94: 34–46.

———. 1987. "L'Entourage royal à la cour des Antigonides." In *Le système palatial en Orient, en Grèce et à Rome*, edited by E. Lévy, 316–26. Strasbourg.

———. 1993a. *Antigone Doson, roi de Macédoine.* Nancy.

———. 1993b. "Les reines de Macédoine de la mort d'Alexandre à celle de Persée." *Cahiers du Centre Glotz* 4: 229–45.

Lenschau, T. 1938. "Pharnabazos 3." *RE* 19 (2): 1848.

Leschhorn, W. 1984. *Grunder der Stadt: Studien zu Einem Politisch-religiosen Phanomen der Griechischer Geschichte.* Stuttgart.

Lévêque, P. 1957. *Pyrrhos.* Paris.

Levin, C. 1989. "Power, Politics, and Sexuality: Images of Elizabeth I." In *The Politics of Gender in Early Modern Europe*, 95–110. Sixteenth-Century Essays and Studies 16. Kirksville, Mo.

Lock, R. 1977. "The Macedonian Army Assembly in the Time of Alexander the Great." *CQ* 72: 91–107.

Longega, G. 1968. *Arsinoe II.* Rome.

Lund, H. 1994. *Lysimachus: A Study in Early Hellenistic Kingship.* London.

Lyons, D. 1997. *Gender and Immortality: Heroines in Ancient Greek Myth and Cult.* Princeton.

McClintock, M. K. 1971. "Menstrual Synchrony and Suppression." *Nature* 229: 244–45.

Macurdy, G. H. 1927. "Queen Eurydice and the Evidence for Woman-Power in Early Macedonia." *AJP* 48: 201–14.

———. 1928. "*Basilinna* and *Basilissa*, the Alleged Title of the Queen Archon in Athens." *AJP* 49: 276–82.

———. 1929. "The Political Activities and the Name of Cratesipolis." *AJP* 50: 273–8.

———. 1932a. *Hellenistic Queens*. Baltimore.

———. 1932b. "Roxane and Alexander IV in Epirus." *JHS* 52: 256–61.

Magie, D. 1950. *Roman Rule in Asia Minor.* Vol. 1. Princeton.

Malkin, I. 1985. "What's in a Name? The Eponymous Founders of Greek Colonies." *Athenaeum* 63: 114–30.

Mallwitz, A. 1972. *Olympia und Seine Bauten*. Munich.

Markle, M. M. 1977. "The Macedonian Sarissa, Spear and Related Armor." *AJA* 81: 323–29.

———. 1978. "The Use of the Sarissa by Philip and Alexander of Macedon." *AJA* 82: 483–97.

Marquandt, P. 1985. "Penelope POLYTROPOS." *AJP* 106: 32–48.

Martin, T. R. 1982. "A Phantom Fragment of Theopompus and Philip II's First Campaign in Thessaly." *HSCP* 86: 55–78.

Meiggs, R., and D. Lewis. 1969. *A Selection of Greek Historical Inscriptions*. Oxford.

Mendels, D. 1984. "Aetolia 331–301: Frustration, Political Power, and Survival." *Historia* 33: 129–80.

Mikrogiannakes, E. I. 1973. "To Politikon Ergon Tou Kassandrou." *AM* 2: 103–8.

Miller, Stella G. 1973. "The Philippeion and Macedonian Hellenistic Architecture." *MDAI(A)* 88: 189–218.

———. 1993. *The Tomb of Lyson and Kallikles: A Painted Macedonian Tomb*. Mainz.

Miller, Stephen G. 1978. *The Prytaneion: Its Function and Architectural Form*. Berkeley.

Mirón Pérez, M. D. 1998a. "Cómo convertirse en diosa: Mujeres y divinidad en la Antigüedad Clásica. *Arenal* 5 (1): 23–46.

———. 1998b. "Olimpia, Eurídice y el origen del culto dinástico en la Grecia helenística." *Florentia Iliberritana* 9: 215–35.

———. 1999. "Realeza y labor doméstica en Macedonia antigua." *Gerión*.

Morse, D. 1967. "Tuberculosis." In *Diseases in Antiquity*, edited by Don Brothwell and A. T. Sandison, 249–71. Springfield, Ill.

Mortensen, C. 1991. "The Career of Bardylis." *AncW* 22: 49–59.

———. 1992. "Eurydice: Demonic or Devoted Mother?" *AHB* 6: 155–69.

———. 1997. "Olympias: Royal Wife and Mother at the Macedonian Court." Ph.D. diss., University of Queensland, Brisbane.

Mossé, C. 1981. "La femme dans la société homérique." *Klio* 63: 149–57.

Muhsam, H. V. 1956–57. "Fertility of Polygamous Marriages." *Population Studies* 10: 3–16.

Munz, P. 1969. *Life in the Age of Charlemagne*. London.

Musgrave, J. 1985. "The Skull of Philip II of Macedon." In *Current Topics in Oral Biology*, edited by S. J. W. Lisney and B. Matthews, 1–16. Bristol.

———. 1990. "Dust and Damn'd Oblivion: A Study of Cremation in Ancient Greece." *BSA* 85: 271–99.

———. 1991. "The Human Remains from Vergina Tombs I, II, and III: An Overview." *AncW* 22 (2): 3–9.

———. 1993. "Cremation in Ancient Macedonia." *AM* 5 (2): 1131–42.

———. 1994. "New Human Remains from Vergina." [Abstract] *AJA* 98: 309.

Nelson, J. L. 1977. "Inauguration Rituals." In *Early Medieval Kingship*, edited by I. N. Wood and P. H. Sayer, 50–71. Leeds.

———. 1978. "Queens as Jezebels: The Careers of Brunhild and Balthild in Merovingian History." In *Medieval Women*, edited by D. Baker, 31–77. Oxford.

Nielsen, I. 1994. *Hellenistic Palaces: Tradition and Renewal.* Aarhus.

Neumer-Pfau, W. 1982. *Studien zur Ikonographie und gesellschaft Funktion hellenistischer Aphrodite-Statuen.* Bonn.

Ninou, K. 1980. *Treasures of Ancient Macedonia.* Athens.

Nock, A. D. 1928. "Notes on Ruler Cult, I–IV." *JHS* 48: 21–42.

———. 1930. "Sunnaos Theos." *HSCP* 41: 1–62.

———. 1944. "The Cult of Heroes." *HThR* 37: 141–70.

O'Brien, J. M. 1992. *Alexander the Great: The Invisible Enemy.* London.

O'Brien, J. V. 1993. *The Transformation of Hera: A Study of Ritual, Hero, and the Goddess in the Iliad.* Lanham, Md.

Oikonomedes, A. 1982. "The Epigram on the Tomb of Olympias at Pydna." *AncW* 5: 9–16.

———. 1983. "A New Inscription from Vergina and Eurydice, Mother of Philip II." *AncW* 7: 62–64.

Oliverio, G. 1933. *Cirenaica 2:1: La stela dei nuovi commandamenti e dei cereali.* Bergamo.

Olmstead, A. T. 1948. *History of the Persian Empire.* Chicago.

Palagia, O. 1999. "The Grave Relief of Adea—A Macedonian Princess." Unpublished paper delivered at the Australian Archaeological Institute, Athens, Greece, April 21.

Papazaglou, F. 1965. "Les origines et la destinée de l'état illyrien: Illyrii Proprie Dicti." *Historia* 11: 143–79.

———. 1988. *Les villes de Macédoine à l'époque romaine. BCH* supplement. 16. Paris.

Parke, H. W. 1933. *Greek Mercenary Soldiers.* Oxford.

———. 1977. *Festivals of Athens.* London.

Pearson, L. 1960. *The Lost Histories of Alexander the Great.* New York.

Pedrick, V. 1988. "The Hospitality of Noble Women in the *Odyssey*." *Helios* 15: 85–101.

Petsas, P. 1978. *Pella, Alexander the Great's Capital.* Institute for Balkan Studies, 182. Thessaloniki.

Pirenne-Delforgé, V. 1994. *L'Aphrodite grecque. Contribution à l'étude de ses cultes et de sa personnalité dans le panthéon archaïque et classique.* Kernos supplement. 4. Athens-Liege.

Pollitt, J. J. 1986. *Art in the Hellenistic Age.* Cambridge.

Pomeroy, S. B. 1975. Goddesses, Whores, Wives, and Slaves: Women in Classical Antiquity. New York.

————. 1977. "Technikai kai Mousikai: The Education of Women in the Fourth Century and Hellenistic Period." *AJAH* 2: 51–68.

————. 1984. *Women in Hellenistic Egypt.* New York.

————. 1994. *Xenophon. Oeconomicus: A Social and Historical Commentary.* Oxford.

Préaux, C. 1978. *Le monde hellénistique: La Grèce et l'Orient de la mort d' Alexandre à la conquête romaine de la Grèce (323–146 av, H.-C.).* 2 vols. Paris.

Prestianni-Giallombardo, A. M. 1976–77. "'Diritto' matrimoniale, ereditario et dinastico nella Macedonia di Filippo II." *RSA* 6–7: 81–118.

————. 1981. "Euridika-Kleopatra. Nota ad Arr. Anab. 3, 6, 5." *AnnPisa* 3: 295–306.

Prestianni-Giallombardo, A. M. and B. Tripodi. 1980. "Le tombe regali di Vergina: Quale Filippo?" *AnnPisa* 10 (3): 989–1001.

Price, S. R. F. 1984a. "Gods and Emperors: The Greek Language of the Roman Imperial Cult." *JHS* 104: 79–95.

————. 1984b. *Rituals and Power: The Roman Imperial Cult in Asia Minor.* Cambridge.

Pritchett, W. K. 1993. *The Liar School of Herodotus.* Amsterdam.

Quirke, S. 1992. *Ancient Egyptian Religion.* New York.

Raubitschek, A. 1941. "Phryne." *RE* 20 (1): 893–907.

Renard, M., and J. Servais. 1955. "A propos du mariage d'Alexandre et de Roxane." *AC* 24: 29–50.

Richter, G. M. 1965. *The Portraits of the Greeks.* London.

Ridgway, B. S. 1987. "Ancient Greek Women and Art: The Material Evidence." *AJA* 91: 399–409.

Riginos, Alice S. 1994. "The Wounding of Philip II of Macedon: Fact and Fabrication. "*JHS* 114: 103–19.

Ritter, H. W. 1965. *Diadem und Königsherrschaft.* Vestigia 7. Munich.

————. 1972. "Livia's Erhebung zur Augusta." *Chiron* 2: 313–38.

Ritzakes, T., and G. Touratsoglou. 1985. *Epigraphes ano Makedonias.* Vol. 1. Athens.

Robert, L. 1933. "Notes d'épigraphie hellénistique xl. Inscription de Ptolemée, fils de Lysimaque." *BCH* 57: 485–91.

————. 1946. "Adeimantos et la ligue de Corinthe. Sur une inscription de Delphes." *Hellenica* 2:15–33.

Robert, L., and J. Robert. 1984. "3249 Vergina-Aegai." *REG* 97:450–51.

Robins, G. 1993. *Women in Ancient Egypt.* Cambridge, Mass.

Roccos, L. J. 1995. "The Kanephoros and Her Festival Mantle in Greek Art." *AJA* 99: 641–66.

Roos, A. G. 1950. "Remarques sur un édit d'Antiochos III roi de Syrie." *Mnemosyne* 4: 54–63.

Roux, G. 1992. "The History of the Rotunda." In *Samothrace* Vol. 7, edited by J. R. McCredie, G. Roux, S. M. Shaw, and J. Kurtisch. Princeton.

Ruzicka, S. 1992. *Politics of a Persian Dynasty: The Hecatomnids in the Fourth Century B.C.* Norman.

Saatsaglou-Paliadeli, C. 1987. "Eurydika Sirra Eukleiai." *Ametos* 2: 733–44.

———. 1993. "Skepseis me Aphorme ena Eurema apo ta Palatitsia." *AM* 5 (3): 1339–71.

Saller, R. 1980. "Anecdote as Historical Evidence for the Principate." *G&R* 27: 69–83.

Samuel, A. E. 1988. "Philip and Alexander as Kings: Macedonian Monarchy and Merovingian Parallels." *AHR* 93: 1270–47.

Sancisi-Weerdenberg, H. 1983. "Exit Atossa: Images of Women in Greek Historiography on Persia." In *Images of Women in Antiquity*, edited by A. Cameron and A. Kuhrt, 20–33. Detroit.

———. 1987. "Decadence in the Empire or Decadence in the Sources?" *Achaemenid History* 1: 33–47.

———. 1993. "Alexander and Persepolis." In *Alexander the Great: Reality and Myth*, edited by J. Carlsen, B. Due, O. S. Due, and B. Poulsen, 177–88. Rome.

Sawada, N. 1993. "A Reconsideration of the Peace of Philocrates." Kodai 4: 21–50.

Schachermeyr, F. 1970. *Alexander in Babylon und die Reichsordnung nach seinem Tode.* Sitzb. Vienna 268.3. Vienna.

———. 1973. *Alexander der Grosse: Das Problem seiner Persönlichkeit und seines Wirkens.* Sitzb. Vienna 285. Vienna.

Schaps, D. 1977. "The Women Least Mentioned: Etiquette and Women's Names." *CQ* 27: 323–30.

Schleif, H. 1944. "Das Philippeion: Baubeschreibung." In *Olympische Forschungen*, vol. 1, edited by E. Kunze and H. Schleif, 3–24. Berlin.

Schoch, F. 1924. "Herakles 2." *RE* Supplbd. 4: 731–32.

Scholl, R. 1987. "Alexander der Grosse und die Sklaverei am Hofe." *Klio* 69: 108–21.

Scott, K. 1928. "The Deification of Demetrius Poliorcetes." *AJP* 49: 137–66, 217–39.

———. 1931. "The Significance of Statues in Precious Metals in Emperor Worship." *TAPA* 62: 101–23.

Seibert, J. 1967. *Historische Beiträge zu den dynastischen Verbindungen in hellenistischer Zeit.* Historia Einzelschriften 10. Wiesbaden.

Shafer, B. E. 1991. *Religion in Ancient Egypt: Gods, Myths, and Personal Practice.* Ithaca.

Siganidou, Maria. 1987. "To Anaktoriko Sugkrotema Tes Pellas." *AEMTH* 1: 119–24.

Simon, E. 1983. *Festivals of Attica.* Madison.

Smith, R. R. 1988. *Hellenistic Royal Portraits.* Oxford.

Staehelin, F. 1914. "Roxane 5." *RE* 1 (1A): 1155–56.

———. 1918. "Drypetis." *RE* Supplbd. 3: 415.

———. 1921. "Kleopatra 13." *RE* 11 (1): 737.

———. 1924a. "Lanassa 2." *RE* 12 (1): 617.

———. 1924b. "Langaros." *RE* 12 (1): 677.

———. 1924c. "Laodike 20." *RE* 12 (1): 707–8.

Stafford, P. M. 1978. "Sons and Mothers: Family Politics in the Early Middle Ages." In *Medieval Women*, edited by D. Baker, 79–100. Oxford.

———. 1981. "The King's Wife in Wessex." *P&P* 91: 3–27.

———. 1983. *Queens, Concubines, and Dowagers: The King's Wife in the Early Middle Ages.* Athens, Ga.

Starr, C. G. 1977. *The Economic and Social Growth of Early Greece, 800–500.* New York.

Stewart, A. 1993. *Faces of Power: Alexander's Image and Hellenistic Politics.* Berkeley.

Stipçevic, A. 1977. *The Illyrians, History and Culture.* Park Ridge, N.J.

Strasburger, H. 1939. "Olympias 5." *RE* 18 (1): 177–82.

Svoronos, J. N. 1919. *L'Hellénisme primitif de la Macédoine.* Athens.

Taeger, F. 1957–60. *Charisma. Studien zur Geschichte des antiken Herrscherkultes.* 2 vols. Stuttgart.

Tarn, W. W. 1913. *Antigonos Gonatas.* Oxford.

———. 1921. "Heracles, son of Barsine." *JHS* 41: 18–28.

———. 1924. "Philip V and Phthia." *CQ* 18: 17–23.

———. 1940. "Phthia-Chryseis." *HSCP* Suppl. 1: 483–501.

———. 1949. *Alexander the Great.* 2 vols. Cambridge.

Tataki, A. B. 1988. *Ancient Beroea: Prosopography and Society.* Athens.

Tod, M. N. 1946. *Greek Historical Inscriptions.* 2d ed. Oxford.

Tondriau, J. L. 1948a. "Comparisons and Identifications of the Rulers with Deities in the Hellenistic Period." *Review of Religion* 13: 24–47.

———. 1948b. "Princesses ptolémaïques comparées ou identifiées à des déesses (IIIe–Ier siècles avant J. C.)." *BSRAA* 37: 12–33.

———. 1948c. "Les souveraines lagides en déesses." *EtPap* 7: 1–15.

———. 1956. "La divinisation de la beauté: Figure littéraire et thème religeux." In *Studi in onore de A. Calderin et R. Paribeni*, 1: 15–22. Milan.

Treves, P. 1934, 1935. "Studi su Antigono Dosone." *Athenaeum* 12: 381–411, 13: 22–56.

Tronson, A. 1984. "Satyrus the Peripatetic and the Marriages of Philip II." *JHS* 104: 116–56.

Turner, E. G., J. Rea, L. Koenen, P. Fernandez, and J. M. Pomar. 1962. *The Oxyrhynchus Papyri.* Pt. 27. London.

Unz, R. K. 1985. "Alexander's Brothers?" *JHS* 105: 171–74.

Van Bremen, R. 1996. *The Limits of Participation: Women and Civic Life in the Greek East in the Hellenistic and Roman Periods.* Amsterdam.

Vatin, C. 1970. *Recherches sur le mariage et la condition de la femme mariée à l'époque hellénistique.* Paris.

Vermeule, E. 1979. *Aspects of Death in Early Greek Art and Poetry.* Berkeley.

Vernant, J. P. 1973. "Le mariage en Grèce archaïque." *PP* 28: 51–74.

―――. 1981. *Myth and Society in Ancient Greece.* New York.

Vickers, M. 1972. "Hellenistic Thessaloniki." *JHS* 92: 156–70.

Volkmann, H. 1959. "Ptolemaios." *RE* 23 (2): 1596–97.

Walbank, F. W. 1940. *Philip V of Macedon.* Cambridge.

―――. 1967. *A Historical Commentary on Polybius.* Vol. 2. Oxford.

―――. 1988. "Part Two." In Hammond and Walbank 1988: 199–362.

Walcot, P. 1987a. "Plato's Mother and Other Terrible Women." *G&R* 13–31.

―――. 1987b. "Romantic Love and True Love: Greek Attitudes to Marriage." *AncSoc* 18: 5–33.

Wehrli, C. 1964. "Phila, fille d'Antipater et épouse de Démétrius, roi des Macédoniens." *Historia* 13: 140–46.

―――. 1969. *Antigone et Demetrios.* Geneva.

Weiskopf, M. 1989. *The So-Called "Great Satrap's Revolt," 366–360 B.C.* Historia Einzelschriften, 63. Wiesbaden.

Welles, C. B. 1963. *Diodorus VII.* Cambridge, Mass.

Wemple, S. F. 1981. *Women in Frankish Society: Marriage and the Cloister.* Philadelphia.

Westlake, H. D. 1935. *Thessaly in the Fourth Century B.C.* London.

―――. 1969. "Eumenes of Cardia." In *Essays on Greek Historians and Greek History,* 313–30. Manchester.

Whitehorne, J. 1994. *Cleopatras.* London.

Wiesner, K. 1939. "Olympia (Philippeion)." *RE* 18 (1): 105–7.

Wilcken, U. 1896. "Arsinoe 26." *RE* 2 (1): 1282–87.

Wilhelm, A. 1908. "Eine Inschrift des Königs Epiphanes Nikomedes." *Jahresh* 11: 79–81.

―――. 1949. "Ein Weihgedicht der Grossmutter Alexanders des Grossen." *Mélanges Grégoire,* 2: 625–33.

Wilkes, J. 1992. *The Illyrians.* Oxford.

Will, E. 1979–82. *Histoire politique du monde hellénistique (323–30 v. J.-C.)* 2d ed. 2 vols. Nancy.

Wood, I. N. 1977. "Kings, Kingdoms, and Consent." In *Early Medieval Kingship,* edited by P. H. Sawyer and I. N. Wood, 6–29. Leeds.

Worrle, M. 1978. "Epigraphische Forschungen sur Geschichte Lykiens." *Chiron* 8: 212–46.

Worthington, I., ed. 1994. *Ventures into Greek History.* Oxford.

Xirotiris, N. I., and F. Langenscheidt. 1981. "The Cremations from the Royal Tombs of Vergina." *AE*: 142–60.

Ziegler, K. 1952. "Polykrateia." *RE* 21 (2): 1726.

Zschietzschmann, W. 1944. "Das Philippeion, Baugeschichte." In *Olympische Forschungen,* vol. 1, edited by E. Kunze and H. Schleif, 24–52. Berlin.

Index to Biographical Essays

General Index

Biographical essays are indicated by page numbers printed in *italics*.

Achaemenid dynasty: Alexander III's marriages into, 109–12; names of women of, 266n.135; women of, 96, 100

Ada, 93

Adea Eurydice, wife of Philip Arrhidaeus, 14, 19, 37, 58, 69, 131, *132–37*, 151; Cynnane and, 129, 130; death of, 13, 136, 140, 141; literacy of, 29; and murder of Perdiccas, 138; name of, 33; in period of the Successors, 115, 117, 122, 139, 140; tomb of, 234, 237, 241

Adeimantus of Lampsacus, 218

Aeacid dynasty: Argead dynasty, reconciliation with, 204; demise of, 190

Aeacides, 31, 120, 121, 136, 139, 142, 144

Aegae, 234. *See also* Vergina

Aelian: on Simache, 17

Aeschines: on Cleopatra 2, 89; on Eurydice 1, 43–46; on Ptolemy Alorites, 40

Aetolians, 141, 190

Agalma, 216

Agatharchides: on Stratonice 3, 185, 189

Agathocles, 161, 169, 174, 175, 301n.23, 304n.66, 305n.81; murder of, 307n.95

Aggression, of women, 36

Agriani, 293n.44, 294n.45

Alcestas, 131

Alexander, son of Craterus, 188

Alexander, son of Lanassa and Pyrrhus, 169

Alexander I, 5; and marriage of Gygaea 1, 16

Alexander II, 38, 39, 41, 42, 43, 47; burial of, 238

Alexander III (Alexander the Great), 4, 7, 52, 53, 63, 76, 206; Attalus and, 71; Barsine and, 101–105; *basileus,* use of, 225; childhood nurse of, 30; cities named after, 207; Cleopatra 2 and, 32, 37, 84, 85, 89–93; Cleopatra 2's wedding celebration, 204; cult worship and, 209, 210, 219; Cynnane and, 30, 129; and Darius III's family, 93–97, 108; death of, 114, 141; divine sonship of, 217; education of, 65, 265n.122; Elizabeth I of England compared with, 99–100; and Macedonian monarchy, 82; marriages of, 19, 23, 83, 96–100, 103–8, 111, 112; and murder of Cleopatra 3 and Europa, 78; Olympias and, 84–88, 90–93; parents' relationship with, 30, 31, 64, 66, 67; and Philip II's assassina-

355

tion, 80; as Philip II's heir, 78; polygamy of, 229; prowess in warfare, 35; Roxane and, 106–107; and royal women, 83, 84, 93, 113, 289n.96; sexual restraint of, 285n.41, 286n.42; Stateira 1 and, 94, 95; Stateira 2 and, 108, 109; statue of, in Philippeum, 212; succession crisis following death of, 24

Alexander IV, 6, 8, 117, 118, 125, 134, 137, 146, 147; birth of, 114; Cassander and, 145; Deidameia and, 291n.21; murder of, 147–48, 154; Olympias and, 120, 121, 138, 139; statue base at Thessaloniki, 209; tomb of, 234

Alexander V, son of Cassander, 157, 159–63; death of, 164; Lysandra and, 160–61

Alexander of Epirus, brother of Olympias, 62, 64, 75, 76, 89, 277n.58

Alexander II of Epirus, father of Phthia, 190

Alexander the Lyncestian, 87, 283n.14

Alexis, cult worship in play of, 218

Alorites, Ptolemy. See Ptolemy Alorites

Amastris, city named after, 208

Amphimachus, 276n.45

Amyntas I, 16

Amyntas III, 5, 38; burial of, 236, 238; children of, 25, 41, 46–47, (Eurynoe) 39; marriages of, 23, 24, 25, 46–49; statue of, in Philippeum, 212; wives of, (Eurydice 1) 40–46, (Gygaea 2) 46–47

Amyntas, nephew of Philip II, 69, 70, 71, 84, 129, 132, 278nn.79, 83

Amyntas, son of Andromenes, 87

Andron, 28

Andronicos, Manolis: on burials at Vergina, 44–45, 46, 234, 236–44

Anecdotal sources, 11

Antigonid dynasty, 3, 7, 153, 172, 179–84, 188; avoidance of violence by, 199; cities named after women of, 208; and cult worship, 219; diadem for royal women of, 233; Greek opinion, concern for, 231; last days of, 196; marriage practices of, 184, 186, 192–95; royal wedding extravaganzas of, 206; royal women in period of, 10, 180–81, 197–202, 245

Antigonus, 114, 120, 126, 127, 128, 145; Adea Eurydice and, 133; *basileus* used by, 225; on Cassander's marriage to Thessalonice, 156; cult worship of, 218, 219, 224; Cynnane and, 130; murder of Cleopatra 2 by, 151; royal diadem and, 232

Antigonus Doson, 179, 191, 192

Antigonus Gonatas, 153, 154, 166, 173, 171, 176, 179, 181, 200; and death of Alexander, son of Craterus, 188; Demo and, 181–82; and great mound at Vergina, 234; monogamy of, 182; Phila 3 and, 182–83

Antiochus I, 171, 184

Antiochus II, 171, 183

Antipater, father of Cassander, 70, 74, 82, 86, 87, 88, 90–93, 97, 99, 113, 114, 120, 137; Adea Eurydice and, 133, 134; and Antigonid dynasty, 179; Cleopatra 2 and, 126; Cynnane and, 129, 130; death of, 138; marriage alliances and, 131; Perdiccas and, 125, 291n.15; Phila 2 and, 165; rivalry with Olympias and Cleopatra 2, 123, 124; Roxane and, 147

Antipater, son of Cassander, 153, 158, 163; Eurydice 2 and, 159, 160;

marriage of, 159, 160; Thessalonice's murder by, 157, 161–64

Antipater Etesias, nephew of Cassander, 301n.14

Antipatrid dynasty, 7, 153, 164; collapse of, 158, 159

Apama, daughter of Antiochus I and wife of Magas of Cyrene, 171

Apamea, wife of Seleucus, 225

Apamea 1, daughter of Demetrius II, 185, *187*

Apamea 2, sister of Perseus, *197*

Aphrodite, 210, 218–25

Aphrodite Hetairia, 223

Aphrodite Lamia, 218

Apollo, cult of, 171–72

Apollonides, 296n.80

Appian: on Eumenes, 196

Aratus of Sicyon, 193

Aratus of Soli, 183

Archaeology, 6; Eucleia temple site, 44–45. *See also* Burial sites; Palaces

Archaic period, women in, 14

Archelaus, son of Amyntas III, 47

Archelaus, son of Perdiccas II, 5, 17, 38; and Cleopatra 1, 21, 22

Argead dynasty, 3–4, 4–8; and Aeacid dynasty, reconciliation of, 204; army's loyalty to, 134; collapse of, 8, 115–19, 137, 141, 144, 151–52, 153, 200; and cult worship, 209, 210; death of last of Argeads, 158, 164; female line, 151; gender roles in, 35–37; household monarchy in period of, 201; marriage practices of, 18–21, 23–27, 184; names and titles in, 32–34; Olympias' death and collapse of, 144; patronage of women of, 34; polygamy of, 228, 229, 231; Polyperchon's military failures and collapse of, 138; racist attitudes and, 26; religious practices of, 34–35; royal women in, 8–37, 198, 245; scholarship and sources for, 8–13; succession patterns of, 23–24, 31–32; and the Successors, 150–51; titles of kings in, 7; violence of, 117

Argive, house of, 194

Ariarathres V, king of Cappadocia, 197

Aristobulus: on Alexander and Barsine, 104; on Parysatis and Alexander, 110

Aristonous, 142, 143

Aristotle, 265n.122; on Cleopatra 1, 21–22

Arrabaeus of Lyncestis, 41

Arrhidaeus, son of Amyntas III,.47

Arrhidaeus, son of Philip II. *See* Philip Arrhidaeus

Arrian: on Adea Eurydice, 133; on Antipater and Olympias, 92; on Audata, 58; on Cleopatra 2, 126, 128; on Eurydice or Cleopatra 3, 74; on Parysatis and Alexander, 110; on Stateira 2 and Alexander, 109

Arsinoe, wife of Lysimachus and Ptolemy Ceraunus, 10, 171, *173–77,* 206; *basilissa* used for, 227, 233; cult worship of, 219–20, 222, 223, 224; marriage to Ptolemy Ceraunus, 230, 231; *regina* as title for, 228; religious practices of, 34; royal trappings of, 232, 233

Arsinoe Philadelphus, 210

Arsinoeum, at Samothrace, 174

Artabazus, 15, 100–105

Arybbas, 63, 64

Asclepiodorus, 133

Asian culture: Graeco-Macedonian contempt for, 149; women, stereotype of, 298n.97

Aspasia, 222
Assimilation, in cult worship, 220–24, 322n.90
Athenaeus, 15, 30; on Audata, 57, 58; on Cleopatra 3, 72, 77; on cults, 218–19, 220, 224, 225; on Cynnane, 41; on Demetrius Poliorcetes, 233; on Halcyoneus, 181; on Harpalus, 217–18, 224; on Meda, 68; on Nicesipolis, 60; on Phila 1, 59; on Phila Aphrodite, 218; on Philinna, 61; on Philip II's marriages, 52–55; on Ptolemy, son of Amyntas III, 42
Athens: cult worship in, 218–19, 224; gender roles in, 36; Macedonia's alliance with, 5; marriage practices in, 19; Philip II's defeat of, 51; women in, 3, 9–10, 27
Attalus, 70–76, 79, 85, 133, 278nn.85, 86, 279nn.88, 89, 90
Audata, wife of Philip II, 14, 53, 54, *57–58*, 69

Babylon, Alexander's death at, 82
Babylonians (Philemon), 217–18
Bactria, revolt of, 106–107
Bagoas, 97
Balacrus, 165, 303n.45
Bardylis, 39, 57–58, 274n.24
Barsine, mother of Heracles, 95, 97, 100, *101–105*, 112, 114, *149–50*, 246; murder of, 148, 149
Basileus, 7, 225, 226; and the Successors, 115, 118, 139, 152; women as part of, 37
Basilissa, 166, 189, 190, 225–28, 231–32; Glycera, 218; Thessalonice, 209; and wearing of the diadem, 233
Beloch, Karl Julius: on Antipater, son of Cassander, 158; on Polycrateia, 194

Berenice, wife of Ptolemy I, 174; *basilissa* used for, 225, 226; cult worship of, 219
Bilistiche, 220, 224
Borza, E. N.: on Eucleia cults, 45; on tomb at Vergina, 243
Briseis, 210
Brother-sister marriages. *See* Sibling marriages
Bubares, 16
Burial sites, 29, 46, 214, 234–44, 264n.120; of Cleopatra 3, 72, 78; of Meda, 68

Cadmeia, 89
Callisthenes, 96
Caranus, 77
Caria, 15, 93; public images of women of, 214
Cassander, 7, 121, 137, 138; Adea Eurydice and, 135, 136, 294n.61; Alexander IV and, 145; Antipater and Eurydice 2, marriage of, 159–60; Barsine, murder of, 148; and burials at Vergina, 241; cult for, 219; death of, 159, 301n.16; eponymous foundations of, 157, 158, 207, 208; Heracles and Barsine, murder of, 150; Macedonia ruled by, 153, 154, 155; Olympias, propaganda campaign against, 63; Olympias' slaughter of followers of, 122, 141, 142; and Olympias' trial and death, 123, 143–44; Olympias' war with, 142–43; Phila 2's diplomatic mission to, 166, 167; Polyperchon's campaign against, 148–49; Roxane and, 147; Roxane and Alexander IV, murder of, 148, 150; sons of, 158, 159, 161, 162–63; Thessalonice and, 155–58, 300n.11

Cassandra, 210
Cassandreia, 207, 208, 219
Ceraunus, Ptolemy. *See* Ptolemy Ceraunus
Chaeroneia, battle of, 45, 51, 212
Charlemagne, daughters of, 284n.22
Children: care of, 30; mother-child relationships, 31–32, 36, 37; from polygamous marriages, 27, 29, 30
Chryseis, wife of Antigonus Doson, 186, *191,* 192, 311n.44
Clan, 214; and Macedonian kingship, 6, 7, 8, 200; women and, 37
Cleopatra 1, wife of Perdiccas II, *21–22*
Cleopatra 2, daughter of Philip II, 14, 30, 31, 37, 53, 63, *75–76,* 80, *89–90, 123–28;* Alexander III's relationship with, 84–85, 87, 90–93; children of, 30; literacy of, 28–29; murder of, 151; and murder of Perdiccas, 138; patronage of, 34, 35; as regent in Epirus, 86; search for husband for, in period of the Successors, 119, 120, 131; wedding celebration for, 203–205, 213
Cleopatra 3, wife of Philip II, 28, 30, 53–56, 66, 70–71, *72–75,* 279n.96, 280n.104; and assassination of Philip II, 79; and Europa, 77; murder of, 12, 30, 84, 85, 86, 282n.4; patronage of, 34; tomb of, 72, 78, 234, 236, 237, 239, 240, 241
Competition, 35, 36
Concubines, 17
Connor, W. R.: on international festivals, 205
Corcyra, island of, 169, 170
Corinth, citadel of, 188, 206
Corinth, League of, 51, 73, 204
Corupedion, battle of, 175, 176
Courtesans, 28. *See also* Hetairai

Craterus, husband of Phila 2, 88, 113, 114, 115, 125, 165
Craterus, son of Phila 2, 165, 188
Cratesipolis, 229
Cratinus, 222
Cremation, 237
Cult worship, 209–25; of Arsinoe, 177; assimilation to divinities, 220–24; Dionysiac cults, 65, 222, 291–92n.22; Eucleia, cult of, 41, 44, 45, 49, 214; of Lanassa, 170; of Phila 2, 169; ruler cults, 210–11; statues and, 215, 216; of Stratonice 2, 171; of women after whom cities were named, 208
Curtius: on Alexander III and Olympias, 217; on Barsine and other captives after battle of Issus, 102; on Roxane and Alexander, 106, 107
Cynnane, daughter of Philip II, 14, 30, 31, 53, 57, 58, *69–70,* 76, *129–31,* 151, 246, 275n.27; Alexander III's death and, 128; burial of, 241; ethnicity of, 41; and marriage of Adea Eurydice and Arrhidaeus, 131–32; murder of, 125; political violence of, 117

Darius III, 108, 109; Alexander III's treatment of family of, 93–97, 108; Roxane's supposed murder of the daughters of, 107
Deianeira, 222
Deidameia, 147, 166, 167, 206, 229, 291n.21
Deipnosophistai (Athenaeus), 52
Delian cults, 172, 219; Laodice's inscription, 196
Demetrius, son of Philip V, 193, 194; execution of, 199
Demetrius I, brother of Laodice, 197
Demetrius II, son of Antigonus Go-

natas, 179, 181, 182, 183; Apamea 1 and, 187; Chryseis and, 191–92; city named for mother of, 208; marriages of, 184, 192–93, 199, 230; Nicaea and, 188–89; Phthia and, 190, 191–92, 232; Stratonice 3 and, 184–86, 189

Demetrius Poliorcetes, 153, 164–69, 172, 176, 179; and Alexander V's murder, 157, 160, 163; *basileus* used by, 225; cult worship of, 218, 219; cult worship of *hetairai* of, 218–19; and Dionysus, 222; Lanassa and, 170–71, 229–30; marriages of, 229, 302–303n.42; royal diadem and, 232, 233; Stratonice 2 and, 171; wedding festival of, 206

Demo, *hetaira* or wife of Antigonus Gonatas and mother of Halcyoneus, *181–82*

Demochares: on cult worship of *hetairai,* 218

Derdas, brother of Phila 1, 59

Diadems, 232–33; in Vergina burial sites, 239, 244

Diadochi. *See* Successors

Diodorus: on Adea Eurydice, 133, 135, 136, 137; on Alexander III, 97; on Alexander IV, 120, 121, 145–48, 150; on Amyntas III, 42; on Attalus, 71; on Cassander, 135, 136, 141, 144, 145, 147–48, 150, 154; on Cleopatra 2, 127, 128, 151, 204, 205; on Heracles, 104, 150; on Memnon and Barsine, 102; on Olympias, 37, 88, 97, 120–23, 139–44; on Phila 2, 165, 168, 169; on Polyperchon, 138, 139, 142–43; on Ptolemy, son of Amyntas III, 42; on Ptolemy Alorites, 39; on Roxane, 145–48; on royal diadem, 232; on Sisygambis, 97;

the Successors, 118; on Thessalonice, 163; on wedding celebration for Cleopatra 2, 204, 205

Diogenes: on *hetairai* of kings, 328n.145

Dionysiac cults, 65, 222, 291–92n.22

Dionysius, son of Tryphon: on Phila Aphrodite, 218

Dionysius of Heracleia, 89, 92

Divorce, 228

Domestic occupations, 29, 30

Dress of royal women, 232–33

Drypetis, widow of Hephaestion, 110, 111

Dual monarchy: Macedonia ruled by Cassander's sons, 162–63

Dunasteia, dynasty and, 3, 8

Duris: on Olympias and Adea Eurydice, 121

Egypt: brother-sister marriage in, 231, 245; cult worship in, 219–20, 221

Eikon, 216

Eleusinian mysteries, 214

Eleusinian Painter, 242

Elimeia, house of, 58, 59, 60

Elimiotis, 38

Elizabeth I, Queen of England: Alexander III compared with, 99–100

Epigraphic sources, 10

Epimeleia, 138, 139

Epirus, 86, 87, 89, 90, 91

Eratosthenes: on Olympias, 217

Errington, R. Malcolm: on Cleopatra 2 and Leonnatus, 124; on Polyperchon, 138

Eucleia, cult of, 41, 44, 45, 49, 214

Eumenes, 103, 123, 125, 126, 128; Olympias and, 88, 121, 139, 143

Eumenes of Pergamum (Eumenes II), 195, 196, 206

Europa, daughter of Philip II, 33, 53, 70, 72, 74, *77–78*, 84, 85

Eurydice: significance of name, 33, 280–81n.113

Eurydice, daughter of Antipater and wife of Ptolemy I, 160, 174; festival in honor of, 321n.80

Eurydice, wife of Demetrius, 166

Eurydice, wife of Philip II. *See* Cleopatra 3

Eurydice, wife of Philip Arrhidaeus. *See* Adea Eurydice

Eurydice 1, wife of Amyntas III, 18, 26, *40–46*, 47, 48, 49, 78; cult of, 317n.37; Eurynoe and, 39; literacy of, 28; religious practices of, 34; statue of, in Philippeum, 212, 213, 214; tomb of, 242, 243

Eurydice 2, daughter of Lysimachus and wife of Antipater, *159–60*

Eurynoe, daughter of Amyntas III, *39–40;* Eurydice 1 and, 42

Eusebius: on Antipater and Eurydice 2, 159; on Cassander's sons, 162; on Chryseis, 191

Faklaris, P. B.: on Vergina, 234

Foreign royal wives, 10, 14, 21, 26

Fraser, P. M.: on cult worship, 220, 221

Gender roles, in Argead period, 35–37

Getae, 68

Glaucias, 147, 148

Glycera, *hetaira,* 218

Gnaethaenion, mother of Perseus, 194

Greece: cults of, 45, 210, 211, 215; deification of rulers in, 211; influence on Antigonids, 201; marriage practices in, 19, 23; names of cities of, 208; objections to monarchy in, 214; portraiture and statuary of, 213–15; sources

from, 4, 10; unpopularity of polygamy in, 231; women in, 3, 4, 9–10, 11, 15, 27, 28, 37

Greek language: study of, by daughters of Darius, 109

Greenwalt, W. S.: on marriage practices, 19, 23, 26

Gygaea 1, daughter of Amyntas I, 15, 16

Gygaea 2, wife of Amyntas III, 42, *46–47,* 48

Halcyoneus, 181

Hammond, N. G. L., 14; on burials at Vergina, 236, 238, 239, 243; on Cleopatra 1, 22; on Meda, 68; on Olympias and Cleopatra 2, 91; on Philip V, 194; on Polyperchon, 138

Harpalus, 15, 59, 87, 217–18, 224

Hathor, 221, 322n.85

Headdress, 232–33

Hecatomnid dynasty, 15, 214

Heckel, Waldemar: on Attalus, 71; on Macedonian marriages, 19

Hegemon, Philip II's role as, 204

Hellenic League. *See* Corinth, League of

Hellenistic period, 203. *See also* Successors

Hellenistic Queens (Macurdy), xii–xiii

Hephaestion, 87, 88, 94

Hera, 206, 221–24

Hera Basileia, 220

Heracles, myth of, 210, 222

Heracles, son of Alexander III, 100, 102–104, 114, 118, 148–50, 154

Hermippus: on Prusias I, 187

Herodotus: on Gygaea 1, 16

Hetairai: Aphrodite's association with, 223; cult worship of, 218–19, 220, 223, 224, 225; Demo, *181–82;* in Diogenes' anecdote, 328n.145;

Harpalus' relationship with, 217–18; Lamia, 165, 169; Phryne, 214; royal diadem and, 233

Hetairoi, 5

Hieronymus: on Phila 2, 168; on the Successors, 118

Hippostratus, 280n.104

Homer: accessibility of women in, 28; Aphrodite in, 223; royal women in, 13–14; warriors as godlike in, 210

Homeric monarchy and society, 5

Homosexual relationships, 35–36

Household management, 29–30

Hunting, 35

Hyperides, 86

Illyria, 38, 39, 41, 44, 45, 48, 57, 58; Philip II's defeat of, 51; role of women in, 69

Inequality, between men and women, 3

International festivals: political disturbances and, 205. *See also* Wedding celebrations

Iolaus, 122, 141

Iphicrates, 41, 43, 44, 45

Ipsus, battle of, 167, 206

Isis, 220, 221, 322n.85

Issus, battle of, 102

Jason of Pherae, 60

Jewelry, 232–33; in Vergina burial sites, 239, 240–41, 244

Josephus: on Stratonice 3, 185

Justin: on Adea Eurydice and Cassander, 135, 136; on Alexander's marriages at Susa, 112; on Antipater and Eurydice 2, 159; on Arsinoe, 175, 176, 228, 233; on Barsine, 104; on Cassander's sons, 162; on Cleopatra 3, 78, 85; on Demetrius II, 230; on Europa, 77; on Eurydice 1, 42, 44, 46, 49; on Eurynoe, 39, 40; on Gygaea 2,

46–47; on Heracles, 103, 104; on Olympias, 13, 33, 62, 76, 123, 140, 141; on Philinna, 61; on Phthia, 190; on Ptolemy Ceraunus, 176, 230; on Stratonice 3, 185, 186, 189; on Thessalonice, 162, 163; on wedding celebration for Cleopatra 2, 204

Kingship, in Argead period, 7–8

Kurios, 30, 31

Lamia, *hetaira* of Demetrius Poliorcetes, 165, 169, 223, 224

Lamia Aphrodite, 218

Lampsace, 208

Lanassa, wife of Demetrius Poliorcetes, 164, 167, *169–71,* 229–30

Laodice, wife of Perseus, *195–97,* 198, 202; wedding extravaganza of, 206

Larnakes, in tombs at Vergina, 238, 240, 242

Leaenea Aphrodite, 218

Le Bohec, Sylvie, 192

Leonidas, 65

Leonnatus, 114, 115, 120; Cleopatra 2's interest in, 123, 124

Letter to Alexander (Theopompus), 217

Lincoln Memorial, Washington, D.C., 216

Literacy, 28–29

Livy: on Eumenes, 196; on Olympias, 86; on Perseus, 199, 206; on Philip V and Polycrateia, 194

Lucius the Tarraian, 60

Lyncestian, sister or daughter of Arrhibaeus, 22

Lyncestis, 38, 41

Lysander, 210

Lysandra, wife of Alexander V, *160–61,* 173, 175, 305n.81

Lysimache, Athenian priestess, 214

Lysimachus, husband of Arsinoe, 114, 115, 145, 153, 154, 159, 160; Arsinoe and, 173–77; murder of Antipater by, 157, 164

Lysimachus, son of Arsinoe and Lysimachus, 174

Macedonia: Athens, alliance with, 5; changes in nature of monarchy, 199–202, 245, 246; early monarchy, 4–8; geographical location of, 4; Hellenization of, 5, 10; impact and influence of monarchy, 4; medieval monarchies compared with, 16–17; parallels or models for monarchy, 16–18; Persian dominance of, 4–5; political structure of, 3; scholarship and sources for history of, 5–6, 8–13, 247; violence in politics of, 116–17; women's involvement in monarchy, 49. *See also* Royal women

Machatas, 59

Macurdy, Grace, xii–xiii; on Demetrius Poliorcetes, 170; on Lysandra, 161; on Stratonice 3, 186; on women in Antigonid period, 180, 198

Marriage, 14, 18–21, 23–27; goddesses associated with, 221–23; monogamy, 182, 184, 228, 232; of royal widows, 43; and use of *basilissa*, 227. *See also* Polygamy

Marriage alliances, 19–20, 259n.67; of Alexander III, 83, 97, 111, 112; in Antigonid period, 180–82, 195, 197, 201; of Gygaea 1, 16; in period of the Successors, 124, 131, 160

Marsyas: on Ptolemy, son of Amyntas III, 42; on Ptolemy Alorites, 39

Meda, wife of Philip II, 53, 55, 56, 67, *68;* tomb of, 68, 236

Medieval monarchy, Macedonian monarchy compared with, 16–18

Memnon, 101, 102

Menelaus, son of Amyntas III, 47

Menopause, age range for, 293n.40

Mentor, 101, 102

Merovingian monarchy, 16–17, 258nn.52,53; Fredegund, story of, 257n.33

Messene, 208, 315n.15

Military activities, of royal women, 14, 28, 31, 36, 267n.149; of Adea Eurydice, 132, 133, 134; of Cynnane, 58, 69, 129, 130; of Olympias and Adea Eurydice, 121–22, 136, 137

Military artifacts, in tombs at Vergina, 239–40, 241

Miller, Stella: on tombs at Vergina, 243

Molossia, 14, 62, 63, 64, 119, 120; Cleopatra 2 as regent in, 89

Monimus, 143

Monogamy, 182, 184, 228, 232

Mortensen, Catherine: on Eurydice 1, 44; on sexual relationships between males, 35

Mother-child relationships, 27, 30, 31–32, 36, 37, 200

Musgrave, Jonathan: on burials at Vergina, 237

Musicians, court, 30

Myrleia Apamea, 187, 197

Myrrhine, *hetaira,* 233

Myrtale. *See* Olympias

Names of royal women, 33–34, 63, 266nn.134–38. *See also* Titles

Nausicaa, 14

Nearchus, 102, 149

Neoptolemus, 62, 89

Neumer-Pfau, W.: on cult worship, 221

Nicaea, daughter of Antipater, 125, 131, 160, 174
Nicaea, wife of Demetrius II, 176, 186, *188–89,* 206, 310n.37; royal trappings of, 232
Nicantor, 139, 141
Nicesipolis, wife of Philip II, 53, 56, *60–61,* 155, 156, 276n.38
Nicomedes II, 187, 197

Occupations of royal women, 29–31
Ochus, Artaxerxes, 110
Oikists, 207, 208
Olympias, half sister of Alexander II of Epirus and mother of Phthia, 190
Olympias, wife of Philip II, 9, 10, 12, 13, 14, 18, 53, 55, *62–67, 85–88, 119–23,* 151, 204, 246–47; and Adea Eurydice and Philip Arrhidaeus, 135, 136, 137, 139–41, 237; Aeacides and, 31; Alexander III and, 30, 31, 84–85, 90–93, 119; Cassander's followers, slaughter of, 141; Cassander's war with, 142–43, 143, 144; Cleopatra 2 and, 75, 76, 89, 123, 127; and Cleopatra 3 and Europa, 72, 74, 77–78; cult worship of, 217; dominance of, 26, 78; literacy of, 28–29; names of, 33, 62–63; Nicesipolis and, 155; occupations of, 29–30; patronage of, 34; in period of the Successors, 115–18, 147; and Philip II's assassination, 79–81, 282n.131; Polyperchon and, 138–40; *proskynesis* and *basilissa,* 320n.75; public role of, 37, 87; religious practices of, 34; return to Macedonia, motive for, 290n.4; and snake story, 256n.26, 277n.61; statue of, in Philippeum, 212, 213, 214; Thessalonice and, 155, 156; trial and execution of, 143–44, 153

Omphale, 222
Oral cultures, literacy in, 28
Orestes, 260n.75
Oxyartes, 106

Palaces, 28, 29, 262nn.106,107
Panathenaic amphora, from tomb at Vergina, 242, 243
Paneguris, wedding celebration for Cleopatra 2 as, 205
Panhellenic festival, wedding celebration for Cleopatra 2 as, 205, 206
Parmenio, 70, 71, 74, 97, 99, 104, 110; Barsine's capture by, 102; murder of, 141
Parysatis, wife of Alexander III, *110–11;* murder of, 146, 148
Patronage of royal women, 34
Pausanias, Argead rival during regency of Ptolemy Alorites, 39, 41, 43
Pausanias, assassin of Philip II, 66, 71, 73, 74, 79, 81, 280n.107
Pausanias, Greek geographer, 12; on Cleopatra 3, 77, 78, 86; on cult statues, 215, 216; on murder of Thessalonice, 163; on Olympias, 86; on the Philippeum, 212
Peisistratus, 262n.96
Peithon, 133
Pelopidas, 43
Peloponnesian War, 5
Penelope, 13–14, 264n.120
Perdiccas, regent for Alexander IV, 109, 110, 114, 115, 119, 120, 146; and Cleopatra 2, 124, 125, 131; Cynnane's murder, 131; murder of, 125, 138
Perdiccas II, 46; burial of, 238; marriages of, 23; sister of (Stratonice 1), 20; wives of, (Cleopatra 1) 21–22, (Simache) 17
Perdiccas III, 38, 39, 40, 55; Eurydice 1 and, 42

364

Pericles, Aspasia and, 222
Persephone theme, in Vergina tomb paintings, 238–39, 242
Persepolis, burning of, 95
Perseus, 180, 193, 194, 195, 198; and Apamea 2, 197; defeat at Pydna, 196; Laodice and, 195, 196; wedding extravaganza of, 206
Persia, 4–5, 15; Alexander's invasion of, 82; Philip II's campaign against, 51, 67; royal women of, 105; wives and children from, 26
Pharnabazus, 102
Pherae, 60, 61
Phila 1, wife of Philip II, 53, 54, 58, *59–60*
Phila 2, wife of Demetrius Poliorcetes, 164, *165–69*, 171, 172, 229, 303n.45; *basilissa* used for, 225, 226; cult worship of, 218, 219, 220, 223; death of, 247
Phila 3, wife of Antigonus Gonatas, 171, 181, *182–83*, 201, 247; city named after, 208; cult worship of, 219
Phila, city, 208
Phila Aphrodite, 218, 224
Philaeum, 218
Philemon: on Pythionice and Harpalus, 217–18
Philetarus, 306n.90
Philinna, wife of Philip II, 53, 60, *61–62*
Philip, son of Arsinoe and Lysimachus, 174
Philip II, 4, 15, 35, 39, 47, 51–52, 151; Alexander III and, 31, 64, 66, 67; Artabazus and, 101; assassination of, 9, 51, 66–67, 75, 76, 79, 80, 81, 204, 205; children of, 25, 30, 53, 67; city named after, 207; court of, 37; and cult worship, 210; daughters of, (Cynnane)

69–70, (Cleopatra 2) 75–76, (Europa) 77–78, (Thessalonice) 155–58; marriages of, 23, 24, 25, 27, 52–62, 67, 68, 70, 229; and names of royal women, 33, 77, 78; Philippeum, construction of, 212, 213; polygamy of, 183–84; royal women used by, 76–78, 83; tomb of, 234, 236–40, 243; wedding celebration for Cleopatra 2, 203–206, 213; wives of, (Audata) 57–58, (Phila 1) 59–60, (Nicesipolis) 60–61, (Philinna) 61–62, (Olympias) 62–67, (Meda) 68, (Cleopatra 3) 72–75
Philip IV, son of Cassander, 157, 159, 161
Philip V, 179, 180, 186, 187, 190–95, 198, 230; execution of son by, 199
Philip Arrhidaeus, 8, 31, 53, 61–64, 66, 68, 76, 98; Adea Eurydice and, 131–34; Alexander III's death and, 114, 115; Cynnane and, 129, 130; murder of, 13, 122, 136–37, 140, 141; name of, 33; tomb of, 234, 236, 237, 238, 241
Philippeum, 77, 212–15, 216, 220, 233; size of statues in, 319n.67
Philotas, 87
Philoxenus, 40, 87
Phocis, 51
Photius: on Audata, 58
Phryne, *hetaira*, 214, 324n.105
Phthia, wife of Demetrius II, 185, 186, 189, *190*, 192, 230, 232; as *basilissa*, 326n.123
Pityoessa, 208
Pixodarus, 62, 66, 76, 79, 93, 98
Plato: on Cleopatra 1, 21; on Simache, 17
Pleistarchus, 167
Plutarch: on Ada, 93; on Alexander III, 93, 94, 102, 103, 104; on Antipater,

father of Cassander, 124; on Antipater, son of Cassander, 158; on Barsine, 101–4; on Barsine's sisters, 103; on Berenice, 174; on change in Macedonian monarchy, 199; on cities named after royal women, 208; on Cleopatra 2, 87, 90, 93, 123, 124, 126; on Cleopatra 3, 71, 72, 74, 78; on cult to Bilistiche, 224; on Demetrius Poliorcetes, 164, 165, 168, 169, 229; on Eurydice 1, 41, 44, 46; on Lanassa, 170; on Leonnatus, 123; on Nicaea, 188–89, 232; on Nicesipolis, 155; on Olympias, 33, 34, 62–65, 73, 86–88, 92, 93, 124, 217; on Olympias and the snake, 277n.61; on Pericles and Aspasia, 222; on Perseus, 194, 196; on Philinna, 61; on Philip II, 37, 229; on Ptolemy, son of Amyntas III, 43; on Ptolemy Alorites, 39; on Roxane, 109, 110, 146; on royal diadem, 232; on Stateira 1, 94

Poisonings, 12
Polemon: on Aphrodite Lamia, 218
Politics, women's involvement in. *See* Public life and politics, women's involvement in
Polyaenus: on Amyntas, 69; on Antigonus, 133; on Arsinoe, 232; on Cynnane, 129
Polybius: on Apamea 1, 187
Polycrateia, wife of Philip V, *193–94*
Polycrates of Argos, 194
Polygamy, 14, 17, 18, 19, 21, 23–27, 32, 117, 183–84, 228–32; of Amyntas III, 42, 47–48; of Antigonids, 192, 199; decline of, 178, 184, 186, 199, 229, 230, 231; of Demetrius II, 192, 193, 199; of Demetrius Poliorcetes, 168–69, 170, 171; Hellenization and, 201;

and Macedonian succession patterns, 81; and mother-son alliances, 30; of Philip II, 55, 57, 79, 80; of Successors, 158
Polyperchon, 120, 121, 122, 134, 135, 136, 138; military campaign against Cassander, 148–49; murder of Heracles and Barsine, 150; and Olympias, 138–44, 147
Polyxena. *See* Olympias
Pomeroy, Sarah B.: on women's influence, 10
Porphyry: on Antipater, son of Cassander, 158
Porus, 83
Pottery, from tombs at Vergina, 242
Power: of Argead royal women, 3, 4, 12; of Macedonian kings, 6, 7
Prejudices of sources, 12–13
Prestianni-Giallombardo, Anna Maria: on polygamy, 14
Price, Simon: on cults, 205, 210, 219
Primogeniture, 24
Property, control of, 30
Proskynesis, 95, 256n.25; *hetaira's* reception of, 218
Prostasia, 139
Prusias I, 187
Prusias II, 187, 197
Ptolemaic cults, 210, 219–23
Ptolemaic rulers: *basilissa* used for wives and daughters of, 226, 227; diadem for royal women, 233
Ptolemaïs, 167
Ptolemy, husband of Barsine's sister, 103
Ptolemy, son of Agesarchus: on Halcyoneus, 181; on Philinna, 61
Ptolemy, son of Amyntas, 42–43
Ptolemy, son of Arsinoe and Lysimachus, 174–77
Ptolemy I, 114, 115, 127, 128, 145, 160, 161, 173

Ptolemy II, 177

Ptolemy Alorites, 39, 40, 43, 44

Ptolemy Ceraunus, 154, 173, 174; Arsinoe and, 176–77, 228, 230, 233

Public life and politics, women's involvement in, 28, 32, 35, 36, 37, 49–50, 79, 257n.28, 258n.41, 296n.79; in Antigonid period, 180, 197–202; of Cleopatra 2, 87, 128; of Eurydice 1, 40, 46, 48; of Olympias, 87; in period of the Successors, 118, 119, 154; of Phila 2, 166

Pydna: defeat of Perseus at, 196; siege of, 142, 155, 296n.81

Pyrrhus, 153, 161, 167; death of, 181; Lanassa and, 169, 170, 229, 230

Pythionice, *hetaira,* 217

Racist attitudes, 26

Regency, 8

Regicide, 6

Regina, title, 228

Religion, 34–35. *See also* Cult worship

Rhodian navy, at wedding of Perseus and Laodice, 195, 206

Rome, 180; capture of Perseus and Laodice by, 196; conquest of Macedonia by, 4; deification of rulers in, 211; and marriage of Perseus and Laodice, 195, 196, 206

Roxane, wife of Alexander III, 74, 100, 103, 104, 105, *106–107,* 112, 114, 134, 139–40, *146–48,* 229; Cassander and, 145; murder of Drypetis or Parysatis by, 110–11; *proskynesis* and *basilissa,* 320n.75; Stateira 2's murder by, 109

Royal women: accessibility of, 27–29; in Antigonid period, 180–81, 197–202; in Argead period, 8–37, 201; burial places of, 234–44; children of, 26, 27, 30; cities

names after, 207–209; dress of, 232–33; and end of Argead dynasty, 151; in era of the Successors, 203; foreign, 10, 14, 21, 26; influences on roles and actions of, 13–15; literacy of, 28–29; male guardians of, 30; marriages of, 18–21, 23; models and parallels for, 16–18; mother-child relationships, 31–32, 200; names of, 33–34, 63, 266nn.134–38; occupations of, 29–31; patronage of, 34; and polygamy, 25–27; portraiture and statuary, 213–14, 216; religious practices of, 34–35, 65; role of, 36–37; scholarship and sources for, 8–13; wedding festivals and extravaganzas for, 203–207. *See also* Cult worship; Military activities; Public life and politics, women's involvement in; Titles

Ruler cults, 210–11

Saatsoglou-Paliadeli, Chryssoula: on Vergina inscriptions, 45

Samuel, Alan, 16

Sardis, 131

Satyrus the Peripatetic, 272n.3; on Audata, 58; on Cleopatra 3, 77; on Nicesipolis, 60; on Philip II, 52–56

Seleucid dynasty: Antigonid alliances with, 182, 184, 195; marriage practices of, 231; royal diadem and, 232

Seleucus, son of Antiochus I, 171

Seleucus I, 114, 115, 154; Adea Eurydice and, 133; at battle of Corupedion, 175; Lysandra and, 161; murder of, 173; Phila 3 and, 182; Stratonice 2 and, 164, 167, 171; wedding festival of, 206

Seleucus II, nephew of Stratonice 3, 185

Seleucus IV, 195, 206

Seuthes, 20

Sexuality: and cult worship, 223–25; gender roles, in Argead period, 35–37; sexual relationships between males, 35–36; stereotyping of politically powerful women, 44

Sexual segregation, 3, 36

Sibling marriages, 177, 202, 214, 231, 245

Simache, wife of Perdiccas II, *17*

Sirras, 41

Sisygambis, 94, 96, 97, 108, 113, 290n.108

Slavery, 29, 30

Sogdiana, revolt of, 106–107

Sosthenes, 200, 301n.14

Stafford, Pauline: on medieval royal women, 18

Stateira 1, wife of Darius III, *94–96*, 108, 285n.35

Stateira 2, wife of Alexander III, *108–109*, 111, 112; murder of, 146, 148

Statues, impact and perception of, 213–16

Stephanus Byzantinus: on Myrleia Apamea, 187; on Nicesipolis, 60

Strabo: on Prusias I, 187

Stratonice, wife of Philip II. *See* Olympias

Stratonice 1, sister of Perdiccas II, *20*

Stratonice 2, daughter of Demetrius Poliorcetes, 164, 166, 167, *171–72*, 182, 184; cult worship of, 219; in inscriptions, 326n.123; as political symbol, 305n.70; wedding festival of, 206

Stratonice 3, wife of Demetrius II, 171, *184–87*, 189, 198, 199, 202, 230; Apamea 1 and, 187

Succession patterns, 23–24; mother-son relationships and, 31

Successors, 4, 7, 82, 113–19, 138–46, 148–52; atrocities of, 12, 163, 256n.28, 296n.80; *basilissa* used for wives of, 226; cities named after, 207; and continuity with the Argead past, 150–51; cult worship and, 210, 211, 222; and dual monarchy, 162; marriages and wedding festivals of, 23, 206, 207; polygamy of, 228, 231; and royal diadem, 232, 233; royal titles, taking of, 154; royal women in period of, 203, 245

Susa, mass weddings at, 206; of Alexander III, 109, 110, 112; Barsine's daughter and Nearchus, 102

Suttee, 236

Symposia, 35, 36; absence of women from, 28

Syncellus: on Philip V, 191

Tarn, W. W.: on Demo and Antigonus Gonatas, 181; on Phila 2 and Demetrius, 166–67; on Phthia and Chryseis, 192

Temple prostitution, 223

Teuta, 69

Thearodoch, 89

Thebes: cult worship in, 218, 224; Philip II's defeat of, 51

Theopompus: on Harpalus, 217, 218, 224

Thessalonice, daughter of Philip II, 53, 60, 61, 98, 115, *155–58*, 159, 161–64; Cassander's marriage to, 145, 154, 300n.11; city named after, 207, 208, 209; cult for, 209, 219; name of, 33; statue base for image of, 214

Thessaloniki, city, 157, 207, 208, 209, 315–16n.26

Thessaly, 60, 61; Philip II's annexation of, 51

Thrace, 68; Philip II's victory over, 51

Titles: in Antigonid period, 189, 201; in Argead period, 32–34, 63; of Macedonian kings, 7; of Macedonian women, 166, 169. *See also* *Basileus; Basilissa*

Tombs. *See* Burial sites

Troas, sister of Olympias, 62

Tuberculosis, 301nn.16–18

Tumpanon drum, 291–92n.22

Tutankhamun, King: burial of, 237; exhibit, Metropolitan Museum, New York CIty, 216

Tyrants, Greek: marriages of, 23; women in families of, 14

Vergina, 28, 46, 214, 234–44, 264n.120; Cleopatra 3, tomb of, 72, 78; Eucleia temple site at, 41, 44, 45; *Eurydika Sirra* inscription at, 269n.10; jewelry found at, 232; Meda, tomb of, 68; palace at, 262n.106, 263n.107; statue base at, 214

Vietnam War Memorial, Washington, D.C., 215

Walbank, F. W.: on Apamea 1, 187

Warfare, 35

Weaponry, in tombs at Vergina, 239–40, 241

Wedding celebrations: international festivals, 203–207; at Susa, 102, 109, 110, 112

Whitehorne, John: on Cleopatra 1, 22

Widows, royal, 32; marriages of, 43, 231

Witchcraft, 12

Zeus, 222, 322n.91